P9-CRX-715

Fodor's

VANCOUVER & VICTORIA

2nd Edition

Fodor's Travel Publications · New York, Toronto, London, Sydney, Auckland

www.fodors.com

Be a Fodor's Correspondent

Your opinion matters. It matters to us. It matters to your fellow Fodor's travelers, too. And we'd like to hear it. In fact, we need to hear it.

When you share your experiences and opinions, you become an active member of the Fodor's community. That means we'll not only use your feedback to make our books better, but we'll publish your names and comments whenever possible. Throughout our guides, look for "Word of Mouth," excerpts of your unvarnished feedback.

Here's how you can help improve Fodor's for all of us.

Tell us when we're right. We rely on local writers to give you an insider's perspective. But our writers and staff editors—who are the best in the business—depend on you. Your positive feedback is a vote to renew our recommendations for the next edition.

Tell us when we're wrong. We're proud that we update most of our guides every year. But we're not perfect. Things change. Hotels cut services. Museums change hours. Charming cafés lose charm. If our writer didn't quite capture the essence of a place, tell us how you'd do it differently. If any of our descriptions are inaccurate or inadequate, we'll incorporate your changes in the next edition and will correct factual errors at fodors.com immediately.

Tell us what to include. You probably have had fantastic travel experiences that aren't yet in Fodor's. Why not share them with a community of like-minded travelers? Maybe you chanced upon a beach or bistro or B&B that you don't want to keep to yourself. Tell us why we should include it. And share your discoveries and experiences with everyone directly at fodors.com. Your input may lead us to add a new listing or highlight a place we cover with a "Highly Recommended" star or with our highest rating, "Fodor's Choice."

Give us your opinion instantly at our feedback center at www.fodors.com/feedback. You may also e-mail editors@fodors.com with the subject line "Vancouver and Victoria Editor." Or send your nominations, comments, and complaints by mail to Vancouver and Victoria Editor, Fodor's, 1745 Broadway, New York, NY 10019.

You and travelers like you are the heart of the Fodor's community. Make our community richer by sharing your experiences. Be a Fodor's correspondent.

Happy traveling!

Tim Jarrell, Publisher

FODOR'S VANCOUVER & VICTORIA

Editor: Caroline Trefler

Editorial Contributors: Crai S. Bower, Carolyn B. Heller, Sue Kernaghan, Chris McBeath

Production Editor: Jennifer DePrima

Maps & Illustrations: David Lindroth, Ed Jacobus, Mark Stroud, and Henry Colomb, *cartographers;* Bob Blake, Rebecca Baer, *map editors;* William Wu, *information graphics*

Design: Fabrizio La Rocca, *creative director;* Guido Caroti, Siobhan O'Hare, *art directors;* Tina Malaney, Chie Ushio, Ann McBride, Jessica Walsh, *designers;* Melanie Marin, *senior picture editor*

Cover Photo: (Capilano Suspension Bridge): Rudy Sulgan/Corbis

Production Manager: Angela L. McLean

2nd Edition

ISBN 978–1–4000–0419–5

ISSN 1941–0301

SPECIAL SALES

This book is available at special discounts for bulk purchases for sales promotions or premiums. Special editions, including personalized covers, excerpts of existing books, and corporate imprints, can be created in large quantities for special needs. For more information, write to Special Markets/Premium Sales, 1745 Broadway, MD 6-2, New York, New York 10019, or e-mail specialmarkets@randomhouse.com.

AN IMPORTANT TIP & AN INVITATION

Although all prices, opening times, and other details in this book are based on information supplied to us at press time, changes occur all the time in the travel world, and Fodor's cannot accept responsibility for facts that become outdated or for inadvertent errors or omissions. So **always confirm information when it matters,** especially if you're making a detour to visit a specific place. Your experiences—positive and negative— matter to us. If we have missed or misstated something, **please write to us.** We follow up on all suggestions. Contact the Vancouver & Victoria editor at editors@fodors.com or c/o Fodor's at 1745 Broadway, New York, NY 10019.

PRINTED IN SINGAPORE

10 9 8 7 6 5 4 3 2 1

CONTENTS

Be a Fodor's Correspondent 3
About This Book. 7

1 **EXPERIENCE VANCOUVER
AND VICTORIA** 9
Vancouver and Victoria Today . . . 10
What's Where. 12
Vancouver and Victoria
Planner. 14
Like a Local 15
Vancouver and Victoria
Top Attractions 16
Flavors of Vancouver and
Victoria. 18
With Kids. 20
Free and Almost Free 21
Great Itineraries 22
First Nations Culture. 23
How to Speak B.C. 24

2 **EXPLORING VANCOUVER** 25
Welcome to Vancouver 26
Vancouver Planner. 28
Exploring Vancouver. 31
Downtown and the West End . . . 32
Gastown and Chinatown 38
Yaletown and False Creek 45
Stanley Park 48
Granville Island. 56
The West Side and Kitsilano 60
North Shore 66

3 **VANCOUVER OUTDOORS AND
SPORTS** 71
Vancouver Outdoors and Sports
Planner. 72

4 **VANCOUVER SHOPS AND
SPAS**. 91
Vancouver Shops and Spas
Planner. 92

5 **VANCOUVER NIGHTLIFE AND
THE ARTS** 113
Nightlife and the Arts
Planner. 114

6 **VANCOUVER WHERE TO
EAT**. 127
Vancouver Where to Eat
Planner. 128
Best Bets for Vancouver
Dining 129
A Side Trip to China—
For Dinner 130
A Passage to India. 132
Beyond the Sushi Bar 134
Downtown Vancouver. 137

7 **VANCOUVER WHERE TO
STAY** 159
Vancouver Where to Stay
Planner. 160
Best Bets for Vancouver
Lodging. 161
Downtown. 163
West End. 174
West Side 179
Yaletown. 179

8 **VICTORIA AND VANCOUVER
ISLAND SIDE TRIPS**. 181
Victoria and Vancouver Island
Side Trips 182
Victoria and Vancouver Island
Side Trips Planner 184
Victoria. 189
Where to Eat 207
Where to Stay. 218
Nightlife and the Arts 227
Sports and the Outdoors 230
Shopping. 236
Side Trips from Victoria 239

9 WHISTLER, THE OKANAGAN,
  TOFINO AND THE
  PACIFIC RIM 257
    Welcome to Whistler 258
    Whistler Planner 260
    Whistler 262
    Okanagan Wine Country
    Planner. 282
    The Okanagan Wine Country. . . 284
    Tofino, Ucluelet, and the Pacific
    Rim Planner 306
    Tofino, Ucluelet, and the Pacific
    Rim 308

TRAVEL SMART 323
    Getting Here and Around. 324
    Essentials 331

INDEX 342
ABOUT OUR WRITERS. 348

MAPS

Downtown and the West End 35
Gastown and Chinatown. 40
Yaletown and False Creek. 46
Stanley Park 50
Granville Island 58
Shopping Neighborhoods 94
Where to Eat in Downtown
Vancouver. 138–139
Where to Eat in
Greater Vancouver 153
Where to Stay in Downtown
Vancouver. 166–167
Victoria and Vancouver Island
Side Trips 182
Downtown Victoria 192–193
Where to Eat and Stay in
Downtown Victoria 216–217
Welcome to Whistler. 258
Whistler Mountain and
Surrounding Areas 264
Wineries of the Okanagan
Valley 286
Tofino, Ucluelet, and the Pacific Rim
National Park 309

ABOUT THIS BOOK

Our Ratings

Sometimes you find terrific travel experiences and sometimes they just find you. But usually the burden is on you to select the right combination of experiences. That's where our ratings come in.

As travelers we've all discovered a place so wonderful that its worthiness is obvious. And sometimes that place is so unique that superlatives don't do it justice: you just have to be there to know. These sights, properties, and experiences get our highest rating, **Fodor's Choice,** indicated by orange stars throughout this book.

Black stars highlight sights and properties we deem **Highly Recommended,** places that our writers, editors, and readers praise again and again for consistency and excellence.

By default, there's another category: any place we include in this book is by definition worth your time, unless we say otherwise. And we will.

Disagree with any of our choices? Care to nominate a place or suggest that we rate one more highly? Visit our feedback center at www.fodors.com/feedback.

Budget Well

Hotel and restaurant price categories from ¢ to $$$$ are defined in the opening pages of each chapter. For attractions, we always give standard adult admission fees; reductions are usually available for children, students, and senior citizens. Want to pay with plastic? **AE, D, DC, MC, V** following restaurant and hotel listings indicate whether American Express, Discover, Diners Club, MasterCard, and Visa are accepted.

Restaurants

Unless we state otherwise, restaurants are open for lunch and dinner daily. We mention dress only when there's a specific requirement and reservations only when they're essential or not accepted—it's always best to book ahead.

Hotels

Hotels have private bath, phone, TV, and air-conditioning and operate on the European Plan (aka EP, meaning without meals), unless we specify that they use the Continental Plan (CP, with a Continental breakfast), Breakfast Plan (BP, with a full breakfast), or Modified American Plan (MAP, with breakfast and dinner) or are all-inclusive (AI, including all meals and most activities). We

always list facilities but not whether you'll be charged an extra fee to use them, so when pricing accommodations, find out what's included.

Listings

★	Fodor's Choice
★	Highly recommended
⊠	Physical address
✛	Directions or Map coordinates
⌖	Mailing address
☎	Telephone
🖷	Fax
⊕	On the Web
✍	E-mail
🖃	Admission fee
◷	Open/closed times
Ⓜ	Metro stations
🖃	Credit cards

Hotels & Restaurants

🏠	Hotel
⤳	Number of rooms
⚲	Facilities
❨◎❩	Meal plans
✕	Restaurant
⌖	Reservations
🏛	Dress code
⤳	Smoking
₿	BYOB

Outdoors

⛳	Golf
⛺	Camping

Other

☻	Family-friendly
⇨	See also
⊠	Branch address
☞	Take note

Experience Vancouver and Victoria

VANCOUVER AND VICTORIA TODAY

Separated from the rest of the country by the Canadian Rockies, Vancouver and Victoria have always marched to a West Coast rhythm that is in many ways more similar to Seattle, Portland, and even parts of California than to their Canadian heritage. Add to this their proximity to the sea and coastal mountains and you have winters that are mild, summers that are balmy, and landscapes lush with temperate forest and gardens. Nowhere else in Canada do daffodils bloom in February! And despite Victoria's old-English facades, these are young cities with active, outdoorsy, and health-conscious populations. Residents may exude a slightly smug, laissez-faire attitude but who can blame them? They live in a place that is consistently ranked as one of the most beautiful and livable in the world.

Today's Vancouver and Victoria . . .

. . . are booming. Ever since Vancouver hosted the World's Fair in 1986, the city had been waiting for the next big event to strut its stuff and the 2010 Winter Olympics literally reshaped the city. Rapid-transit systems were expanded, entire infrastructures were upgraded, and Olympic venues redefined neighborhoods, upping already high real estate values to stratospheric heights (and it all happened during one of the worst global economies). There's no doubt that the Olympics showcased the unparalleled beauty of the region and that the area will continue to prosper, but once Vancouver emerges from its postevent haze, it *will* need to grapple with the debt (thinking back, it took Montreal decades to clear their books of Olympic expenditures). Although separated from Vancouver by the Strait of Georgia, Victoria also got an economic shot in the arm from Olympic activity. Condo developments that once attracted mainly Albertans and Vancouverites to Victoria's more temperate lifestyle now have Americans and Europeans lining up to buy. As a result, urban development is hot and heavy all along the coast, far beyond Victoria's picturesque harbor, so as foundation industries like logging continue their downward slide in many island communities, there are pockets of growth in others.

. . . are greener than ever. West Coasters are more eco-conscious than your average bear. Commercial ventures have pioneered green as the new black: new construction embodies eco-oriented practices from thermal heating to energy-saving fixtures; rooftop gardens add to the cities' relatively pristine air; and recycling is a daily

WHAT'S HOT IN VANCOUVER AND VICTORIA TODAY

With Olympic fervor subsiding, Vancouverites are taking stock of their newly invigorated city. The most controversial venue is the Athletes Village, promised pre-Games to be an environmentally self-sustaining, mixed-use community, but rapidly turning into upscale housing units to help pay off Olympic debt. Other venues are less contentious: the stunning convention-center expansion transformed the downtown waterfront; Cypress Mountain went from being a small family-ski destination to having Olympic status; and the award-winning Richmond Oval that houses two international-size ice rinks, eight gymnasiums, a 200-meter running track, and a fitness center this is an incomplete sentence. And beyond the venues themselves, the city's transit system and infrastructure also

ritual in business and at home. Hoteliers out here were among the first to introduce green practices when they started installing dual-flush toilets (that's two kinds of flushes, not flushing twice) and asking guests to use linens more than once. Car pools and co-op rentals are commonplace, bicycle lanes rule (bike trips into downtown Vancouver number about 2,700—equivalent to 40 full buses), and companies often provide free bus passes to employees who give up commuting by car. Be sure to carry an eco-friendly water bottle and use a reusable carrying bag to fit in with the locals and do your part.

. . . have ethnic diversity. While Victoria is still fairly WASPy, Vancouver's easy access to Asia-Pacific destinations has generated a great influx of Asian immigrants. News is delivered in 22 different languages; shops and ATM machines post signs in English, Mandarin, Cantonese (by far the largest visible minority group in B.C. is Chinese), Punjabi, Farsi, and even Vietnamese. Ironically, French, Canada's other official language, is rarely seen or heard. While this diversity has serious social implications in schools and business, it creates a cultural mosaic that comes vibrantly to life in various festivals and above all, in a range of superb restaurants.

. . . are very outdoorsy. Few cities in the world have mountains, oceans, and wilderness rain forest all on their doorstep. The locals have been taking full advantage of these options themselves, and have also realized the incredible opportunities in promoting ecotourism. Whatever your age or ability, the range of activities includes family spelunking and whale-watching excursions, stellar golf and fishing, white-knuckle rafting expeditions, and no-holds-barred extreme wilderness experiences. Victoria is a popular transit point to explore the myriad of eco-adventures on Vancouver Island, while Vancouver is the gateway to the more sophisticated regions of Whistler and the B.C. Interior. It's fair to say that all this fresh air makes for an extremely health-oriented population and fitness is serious business: gyms are part and parcel of most office and condo high-rises; fitness-club memberships are valued employee benefits and health-gear outlets are plentiful. Is it any wonder that Vancouver and Victoria have some of the toughest no-smoking-in-public-places bylaws in Canada?

saw significant upgrades. The result? Many more Vancouverites have adopted public transit and newly landscaped walkways as a regular modus operandi.

Gastown is the new Yaletown. They're both hip 'hoods but tourist-oriented Gastown is spreading its wings as developers convert seedy hotels into chic urban dwellings with must-have views. Robson Street is still the place for fashionistas, but some of Vancouver's best clothes designers are in Gastown's revamped studio warehouses.

Victoria might be best known for its hanging flower baskets, but it's making its mark as the first city in North America to install pop-up public urinals for drunken bar patrons. By day the devices, installed underground and connected to the sewer system, appear much like a manhole cover. At night they're raised as an invitation to pee in private.

WHAT'S WHERE

1 **Vancouver.** Many people say that Vancouver is the most gorgeous city in North America and situated as it is, between mountains and water, it's hard to disagree. The Vancouver area actually covers a lot of ground but the central core—Downtown, Gastown, Yaletown, Chinatown, Stanley Park, and Granville Island—is fairly compact. An excellent public transportation system makes getting around a snap. When in doubt, remember the mountains are north.

2 **Victoria.** At the southern tip of Vancouver Island, British Columbia's capital city, Victoria, is a lovely walkable city with waterfront paths, lovely gardens, fascinating museums, and splendid 19th-century architecture. In some senses remote, it's roughly midway between Vancouver and Seattle and about three hours by car and ferry from either city.

3 **Whistler.** Just 120 km (75 mi) north of Vancouver—about a two-hour drive along the stunning Sea-to-Sky Highway (Highway 99)—Whistler is outdoor paradise, winter and summer. The two mountains, Whistler and Blackcomb, are the focus of activities, and Whistler Village, at their base, is a compact mecca of lodgings, restaurants, shops, and cafés.

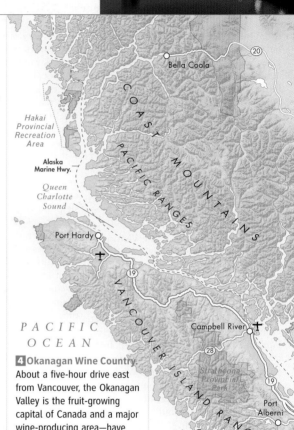

Bella Coola

Hakai Provincial Recreation Area

Alaska Marine Hwy.

Queen Charlotte Sound

Port Hardy

Campbell River

PACIFIC OCEAN

4 **Okanagan Wine Country.** About a five-hour drive east from Vancouver, the Okanagan Valley is the fruit-growing capital of Canada and a major wine-producing area—have you heard of the "Napa of the North"? This, and the sandy beaches and hot dry climate, make it a popular summer destination.

5 **Tofino, Ucluelet, and the Pacific Rim.** British Columbia's Pacific Rim region, on the west coast of Vancouver Island, is known for its dramatically crashing Pacific Ocean waves and its fabulous

COAST MOUNTAINS

PACIFIC RANGES

VANCOUVER ISLAND RANGES

Strathcona Provincial Park

Port Alberni

Tofino

5 Ucluelet

Pacific Rim National Park

VANCOUVER ISLAND

wildlife-watching opportunities. Of the two coastal towns in the region, Tofino is slightly north of Ucluelet and is a bit more established in terms of tourism, with upscale lodgings and fine-dining destinations.

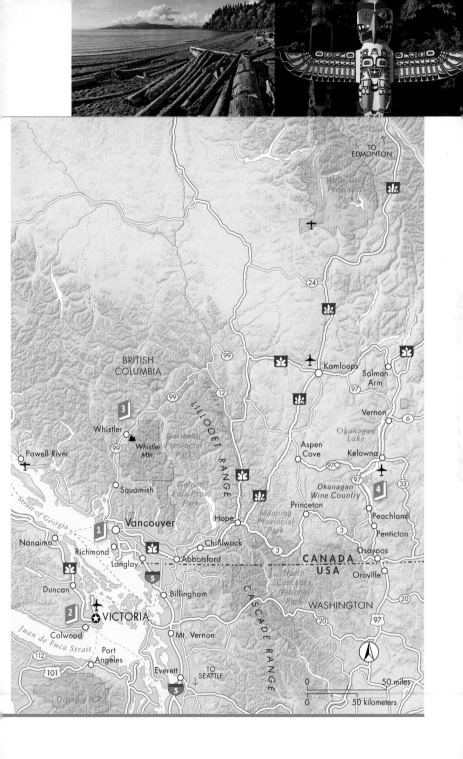

TO
EDMONTON

Wells Gray
Provincial
Park

BRITISH
COLUMBIA

LILLOOET RANGE

24

99

12

99

99

3

Whistler

Whistler
Mtn.

Garibaldi
Provincial
Park

Golden
Ears Prov.
Park

Kamloops

Salmon
Arm

97

Vernon

6

Okanagan
Lake

Aspen
Cove

Kelowna

97C

97

4

33

Powell River

Squamish

Manning
Provincial
Park

Okanagan
Wine Country

Princeton

Peachland

Penticton

Hope

1

Vancouver

Nanaimo

Richmond

Langlay

5

Chilliwack

Abbotsford

3

3

Osoyoos

**CANADA
USA**

Oroville

Strait of Georgia

Duncan

Billingham

North
Cascades
National
Park

CASCADE RANGE

20

97

2

VICTORIA

Colwood

Mt. Vernon

WASHINGTON

20

Juan de Fuca Strait

112

101

Port
Angeles

Everett

TO
SEATTLE

5

Olympic N.P.

0   50 miles

0   50 kilometers

VANCOUVER AND VICTORIA PLANNER

Both Vancouver and Victoria are cosmopolitan, year-round destinations with an outdoor vibe that kicks into high gear whenever the sun shines.

When to Go

In summer (June through September), it seems like the entire populace of Vancouver and Victoria migrates to the beaches, parks, and water. Daffodils and cherry blossoms transform city streets March to May. Despite the risk of rain, October's cool crisp mornings almost invariably give way to marvelous sunshine sparkling through multicolored leaves. Come winter, expect lots of hotel and restaurant bargains, the exceptions being glorious Whistler and along Vancouver Island's westernmost coast where storm watching is a luxury.

Canadian money

U.S. dollars are widely accepted but usually at par, so carry local cash. ATMs are in abundance. Canadian currency uses one- and two-dollar coins and colorful notes for larger denominations.

Getting Here

Air Travel. There are direct flights from most major U.S. and international cities to Vancouver International Airport (YVR), with connecting services to Victoria. You can sometimes get good deals on flights to Seattle (a 2 ½ hour drive south) and then rent a car or take Amtrak to Canada.

Car Travel. Interstate highway I-5 heads straight up the U.S. coast into Vancouver.

However you travel, carry a passport. Without one, even U.S. citizens might not be allowed home. That includes minors. Check out full details in the Travel Smart chapter.

Getting Around

Both Victoria and Vancouver have easy-to-use transit options, and Vancouver's rapid transit makes airport transfers to the downtown core a cinch. A car can be a hindrance: parking is expensive (usually not included in your room rate) and tow trucks prowl the streets for meter violators. Bike rentals are numerous; miniferry rides are practical; and there are taxis for when all else fails. Use a car for out-of-town excursions.

What to Pack

Layering is the best solution to the region's variable weather. And unless "swank" is on your to-do list, ditch the tie because West Coast casual means smart cotton dress pants or jeans and tees. Ward off cool summer breezes with a light jacket or pashmina; bring Gore-Tex for warmth in winter and, year-round, it's never a bad idea to stash something waterproof. Vancouver and Victoria are walking cities, so pack comfortable shoes and if you forget an umbrella, they're a dime a dozen at every corner store.

LIKE A LOCAL

Heading out to Vancouver or Victoria? Here are a few helpful tips for appreciating this unique part of western Canada just like the locals do.

Eat Local . . .

Supporting local producers is part of the West Coast lifestyle so when two Vancouver writers originated the 100-mile diet in 1995, they didn't expect it would catch on across North America let alone the world. Look for neighborhood farmers' markets, now open year-round, with products such as handcrafted island cheeses, organic meats, fish, homemade jams and honey, and seasonal fresh produce.

Layer Up . . .

Dressing for success out here means layering to suit the sea breezes and rain—especially rain. Local mythology says that real natives don't carry umbrellas, they just wear a lot of Gore-Tex, but some reliable insider info says the locals do use their "brollies," though as elsewhere in the world, they never seem to be handy when you need 'em—which probably accounts for why you can find so many inexpensive umbrellas for sale whenever it rains. Sure, there are folks out here who opt for laser eye surgery to eliminate rain-splattered glasses, and certainly those multipurpose Gore-Tex overlays mean you don't have to give in to the umbrella until it really starts to pour. And chances are the locals own at least one pair of quality (not necessarily good-looking) rain boots.

Love your Lattes . . .

West Coasters have a love-hate relationship with the ubiquitous S chain, which has an outlet—sometimes even two as at the Robson–Thurlow intersection—on almost every street corner. Real locals, however, prefer the authenticity of the Italian coffee shops along Commercial Drive and the award-winning creations of the national- and world-champion baristas at the Caffe Artigiano outlets. Locals also like to linger over their lattes at sidewalk tables, at any time of year, rain or shine.

Be Eco-Savvy . . .

Doing your bit for the planet is integral to living like a local in Vancouver and Victoria, so rinse and recycle your cans and bottles; take a reusable bag if you're going shopping; and search out socially responsible products and companies. Lots of locals support local environmental heroes such as David Suzuki, philanthropists Linda and Joel Solomon, as well as organizations such as Greenpeace and the Western Canada Wilderness Committee.

Read the *Georgia Straight* . . .

This once underground, now mainstream Vancouver weekly tabloid echoes Vancouver's inner cool. Everything's here, from opinion pieces to offbeat travel articles, intelligent restaurant reviews, show schedules, and personal ads of all genres.

Exercise a Passion . . .

Keeping the body healthy is a local preoccupation, as is having the wardrobe to suit the way of life, preferably purchased along 4th Avenue—the Mecca for sporting goods and clothing. Hike the Grouse Grind, scuba dive Howe Sound, kayak Indian Arm (some locals even kayak to work along the Fraser River), sweat in Bikrams, or practice Pilates. Even as a visitor you can partake. Here's a tip: buy a used bike from Westcoast Sports Discount Outlet (1675 West 4th Avenue, 604/732–4810); they'll usually buy it back from you later.

VANCOUVER AND VICTORIA TOP ATTRACTIONS

(A) **The Bill Reid Gallery, Vancouver.** If First Nations heritage is your thing, be sure to visit the new Bill Reid Gallery.

(B) **Museum of Anthropology, Vancouver.** The city's most spectacular museum displays art from the Pacific Northwest and around the world—dramatic totem poles and canoes; exquisite carvings of gold, silver, and argillite; and masks, tools, and textiles from many cultures.

(C) **Granville Island, Vancouver.** Take the foot-passenger ferry across the inlet from downtown and bring your appetite. This small island houses a really popular indoor public market, a marina, theaters, restaurants, park space, and dozens of crafts shops and artisan work spaces. Wander the stalls in the market then grab a bench outside to get your fill of delicacies and the view.

(D) **Dr. Sun Yat-Sen Chinese Garden, Vancouver.** "Life is not measured by the number of breaths we take but by the places and moments that take our breath away" is one of the mottos that sums up this elegant downtown site. It's the first authentic Ming Dynasty–style garden outside of China to incorporate symbolism and design elements from centuries-old Chinese gardens and a visit is almost guaranteed to bring tranquility.

(E) **Stanley Park, Vancouver.** An afternoon in this gorgeous 1,000-acre wilderness on the water, just blocks from downtown Vancouver, can include beaches, the ocean, the harbor, Douglas fir and cedar forests, attractions for kids, First Nations sculptures, and a good look at the North Shore Mountains. Walk, bike, picnic, or just take the trolley tour around the perimeter, but don't miss it.

(F) Whistler. At the base of Whistler and Blackcomb mountains, which have the two longest vertical ski drops on the continent, this ski-in, ski-out village has enough shops, restaurants, nightlife, and other activities to fill a vacation without even hitting the slopes.

(G) The Inner Harbour, Victoria. The lovely capital of British Columbia has a remarkably intimate and walkable downtown, focused around the harbor and its sites. Street entertainers and crafts vendors—and lots of people—come out to stroll the waterfront walkway in summer.

(H) The Butchart Gardens, Victoria. Just twenty minutes from downtown Victoria, the 55-acre Butchart Gardens planted in a limestone quarry in 1904 shouldn't be missed; there are plenty of public-transportation and bus-tour options. Highlights include the Japanese, Italian, rose, and sunken gardens; there are more than 700 varieties of flowers.

(I) Pacific Rim National Park Reserve, Vancouver Island. This park on Canada's far west coast has a 16-km-long (10-mi-long) white-sand beach and hiking trails with panoramic views of the sea and rain forest. More and more visitors go in the winter to witness the dramatic storms coming off the water—and to take advantage of the off-season rates. Adventurous souls can try a kayak trip out to the Broken Group Islands.

(J) The Okanagan Valley. East of Vancouver, Canada's premier fruit-growing region is an experience for the senses: the "beaches and peaches" slogan is rapidly taking on a different element as the plethora of wineries continues to grow and produce a wide variety of notable wines. The opportunities for tasting are many, so you might want to choose a designated driver at breakfast. The bountiful resources and gifted chefs in the area also mean the food is on par with the quality of the wines.

FLAVORS OF VANCOUVER AND VICTORIA

For an entire year, from March 2005 through February 2006, one Vancouver couple ate only food that had been raised within 100 miles of their Kitsilano home—going without coffee, lemons, or bananas, but stocking their pantry with abundant local seafood, vegetables, and nuts. Their "100-mile diet" project, later chronicled in a book, became a rallying cry for the region's emerging "locavore" movement—a philosophy that's come to define the current dining scene in Vancouver and Victoria. If it's fresh, in season, and locally grown, it'll be on your plate.

So what's local in Vancouver and Victoria? Seafood is a good starting point, with salmon, Dungeness crab, spot prawns (flavorful, large shrimp), oysters, and scallops fished from B.C. waters. Locally-raised pork and chicken, handcrafted cheeses, and hazelnuts grown nearby, round out the protein options. You'll also find mushrooms, a variety of greens, and in summer, locally-grown strawberries, blueberries, and blackberries. And to drink? B.C. wines, of course.

Yet even as local ingredients are all the rage, Vancouver and Victoria continue to look for culinary inspiration beyond their borders. Positioned on Canada's west coast, British Columbia is the country's gateway to the Pacific Rim, and Asian influences abound in the region's food. B.C. draws on its European roots, too, with many chefs updating classic cuisine with local products.

All the restaurants below have full listings in the Vancouver Where to Eat or Victoria chapters.

Eating Local

Local eating has become almost a religion in Vancouver restaurants, and diners across the city are benefiting from the emphasis on fresh, locally-sourced products. And even when the 100-mile ideal is unattainable, restaurateurs still often choose from local bounty, whether it's fresh fruit from the Okanagan Valley or fish from B.C.'s coastal waters.

■ **Bishop's, Vancouver.** Before "local" became fashionable, owner John Bishop was championing seasonal eating, and his Kitsilano restaurant still emphasizes regional products.

■ **Raincity Grill, Vancouver.** Another early adopter of local ingredients, this romantic restaurant near English Bay offers a 100-mile tasting menu.

■ **Blue Water Cafe, Vancouver.** Chef Frank Pabst often features underappreciated (and more abundant) varieties of seafood, many from local waters, at this fashionable Yaletown spot.

■ **West, Vancouver.** Contemporary regional cuisine is the theme at this chic South Granville restaurant, one of the city's most innovative spots.

Drinking Local

British Columbia has a rapidly maturing wine industry, concentrated in the sunny and dry Okanagan Valley 400 km (250 mi) east of Vancouver. Vancouver Island also is emerging as a wine-producing area. In Vancouver and Victoria, many local restaurants are passionate purveyors of local wines, and wine bars, pairing B.C. vino with artisanal cheeses and house-cured charcuterie, are all the rage.

■ **Cru, Vancouver.** A lengthy by-the-glass list delights diners who flock to this stylish South Granville storefront for small plates and big wines.

■ **Salt Tasting Room, Vancouver.** Hidden in a Gastown alley, this popular spot focuses

on the essentials: cheese, cured meats, and wine.

- **Uva Wine Bar, Vancouver.** A hip downtown hangout for sipping and grazing, Uva offers plenty of local wines by the glass.

- **Stage, Victoria.** Packed with locals, this comfortable wine bar offers Victoria's take on small plates and B.C. wines.

Asian Fine Dining

Vancouver's large population of Asian expats and immigrants has created a demand for Asian fine dining that rivals the best of Hong Kong, Shanghai, and Taipei. Homegrown chefs, such as Maenam's Angus An, are getting into the act, too; his modern Thai bistro takes Southeast Asian dishes to new levels.

- **Kirin, Vancouver.** One branch of this stylish restaurant specializes in northern Chinese cuisine; the others serve up refined Cantonese fare.

- **Sun Sui Wah Seafood Restaurant, Vancouver.** With locations on Main Street and in suburban Richmond, these popular spots are favorites for dim sum.

- **Vij's, Vancouver.** This South Granville dining room packs in the crowds for its innovative Indian creations.

- **Tojo's, Vancouver.** Book a seat at the sushi bar, order *omakase* (chef's choice), and legendary chef Hidekazu Tojo will regale you with a parade of creative Japanese bites.

- **Maenam, Vancouver.** Local ingredients, fresh herbs, and vibrant seasonings spice up traditional Thai dishes at this Kitsilano bistro.

European Renaissance

Vancouver kitchens have long incorporated Asian influences into their dishes, reflecting the region's position as a gateway to the Pacific Rim. More recently, though, local chefs are rediscovering European flavors, with classic French bistros, regional Italian dining rooms, and Mediterranean-style dishes taking on renewed importance.

- **Le Crocodile, Vancouver.** A classic for French fare that's, well, classic.

- **Mistral French Bistro, Vancouver.** The sunny flavors of Provence light up this Kitsilano bistro, even on winter's longest days.

- **Cibo Trattoria, Vancouver.** This sleek, funky trattoria makes Italian fare fun again.

- **Campagnolo, Vancouver.** Take the traditional dishes of Emiglia-Romana and Piedmonte, perk them up with B.C. products, and add a dose of hip. The result? An out-of-the-way eatery that's worth seeking out.

Island Appetites

Much of the produce, seafood, cheese, and wine that Vancouver restaurants are serving comes from Vancouver Island or the surrounding Gulf Islands, so it's no surprise that Victoria and vicinity are developing a culture of local eating as well.

- **Cafe Brio, Victoria.** Highlighting regional, organic fare and B.C. wines, this long-time favorite manages to be both comfortable and hip.

- **Brasserie L'école, Victoria.** French country classics made with locally-sourced provisions—what's not to love?

- **Sooke Harbour House, Victoria environs.** If you can make one foodie side trip from Victoria, this should be it. A passionate purveyor of creative cuisine based on the freshest local ingredients, this inn-restaurant is a romantic hideaway, too.

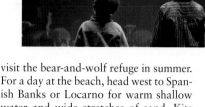

WITH KIDS

Vancouver and Victoria are great places to entertain children, especially ones who like the outdoors. Check the calendar, too, for family-oriented special events, like the Vancouver International Children's Festival in May and the Vancouver Folk Music Festival in July.

Downtown Vancouver

Allow a day to enjoy the kid-friendly activities in Stanley Park: the aquarium, pool, water park, miniature train, and beaches are great for all ages. And getting around this huge park—on a horse-drawn wagon or the free Stanley Park Shuttle—is half the fun. Make sure you also plan a trip on the foot-passenger AquaBus to Granville Island, home of North America's largest free public water park and the Kids' Market, a two-story complex of toy stores and play areas. The Granville market is a great place for lunch or snacking; even the pickiest kids will find something. Also downtown you can check out the interactive displays at Science World, catch an IMAX film at Science World or Canada Place, or hop a foot-passenger ferry to see one (or more) of the three kid-friendly museums at Vanier Park: the Vancouver Museum, the Maritime Museum, or the H.R. Mac-Millan Space Centre.

And beyond downtown

Outside downtown Vancouver, the North Shore is a wilderness playground. Older kids will no doubt enjoy terrifying their parents by trying to wobble the Capilano Suspension Bridge (or the Lynn Valley Suspension Bridge). And the Treetops Adventure at Capilano Suspension Bridge Park and the salmon-spawning displays at the nearby Capilano Salmon Hatchery are big hits. Finish with a Skyride trip up Grouse Mountain, where you can skate or take a sleigh ride in winter, or hike and

visit the bear-and-wolf refuge in summer. For a day at the beach, head west to Spanish Banks or Locarno for warm shallow water and wide stretches of sand. Kits Beach is busier, but has a playground and a seaside pool.

Don't underestimate the entertainment power of public transportation. For a few dollars, a SeaBus ride across Burrard Inlet (a larger ferry than the Granville Island Aquabus) provides a water-level view of the harbor; the same ticket gets you on an elevated SkyTrain ride across town.

Victoria

Like Vancouver, Victoria has small foot-passenger ferries zigzagging across the harbor, and Fisherman's Wharf, with its houseboats and fish-and-chips stands, is popular. Preschoolers are mesmerized by the tiny displays at Miniature World and charmed by the friendly critters at the Beacon Hill Park Petting Zoo, while older kids enjoy the Bug Zoo, the Royal BC Museum, and shopping for allowance-priced souvenirs in Chinatown, as well as easy hikes, bike rides, and picnics. For serious "what I did on my summer vacation" material, you can't beat a whale-watching trip. For a night out, try the IMAX theater, or stargazing at the Dominion Astrophysical Observatory.

Butchart Gardens

If Victoria's Butchart Gardens is on your to-do list, you can make a full day of it by meandering through the peninsula's wine country—Sea Cider (about a 10-minute drive from the ferry and about 15 minutes from the gardens) is the place for munchies. Nearby, the new Shaw Ocean Discovery Center has amazing touchy-feely exhibits to entertain everyone from 8- to 80-year-olds.

FREE AND
ALMOST FREE

The best things in life are free and a surprising number of them are in Vancouver, Victoria, and Whistler. In fact, most of what's enjoyable in this part of the world—including beaches, parks, hiking trails, interesting architecture, great views, and fun-and-funky neighborhoods—is available free of charge.

Vancouver

In Vancouver, you can visit Stanley Park, Granville Island, Downtown, Gastown, Chinatown, and Yaletown and rarely have to open your wallet to pay admission fees—except for such worthwhile exceptions as the Vancouver Aquarium and the Dr. Sun Yat-Sen Garden. Granville Island's markets and galleries are all free, as are Canada Place and Stanley Park. Even the shuttle bus around Stanley Park and guided walking tours of Gastown (604/683–5650 for details) are free.

If that's not enough, here are a few lesser-known ways to stretch those loonies and toonies.

On Tuesday evenings between 5 and 9 the Vancouver Art Gallery charges admission by donation while the Museum of Anthropology has reduced rates. In North Vancouver, most visitors head for the fun, if pricey, Capilano Suspension Bridge. A few miles away, though, the equally thrilling Lynn Canyon Suspension Bridge, in Lynn Canyon Park, is absolutely free. It might be a bit of a trek, but also free on the North Shore are the Capilano Salmon Hatchery, where you can learn about the life cycle of salmon, and, in fall, watch them struggling upstream to spawn; and Lonsdale Quay Public Market, home to street entertainers, tugboats, and great city views.

Public transit

And don't forget one of Vancouver's great unsung bargains: an off-peak, two-zone SkyTrain ticket. For just a few dollars, you can see much of the city's east side and mountains from a clean, efficient elevated train. Then (using the same ticket) you can transfer to the SeaBus for a 15-minute ride across the harbor. The tiny foot-passenger ferries across False Creek are also great bargains at just a few dollars a ticket.

Victoria

In Victoria, Beacon Hill Park or any of the city's parks and beaches are free, as are most of the city's iconic buildings: a stroll through the public areas of the venerable Fairmont Empress Hotel, or even a guided tour of the Parliament Buildings won't cost a dime. The Inner Harbour Walk, providing views of Victoria's Edwardian architecture, boats at harbor, and great people-watching is also free. And if you're there on a Sunday morning in summer, you can even watch the foot-passenger ferries perform a water ballet. Admission: a whopping C$0.

Bargains in Whistler?

Even in jet-set Whistler you can find a few bargains. In the village, you can make like the glitterati for the price of a latte: start with people-watching from a café patio, enjoy the street entertainers, then move on to a stroll through the village's half dozen or so art galleries or join a free brewery tour at the Brewhouse. Even the village shuttle buses are free, while WAVE buses can get you pretty much anywhere in the valley for C$1.50.

GREAT ITINERARIES

See the Cities: 7–10 days

It's still possible to see Vancouver, Whistler, and Victoria, even if you just have time to hit the highlights. Start with two or three days in Vancouver, seeing Stanley Park and strolling through some neighborhoods like Granville Island, Yaletown, Chinatown, and Gastown. Add a day to explore the mountains and parks of the North Shore (Capilano, Grouse, or Lynn Canyon) or the museums on the city's west side before heading north to Whistler. Be sure to do the drive in daylight as the route, along Howe Sound and into the Coast Mountains, is too stunning to miss. After a day or two of biking, hiking, skiing, spa'ing or just shopping and café sitting in Whistler, head back down Highway 99 to Horseshoe Bay, where you can board a car ferry to Nanaimo. From there, a two-hour drive south takes you to Victoria, B.C.'s lovely seaside capital, where the museums, restaurants, and shopping warrant at least two or three days of browsing. A ferry from nearby Swartz Bay will have you back in Vancouver in half a day.

Wilderness and Wildlife: 7–10 days

To get in some serious outdoors time, spend a few days in Vancouver—you can follow the See the Cities outline above and include some hiking in the North Shore Mountains or kayaking in Indian Arm—then head up Highway 99, one of the world's great scenic drives, to Whistler. Here, lift-accessed hiking, mountain biking, or snowshoeing are easy ways into the backcountry. If you've ever wanted to try an outdoor sport, this is the place to do it: summer options run from rafting, golf, and fishing to mountaineering, ziplining, and rock climbing. And in winter, skiing is just the start. From Whistler, if you have time (it's a full day's drive each way), Highway 99 continues through the mountains to link with Highway 1 to the Okanagan, where more parks, hiking, and water sports (and wineries) await. Otherwise, retrace your steps down Highway 99 to Horseshoe Bay, where you can catch a ferry to Nanaimo, then make the three-hour drive across the mountains of Vancouver Island to Tofino and Ucluelet. Finish with several days of whale-watching, bear watching, kayaking, surfing, beachcombing, and perhaps some spa time, in and around the Pacific Rim National Park Reserve.

Food and Wine: 5–10 days

So many restaurants, so many wineries, so little time! A food-and-wine tour of British Columbia would start with several days of browsing Vancouver's markets and specialty shops, followed by evenings in a selection of its 3,000 or so restaurants (⇨ *the Where to Eat chapter will help you choose*). Then you can head to the source of the bounty you've just sampled, traveling east (Highway 5 is the quickest at five hours) to the Okanagan Valley, where more than 125 wineries line a 200-km (120-mi) string of lakes. The dozen vineyards around Oliver, known as the Golden Mile, make a good focus if you're short on time. Another option is a visit to B.C.'s newest wine region, around Victoria. Dubbed the Wine Islands, southern Vancouver Island and the offshore Gulf Islands are home to about a dozen wineries (see the Wine Islands CloseUp box in the Victoria chapter), as well as organic farms, farmers' markets, cideries, cheese makers, and some of B.C.'s best country inns.

FIRST NATIONS CULTURE

Home to more than 30 First Nations, each with its own language, history, and culture, B.C. has the most varied, and vibrant, range of aboriginal cultures in North America. It's also one of the best places to experience these cultures, whether in a museum, at a cultural center, or while exploring the wilderness with a First Nations guide.

Museums
Southern B.C. has several First Nations museums—in Vancouver, the Bill Reid Gallery of Northwest Coast Art is an exceptional legacy to this famous artist and includes a wide range of aboriginal art. Vancouver's Museum of Anthropology and Victoria's Royal British Columbia Museum in Victoria each have a renowned collection of First Nations artifacts, from archaeological finds to modern-day works, that represent a cross section of B.C. aboriginal groups.

Cultural Centers
Another way to experience aboriginal culture is to visit one of the province's cultural centers run by First Nations people. There are several easy day-trip destinations from Vancouver, including the impressive Squamish Lil'wat Cultural Centre (⊕ www.slcc.ca) in Whistler and the Xá:ytem (pronounced "HAY-tum") Longhouse Interpretive Centre (⊕ www.xaytem.ca), about an hour east of Vancouver. On Vancouver Island, the Quw'utsun' Cultural and Conference Centre (⊕ www.quwutsun.ca) is an hour north of Victoria, in Duncan, and the riverside site's cedar longhouses include the Riverwalk Café, open June to September, where you can sample traditional First Nations cuisine—perhaps some intriguingly prepared salmon or stew with bannock (unleavened bread). If you're heading east to the Okanagan, you can stop en route in Kamloops at the Secwepemc Museum and Heritage Park (⊕ www.secwepemc.org/museum), a traditional gathering place now home to replica homes and indigenous gardens. Also in the Okanagan, in Osoyoos, is Nk'Mip Spirit of the Desert (⊕ www.nkmipdesert.com), a resort complex that includes North America's first aboriginal-owned winery. Further east, in Cranbrook, the Kunaxa Interpretive Centre is housed in St. Eugene Mission, a former residential school.

Powows
To experience a powwow, check out Chilliwack's Spirit of the People Pow Wow (⊕ www.tourismchilliwack.com): a huge gathering of First Nations groups complete with drumming circles, dancing, traditional foods, and exhibits. Or, each August, Kamloops hosts the annual Kamloopa Pow Wow, British Columbia's biggest festival of First Nations dance (⊕ www.tourismkamloops.com).

Exploring with a First Nations guide
For more of a get-out-and-do-it kind of experience, sign up with a First Nations guide. A growing number of First Nations'-owned tourism operators offer everything from kayaking to hiking to whale-watching or jet-boat tours, typically with traditional songs, legends, historic insights, and food (think waterfront salmon barbecues) thrown in. Experiences range from paddling a traditional oceangoing canoe near Vancouver, to desert tours around Osoyoos, to hiking and whale-watching near Tofino.

The Aboriginal Tourism Association of British Columbia (⊕ www.aboriginalbc.com) has more details about sites, tours, and experiences.

HOW TO SPEAK B.C.

"In Canada we have enough to do keeping up with two spoken languages without trying to invent slang, so we just go right ahead and use English for literature, Scotch for sermons, and American for conversation." —Stephen Leacock (1869–1944), Canadian humorist

Stephen Leacock was right: Canadians don't like to confuse visitors with obscure regional dialects. For that, we have the metric system. Still, we have our eccentricities, and a brief primer may help avoid some confusion.

Terms useful in B.C. include the words for money: loonies for the dollar coin (because of the loon that graces the coin) and toonies for the 2-dollar version. British Columbians, like other Canadians, spell many things the British way (colour instead of color, for example), pronounce the letter "z" as "zed," and occasionally (okay, more than occasionally) tack an "eh?" to the end of a sentence—to turn it into a question, to invite a response, or just out of habit.

The Canadianisms toque (woolly cap) and Zamboni (ice-rink cleaning machine) are also used here, albeit less frequently given the temperate weather. What you will hear are many words for precipitation. A Vancouverite might observe that it's drizzling, spitting, pouring, or pissing down, but will avoid saying "Yup, it's raining again." That just shows a lack of imagination. Oh, and if someone does say "It's raining again, eh?" he's not asking a question; he's just inviting you to discuss the situation.

A few words are uniquely West Coast, including some derived from Coast Salish, a First Nations trading language. *Skookum*, for example, means big or powerful; *chuck* means water (as in a body of water); salt *chuck* is seawater. Chinook, which means a warm wind in Alberta, is a species of salmon in B.C. Thus you might find: "He caught a skookum chinook then chucked it right back in the salt chuck."

Probably the best sources of confusion out in B.C. are geographical. The Okanagan, and anything else not on the coast, is called "the Interior" by Vancouverites—unless it's north of, say, Williams Lake, in which case it's "Up North." There are thousands of islands in B.C., but "the Island" refers to Vancouver Island—remember, though: Vancouver isn't on Vancouver Island; Victoria is.

Food and drink offer more room for misunderstanding: order soda and you'll get soda water (Canadians drink pop). Homo milk? It's short for homogenized milk and it means whole milk. Bacon is bacon, but Canadian bacon is called back bacon in Canada. Fries are generally fries, but will be called chips if they come with fish, in which case they'll also come with vinegar.

And beer? You can just order "beer," but be prepared to discuss with the bartender your preference for lager, ale, porter, et cetera. You'll probably also be told that Canadian beer is stronger than American. This is a widely held belief that simply doesn't hold water. According to *Beverage Business Magazine*, the alcohol levels are the same—they're just measured differently. That, and the fact that Canadian beer has more flavor, has led generations of cross-border drinkers to believe that the northern brew packs more punch. That's simply not true; it just tastes better.

Exploring Vancouver

WORD OF MOUTH

"I had a terrific time in Vancouver. My hotel, the Fairmont Waterfront, lent me a bicycle late one afternoon, and I rode all around
the waterfront and Stanley Park. Another afternoon, I took the False
Creek Aquabus from start (Science World) to finish (the Kitsilano
beach area) crisscrossing False Creek numerous times with views
of the downtown all the way."

—jrpfeiffer

WELCOME TO VANCOUVER

TOP REASONS TO GO

★ **Stanley Park:** The views, the activities, and the natural wilderness beauty here are quintessential Vancouver.

★ **Granville Island:** Ride the mini-ferry across False Creek to the Granville Island Public Market where you can shop for delicious lunch fixings; eat outside when the weather's fine.

★ **Kitsilano beaches:** Options range from beaches with grass-edged shores to windswept stretches of sand, to cliffside coves so private that clothing is optional.

★ **Museum of Anthropology at University of British Columbia:** The phenomenal collection of First Nations art and cultural artifacts, and the incredible backdrop, make this a must-see.

★ **Rain-forest intimacy:** Traverse the canopies at UBC Botanical Garden and Capilano Suspension Bridge Park; you can even zip-line from the treetops.

1 Downtown and the West End. The city's downtown commercial heart has the Pacific Centre Mall, most of the city's high-fashion shops, major hotels, and transit hubs. The compact layout is easy to walk and navigate, and it borders the West End, a residential neighborhood that edges beaches and Stanley Park.

2 Gastown and Chinatown. These adjoining 'hoods have been redone a bit but their ornamental architecture, nooks, and alleyways give clues to Vancouver's earliest history. Chinatown feels like a Hong Kong street market with its mishmash of exotic sights and smells.

3 Yaletown and False Creek. Colossal glass high-rises are juxtaposed against converted loft-style warehouses in this urbanly hip and happening neighborhood best known for its specialty shops and eateries.

4 Stanley Park. A rain-forest with top-quality attractions, hikes, and views—all within blocks of the cosmopolitan city skyscrapers.

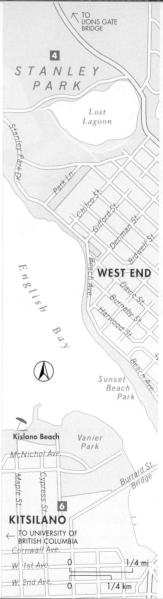

5 **Granville Island.** The city's most eclectic destination puts art alongside cement works alongside fresh-produce markets, with floating homes and busker entertainment to boot. Nothing disappoints.

6 **The West Side and Kitsilano.** This is the catchall name for the neighborhoods southwest of downtown, including the university area of Point Grey with its stunning Pacific Spirit Park; old-money Shaughnessy with its posh, seemingly multi-acre stone mansions; the busy Cambie Corridor; and trendy Kitsilano, with its boutiques, converted beach houses, hip restaurants, and terrific beaches.

7 **North Shore.** Across Burrard Inlet, on the North Shore, are residential and scenic West Vancouver and the more bustling North Vancouver; the mountains, your constant compass-point of reference, are the backdrop.

GETTING ORIENTED

For the most part, Vancouver central sits on a peninsula, which makes it compact and easy to explore on foot, especially since most streets are laid out on a grid system. To get your bearings, use the mountains as your "true north" and you can't go too far wrong. All the avenues, which are numbered, have east and west designations; the higher the number, the farther away from the inlet you are.

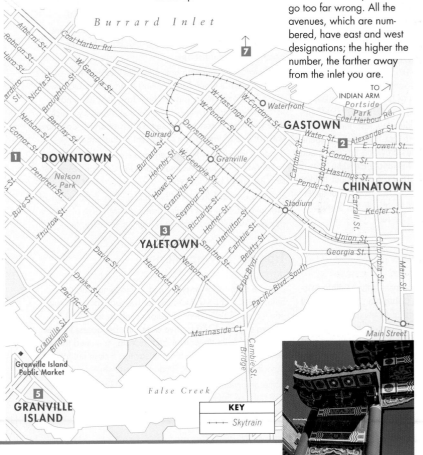

VANCOUVER PLANNER

Rainy-Day Activities

While most Vancouverites don't let a little drizzle stop them, heavier rains might inspire you to seek indoor activities. Obvious options include museums—the Museum of Anthropology at UBC is a worthwhile trek. If you're downtown, the Vancouver Art Gallery is good for an hour or two, as is the Vancouver Aquarium and Science World. Less obvious choices are the Bill Reid Gallery, the Dr. Sun Yat-Sen Classical Chinese Garden (it has covered walkways), or Granville Island Market (it's inside; you just have to get there, but then you can spend hours browsing the goods and having lunch). Lonsdale Quay is another colorful indoor market on the North Shore and getting there, via the SeaBus, is half the fun.

Making the Most of Your Time

If you don't have much time in Vancouver, you'll probably still want to spend at least a half day in Stanley Park: start out early for a walk, bike, or shuttle ride through the park to see the Vancouver Aquarium Marine Science Centre, enjoy the views from Prospect Point, and stroll the seawall. If you leave the park at English Bay, you can have lunch on Denman or Robson Street, and meander past the trendy shops between Jervis and Burrard streets. Or, exit the park at Coal Harbour and follow the Seawall Walk to Canada Place, stopping for lunch at a harbor-front restaurant.

A couple hours at the Granville Island Public Market are also a must—plan to have lunch, and, if you have time, check out the crafts stores.

Walking the downtown core is a great way to get to know the city. Start at Canada Place and head east to Gastown and Chinatown; that's a good half day. Then head north to Yaletown and travel back via Robson Street, by which time you'll have earned yourself a glass of British Columbia wine at one of Vancouver's excellent restaurants.

If you're traveling with children, make sure to check out Science World, Grouse Mountain, and the Capilano Suspension Bridge or Lynn Canyon.

For museums, adults and older children love the displays of Northwest Coast First Nations art at the Museum of Anthropology. The Bill Reid Gallery is pretty impressive, too.

Tours

A company called **Edible British Columbia** provides guided tours of Granville Island, with the market as its focus. They also have culinary tours around Vancouver's Chinatown as well as the coffee shops, delis, and bakeries of Little Italy, aka Commercial Drive. ☎ *604/662-3606* ⊕ *www.edible-britishcolumbia. com.*

Tips for Saving Money

If you're in for an energy-packed sight-seeing visit, the Smartvisit Card (⊕ *www.seevancouvercard.com*) can save you money. Sold in denominations ranging from C$119 for two days to $219 for five days, you get access to over 50 attractions in Vancouver and Victoria. You need to visit about four attractions before the savings kick in but for stays longer than 2 days, it can be worthwhile.

Some attractions, like the Vancouver Art Gallery (Tues. 5–9 PM) and the Museum of Anthropology (Tues. 5–9 PM) have reduced rates or "by donation" evenings.

Getting Around

Central Vancouver is extremely walkable and the public transit system—a mix of bus, ferry, and the SkyTrain (a fully automated rail system)—is easy and efficient to use. Transfer tickets enable you to travel from one mode of transport to the other. The hop-on-hop-off Vancouver Trolley buses circle the city in a continuous loop, and are a great way to see the sites—especially on a rainy day.

Contacts Vancouver Trolley (☎ 888/451–5581 ⊕ www.vancouvertrolley.com).

By Bus and Rapid-Transit

TransLink, Metro Vancouver's public transport system, includes regular bus service, rapid transit (known as SkyTrain), and a 400-passenger commuter ferry (SeaBus) that connects downtown to the North Shore.

Fares are based on zones: one zone (C$2.50), two zones (C$3.75), or three zones (C$5). Day passes (C$9) and FareSaver tickets (sold in books of 10, at outlets such as 7/11, Safeway, and London Drugs) can also be purchased. Transfers (ask for one when you board) are valid for 90 minutes and allow travel in any direction. Tickets for bus travel requires exact change at time of embarkation, while SkyTrain and SeaBus tickets are purchased from machines (correct change isn't necessary). Tickets must be carried with you as proof of payment.

There are three SkyTrain lines: the Expo Line and the Millennium Line share the same stations between downtown and Commercial Drive, so unless you're going east of Commercial Drive, you can use either line. Trains leave about every two to five minutes. The Canada Line travels to Richmond's commercial hub (for great shopping) and to Vancouver International Airport, a ride that's less than 30 minutes. Canada Line trains leave about every 8 to 10 minutes.

■ TIP→ SkyTrain is convenient for transit between downtown, B.C. Place Stadium, Pacific Central Station, Science World, and Vancouver International Airport. SeaBus is the fastest way to travel between downtown and the North Shore (there are bus connections to Capilano Suspension Bridge and Grouse Mountain).

Contacts SkyTrain (☎ 604/953–3333 ⊕ www.translink.bc.ca). **Translink** (⊕ www.translink.bc.ca).

By Ferry

Twelve-passenger ferry boats bypass busy bridges and are a key reason why you don't need a car in Vancouver. Aquabus Ferries and False Creek Ferries are private commercial enterprises that provide passenger services between key locales on either side of False Creek. Tickets average C$5 depending on the route; day passes are C$14. Aquabus Ferries connections include Science World, Plaza of Nations, Granville Island, Stamp's Landing, Spyglass Place, Yaletown, and the Hornby Street dock. False Creek Ferries provides service between the Aquatic Centre on Beach Avenue, Granville Island, Science World, Stamp's Landing, and Vanier Park. False Creek and Aquabus ferries are not part of the TransLink system.

Contacts Aquabus Ferries (☎ 604/689-5858 ⊕ www.theaquabus.com). **False Creek Ferries** (☎ 604/684-7781 ⊕ www.granvilleislandferries.bc.ca). **SeaBus** (☎ 604/953-3333 ⊕ www.translink.bc.ca).

By Taxi

It can be hard to hail a cab in Vancouver. Unless you're near a hotel or find a taxi rank (designated curbside parking areas), you'll have better luck calling a taxi service. Try Black Top or Yellow Cab.

Taxi Companies Black Top Cabs (☎ 604/681–2181). **Yellow Cab** (☎ 604/681–1111).

By Chris
McBeath

Consistently ranked as one of the world's most livable cities, Vancouver lures visitors with its abundance of natural beauty, multicultural vitality, and cosmopolitan flair. The attraction is as much in the range of food choices—the fresh seafood and local produce are some of North America's best—as it is in the museums, shopping opportunities, and beaches, parks, and gardens. Indeed, the Vancouver package is a delicious juxtaposition of urban sophistication and on-your-doorstep wilderness adventure.

The mountains and seascape make Vancouver an outdoor playground for hiking, skiing, kayaking, cycling, and sailing—and so much more—while the cuisine and arts scenes are equally diverse, reflecting the makeup of Vancouver's ethnic (predominantly Asian) mosaic. Yet despite all this vibrancy, the city still exudes an easy West Coast style that can make New York or London feel, in comparison, edgy and claustrophobic to some.

More than 8 million visitors each year come to this, Canada's third-largest metropolitan area, and thousands more are expected now that it has strutted its stuff on the Olympic world stage. Because of its peninsula location, traffic flow is a contentious issue. Thankfully, Vancouver is wonderfully walkable, especially in the downtown core. The North Shore is a scoot across the harbor, and the new rapid-transit system to Richmond and the airport means that staying in the more affordable 'burbs doesn't have to be synonymous with sacrificing convenience. The mild climate, exquisite natural scenery, and relaxed outdoor lifestyle keep attracting residents, and the number of visitors is increasing for the same reasons. People often get their first glimpse of Vancouver when catching an Alaskan cruise, and many return at some point to spend more time here.

CLOSE UP

Vancouver History

Vancouver's history, such as it is, remains visible to the naked eye at every corner: eras are layered east to west along the waterfront, from the origins in late-Victorian Gastown to the shiny, postmodern glass cathedrals of commerce that spread north and west.

The history of Vancouver is integrally linked with the taming of western Canada: the trappers working for the Hudson's Bay Company (the oldest retail store still operating in North America) explored the area; then the Canadian Pacific Railway, which crossed the country, chose the ramshackle site of Granville as its Pacific terminus. The coming of the railway inspired the loggers and saloon owners of Granville to incorporate as a

city: on April 6, 1886, Granville Townsite, with a population of about 400, became the City of Vancouver, named after the British explorer who had toured the inlet here in 1792.

The railway, along with Canadian Pacific's fleet of clipper ships, gave Vancouver a full week's edge over the California ports in shipping tea and silk from the Orient to New York. Lumber, fish, and coal from British Columbia's hinterland—resources that are still the backbone of the provincial economy, also flowed through the port to world markets. The same ships and trains brought immigrants from all corners of the earth, helping the population grow exponentially to today's 2.5 million.

EXPLORING VANCOUVER

The city's downtown core includes the main business district between Robson Street and the Burrard Inlet harbor front; the West End that edges up against English Bay; Stanley Park; trendy Yaletown; and Gastown and Chinatown, which are the oldest parts of the city. Main Street, which runs north-south, is roughly the dividing line between the east and west sides. The entire downtown district sits on a peninsula bordered by English Bay and the Pacific Ocean to the west; by False Creek to the south; and by Burrard Inlet, the city's working port, to the north, where the North Shore Mountains loom.

One note about printed Vancouver street addresses: suite numbers often appear *before* the street number, followed by a hyphen.

Elsewhere in the city you'll find other places of interest: the North Shore is across Burrard Inlet (Whistler is a two-hour drive from here); Granville Island is south of downtown across False Creek; the West Side comprises several neighborhoods across from English Bay in the West End. Richmond, where the airport is, is to the south; the suburbs of Burnaby and the Fraser Valley are to the east.

DOWNTOWN AND THE WEST END

Vancouver's compact downtown juxtaposes historic architecture with gleaming brand-new buildings. Sightseeing venues include museums, galleries, and top-notch shopping, most notably along Robson Street, and in and around couture-savvy Sinclair Centre. The harbor front, with the convention center expansion, has a fabulous water's edge path all the way to Stanley Park, epitomizing what Vancouver is all about.

At the top of a gentle rise up from the water, the intersection of Georgia and Granville streets is considered the city's epicenter and it's always bustling with activity. Georgia Street runs east-west, past Library Square and General Motors Place (home of the NHL's Vancouver Canucks), straight through to Stanley Park and the Lions Gate Bridge (which leads to the North Shore and on to Whistler, a two hour drive away). North-south Granville Street is shedding its previous shabbiness and evolving into a pedestrian-friendly area of neon-lit sidewalks, funky shops, nightclubs, and street-side cafes. There may be pockets of grunge still visible but the Olympics spurred a remarkable renaissance and the street has taken on a vitality of its own. So, from the corner of Georgia and Granville, you'll find many key attractions within a five-minute walk, including the Vancouver Art Gallery, Robson Square, and Pacific Centre Mall.

Vancouver's landscaping adds to the city's walking appeal. In spring, flowerbeds spill over with tulips and daffodils while sea breezes scatter scented cherry blossoms throughout downtown; in summer, office workers take to the beaches, parks, and urban courtyards for picnic lunches and laptop meetings. The West End has the prettiest streetscapes and hark back to the early 1930s when it housed the affluent middle class: trees are plentiful, gardens are lushly planted, and homes and apartment buildings exude the character of that era. Even in winter the West End makes for an idyllic walk. On rainy days, many downtown buildings have overhangs, so that you don't have to get as wet as the weather.

TOP ATTRACTIONS

8 **The Bill Reid Gallery of Northwest Coast Art.** Vancouver's newest aborigi-
Fodor's Choice nal art gallery, named after one of B.C.'s pre-eminent artists, Bill Reid
★ (1920–98), is as much a legacy of his works as it is a showcase of current artists. Displays include wood carvings, jewelry, print, and sculpture. The gallery may be small but its expansive offerings often include
artist talks and noon-hour presentations. Bill Reid is best known for
his bronze statue, "The Spirit of Haida Gwaii, The Jade Canoe"—
measuring 12 ft x 20 ft, the original is an iconic meeting place at the
Vancouver International Airport and its image is on the back of the
Canadian $20 bill. ⊠ *639 Hornby St., Downtown* ☎ *604/682–3455*
⊕ *www.billreidgallery.ca.* ⊠ *C$10* ☉ *Wed.-Sun. 11–5.*

10 **Canada Place.** Extending four city blocks (about a mile and a half) north
★ into Burrard Inlet, this complex (once a cargo pier) mimics the style
and size of a luxury ocean liner, with exterior esplanades. The Teflon-
coated fiberglass roof, shaped like five sails (the material was invented
by NASA and once used in astronaut space suits), has become a Vancouver skyline landmark. Home to Vancouver's main cruise-ship terminal,
Canada Place can accommodate up to four luxury liners at once. It's
also home to the luxurious **Pan Pacific Hotel** and the **Vancouver Convention and Exhibition Centre** (☎ *604/647–7390*), which links to an
even-more-impressive expansion via outdoor plazas and an underground
art gallery–themed tunnel. The promenades, which wind all the way to
Stanley Park, present spectacular vantage points to view Burrard Inlet
and the North Shore Mountains; plaques posted at intervals offer historical information about the city and its waterfront. At the north end of
the complex, at the **Port Authority Interpretive Centre** (☎ *604/665–9179*
⊠ *Free* ☉ *Weekdays 9–4*), you can catch a video about the workings
of the port, see some historic images of Vancouver's waterfront, or try
your hand at a virtual container-loading game. Also at the north end, the
CN IMAX Theatre (☎ *604/682–4629* ⊠ *C$14, higher prices for some
films*) shows films on a five-story-high screen. ⊠ *999 Canada Place Way,
Downtown* ☎ *604/775–7200* ⊕ *www.canadaplace.ca.*

7 **Christ Church Cathedral.** The oldest church in Vancouver was built between
1889 and 1895. Constructed in the Gothic style, this Anglican church
looks like the parish church of an English village from the outside,
though underneath the sandstone-clad exterior it's made of Douglas
fir from what is now south Vancouver. The 32 stained-glass windows
depict Old and New Testament scenes, often set against Vancouver
landmarks (St. Nicholas presiding over the Lions Gate Bridge, for example). The building's excellent acoustics enhance the choral evensong
and carols frequently sung here. Gregorian chants are performed every
Sunday evening at 9:30. There's also a labyrinth to enjoy and special-
event walks are usually scheduled around seasonal equinoxes. ⊠ *690
Burrard St., Downtown* ☎ *604/682–3848* ⊕ *www.cathedral.vancouver.
bc.ca* ☉ *Weekdays 10–4. Services Sun. at 8* AM, *10:30* AM; *weekdays
at 12:10* PM.

9 **Marine Building.** Inspired by New York's Chrysler Building, the terra-
★ cotta bas-reliefs on this 21-story, 1930s art deco structure depict the
history of transportation—airships, steamships, locomotives, and

submarines—as well as Mayan and Egyptian motifs and images of marine life. Step inside for a look at the beautifully restored interior, then walk to the corner of Hastings and Hornby streets for the best view of the building. It serves as the headquarters of the *Daily Planet* in the TV show, *Smallville*. ⊠ *355 Burrard St., Downtown.*

❶ Robson Street. Robson, Vancouver's busiest shopping street, is lined with see-and-be-seen sidewalk cafés, chain stores, and high-end boutiques. The street, which links downtown to the West End, is particularly lively between Jervis and Burrard streets and stays that way into the evening with buskers and entertainers.

OFF THE BEATEN PATH

Roedde House Museum. Two blocks south of Robson Street, on Barclay, is the Roedde (pronounced *roh*-dee) House Museum, an 1893 house in the Queen Anne Revival style, set among Victorian-style gardens. Tours of the restored, antiques-furnished interior take about an hour. On Sunday, tours are followed by tea and cookies. The gardens (free) can be visited anytime. ⊠ *1415 Barclay St., between Broughton and Nicola, West End* ☎ *604/684–7040* ⊕ *www.roeddehouse.org* ⊠ *C$5; Sun. C$6, including tea* ⊗ *Tues.– Sun. 2–4.*

⑬ Vancouver Lookout! The lookout looks like a flying saucer stuck atop a high-rise and at 553 feet high, it affords one of the best views of Vancouver. A glass elevator whizzes you up 50 stories to the circular observation deck, where knowledgeable guides point out the sights and give a tour every hour on the hour. On a clear day you can see Vancouver Island and Mt. Baker in Washington State. The top-floor restaurant makes one complete revolution per hour; the elevator ride up is free for diners. ■ TIP➡ Tickets are good all day, so you can visit in daytime and return for another look after dark. ⊠ *555 W. Hastings St., Downtown* ☎ *604/689–0421* ⊕ *www.vancouverlookout.com* ⊠ *C$13* ⊗ *May–mid-Oct., daily 8:30 AM–10:30 PM; mid-Oct.–Apr., daily 9–9.*

WORTH NOTING

❺ Cathedral Place. One of Vancouver's most handsome postmodern buildings, Cathedral Place is an impressive 23-story tower with a faux-copper roof that mimics that of the Fairmont Hotel Vancouver nearby. The three large sculptures of nurses at the corners of the building are replicas of the statues that adorned the Georgia Medical–Dental Building, the art deco structure that previously occupied this site. Step into the lobby to see another interesting sculpture: Robert Studer's *Navigational Device,* suspended high up on the north wall. The small garden courtyard is an unexpected respite from the downtown bustle. ⊠ *925 W. Georgia St., Downtown* ☎ *604/669–3312* ⊕ *www.925westgeorgia.com.*

❹ Fairmont Hotel Vancouver. One of the last railway-built hotels in Canada, the Fairmont Hotel Vancouver was designed in the château style, its architectural details reminiscent of a medieval French castle. Similar chateâu properties are in the Canadian Rockies and across the country; each is an iconic Canadian landmark. Construction began in 1929 and wrapped up just in time for King George VI of England's 1939 visit. The exterior of the building, one of the most recognizable in Vancouver's skyline, has carvings of malevolent-looking gargoyles at the corners, native chiefs on the Hornby Street side, and an assortment of figures from classical

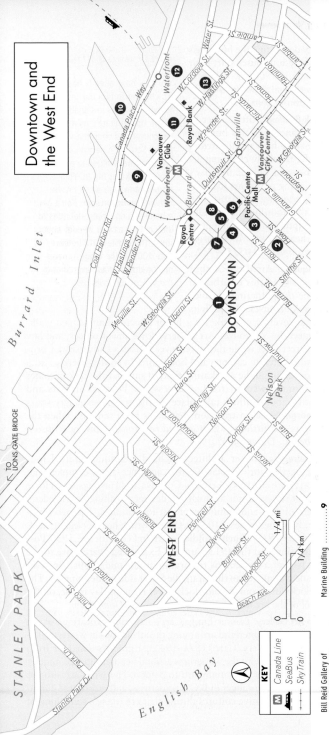

Downtown and the West End

STANLEY PARK

Burrard Inlet

English Bay

WEST END

DOWNTOWN

TO LIONS GATE BRIDGE

Nelson Park

Pacific Centre Mall

Royal Centre

Vancouver Waterfront Centre

Vancouver Club

Royal Bank

Vancouver City Centre

Waterfront

Streets:
Park Ln.
Stanley Park Dr.
Chilco St.
Gilford St.
Denman St.
Cardero St.
Nicola St.
Broughton St.
Barclay St.
Nelson St.
Jervis St.
Bute St.
Thurlow St.
Burrard St.
Hornby St.
Howe St.
Granville St.
Seymour St.
Richards St.
Homer St.
Hamilton St.
Cambie St.
Park Ln.
Pendrell St.
Davie St.
Burnaby St.
Harwood St.
Beach Ave.
Comox St.
Haro St.
Robson St.
Alberni St.
W. Georgia St.
Melville St.
W. Hastings St.
W. Pender St.
Coal Harbor Rd.
Canada Place Way
W. Cordova St.
Water St.
W. Hastings St.
W. Pender St.
Dunsmuir St.
W. Georgia St.
Smithe St.

KEY

Ⓜ Canada Line
SeaBus
SkyTrain

Bill Reid Gallery of Northwest Coast Art **8**
Canada Place **10**
Cathedral Place **5**
Christ Church Cathedral **7**
Fairmont Hotel Vancouver **4**
HSBC Bank Building **6**

Marine Building **9**
Robson Square **2**
Robson Street **1**
Sinclair Centre **11**
Vancouver Art Gallery **3**
Vancouver Lookout! **13**
Waterfront Station **12**

0 — 1/4 mi
0 — 1/4 km

mythology decorating the building's facade. Many tour buses start their circuits here. ✉ *900 W. Georgia St., Downtown* ☎ *604/684–3131* ⊕ *www.fairmont.com.*

6 HSBC Bank Building. Kitty-corner to the Hotel Vancouver, this building has a five-story-high public atrium with a café, regularly changing art exhibitions, and one of the city's more intriguing public-art installations: *Pendulum,* by B.C. artist Alan Storey, is a 90-foot-long hollow aluminum sculpture that arcs hypnotically overhead. ✉ *885 W. Georgia St., Downtown* ☎ *604/525–4722.*

2 Robson Square. Architect Arthur Erickson designed this refurbished plaza to be *the* gathering place of downtown Vancouver, although its

below-street-level access makes it a bit of a secret. Landscaped walkways connect the Vancouver Art Gallery, government offices, and law courts at street level while the lower level houses a University of British Columbia satellite campus and bookstore. In winter, there's also a covered, outdoor, public ice skating rink; in summer the rink becomes a dance floor for weekly (free) salsa sessions. Political protests and impromptu demonstrations take place on the grandiose gallery stairs facing Georgia Street, a tradition that dates from the days when the building was a courthouse. ✉ *Bordered by Howe, Hornby, Robson, and Smithe sts., Downtown.*

11 Sinclair Centre. Vancouver architect Richard Henriquez knitted four buildings together into Sinclair Centre, an office–retail complex that takes up an entire city block between Cordova and Hastings, and Howe and Granville streets. Inside are high-end designer-clothing shops, federal government offices, and a number of fast-food outlets. The two Hastings Street buildings—the 1910 **Post Office,** which has an elegant clock tower, and the 1911 **Winch Building**—are linked with the 1937 **Post Office Extension** and the 1913 **Customs Examining Warehouse** to the north. As part of a meticulous restoration in the mid-1980s, the post-office facade was moved to the Granville Street side of the complex. The original clockwork from the old clock tower is on display inside, on the upper level of the arcade. ✉ *757 W. Hastings St., Downtown.*

3 Vancouver Art Gallery. Painter Emily Carr's haunting evocations of the British Columbian hinterland are among the attractions at western Canada's largest art gallery. Carr (1871–1945), a grocer's daughter from Victoria, fell in love with the wilderness around her and shocked middle-class Victorian society by running off to paint it. Her work accentuates the mysticism and the danger of B.C.'s wilderness, and records the diminishing presence of native cultures during that era (there's something of

Robson Square, in front of the Vancouver Art Gallery, is a downtown focal point; there's a skating rink here in winter.

a renaissance now). The gallery, which also hosts touring historical and contemporary exhibitions, is housed in a 1911 courthouse that Canadian architect Arthur Erickson redesigned in the early 1980s as part of the Robson Square redevelopment. Stone lions guard the steps to the parklike Georgia Street side; the main entrance is accessed from Robson Square at Hornby Street. ⊠ *750 Hornby St., Downtown* ☎ *604/662–4719* ⊕ *www.vanartgallery.bc.ca* ✍ *C$19.50; higher for some exhibits; by donation Tues. 5–9* ⊙ *Daily 10–5:30, Tues. and Thurs. 10–9.*

NEED A BREAK? The culinary artists at **Gallery Café** (⊠ *750 Hornby St., Downtown* ☎ *604/688–2233*) create delicious homemade soups, salads, pies, and other sinful desserts. Try to avoid the noon-hour crush, though, and if the sun is shining, opt for a patio seat overlooking the square.

⑫ **Waterfront Station.** This former Canadian Pacific Railway passenger terminal was built between 1912 and 1914 as the western terminus for Canada's transcontinental railway. After Canada's two major railways shifted their focus away from passenger service, the station became obsolete, but a 1978 renovation turned it into an office–retail complex and depot for SkyTrain, SeaBus, and West Coast Express passengers. In the main concourse, murals up near the ceiling depict the scenery travelers once saw on journeys across Canada. This is where you catch the SeaBus for the 13-minute trip across the harbor to the waterfront public market at Lonsdale Quay in North Vancouver. ⊠ *601 W. Cordova St., Downtown* ☎ *604/953–3333 SeaBus and SkyTrain, 604/488–8906 or 800/570–7245 West Coast Express.*

GASTOWN AND CHINATOWN

Gastown and Chinatown are favorite destinations for visitors and residents alike. Gastown is fast becoming the new Yaletown as überhip stores, ad agencies, and restaurants take over refurbished brick warehouses. Chinatown's array of produce stalls and curious alleyways make it look as if they're resisting gentrification, but inside many of the historic buildings are getting a new lease on life.

Gastown is best known for its cobblestone streets, Victorian era–style streetlamps and an overabundance of souvenir shops from tacky to tasteful. Nicknamed for the garrulous ("Gassy") Jack Deighton who opened his saloon where his statue now stands on Maple Tree Square, this is where Vancouver originated. A fire burned the fledgling community to the ground in 1886, but it was quickly resurrected. By the time the first transcontinental train arrived less than a year later, in May 1887, Vancouver had become an important transfer point for trade with the Far East and a stopping point for those en route to the gold rushes. The waterfront was crowded with hotels, warehouses, brothels, and dozens of saloons—place names such as Gaoler's Mews and Blood Alley can only hint to those early rough-and-tumble days. As commerce shifted toward Hastings Street and the Depression took its toll, though, Gastown fell into general neglect: hotels were converted into low-rent rooming houses and "the East Side," which includes Chinatown, gradually earned the reputation as having the poorest demographic in the country.

In 1971, the area was declared a historic district and it became the focus of a huge revitalization effort. Warehouses that once lined the shorefront were remodeled to house boutiques, cafés, loft apartments, and shops. Gastown became a visitor destination once again and today also attracts hip professional residents, and gentrification is extending into Chinatown.

Chinatown still has a completely distinct vibe, and although a large percentage of Vancouver's Chinese community has shifted to suburban Richmond, there's still a wonderful buzz of authenticity in the open-front markets, bakeries, and herbalist and import shops. Street signs are in Chinese lettering, streetlights look like lanterns topped with decorative dragons, and much of the architecture is patterned on that of Guangzhou (Canton).

> **NIGHT MARKET**
>
> If you're in the area in summer on a Friday, Saturday, or Sunday, check out Chinatown's bustling Night Market for food and tchotchkes: the 200 block of East Pender and Keefer are closed to traffic from 6:30–11 PM (until midnight on Saturday).

GETTING HERE AND AROUND

Getting to Gastown is easy: head for the waterfront. It's just east of the Waterfront Station. Allow about an hour to explore Gastown—that's without shopping too much. Then, if you have time, continue on to Chinatown, where you could spend an hour or two just wandering around, checking out the architecture and exotic wares; add about 45 minutes each if you also want to visit the Dr. Sun Yat-Sen Classical Chinese Garden and the Chinese Cultural Centre Museum.

Be aware that you might come across one or two seedy corners: it's all pretty safe by day, but you might prefer to cab it at night. The No. 19 Metrotown and No. 22 Knight buses travel east to Chinatown from stops along West Pender Street; the No. 3 Main and No. 8 Fraser serve Gastown and Chinatown from Cordova and Seymour near Waterfront Station. The Stadium SkyTrain station is a five-minute walk from Chinatown. From the station head down the Keefer Street steps, and turn left at Abbott Street. This will take you to the Millennium Gate.

Another option is to take the Silk Road Walking Tour, a self-guided route marked with colorful banners. It starts at the Vancouver Public Library downtown and leads north and east to the main attractions in Chinatown, before the banners lead you back to the library.

TOP ATTRACTIONS

❾ ★ Dr. Sun Yat-Sen Classical Chinese Garden. The first authentic Ming Dynasty–style garden outside China, this small garden was built in 1986 by 52 artisans from Suzhou, China. It incorporates design elements and traditional materials from several of Suzhou's centuries-old private gardens. No power tools, screws, or nails were used in the construction. Guided tours (45 minutes long), included in the ticket price, are conducted on the hour between mid-June and the end of August (call ahead for off-season tour times); they are valuable for understanding the philosophy and symbolism that are central to the garden's design. A concert series, including classical, Asian, world, jazz, and sacred music, plays on Friday evenings in July, August, and September. The free public park next door is also designed as a traditional Chinese garden. ■TIP➜ **Covered walkways make this a good rainy-day choice.** ✉ *578 Carrall St., Chinatown* ☎ *604/662–3207* ⊕ *www.vancouverchinesegarden.com* ☜ *C$10*

Byrnes Block **4**

Chinese Cultural Centre Museum and Archives **10**

Chinese Freemasons Building **6**

Dr. Sun Yat-Sen Classical Chinese Garden **9**

Gaoler's Mews ... **3**

Hotel Europe **5**

The Landing **1**

Millennium Gate **7**

Sam Kee Building **8**

Steam Clock **2**

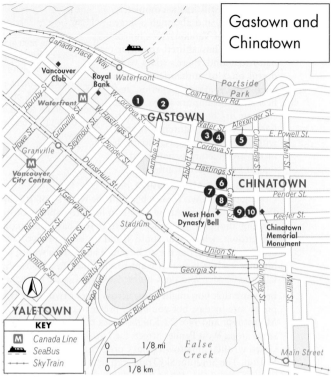

⊙ *May–mid-June and Sept., daily 10–6; mid-June–Aug., daily 9:30–7; Oct., daily 10–4; Nov.–Apr., Tues.–Sun. 10–4.*

❸ Gaoler's Mews. Once the site of the city's first civic buildings—the constable's cabin and customs house, and a two-cell log jail—this atmospheric brick-paved courtyard is home to cafés, an Irish pub, and architectural offices. ⊠ *Behind 12 Water St., Gastown.*

❺ Hotel Europe. Once billed as the best hotel in the city, this 1908 flatiron building is one of the world's finest examples of triangular architecture. Now used for government-subsidized housing and not open to the public, the hotel still has its original Italian tile work and lead-glass windows. The glass tiles in the sidewalk on Alexander Street were the former "skylight" for an underground saloon. ⊠ *43 Powell St., Gastown.*

❷ Steam Clock. An underground steam system, which also heats many local buildings, supplies the world's first steam clock—possibly Vancouver's most-photographed attraction. On the quarter hour a steam whistle rings out the Westminster chimes, and on the hour a huge cloud of steam spews from the apparatus. The ingenious design, based on an 1875 mechanism, was built in 1977 by Ray Saunders of Landmark Clocks (at 123 Cambie Street) to commemorate the community effort that saved Gastown from demolition. ⊠ *Water St., Gastown.*

Vancouver Police Centennial Museum. It's not in the best neighborhood, and its morgue and autopsy areas may be off-putting to some, but this museum provides an absorbing glimpse into the history of the Vancouver police. Firearms and counterfeit money are on exhibit, as are clues from some of the city's unsolved crimes: one of the more compelling mysteries, "Babes in the Woods," is about two children whose remains were found in Stanley Park in the 1950s. ⊠ *240 E. Cordova St., Gastown/Chinatown* ☎ *604/665–3346* ⊕ *www.vancouverpolicemuseum. ca* ⊠ *C$7* ۩ *Mon.–Sat. 9–5.*

WORTH NOTING

④ Byrnes Block. George Byrnes constructed Vancouver's oldest brick building on the site of Gassy Jack Deighton's second saloon after the 1886 Great Fire, which wiped out most of the fledgling settlement of Vancouver. For a while this two-story building was Vancouver's top luxury hotel, the Alhambra Hotel, charging a dollar a night. The site of Deighton's original saloon, east of the Byrnes Block where his statue now stands, is the zero point from which all Vancouver street addresses start. ⊠ *2 Water St., Gastown.*

⑩ Chinese Cultural Centre Museum and Archives. The Chinese have a rich, grueling, and enduring history in British Columbia, and it's well represented in this Ming Dynasty–style facility. The art gallery upstairs hosts traveling exhibits by Chinese and Canadian artists, and an on-site military museum recalls the role of Chinese Canadians in the last two world wars. Across the street is the Chinatown Memorial Monument, commemorating the Chinese-Canadian community's contribution to the city, province, and country. The monument, shaped in the Chinese character "zhong," symbolizing moderation and harmony, is flanked by bronze statues of a railroad worker and a World War II soldier. ⊠ *555 Columbia St., Chinatown* ☎ *604/658–8880* ⊕ *www.cccvan.com* ⊠ *C$4, Tues. by donation* ۩ *Tues.–Sun. 11–5.*

⑥ Chinese Freemasons Building. Two completely different facades distinguish this structure on the northwest corner of Pender and Carrall streets. The side facing Pender represents a fine example of Cantonese recessed balconies. The Carrall Street side displays the standard Victorian style common throughout the British Empire. Dr. Sun Yat-Sen hid for months in this building from agents of the Manchu Dynasty while he raised funds for its overthrow, which he accomplished in 1911. ⊠ *3 W. Pender St., Chinatown.*

① The Landing. Built in 1905 with gold-rush money, this brick warehouse was elegantly renovated in 1988 to include shops and Steamworks, a popular brewpub *(⇨ see the review in the Nightlife chapter).* From the oversized bay window at the rear of the lobby you can appreciate where the shoreline was 100 years ago, as well as enjoy terrific views of Burrard Inlet and the North Shore Mountains. ⊠ *375 Water St., Gastown.*

⑦ Millennium Gate. This four-pillar, three-story high, brightly painted arch spanning Pender Street was erected in 2002 to mark the millennium and commemorate the Chinese community's role in Vancouver's history. The gate incorporates both Eastern and Western symbols, and both

DID YOU KNOW?

Gastown's steam clock is one of Vancouver's most famous landmarks. Rather than bells, a steam whistle sounds on the quarter hour.

Top Asphalt Strolls: Vancouver

Robson Street: A shopaholics' dream come true, Robson has everything from finger-licking good fudge to fashionista shopping.

Granville Island: It's always a voyage of discovery for fabulous local art, foodstuffs, boutique shops, street entertainment, and more.

Main Street: This is the undisputed antiques capital of the city, where you'll also find folk art, fine art, and retro 1950s appliances—you might not be in the market for any of it, but it's fun to browse.

Chinatown: The variety of Asian treats and delicacies along Keefer and East Pender streets is spectacular—take your pick of exotic teas, sea cucumbers, dried seahorses, and nifty gifts.

Commercial Drive: From the coffee-houses to the cantinas, The Drive has a healthy serving of cultural cool with an eclectic array of people and shops.

The West End: This pleasing, tree-lined neighborhood is a refreshing change of pace from the urban commotion steps away.

Harbor-front Shoreline: With the water's edge on one side and glassy, million-dollar condo developments and commercial high-rises on the other, a walk along the harbor front epitomizes the future of this city.

Marinaside: Residents of Yaletown's intense-density condos flock to this walking and cycling path around False Creek. Combine your walk with a ride on an Aquabus ferry if time is short or your feet get weary.

---

traditional and modern Chinese themes. Just east of the Millennium Gate, a right turn will take you into Shanghai Alley. Also known as Chinatown Heritage Alley, this was the site of the first Chinese settlement in the Vancouver area. By 1890 Shanghai Alley and neighboring Canton Alley were home to about 1,000 Chinese residents. At the end of the alley is a replica of the West Han Dynasty Bell, a gift to Vancouver from the city of Guangzhou, China. Surrounding the bell are a series of panels relaying some of the area's early history.

8 **Sam Kee Building.** *Ripley's Believe It or Not!* recognizes this 6-foot-wide structure as the narrowest office building in the world. In 1913, after the city confiscated most of the then-owner's land to widen Pender Street, he built a store on what was left, in protest. Customers had to be served through the windows. These days the building houses an insurance agency, whose employees make do within the 4-foot-10-inch-wide interior. The glass panes in the sidewalk on Pender Street once provided light for Chinatown's public baths, which, in the early 20th century, were in the basement here. The presence of this and other underground sites has fueled rumors that Chinatown and Gastown were connected by tunnels, enabling residents of the latter to anonymously enjoy the vices of the former. No such tunnels have been found, however. ⊠ *8 W. Pender St., Chinatown.*

YALETOWN AND FALSE CREEK

Back around 1985–86 the B.C. provincial government cleaned up a derelict industrial site on the north shore of False Creek, built a world's fair, and invited everyone; 20 million people showed up for Expo '86. Now, the site of the fair, Yaletown, has become one of the largest and most densely populated, urban-redevelopment projects in North America. It's now one of the city's most fashionable neighborhoods, and the Victorian-brick loading docks have become terraces for cappuccino bars.

First settled by railroad workers who followed the newly laid tracks from the town of Yale in the Fraser Canyon, Yaletown in the 1880s and '90s was probably the most lawless place in Canada: it was so far into the woods that the Royal Canadian Mounted Police complained they couldn't patrol it. The area—which also has restaurants, brewpubs, day spas, retail and wholesale fashion outlets, and shops selling upscale home decor—makes the most of its waterfront location, with a seaside walk and cycle path that completely encircles False Creek.

On the south shore, note the matchbox cubelike buildings. Purposely designed to house the Winter Olympics Athlete's Village, they remain controversial—for construction-cost overruns and displeasing aesthetics. The village has fallen short of promises to be a totally self-sustaining, eco-aware community, though it should be noted that many of the "boxes" are made from recycled ship containers.

GETTING HERE AND AROUND
Parking is tight in Yaletown; your best bet is the lot at Library Square nearby. It's easy to walk here from downtown, though, and you can scoot to Yaletown from other locations aboard the False Creek and Aquabus ferries (☎ *604/689–5858*), which run every 15 minutes from

B.C. Sports Hall of
Fame and
Museum **3**

Contemporary Art
Gallery **2**

Library Square ...**1**

Science World ...**4**

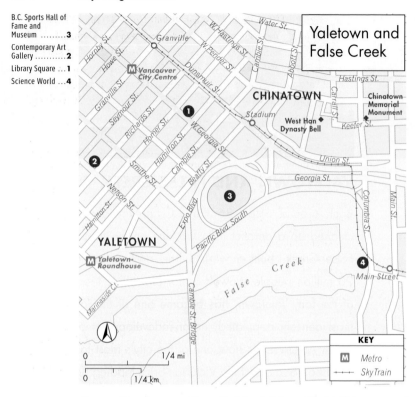

7 AM to 10 PM between Granville Island, Science World, Yaletown, and the south shore of False Creek.

If you're at Science World on a summer weekend, you might be able to catch the **Downtown Historic Railway** (☎ 604/665–3903 ⊕ *www.trams.bc.ca*) to Granville Island—we say "might" because the antique trams had to suspend service during the construction of the airport SkyTrain line and other Olympic-related projects. The hope is to see the trams running again (on summer weekends only) in 2010.

TOP ATTRACTIONS

❹ Science World. In a gigantic shiny dome built over the Omnimax theater, this hands-on science center encourages children to participate in interactive exhibits and demonstrations. Exhibits change throughout the year, so there's always something new to see. It's an easy walk (and mini-ferry ride) from Yaletown; there's a SkyTrain station on its doorstep, and there's plenty of parking though the lot is prone to bicycle theft. ✉ *1455 Québec St., False Creek* ☎ *604/443–7443 or 604/443–7440* ⊕ *www.scienceworld.bc.ca* 🎟 *Science World C$19.75, Science World and Omnimax theater C$24.75* ☉ *July–Labor Day, daily 10–6; Sept.– June, weekdays 10–5, weekends 10–6.*

NEED A BREAK?

Urban Fare (✉ *177 Davie St., Yaletown* ☎ *604/975–7550*) supplies, among other things, truffles, foie gras, and bread air-freighted from France to Yaletown's Francophiles and foodies. It's open daily 6 AM–midnight and is considered *the* destination for gastronomes. You can sample the wares at the café or purchase a take-out snack and eat it at the water's edge over-looking an idyllic marina. Additional Urban Fare outlets are at Coal Harbour and on Alberni Street next to the posh Shangri-la Hotel.

WORTH NOTING

❸ **B.C. Sports Hall of Fame and Museum.** Inside the B.C. Place Stadium com-plex, this museum celebrates the province's sports achievers in a series of historical displays. You can test your sprinting, climbing, and throwing prowess in the high-tech participation gallery. The Scavenger History Hunt quiz is equally engaging though not as energetic. An hour-long audio tour is included with admission. As you leave the museum, the Terry Fox Memorial is to your left. This archway at the foot of Rob-son Street was built in honor of Terry Fox (1958–81), a local student whose cross-Canada run raised millions of dollars for cancer research. A memorial fund-raising run is now held annually in 58 countries around the world. ✉ *B.C. Place, 777 Pacific Blvd. S, Gate A, at Beatty and Robson sts., Downtown* ☎ *604/687–5520* ⊕ *www.bcsportshalloffame. com* 🎫 *C$10* 🕙 *Daily 10–5.*

❷ **Contemporary Art Gallery.** This nonprofit public gallery in a purpose-built modern building has regularly changing exhibits of the latest in contemporary local and international visual art. Events include artists' talks, lectures, and tours. ✉ *555 Nelson St., Downtown* ☎ *604/681–2700* ⊕ *www.contemporaryartgallery.ca* 🎫 *By donation* 🕙 *Wed. and Fri. noon–6, Thurs. noon–8, weekends noon–5.*

❶ **Library Square.** The spiraling library building, open plazas, and lofty atrium of Library Square, completed in the mid-1990s, were built to evoke images of the Colosseum in Rome. A high-tech public library is the core of the structure; the outer edge of the spiral houses cafés and a handful of boutiques. ✉ *350 W. Georgia St., Downtown* ☎ *604/331–3600* ⊕ *www.vpl.vancouver.bc.ca* 🕙 *Mon.–Thurs. 10–9, Fri. and Sat. 10–6, Sun. 12–5.*

STANLEY PARK

A 1,000-acre wilderness park, only blocks from the downtown section of a major city, is a rare treasure. Vancouverites use it, protect it, and love it with such zeal that when it was proposed that the 120-year-old Hollow Tree be axed due to safety concerns, citizens rallied, raised funds, and literally engineered its salvation.

The fact that Stanley Park is so close to the city is actually all thanks to the Americans—sort of! In the 1860s, because of a threat of American invasion, this oceanfront peninsula was designated a military reserve, though it was never needed. When the City of Vancouver was incorporated in 1886, the council's first act was to request the land be set aside as a park. Permission was granted two years later and the grounds were named Stanley Park after Lord Stanley, then governor general of Canada. The only military vestige is Deadman's Island, a former burial ground for local Salish First Nations people and early settlers; the small naval installation here, HMCS *Discovery*, is not open to the public.

Stanley Park is, perhaps, the single most prized possession of Vancouverites, who make use of it fervently to cycle, walk, jog, Rollerblade, play cricket and tennis, and enjoy outdoor art shows and theater performances alongside attractions such as the renowned aquarium.

When a storm swept across the park's shores in December 2006, it destroyed close to 10,000 trees as well as parts of the perimeter seawall. Locals contributed thousands of dollars to the clean-up and replanting effort in addition to the monies set aside by local authorities. The storm's silver lining was that it cleared some dead-wood areas, making room for the reintroduction of many of the park's original species of trees. It also gave rise to an unusual ecological arts program in which ephemeral sculptures have been placed in various outdoor locations. Made of natural and organic materials, the elements are constantly changing the look of each piece which, over the course of its 24-month "display period," will decay and return to the earth.

The **Stanley Park Shuttle** (☎ 604/257–8400 ⊕ www.vancouver.ca/parks/) operates mid-June to mid-September between 10 AM and 6:30 PM, providing frequent (every 15 minutes) transportation to 15 major park sights. Pick it up on Pipeline Road, near the Georgia Street park entrance, or at any of the stops in the park. The fare is C$2.

For information about guided nature walks in the park, contact the **Lost Lagoon Nature House** (☎ 604/257–8544 ⊕ www.stanleyparkecology.ca) on the south shore of Lost Lagoon, at the foot of Alberni Street. They operate May to September, Tuesday through Sunday, 9–4:30.

GETTING HERE AND AROUND

If you're driving to Stanley Park, head northwest on Georgia Street from downtown. Parking is available at or near all the major attractions; one ticket (C$8 April–September, C$4 October–March) allows you to park all day and to move between lots. Tickets are purchased from automated dispensers in lots, and should be displayed on your dashboard.

If you're taking public transit, catch any bus labeled STANLEY PARK at the corner of Pender and Howe streets downtown. You can also catch North Vancouver Bus 240 or 246 from anywhere on West Georgia Street to the park entrance at Georgia and Chilco streets, or a Robson Bus 5 to Robson and Denman streets, where there are a number of bicycle-rental outlets.

Once at the park, you can bike, walk, drive, or take the park shuttle to reach the main attractions.

Numbers in the text correspond to numbers in the margin and on the Stanley Park map.

TOP ATTRACTIONS

❼ Prospect Point. At 211 feet, Prospect Point is the highest point in the park and provides striking views of the Lions Gate Bridge (watch for cruise ships passing below), the North Shore, and Burrard Inlet. There's also a year-round souvenir shop, a snack bar with terrific ice cream, and a restaurant (May–September only). From the seawall, you can see where cormorants build their seaweed nests along the cliff ledges.

❶ Seawall. The seawall path, a 9-km (5½-mi) paved shoreline route popular with walkers, cyclists, and in-line skaters, is one of several car-free

Fodor's Choice
★

zones within the park. If you have the time (about a half day) and the energy, strolling the entire seawall is an exhilarating experience. It extends an additional mile east past the marinas, cafés, and waterfront condominiums of Coal Harbour to Canada Place downtown, so you could start your walk or ride from there. From the south side of the park, the seawall continues for another 28 km (17 mi) along Vancouver's waterfront, to the University of British Columbia, allowing for a pleasant, if ambitious, day's bike ride. Along the seawall, cyclists must wear helmets and stay on their side of the path. Within Stanley Park, cyclists must ride in a counterclockwise direction.

The seawall can get crowded on summer weekends, but inside the park is a 28-km (17-mi) network of peaceful walking and cycling paths through old- and second-growth forest. The wheelchair-accessible Beaver Lake Interpretive Trail is a good choice if you're interested in park

Lumberman's
Arch **4**

Miniature Railway
and Children's
Farmyard **6**

Nine O'Clock
Gun **3**

Prospect
Point **7**

Seawall **1**

Second
Beach **9**

Siwash
Rock **8**

Totem
poles **2**

Vancouver
Aquarium **5**

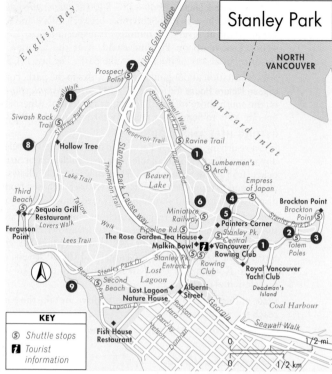

ecology. Take a map—they're available at the park-information booth and many of the concession stands—and don't go into the woods alone or after dusk.

Totem poles. Totem poles are an important art form among native peoples along British Columbia's coast. These eight poles, all carved in the latter half of the 20th century, include replicas of poles originally brought to the park from the north coast in the 1920s, as well as poles carved specifically for the park by First Nations artists. The several styles of poles represent a cross section of B.C. native groups, including the Kwakwaka'wakw, Haida, and Nisga'a. The combination of carved animals, fish, birds, and mythological creatures represents clan history. An information center near the site has a snack bar, a gift shop, and information about B.C.'s First Nations.

Vancouver Aquarium Marine Science Centre. Massive pools with windows below water level let you come face to face with beluga whales, sea otters, sea lions, dolphins, and harbor seals at this research and educational facility. In the Amazon rain-forest gallery you can walk through a jungle populated with piranhas, caimans, and tropical birds, and in summer, you'll be surrounded by hundreds of free-flying butterflies. Other displays, many with hands-on features for kids, show the underwater life of coastal British Columbia and the Canadian Arctic. A

Tropic Zone is home to exotic fresh-water and saltwater life, including clown fish, moray eels, and black-tip reef sharks. Beluga whale, sea lion, and dolphin shows, as well as dive shows (where divers swim with aquatic life, including sharks) are held daily. Make sure to check out the 4-D film experience; it's a multisensory show that puts mist, smell, and wind into the 3-D equation. For an extra fee, you can help the trainers feed and train otters, belugas, and sea lions. There's also a café and a gift shop. Be prepared for lines on weekends and school holidays. ■TIP→ The quietest time to visit is before 11 AM or after 3 PM ⊠ 841 Avison Way, Stanley Park ☎ 604/659–3474 ⊕ www.vanaqua. org ⊠ C$22 ⊙ July–Labor Day, daily 9:30–7; Labor Day–June, daily 9:30–5:30.

WORTH NOTING

4 **Lumbermen's Arch.** Made of one massive log, this archway, erected in 1952, is dedicated to the workers in Vancouver's first industry. Beside the arch is an asphalt path that leads back to Lost Lagoon and the Vancouver Aquarium. There's a picnic area, a snack bar, and small beach here, too. The Children's Water Park is across the road.

6 **Miniature Railway and Children's Farmyard.** A child-size steam train takes kids and adults on a ride through the woods. Next door is a farmyard full of some 200 critters, including goats, rabbits, and pigs. At Christmastime, an elaborate light display illuminates the route, and Halloween displays draw crowds throughout October. ■TIP→ A family ticket gets everyone in for the child's rate. ⊠ Off Pipeline Rd., Stanley Park ☎ 604/257–8531 ⊠ Each site C$6, C$3 children; C$10 for a combination ticket ⊙ Feb.–May, weekends 11–4, weather permitting; June–Sept., daily 10:30–5; call for holiday and off-season hours.

3 **Nine O'Clock Gun.** This cannonlike apparatus by the water was installed in 1890 to alert fishermen to a curfew ending weekend fishing. Now it signals 9 o'clock every night.

NEED A BREAK? **Stanley's Park Bar and Grill** (☎ 604/602–3088), in a 1911 manor house, is a family-friendly veranda serving burgers, wraps, soups, and salads. Open May through September, it overlooks the Rose Garden and is near the Children's Farmyard and Malkin Ball, where outdoor theater and concerts are held in summer. There's also a gift and souvenir shop here.

9 **Second Beach.** The 50-meter pool, which has lifeguards and waterslides, is a popular spot in summer. The sandy beach has a playground and

Stanley Park › 51

CLOSE UP

A Tour of Stanley Park

Stanley Park Drive is a scenic road that circles the park, often parallel to the Seawall walking/cycling path ❶. If you're walking or cycling, start at the foot of Alberni Street, beside Lost Lagoon. Go through the underpass and veer right, following the cycle-path markings, to the seawall.

Whichever route you travel, the old wooden structure that you pass on your right is the Vancouver Rowing Club, a private athletic club established in 1903. Just ahead and to your left is a parking lot, an information booth (staffed year-round, weather permitting), and a turnoff to the aquarium and Painters Corner, where artists sell their work. A Salmon Demonstration Stream, near the information booth, presents facts about the life cycle of the fish.

Continue along past the Royal Vancouver Yacht Club, and after ½ km (¼ mi) you'll reach the causeway to Deadman's Island. The totem poles ❷, which are a bit farther down Stanley Park Drive and on your left, are a popular photo stop. The Nine O'Clock Gun ❸ is ahead at the water's edge, just past the sign for Hallelujah Point. Brockton Point and its small lighthouse and foghorn are to the north. Brockton Oval, where you can catch a rugby game in winter or cricket in summer, is inland on your left. On the waterside, watch for the *Girl in a Wetsuit*, a sculpture on a rock offshore that mimics Copenhagen's *Little Mermaid*. A little farther along the seashore stands a replica of the dragon-shaped figurehead from the SS *Empress of Japan*, which plied these waters between 1891 and 1922.

Lumbermen's Arch ❹, a log archway, is at km 3 (mi 2) of the drive. There's a picnic area, a snack bar, and a small beach. The Children's Water Park, across the road, is a big draw in summer. Cyclists and walkers can turn off here for a shortcut back to the Vancouver Aquarium ❺, the Miniature Railway ❻ and Children's Farmyard, and the park entrance.

At the Lions Gate Bridge: cyclists go under the bridge, past Prospect Point ❼; drivers go over the bridge to a viewpoint–café at the top of Prospect Point. Both routes then continue to the English Bay side of the park and its sandy beaches. Keep an eye open for the Hollow Tree (you can't miss the signs). The imposing monolith offshore (not visible from the road) is Siwash Rock ❽, the focus of a native legend. Continue to the swimming area and snack bar at Third Beach, then the heated pool at Second Beach ❾. If you're walking or cycling, you can shortcut from here back to Lost Lagoon by taking the perpendicular pathway behind the pool that cuts into the park. Either footbridge ahead leads to a path along the south side of the lagoon that will take you to Alberni and Georgia streets. If you continue along the seawall from Second Beach, you'll emerge from the park into a residential part of the West End.

An underwater view of a beluga whale at the Vancouver Aquarium.

covered picnic areas. If you like romantic beachside sunsets, this is one for the books. ☎ *604/257–8371 summer only* ⊕ *www.vancouver.ca/ parks/* ✉ *Beach free, pool C$5* ☉ *Pool mid-May–mid-June, weekdays noon–8:45, weekends 10–8:45; mid-June–late July, daily 10–8:45; late July–Labor Day, Mon., Wed., Fri. 7 AM–8:45 PM, Tues., Thurs., and weekends 10–8:45.*

⑧ Siwash Rock. According to a local First Nations legend, this 50-foot-high offshore promontory is a monument to a man who was turned into stone as a reward for his unselfishness. The rock is visible from the seawall; if you're driving, you need to park and take a short path through the woods. Watch for the Hollow Tree nearby. This 56-foot-wide burnt cedar stump has shrunk over the years but still gives an idea of how large some of the old-growth trees can be.

NEED A BREAK?

Prospect Point Café (☎ *604/669–2737*), open only in summer, is at the top of Prospect Point, with a deck overlooking the Lions Gate Bridge. It specializes in salmon dishes and is a good lunch stop, though it's often fully booked with tour groups ($–$$$).

GRANVILLE ISLAND

Fodor's Choice
★

The creative redevelopment of this former industrial waste-
land vies with Stanley Park as the city's top attraction. An
active cement works remains at its heart, and is oddly com-
plemented with a thriving diversity of artist studios, performing arts spaces, an indoor farmers' market, specialty shops,
and a jammed-to-the-gunnels marina. There's not a chain
store or designer label in sight.

In the early 20th century False Creek was dredged for better access
to the sawmills that lined the shore and the sludge was heaped onto a
sandbar that grew large enough to house much-needed industrial and
logging-equipment plants. Although business thrived in the twenties,
most fell into derelict status by the 1960s. In the early '70s, though,
the federal government came up with a creative plan to redevelop the
island with a public market, marine activities, and artisans' studios. The
refurbished Granville Island opened to the public in 1979 and was an
immediate hit with locals and visitors alike.

Explore Granville Island at your leisure but try to plan your expedition
over a meal, since the market is an excellent place for lunch, snacks,
and shopping. The buildings behind the market are as diverse as the
island's main attractions and house all sorts of crafts shops. The waterside boardwalk behind the Arts Club and around the Creekhouse building will bring you to Ocean Art Works, an open-sided longhouse-style
structure where you can watch First Nations artists at work. Be sure
to visit the free contemporary galleries beside the covered walkway
to Sea Village, one of the few houseboat communities in Vancouver.
Other nooks and alleys to note are Ron Basford Park, a natural amphitheater for outdoor performances, and Railspur Alley, home to about
a dozen studios and galleries that produce everything from guitars to
leather work and model dragons. Granville Island is also a venue for

Vancouver's many performing arts festivals—and a great place to catch top-quality street entertainment at any time.

Though the 35-acre island is now technically a peninsula, connected years ago by landfill to the south shore of False Creek, it still feels like an island with its own distinct character.

Numbers in the text correspond to numbers in the margin and on the Granville Island map.

GETTING HERE AND AROUND

The mini Aquabus ferries are a favorite way to get to Granville Island (it's about a two-minute ride); they depart from the south end of Hornby Street, a 15-minute walk from downtown Vancouver. The Aquabus delivers passengers across False Creek to the Granville Island Public Market *(see below)*. The larger False Creek ferries leave every five minutes for Granville Island from a dock behind the Vancouver Aquatic Centre, on Beach Avenue. Still another option is to take a 20-minute ride on a TransLink bus: from Waterfront Station or stops on Granville Street, take False Creek South Bus 50 to the edge of the island. Buses 4 UBC and 7 Dunbar will also take you within a few minutes' walk of the island. The market is a short walk from the bus, ferry, or tram stop. If you drive, parking is free for up to three hours, and paid parking is available in four garages on the island.

Look out for the **Downtown Historic Railway** (☎ *604/665–3903* ⊕ *www. trams.bc.ca*), two early-20th-century electric trams scheduled to run on summer weekends and holiday afternoons from Science World to Granville Island. Olympics-related construction forced the railway to cease operation for a few years but it's scheduled to resume in 2010.

TIMING
If your schedule is tight, you can tour Granville Island in two to three hours. If you like to shop you could spend a full day.

TOP ATTRACTIONS

❶ **Granville Island Public Market.** Because no chain stores are allowed in this Fodor's Choice 50,000-square-foot building, each shop here is unique. Dozens of stalls ★ sell locally grown produce direct from the farm; others sell crafts, chocolates, cheese, fish, meat, flowers, and exotic foods. On Thursdays in summer, market gardeners sell fruit and vegetables from trucks outside. At the north end of the market you can pick up a snack, lunch, or coffee at one of the many food stalls. The Market Courtyard, on the waterside, is a good place to catch street entertainers—be prepared to get roped into the action, if only to check the padlocks of an escape artist's gear. Weekends can get madly busy. ⊠ *1689 Johnston St., Granville Island* ☎ *604/666–5784* ⊕ *www.granvilleisland.com* ☉ *Daily 9–7.*

WORTH NOTING

❻ **Emily Carr University of Art and Design.** The university's three main buildings—tin-plated structures formerly used for industrial purposes—were renovated in the 1970s. The **Charles H. Scott Gallery** to the right of the main entrance hosts contemporary exhibitions in various media. Two other galleries showcase student work. Note that there isn't any Emily Carr work on display here; the building is simply named in her honor. ⊠ *1399 Johnston St., Granville Island* ☎ *604/844–3811* ⊕ *www.ecuad. ca* 🎟 *Free* ☉ *Weekdays noon–5, weekends 10–5.*

Emily Carr
Institute of Art
and Design **6**

Granville Island
Brewing **3**

Grandville Island
Public Market **1**

Granville Island
Water Park **5**

Kids' Market **4**

Net Loft **2**

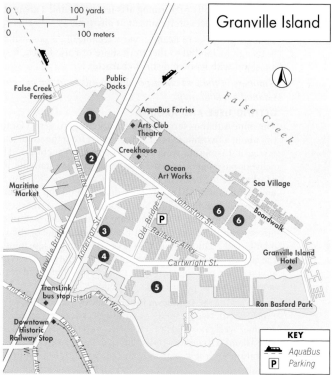

3 Granville Island Brewing. Tours of Canada's first modern microbrewery last about 45 minutes and include a taste of four brews. Kids are welcome; they get a taste of root beer. ✉ *1441 Cartwright St., Granville Island* ☎ *604/687–2739* ⊕ *www.gib.ca* ✍ *C$9.75* ☉ *Daily 10–8; tours daily at noon, 2, and 4.*

5 Granville Island Water Park. North America's largest, free public water park has slides, pipes, and sprinklers for children to shower one another. Kids can also join free daily craft activities. There's a grassy patch for picnics and clean washrooms at the nearby community center. ✉ *1318 Cartwright St., Granville Island* ☎ *604/257–8195* ✍ *Free* ☉ *Mid-May– Labor Day, daily 10–6; slides open mid-June.*

4 Kids' Market. A converted factory warehouse sets the stage for a slice of kids' heaven on Granville Island. The Kids' Market has an indoor play area and two floors of small shops that sell all kinds of toys, magic gear, books, and other fun stuff. ✉ *1496 Cartwright St., Granville Island* ☎ *604/689–8447* ⊕ *www.kidsmarket.ca* ☉ *Daily 10–6.*

2 Net Loft. This blue-and-red building—a former loft where fishermen used to dry their nets—includes a bookstore, a café, and a collection of high-quality boutiques selling imported and locally made crafts, exotic fabrics, handmade paper, and First Nations art. ✉ *1666 Johnston St., Granville Island* ☎ *No phone* ☉ *Daily 10–7.*

DID YOU KNOW?

Cooking demonstrations are part of the fun at Granville market, where you can also shop for produce, baked goods, and prepared foods.

THE WEST SIDE AND KITSILANO

Once a hippie haven, Kitsilano has gone upmarket. Character homes and specialty shopping now make up some of the country's most expensive few square miles of real estate. The West Side has the city's best gardens and natural sights; "Kits," however, is really where all the action is.

Leave downtown via Burrard, Granville, or Cambie Street bridges and you'll be on the West Side, an area of diverse neighborhoods just south of the downtown core. Any reference to "the West Side" usually has moneyed connotations, as in South Granville's chic galleries and upscale shopping, the old-family mansions of Shaughnessy, the tony university district, and even the up-and-coming, albeit yet to arrive, area surrounding Cambie Street. The West Side is the antithesis of the low-income East Side of Vancouver. Some of Vancouver's best gardens, natural sights, and museums, including the renowned Museum of Anthropology on the campus of the University of British Columbia, are south of downtown Vancouver. Established in 1908, UBC is the city's main university campus with a student population of approximately 44,000. The university is where you'll also find the Chan Centre for the Performing Arts (⇨ *See the Nightlife and Performing Arts chapter*), the Botanical Gardens, and Pacific Spirit Regional Park—the latter, although it can't compare with Stanley Park, is where the locals go for meandering forested trails that put you in touch with nature. Except during rush hour, it takes about 30 minutes to drive from downtown to the University of British Columbia.

The beachfront district of Kitsilano (popularly known as Kits), is among the trendiest of Canadian neighborhoods. Originally inhabited by the Squamish people, whose Chief Khahtsahlanough gave the area its name, Kitsilano began to attract day-trippers from Vancouver in the early part of the 20th century. Some stayed and built lavish waterfront mansions; others built simpler Craftsman-style houses farther up the slope. After a period of decline in the mid-20th century, Kits became a haven for hippies and their yuppie offspring who have since restored many of the

2

wood-frame houses, and the neighborhood is once again chic. Kitsilano is home to three museums, some fashionable shops, and popular pubs and cafés. Kits has hidden treasures, too: rare boats moored at Heritage Harbour, stately mansions on forested lots, and, all along the waterfront, quiet coves and shady paths within a stone's throw of Canada's liveliest beach. Vanier Park, the grassy beachside setting for three museums and the best kite-flying venue in Vancouver, is the logical gateway to Kits. Every summer, it also hosts the Children's Festival, and Bard on the Beach theater—both presented under colorful tents. Because Vanier Park is home to three indoor attractions, it's also a great rainy-day activity center.

GETTING HERE AND AROUND

Individual attractions on the West Side are easily reached by TransLink buses, but a car makes things easier, especially if you want to see more than one of these sites in a day.

The most enjoyable way to get to Kitsilano is by a False Creek ferry from Granville Island or from the dock behind the Vancouver Aquatic Centre, on Beach Avenue. The ferries dock at Heritage Harbour in Kitsilano, behind the Vancouver Maritime Museum. You can also walk or cycle the 1 km (½ mi) or so along the waterfront pathway from Granville Island (leave the island by Anderson Street and keep to your right along the waterfront, following the Seaside Bike Path signs). If you prefer to come by road, drive over the Burrard Street Bridge, turn right at Chestnut Street, and park in either of the museum parking lots; or take bus 2, or 22, traveling south on Burrard Street downtown, get off at Cypress Street and Cornwall Avenue, and walk over to the park.

TOP ATTRACTIONS

Fodor's Choice
★

Museum of Anthropology. Part of the University of British Columbia, the MOA has one of the world's leading collections of Northwest Coast First Nations art. The Great Hall displays dramatic cedar poles, bent-wood boxes, and canoes adorned with traditional Northwest Coast–painted designs. On clear days, the gallery's 50-foot-tall windows reveal a striking backdrop of mountains and sea. Another highlight is the work of the late Bill Reid, one of Canada's most respected Haida artists. In *The Raven and the First Men* (1980), carved in yellow cedar, he tells a Haida story of creation. Reid's gold-and-silver jewelry work is also on display, as are exquisite carvings of gold, silver, and argillite (a black shale found on Haida Gwaii, also known as the Queen Charlotte Islands) by other First Nations artists. The museum's visible storage section displays, in drawers and cases, contain thousands of examples of tools, textiles, masks, and other artifacts from around the world. The Koerner Ceramics Gallery contains 600 pieces from 15th- to 19th-century Europe. Behind the museum are two Haida houses, set on the cliff over the water. Free guided tours—given twice daily in summer, usually at 11 and 2 (call to confirm times)—are immensely informative. For an extra C$5 you can rent a VUEguide, an electronic device which senses where you are in the museum and shows relevant artist interviews, archival footage, and photographs of the artifacts in their original contexts, on a hand-held screen. Arthur Erickson designed the cliff-top structure that houses the MOA, which also has a book and fine-art shop

Part of the attraction of the Museum of Anthropology are the exhibits outside the museum, on the cliffs overlooking the water.

and a summertime café. To reach the museum by transit, take UBC bus 4 from Granville Street or bus 44 from Burrard Street downtown to the university loop, a 10-minute walk from the museum. ■TIP→ Pay parking is available in the Rose Garden parking lot, across Marine Drive from the museum. ⊠ *University of British Columbia, 6393 N.W. Marine Dr., Point Grey* ☎ *604/822–5087* ⊕ *www.moa.ubc.ca* ✉ *C$11, Tues. 5–9 C$6* ☺ *Memorial Day–Labor Day, Tues. 10–9, Wed.–Mon. 10–5; Labor Day–Memorial Day, Tues. 11–9, Wed.–Sun. 11–5.*

Nitobe Memorial Garden. Opened in 1960 in memory of Japanese scholar and diplomat Dr. Inazo Nitobe (1862–1933), this 2½-acre walled garden, which includes a pond, a stream with a small waterfall, and a ceremonial teahouse, is considered one of the most authentic Japanese tea and strolling gardens outside Japan. Designed by Professor Kannosuke Mori of Japan's Chiba University, the garden incorporates many native British Columbia trees and shrubs, pruned and trained Japanese style, and interplanted with Japanese maples and flowering shrubs. The circular path around the park symbolizes the cycle of life and provides a tranquil view from every direction. Cherry blossoms are the highlight in April and May, and in June the irises are magnificent. Because the garden is so exotic, renting an audio guide is worth the C$2. ■TIP→ Japanese tea ceremonies are held the last Saturday of every month, June through October. Space is limited to 8 people; call ☎ 604/939–7749 for reservations. ⊠ *University of British Columbia, 1903 West Mall, Point Grey* ☎ *604/822–9666* ⊕ *www.nitobe.org* ✉ *C$5 mid-Mar.–mid-Oct., C$10 includes admission to the UBC Botanical Gardens; by donation mid-Oct.–mid-Mar.* ☺ *Mid-Mar.–mid-Oct., daily 10–6; mid-Oct.–mid-Mar., weekdays 10–2:30.*

EN **ROUTE**	**Old Hastings Mill Store Museum.** Vancouver's first store and oldest building was built in 1865 at the foot of Dunlevy Street in Gastown and moved to this seaside spot near the Royal Vancouver Yacht Club in 1930. It's a little wooden structure at the corner of Point Grey Road and Alma Street—about midpoint between downtown and UBC—and is the only building to predate the 1886 Great Fire. The site is now a museum with displays of First Nations artifacts and pioneer household goods. ☒ *1575 Alma St., Point Grey* ☎ *604/734–1212* ☒ *By donation* ☉ *Mid-June–mid-Sept., Tues.–Sun. 1–4; mid-Sept.–mid-Dec. and Feb.–mid-June, weekends 1–4.*

☼ **Queen Elizabeth Park.** At the highest point in the city, showcasing 360-degree views of downtown, this 52-hectare (130-acre) park has lavish sunken gardens (in a former stone quarry), a rose garden, and an abundance of grassy picnicking spots. Other park facilities include 20 tennis courts, pitch and putt (an 18-hole putting green), and a restaurant. On summer evenings there's free outdoor dancing on the Plaza—everything from Scottish country dance to salsa, for all ages and levels. In the **Bloedel Floral Conservatory** you can see tropical and desert plants and 100 species of free-flying tropical birds in a glass geodesic dome—the perfect place to be on a rainy day. To reach the park by public transportation, take a Cambie Bus 15 from the corner of Robson and Burrard streets downtown to 33rd Avenue; it should take about 20 minutes. Hop on board the SkyTrain for an even faster trip although the stop requires a six-block walk. ■TIP→ Park activities make for a great family excursion as well as being a gardener's delight, and unlike Stanley Park with its acres of rain forest, Queen Elizabeth's floral showcases are the focal point for bridal parties galore—particularly on Saturday afternoons. ☒ *Cambie St. and 33rd Ave., Cambie Corridor* ☎ *604/257–8584* ⊕ *www.vancouver.ca/parks/* ☒ *Conservatory C$5* ☉ *Apr.–Sept., weekdays 9–8, weekends 10–9; Oct.–Mar., daily 10–5.*

★ **University of British Columbia Botanical Garden.** Ten thousand trees, shrubs, and rare plants from around the world thrive on this 70-acre research site on the university campus, which edges on Pacific Spirit Park. The complex feels as far away from the city as you can get, with forested walkways through an Asian garden, a garden of medicinal plants, and an alpine garden with some of the world's rarest plants. A Walk in the Woods is a 20-minute loop that takes you through more than 1,000 species of coastal plant life while a fabulous 17 ½-mile-high, swaying canopy crossing takes you over them, weaving its way between ginormous cedars and gargantuan hemlocks. The walkway is open June to September and adds enough thrill factor to get kids interested in garden fare. The garden gift store is one of the best of its kind. Guided tours can be arranged in advance. ☒ *6804 S.W. Marine Dr., Point Grey* ☎ *604/822–4208* ⊕ *www.ubcbotanicalgarden.org* ☒ *Mid-Mar.–mid-Oct., C$8, C$12 includes admission to Nitobe Memorial Garden; mid-Oct.–mid-Mar., free* ☉ *Mid-Mar.–mid-Oct., daily 10–5; mid-Oct.–mid-Mar., daily 10–3.*

★ **VanDusen Botanical Garden.** An Elizabethan maze, a formal rose garden, a meditation garden, and a collection of Canadian heritage plants are among the many themed displays at this 55-acre site. The collections include flora from every continent and many rare and endangered species. The Phyllis Bentall Garden area features hybrid water lilies and carnivorous plants (a hit with kids). From mid-May to early June the Laburnum Walk forms a canopy of gold; in August and September the wildflower meadow is in bloom. The garden is also home to five lakes, a garden shop, a library, and a restaurant, as well as the site for special events throughout the year such as an outdoor flower and garden show, a large outdoor vintage-car exhibit, and a spectacular Christmas-theme Festival of Lights every December (daily 5–9 PM). An Oak Bus 17 gets you here from downtown. Queen Elizabeth Park is a 1-km (½-mi) walk away, along West 37th Avenue. Tip: Because this was once a golf course, pathways make this garden extremely wheelchair accessible. ⊠ *5251 Oak St., at W. 37th Ave., Shaughnessy* ☎ *604/878–9274 garden, 604/261–0011 restaurant* ⊕ *www.vandusengarden.org* ✉ *Apr.–Sept. C$8.85, Oct.–Mar. C$6.50* ☉ *June–Aug., daily 10–9; Sept.– May, daily (call for hrs).*

> ### WHAT IS THAT?
>
> The massive white-and-yellow contraption behind the Maritime Museum is the Ben Franklin submersible. It looks like something a Jules Verne character would put to sea but was actually built in 1968 as a marine research tool to, among other things, chart the Gulf Stream. A more fascinating claim to fame is that it was once the largest of its kind in America and was instructional for NASA: the information about how people lived in such close quarters for extended periods of time provided preliminary research data on the dynamics of living aboard a space station.

WORTH NOTING

☺ **H. R. MacMillan Space Centre.** The interactive exhibits and high-tech learning systems at this museum include a Virtual Voyages ride, where visitors can take a simulated space journey (definitely not for those afraid of flying); GroundStation Canada, showcasing Canada's achievements in space; and the Cosmic Courtyard, full of hands-on space-oriented exhibits including a moon rock and a computer program that shows what you would look like as an alien. You can catch daytime astronomy shows or evening music-and-laser shows at the **H. R. Mac-Millan Planetarium.** When the sky is clear, the ½-meter telescope at the **Gordon MacMillan Southam Observatory** (☎ *604/738–2855*) is focused on whatever stars or planets are worth watching that night. Admission to the observatory is by donation, and it's open year-round Friday and Saturday evenings, from 8 to 11, weather permitting. ⊠ *Vanier Park, 1100 Chestnut St., Kitsilano* ☎ *604/738–7827* ⊕ *www. hrmacmillanspacecentre.com* ✉ *C$15* ☉ *July and Aug., daily 10–5; Sept.–June, Tues.–Sun. 10–5.*

☺ **Kitsilano Beach.** Picnic sites, a playground, tennis courts, beach volleyball, a restaurant, take-out concessions, Vancouver's biggest outdoor pool (open May to September), and some fine people-watching can all be found at Kits Beach. Inland from the pool, the **Kitsilano Showboat,** an outdoor amphitheater, hosts free music and dance performances in summer. ⊠ *2305 Cornwall Ave., Kitsilano* ☎ *604/731–0011 Pool (summer* *only)* ⊕ *www.vancouver.ca/parks/* ⌨ *Beach free, pool C$5.15* ⊙ *Pool: late May–mid-June, weekdays noon–8:45, weekends 10–8:45; mid-June–Labor Day, weekdays 7 AM–8:45 PM, weekends 10–8:45; Labor Day–mid-Sept., weekdays 7 AM–7:15 PM, weekends 10–7:15.*

NEED A BREAK?

Just steps from the sand, **Watermark on Kits Beach** (☎ 604/738–5487) serves lunch and dinner inside and on its big ocean-view deck. There's also a take-out concession at the same site.

2

Vancouver Maritime Museum. About a third of this museum has been turned over to kids, with touchable displays offering a chance to drive a tug, maneuver an underwater robot, or dress up as a seafarer. Toddlers and school-age children can work the hands-on displays in Pirates' Cove and the Children's Maritime Discovery Centre. The museum also has an extensive collection of model ships and is the last moorage for the *RCMP Arctic St. Roch*, the first ship to sail in both directions through the treacherous Northwest Passage and the first to circumnavigate North America. While you're here, take a moment to look at the 100-foot-tall replica Kwakiutl totem pole in front of the museum. ⊠ *Vanier Park, 1905 Ogden Ave., north end of Cypress St., Kitsilano* ☎ *604/257–8300* ⊕ *www.vancouvermaritimemuseum.com* ⌨ *C$10* ⊙ *Mid-May–Labor Day, daily 10–5; Labor Day–mid-May, Tues.–Sat. 10–5, Sun. noon–5.*

Vancouver Museum. Vancouver's short-but-funky history comes to life at this seaside museum. The war-years gallery remembers some poignant episodes involving the Japanese internment, as well as local stories of the war effort. The 1950s Gallery has a 1955 Ford Fairlane Victoria and a Seeburg select-o-matic jukebox. The 1960s-theme Revolution Gallery revisits the city's days as the hippie capital of Canada: visitors can hear local bands from the '60s and poke around a re-created communal house. At the on-site Joyce Whalley Learning Centre, kids and adults can handle artifacts relating to immigration, First Nations, and the history of childhood. There are often intriguing temporary exhibits. ⊠ *Vanier Park, 1100 Chestnut St., Kitsilano* ☎ *604/736–4431* ⊕ *www. museumofvancouver.com* ⌨ *C$11* ⊙ *June–Sept., Fri.–Wed. 10–5, Thurs. 10–9; Oct.–June, Tues., Wed., and Fri.–Sun. 10–5, Thurs. 10–8.*

NORTH SHORE

The North Shore and its star attractions—the Capilano Suspension Bridge, Grouse Mountain, Lonsdale Quay, and, farther east, the lovely hamlet of Deep Cove—are just a short trip from downtown Vancouver.

The North Shore is where to come to kayak up fjords, and hike, ski, and explore mountainous terrain with large swathes of forest. Tony "West Van", as the locals call it, has retained its well-heeled character from the time when the Guinness family developed the area in the 1930s and is a network of English style, winding country roads, and multimillion-dollar homes. West Van is en route to the Horseshoe Bay ferry terminal for ferries to Vancouver Island, the Sea-to-Sky Whistler Highway, and Cypress Mountain, which hosted the Olympic freestyle skiing and snowboard competitions. If you have a car, you can drive to the top for spectacular vistas of Vancouver and beyond. Unlike Grouse Mountain, the views here are free. North Vancouver to the east is a poor relation of sorts and more commercial in nature, including tourist havens of Grouse and Capilano.

GETTING HERE AND AROUND

From downtown, drive west down Georgia Street to Stanley Park and across the Lions Gate Bridge to North Vancouver. Stay in the right lane, take the North Vancouver exit, and then turn left onto Capilano Road. In about 2 km (1 mi), you come to the Capilano Suspension Bridge. A few hundred yards up Capilano Road, on the left, is the entrance to Capilano River Regional Park. About 1½ km (1 mi) along the park access road you'll find the Capilano Salmon Hatchery. Returning to Capilano Road and continuing north, you'll reach Cleveland Dam (also part of the park), where you can stop for great mountain views. As you continue north, Capilano Road becomes Nancy Greene Way, which ends at the base of Grouse Mountain.

If you don't have a car, you can take the SeaBus from Waterfront Station to Lonsdale Quay and then catch a Grouse Mountain Bus 236. This stops at the Capilano Suspension Bridge and near the Salmon

Hatchery on its way to the base of Grouse Mountain. It's an easy trip, but if you only have the Capilano Suspension Bridge on your agenda, take advantage of its complimentary shuttle from downtown.

TIMING You need at least a half day to see the sights around the North Shore; allow a full day if you want to hike at Grouse Mountain or Capilano River Regional Park, or include a meandering drive through West Vancouver. You'll literally pass the entrance of the Capilano Bridge en route to Grouse Mountain, so it makes sense to do both. To save time, avoid crossing the Lions Gate Bridge during weekday rush hours (about 7–9 AM and 3–6 PM). Note that there's also a suspension bridge at Lynn Canyon, though many opt for the more well-known Capilano Suspension Bridge.

> **WORD OF MOUTH**
>
> "A really neat experience for the kids and yourself is a trip to Capilano Suspension bridge on the north shore (around 30 minute drive). Besides the suspension bridge, you're surrounded by the North Shore mountains and forest, and lots of opportunity to explore the park. Also a day trip to Grouse Mountain (same north shore area) is awesome—you take a gondola ride to the top and there is lots to see and do." —loriplain

TOP ATTRACTIONS

Fodor's Choice
★

Capilano Suspension Bridge. At Vancouver's oldest tourist attraction (the original bridge was built in 1889), you can get a taste of rain-forest scenery and test your mettle on the swaying, 450-foot cedar-plank suspension bridge that hangs 230 feet above the rushing Capilano River. Across the bridge is the Treetops Adventure, where you can walk along 650 feet of cable bridges suspended among the trees; there's also a scenic pathway along the canyon's edge, appropriately called Cliff Hanger Walk. Without crossing the bridge, you can enjoy the site's viewing decks, nature trails, totem park, and carving center (where you can watch First Nations carvers at work), as well as history and forestry exhibits, a massive gift shop in the original 1911 teahouse, and a restaurant. May through October, guides in 19th-century costumes conduct free tours on themes related to history, nature, or ecology, while fiddle bands, First Nations dancers, and other entertainers keep things lively. ■ TIP→ Catch the attraction's free shuttle service from Canada Place; it also stops along Burrard and Robson streets. ⊠ 3735 Capilano Rd., North Vancouver ☎ 604/985–7474 ⊕ www.capbridge.com ☞ Mid-May–Oct. C$29.95, Nov.–mid-May C$27.95, plus C$5 for parking ⊙ May–Labor Day, daily 8:30–8; Nov.–Mar., daily 9–5; Sept., Oct., and Apr.–mid-May call for hrs.

Grouse Mountain. North America's largest aerial tramway, the **Skyride** is a great way to take in the city, sea, and mountain vistas (be sure to pick a clear day or evening). The Skyride makes the 2-km (1-mi) climb to the peak of Grouse Mountain every 15 minutes. Once at the top you can watch a half-hour video presentation at the Theatre in the Sky (it's included with your Skyride ticket). Other free mountaintop activities include, in summer, lumberjack shows, chairlift rides, walking tours, hiking, falconry demonstrations, and a chance to visit the grizzly bears and gray wolves in the mountain's wildlife refuge. For an extra fee you

DID YOU KNOW?

The 450-foot-long cedar-plank Capilano suspension bridge hangs 230 feet above the rushing Capilano River, and makes for an exhilarating walk in the woods.

SUBURBAN RICHMOND'S CHINATOWN

Vancouver's city-center Chinatown is its "old" Chinatown, originally settled in the late 1800s, primarily by immigrants who came seeking work in the region's canneries or on the railroads. Beginning in the 1970s, however, the demographics of Vancouver's Chinese community began to change. Increasingly, the Chinese immigrants who settled in Vancouver were well-to-do professionals from Hong Kong and Taiwan, and many of these immigrants avoided the working-class downtown Chinatown, taking up residence elsewhere in the Vancouver region. In particular, the suburban community of Richmond, a suburb just south of Vancouver and home to the city's airport, became a popular destination for these new émigrés. Today, with a population that is more than 50% Asian, Richmond has become Vancouver's "new" Chinatown.

SkyTrain's Canada Line will take you right up to Richmond, where you can explore Asian-style shopping centers—it's almost like being in Hong Kong. ⊕ *www.tourismrichmond.com.*

Nearby you also might be tempted to visit the Oval, the 2010 Olympic venue that's now a multipurpose activity center and a really cool (literally) place to don a pair of ice skates.

can also try zip-lining and tandem paragliding, or take a helicopter tour. In winter you can ski, snowshoe, snowboard, ice-skate on a mountaintop pond, or take Sno-Cat-drawn sleigh rides. A stone-and-cedar lodge is home to a café, a pub-style bistro, and a high-end restaurant, all with expansive city views. ■ **TIP→ The Grouse Grind—a hiking trail up the face of the mountain—is one of the best workouts on the North Shore. Depending on your fitness level, allow between 20 and 80 minutes to complete it. Then you can take the Skyride down. The BCMC Trail is a less crowded, slightly longer alternative.** *(⇨ See the Vancouver Outdoors chapter for more info.)* ✉ *6400 Nancy Greene Way, North Vancouver* ☎ *604/980–9311* ⊕ *www.grousemountain.com* 🎫 *Skyride and most activities C$37.95* ⏲ *Daily 9 AM–10 PM.*

WORTH NOTING

Capilano River Regional Park. The park has hiking trails and footbridges over the Capilano River, where it cuts through a dramatic gorge. At the park's **Capilano Salmon Hatchery** (✉ *4500 Capilano Park Rd., North Vancouver* ☎ *604/666–1790*), viewing areas and exhibits illustrate the life cycle of the salmon. The best time to see the salmon run is between July and November. The **Cleveland Dam** (✉ *Capilano Rd., about 1½ km [1 mi] past main park entrance*) is at the north end of the park. Built in 1954 and named for Dr. E. A. Cleveland, a former chief commissioner of the Greater Vancouver Water District, it dams the Capilano River to create the 5½-km-long (3½-mi-long) Capilano Reservoir. A hundred yards from the parking lot, you can walk across the top of the dam to enjoy striking views of the reservoir and mountains behind it. The two sharp peaks to the west are the Lions, for which the Lions Gate Bridge is named. ✉ *Capilano Rd., North Vancouver* ☎ *604/224–5739* ⊕ *www.britishcolumbia.com/parks/id=486* 🎫 *Free*

☉ *Park: daily 8–dusk. Hatchery: June–Aug., daily 8–8; May and Sept., daily 8–7; Apr. and Oct., daily 8–6; Nov.–Mar., daily 8–4.*

**OFF THE
BEATEN
PATH** ☾

Lynn Canyon Park. With a steep canyon landscape, a temperate rain forest complete with waterfalls, and a suspension bridge 166½ feet above raging Lynn Creek, this 616-acre park provides thrills to go with its scenic views. The on-site Ecology Centre distributes maps of area hiking trails, waterfalls, and pools as well as information about the local flora and fauna. There's also a gift shop and a café on-site. To get to the park, take the Lions Gate Bridge and Capilano Road, go east on Highway 1, take the Lynn Valley Road exit, and turn right on Peters Road. From downtown Vancouver, you can take the SeaBus to Lonsdale Quay, then bus 228 or 229 from the quay; both stop near the park. ✉ *3663 Park Rd., at end of Peters Rd., North Vancouver* ☎ *604/981–3103 Ecology Centre, 604/984–9311 café* ⊕ *www.dnv.org/ecology* ✐ *Ecology Centre by donation, suspension bridge free* ☉ *Park: daily, dawn to dusk; Ecology Centre: June–Sept., daily 10–5; Oct.–May, weekdays 10–5, weekends noon–4.*

☾ **Lonsdale Quay.** Of the many public markets in the Greater Vancouver area, this indoor seaside market is one of the most popular. Stalls selling fresh produce, exotic fare, and ready-to-eat food fill the lower level; upstairs are boutiques, toy stores, and a kids' play area. Outside you can wander the quay, admire the fishing boats and tugs moored here, and enjoy the views of the downtown skyline across the water. You'll also see a number of old dry docks and canneries finding fresh leases on life as modish condominiums. The SeaBus foot-passenger ferry (☎ *604/953–3333* ⊕ *www.translink.bc.ca*), part of the city's public transit system, leaves the quay every 15 to 30 minutes for the 13-minute ride to Waterfront Station downtown. ■**TIP→** This is a great rainy-day activity. ✉ *123 Carrie Cates Ct., at foot of Lonsdale Ave.* ☎ *604/985–6261* ⊕ *www.lonsdalequay.com* ✐ *Free* ☉ *May–Aug., daily 9:30–7; Sept.–Apr., daily 9:30–6:30.*

Vancouver Outdoors and Sports

WORD OF MOUTH

"We made the most of the sunny days we had: we rented bikes and rode all around Stanley Park—fun! The next day we took the ferry and the bus to the Suspension Bridge and then hiked the Grouse Grind. When the Canadians give you warnings about how hard the trip will be, they mean it."

—StantonHyde

VANCOUVER OUTDOORS AND SPORTS PLANNER

Top Outdoors Experiences

Walk or bike the Seawall: The 8.8-km (5.5-mi) walk around Stanley Park is a civilized entrée into the coastal habitat where forest meets sea. The entire 22-km (13.6-mi) Seawall circles the city and is great for biking.

Hike the Grouse Grind: This two-hour climb up Grouse Mountain is a local rite of passage. The city and ocean views from the top are stunning.

White-water kayak the Capilano River: It's a serious tumble along canyons, through rain forest, and over rocks and rapids.

Play volleyball at Kits Beach: Vancouverites play a mean game of beach volleyball. Listen for the shouts of "good kill" on weekends from late spring to fall.

Kayaking into Indian Arm: Barely 30 minutes from downtown, the North Shore's fjordic landscape is stunning and best appreciated under paddle power.

When to Do It

Vancouver has a moderate climate, with temperatures rarely exceeding 90°F or falling below freezing for sustained periods, though winter storms that blend relentless rain with 40°F days can feel colder than the Canadian Rockies. Whatever you're doing, wearing layers is key, as a downpour may abruptly turn into a 60-minute sun break, or marine air can bring a sudden chill to a July day.

Year-round: If Vancouverites postponed jogging, biking, or golfing because of a bit of rain, they'd only get outside half the time; visitors, too, are encouraged to venture out in all but the rare rainstorm to participate in adventure, whether crossing the Capilano Suspension Bridge, hiking in Stanley Park, or kayaking on False Creek. Though water temps in Georgia Strait hardly vary from summer to winter, visibility improves significantly from December to March in what Jacques Cousteau declared the second-best scuba location in the world. Sportfishing and most wilderness tours take place year-round; you should check with operators for peak migration periods of sea mammals and birds.

Summer: True summer weather starts late in Vancouver, around Canada Day (July 1), but warm temperatures and sunshine persist into October. The beach scene is popular when the weather's good.

Winter: Most cities boast plenty of parks, but how many can claim three ski areas within city limits? Welcome to the North Shore, where Cypress Mountain hosted the 2010 Olympic snowboard and freestyle ski events. The winter-sports season starts in November and runs through March—in addition to skiing and boarding, snowshoeing and dogsledding have become increasingly popular.

Special Events

The Bank of Montreal Marathon is early May; the Scotiabank Half-Marathon and 5K are June; the popular Vancouver Sun Run (a 10K, with a minirun) is mid-April.

Polar Bear Swim: Every New Year's Day a phalanx of extremists plunge into the frigid waters at English Bay beach—often in costume.

By Crai S. Bower

Blessed with a mild climate, fabulous natural setting, and excellent public facilities, it's not surprising that Vancouverites are an outdoorsy lot. It's not uncommon for locals to commute to work by foot or bike and, after hours, they're as likely to hit the water, trails, ski slopes, or beach volleyball courts as the bars or nightclubs.

Exceptional for North American cities, the downtown peninsula of Vancouver is entirely encircled by a seawall along which you can walk, in-line skate, cycle, or otherwise propel yourself for more than 22 km (13 mi), with plenty of ideal jumping on and off points. Indeed, it's so popular that it qualifies as an, albeit unofficial, national treasure. There are places along the route where you can hire a bike, Rollerblade, canoe, or kayak, or simply go for a swim. Top-rated skiing, snowboarding, mountain biking, fishing, diving, and golf are just minutes away.

You'll find rental equipment and tour operators in Vancouver for every imaginable outdoor activity, from tandem mountain bikes for Stanley Park trails to fly-fishing rods for English Bay. Lululemon athletic- and yoga-wear began as a boutique in Kitsilano, and you'll find yoga studios around every corner. Hotel concierges can typically recommend the best wilderness trails just as easily as they can top sushi spots.

The **Mountain Equipment Co-op** is something of a local institution, a veritable outdoor-lovers' emporium with every kind of gear imaginable, as well as rentals, books and maps, and information from people in the know. ✉ *130 W. Broadway, Fairview* ☎ *604/872–7858.*

BEACHES

Greater Vancouver is well endowed with beaches—from the pebbly coves of West Vancouver to a vast tableau of sand at Spanish Banks—but the waters are decidedly cool, even in summer, and, aside from the kids and the intrepid, the preferred activity is sunbathing. That said, the city provides several exceptional outdoor pools—right smack on the ocean. The most spectacular is Kitsilano Pool, where you can gander up

Beaches might not be the first thing you think of in Vancouver, but in summer, Kits Beach is quite a hot spot.

at the North Shore Mountains while swimming lengths or lolling in the shallows. Beaches at Kitsilano, Spanish Banks, and nearby Locarno are popular beach-volleyball venues. At the city's historic beach and round-the-clock social venue, English Bay, you can swim, rent a kayak—or simply stroll and people-watch. The area is also known for its clothing-optional beaches that, true to Vancouver's cosmopolitan perspective, are quite celebrated.

All city beaches have lifeguards, washrooms, concession stands, and most have paid parking. Liquor is prohibited in parks and on beaches. With a few exceptions, dogs are not permitted on beaches. For more information check out the Vancouver Parks Web site (⊕ *vancouver.ca/ parks/rec/beaches*).

Ambleside Park. Off Marine Drive, west of the Lions Gate Bridge, this long stretch of sand is West Vancouver's most popular beach. There's a pool here, too.

Fodor's Choice ★

Kitsilano Beach. To the west of the south end of the Burrard Bridge, this is the city's busiest beach—in-line skaters, volleyball games, and sleek young people are ever present. Facilities include a playground, restaurant and concession stand, and tennis courts. **Kitsilano Pool** is also here: at 137 meters (445 feet), it's the longest pool in Canada and one of the few heated saltwater pools in the world. ⊠ *2305 Cornwall Ave., Kitsilano* ☎ *604/731–0011* ⊗ *Late May–mid-September.*

Point Grey beaches. Jericho, Locarno, and **Spanish Banks** beaches begin at the end of Point Grey Road and offer huge expanses of sand backed by wide lawns full of picnic tables. The shallow water, warmed slightly by sun and sand, is good for swimming. Jericho Beach, with Jericho

Sailing Centre complex, is popular for windsurfing. Farther out, toward Spanish Banks, the beach becomes less crowded.

Stanley Park beaches. There are several beaches accessed from Stanley Park Drive in Stanley Park. **Second Beach** has a playground, a small sandy area, and a large heated pool with a slide. **Third Beach** has a larger stretch of sand, fairly warm water, and great sunset views. It's a popular evening picnic spot.

West End beaches. English Bay, the city's best-known beach, lies just to the east of the south entrance to Stanley Park, at the foot of Denman Street. A waterslide, street performers, and artists keep things interesting all summer. Farther along Beach Drive, **Sunset Beach** is too close to the downtown core for clean safe swimming, but is a great spot for an evening stroll. You can catch a ferry to Granville Island here, or swim at the **Vancouver Aquatic Centre** (⊠ *1050 Beach Ave.* ☎ *604/665–3424*), a public indoor pool and fitness center.

West Vancouver. This long shoreline on the north side of Burrard Inlet has a dozen coves, rocky and sandy, that are coveted retreats for the knowing beach-seeker. They include (from west to east) **Whytecliff Park, Kew Beach, Caulfield Cove, Sandy Cove, West Bay,** and **Dundarave.**

Wreck Beach. Canada's largest clothing-optional beach is reached via a steep trail and flight of stairs from Gate 6, off Marine Drive on the University of British Columbia campus. This 6-km-long (4-mi-long) wilderness beach, managed by a team of volunteers, has a delightfully anarchic culture of its own. The driftwood is tangled, bathing suits aren't required, and you can buy a wild array of food, goods, and services: vendors sell pizza, homemade sandwiches, buffalo burgers, and Mexican specialties. They peddle fresh fruit, juices, and alcoholic drinks. You can get a pedicure or massage, or have your hair cut. And there's jewelry, sarongs, and other hippie-inspired beachwear for sale. Up to 14,000 people might visit on a summer weekend. There are no lifeguards.

CYCLING

While Vancouver is relatively bike friendly, its major arteries and busier streets can be uncomfortable and unsafe for all but the experienced cyclist. As a helpful gesture, the city introduced 16 interconnected bikeways, identified by green bicycle signs; although most routes share the road with cars, they're well chosen for safety, and include cyclist-activated signals and other bike-friendly measures. The city has also just introduced protected bike lanes on the Burrard Bridge. Many TransLink buses have bike racks, and bikes are welcome on the SeaBus and on the SkyTrain at off-peak times. Aquabus Ferries transport bikes and riders across False Creek. If cycling is a key component of your visit, check in with the Vancouver Cycling Coalition (⊕ *www.vacc.bc.ca*) for events and cycling-awareness information.

Fodor's Choice The most popular recreational route, much of it off-road, is the **Seaside**
★ **route.** It runs about 32 km (20 mi) from the seawall in Coal Harbour, around Stanley Park and False Creek, through Kitsilano to Spanish Banks. For detailed route descriptions and a downloadable map check

out ⊕ *www.metrovancouver.ca*. Vancouver cycling routes connect with routes on the North Shore, in Richmond and Delta to the south, and in municipalities to the east. For sub-area and region-wide maps go to the regional transportation authority, TransLink (⊕ *www.translink.bc.ca*) or the Metro Vancouver (formerly Greater Vancouver Regional District) Web site (⊕ *www.metrovancouver.ca*). Cycling maps are also available from most bike shops and bike-rental outlets. Helmets are required by law and a sturdy lock is essential.

BIKE RENTALS Most bike-rental outlets also rent Rollerblades and jogging strollers. Cycling helmets, a legal requirement in Vancouver, come with the rentals. Locks and maps are also normally supplied.

Bayshore Bicycles. If you're starting your bike ride near Stanley Park, try this friendly store. It has a range of bikes and Rollerblades as well as baby joggers and bike trailers. ⊠ *745 Denman St., West End* ☎ *604/ 688–2453* ⊕ *www.bayshorebikerentals.ca.*

Reckless Bike Stores. This outfit rents bikes on the Yaletown section of the bike path. To explore the Granville Island and Kitsilano area, a better bet might be their Kitsilano branch. ⊠ *110 Davie St., Yaletown* ☎ *604/648–2600* ⊕ *www.reckless.ca* ⊠ *1810 Fir St., at 2nd Ave., Kitsilano* ☎ *604/731–2420.*

Spokes Bicycle Rentals. Located at Denman and Georgia, near Stanley Park, Spokes has a wide selection of bikes, including kids' bikes, tandems, mountain bikes, and Rollerblades. They also offer 90-minute tours of Stanley Park for C$33 and 3½-hour rides around Stanley Park, False Creek, and Granville Island for C$66; rates include bike rentals. ⊠ *1798 W. Georgia St., West End* ☎ *604/688–5141* ⊕ *www. spokesbicyclerentals.com.*

MOUNTAIN BIKING Mountain biking may be a worldwide phenomenon, but its most radical expression, known as free-riding, was born in the 1990s on the steep-and-rugged North Shore Mountains. Here, the mostly young thrill-seekers ride ultra-heavy-duty bikes through gnarly forest, along log-strewn trails, over rocky precipices, and down stony stream beds (not to mention along self-installed obstacles like planks and teeter-totters)—and live to tell about it. And while this madcap sport has found greater fame at the Whistler Mountain Bike Park, where 100,000 people ride annually (and ascend by lift), North Shore free-riding remains true to its literal roots. This anarchic culture can be explored at the **North Shore Mountain Biking** Web site, ⊕ *www.nsmb.com.*

Lower Seymour Conservation Reserve. Nestled into the precipitous North Shore Mountains, this reserve has 25 km (15.5 mi) of challenging rainforest trails. The **Seymour Valley Trailway** is a 10-km (6-mi) paved pathway, suitable for cyclists, in-line skaters, baby strollers, and wheelchairs; it meanders over streams and through woods. Other trails, like Corkscrew and Salvation, are classified as advanced or even extreme. ⊠ *End of Lillooet Rd., North Vancouver* ☎ *604/432–6286.*

Pacific Spirit Regional Park. Pacific Spirit is beautifully sited on the Point Grey peninsula on Vancouver's west side, close to the University of British Columbia. Open year-round, dawn to dusk, it includes 38 km

(23.5 mi) for cycling and horseback riding. ⌂ *4915 W. 16th Ave., Point Grey* ☎ *604/224–5739.*

MOUNTAIN
BIKE RENTALS

Cove Bike Shop. In the village of Deep Cove on Indian Arm, the Cove Bike Shop pioneered the design and construction of mountain bikes for this punishing terrain and continues to market them worldwide. Given huge insurance costs, it's also the only bike shop that rents them. Bikes of all types and sizes are available March through October. ⌂ *4310 Gallant Ave., North Vancouver* ☎ *604/929–2222 or 604/985–2222* ⊕ *www.covebike.com.*

3

DIVING

The rugged, wildly indented coastline of southwestern British Columbia offers excellent and varied diving opportunities. Especially in winter, when water clarity allows visibility of up to 100 feet, the region delivers some of the most spectacular temperate-water diving in the world, including frequent sightings of the North Pacific Giant Octopus.

BC Dive and Kayak Adventures. This outfit offers day trips from Vancouver to the flora- and fauna-rich waters of Howe Sound and Indian Arm. The trips run weekends, year-round. ⌂ *1695 W. 4th Ave., Kitsilano* ☎ *604/732–1344 or 800/960–0066* ⊕ *www.bcdive.com.*

Rowand's Reef Dive Shop. This Granville Island–based sales-and-rental business specializes in year-round diving trips to Howe Sound. ⌂ *1512 Duranleau St., Granville Island* ☎ *604/669–3483* ⊕ *www.rowandsreef. com.*

ECOTOURS AND WILDLIFE VIEWING

Given a temperate climate and forest, mountain, and marine environments teeming with life, it's no surprise that wildlife watching is an important pastime and growing business in and around Vancouver. Many people walk the ocean foreshores or park and mountain trails, binoculars or scopes in hand, looking for exceptional or rare birds. Others venture onto the water to see seals, sea lions, and whales—as well as the birds that inhabit the maritime world.

Sewell's Marina Horseshoe Bay. This long-time marina at the foot of Howe Sound runs year-round, two-hour ecotours of the surrounding marine and coastal mountain habitat. Sightings range from seals to soaring eagles. High-speed rigid inflatable hulls are used. ⌂ *6409 Bay St., Horseshoe Bay* ☎ *604/921–3474* ⊕ *www.sewellsmarina.com.*

BIRD- AND
EAGLE-
WATCHING

Between mid-November and mid-February, the world's largest concentration of bald eagles gathers to feed on salmon at **Brackendale Eagles' Park** (⌂ *Government Rd. off Hwy. 99, Brackendale*), about an hour north of Vancouver.

Canadian Outback Adventure Company. This outfit runs "eagle safari" trips that allow you to watch and photograph eagles from a slow-moving raft on the Cheakamus River. Transportation from Vancouver is available. ☎ *604/921–7250 or 800/565–8735* ⊕ *www.canadianoutback.com.*

Whale-watching tours from Vancouver (or Victoria) are extremely popular.

George C. Reifel Bird Sanctuary. More than 260 species of migratory birds visit this 850-acre site on Westham Island, about an hour south of Vancouver. A seasonal highlight is the arrival of an estimated 80,000 Lesser Snow Geese in the late fall. ✉ *5191 Robertson Rd., Ladner* ☎ *604/946–6980* ⊕ *www.reifelbirdsanctuary.com* ✎ *C$4* ⊙ *Daily 9–4.*

Steveston Seabreeze Adventures. During the autumn bird migratory season, Seabreeze takes bird-watchers by boat along the Fraser Estuary to the Reifel Bird Sanctuary on Westham Island. ✉ *12551 No. 1 Rd., Richmond* ☎ *604/272–7200* ⊕ *www.seabreezeadventures.ca.*

Vancouver All-Terrain Adventures. Day trips to Brackendale include pickup in Vancouver in a four-wheel drive, and an option to watch the eagles by raft or horseback. ☎ *778/371–7830 or 888/754–5601* ⊕ *www.all-terrain.com.*

SEA LION VIEWING
In April and early May thousands of male California sea lions and larger Steller sea lions settle on rocks near the mouth of the Fraser River to feed on the eulachon, a member of the smelt family. Sightseeing boats make the short trip from Steveston into the estuary.

Steveston Seabreeze Adventures. From docks in Steveston village in Richmond, south of Vancouver, Seabreeze motors into the sea lion's natural habitat. ✉ *12551 No. 1 Rd., Richmond* ☎ *604/272–7200* ⊕ *www.seabreezeadventures.ca.*

WHALE-WATCHING
Between April and October pods of orca whales travel through the Strait of Georgia, near Vancouver. The area is also home to harbor seals, elephant seals, bald eagles, minke whales, porpoises, and a wealth of birdlife.

Lotus Land Tours. High-speed covered boats take you out to watch for whales and other wildlife in the Strait of Georgia. The five-hour cruise costs C$175 and includes pickup anywhere in Vancouver and an on-board lunch. ☎ *604/684–4922 or 800/528–3531* ⊕ *www.Vancouver-NatureAdventures.com.*

Prince of Whales. This established Victoria operator runs four-hour trips from the downtown waterfront (near Waterfront Station) across Georgia Strait to the Victoria area in season. ✉ *812 Wharf St., Victoria* ☎ *888/383–4884* ⊕ *www.princeofwhales.com.*

Wild Whales Vancouver. Boats leave Granville Island in search of orca pods in Georgia Strait, traveling as far as Victoria. Rates are C$125 for a three- to seven-hour trip in either an open or glass-domed boat. Each boat leaves once daily, April through October, conditions permitting. ☎ *604/699–2011* ⊕ *www.whalesvancouver.ca.*

FISHING

You can fish for salmon all year in coastal British Columbia, weather and marine conditions permitting. Halibut, at 50 pounds and heavier, is the area's other trophy fish. Charters ply waters between the Capilano River mouth in Burrard Inlet and the outer Georgia Strait and Gulf Islands. Your fishing license can be purchased from the boat rental or tour operator.

Bonnie Lee Charters. From moorings in the Granville Island Maritime Market, this company runs five-hour fishing trips into Burrard Inlet and Georgia Strait year-round. Guided outings start at C$395 for one person, less per person for groups. ✉ *1676 Duranleau St., Granville Island* ☎ *604/290–7447* ⊕ *www.bonnielee.com.*

Sewell's Marina. Something of a coastal institution at Horseshoe Bay in West Vancouver, this fishing boat–rental outfit also offers guided and self-driven salmon-fishing charters in Howe Sound and to the mouths of the Capilano and Fraser rivers. ✉ *6409 Bay St., Horseshoe Bay* ☎ *604/921–3474* ⊕ *www.sewellsmarina.com.*

Steveston Seabreeze Adventures. From docks in Steveston village in Richmond, just south of Vancouver, Seabreeze operates fishing charters as far west as the Gulf Islands, between mid-June and September. Its 12-passenger boats, with guides, cost C$1,400 on weekends, C$1,300 on weekdays. ✉ *12551 No. 1 Rd., Richmond* ☎ *604/272–7200* ⊕ *www. seabreezeadventures.ca.*

GOLF

Vancouver-area golf courses offer challenging golf with great scenery. Most are open year-round. For advance tee-time bookings at about 20 Vancouver area courses, or for a spur-of-the-moment game, call **Last Minute Golf** (☎ *604/878–1833 or 800/684–6344* ⊕ *www.lastminutegolfbc. com*). The company matches golfers and courses, sometimes at substantial greens-fee discounts.

Fodor's Choice
★
The Vancouver Park Board operates three public courses, all located on the city's south-facing slope. The most celebrated is the 18-hole, par-72, 6,700-yard **Fraserview Golf Course** (⊠ *7800 Vivian Dr., South Vancouver* ☎ *604/257–6923, 604/280–1818 advance bookings*), where facilities include a driving range and a new clubhouse. The greens fee is C$58–C$65. The other two, both 18 holes and with slightly lower greens fees, are **Langara Golf Course** (⊠ *6706 Alberta St.* ☎ *604/713–1816*) and **McCleery Golf Course** (⊠ *7188 Macdonald St.* ☎ *604/257–8191*).

Northlands Golf Course. In North Vancouver just 20 minutes from downtown, Northlands may be Vancouver's best-kept secret. Douglas fir woods line the fairways, which gives it the impression of a Whistler or Vancouver Island track. The greens and fairways are well maintained. Greens fees are C$40–C$45. ⊠ *3400 Anne Macdonald Way, North Vancouver* ☎ *604/924–2950* ⊕ *www.golfnorthlands.com.*

Northview Golf and Country Club. Situated in lovely rolling terrain in the city of Surrey, southeast of Vancouver, this club comprises two Arnold Palmer–designed 18-hole courses (both par 72, and both open year-round). The greens fee for the Ridge course is C$95–C$105; the fee for the more challenging Canal course is C$85–C$95. An optional cart at either course costs C$25–C$40. ⊠ *6857 168th St., Surrey* ☎ *604/576–4653 or 888/574–2211* ⊕ *www.northviewgolf.com.*

Seymour Golf and Country Club. A semiprivate course, its holes wend around towering old-growth fir and cedar trees at the foot of Mt. Seymour. It's open to the public on Monday and Friday, and has a fairly strict dress code. Greens fees run C$80 to C$90. ⊠ *3723 Mt. Seymour Pkwy., North Vancouver* ☎ *604/929–2611* ⊕ *www.seymourgolf.com.*

University Golf Club. Located on the city's west-side, Point Grey peninsula, this historic course is par 71 and 6,560 yards. Facilities include a clubhouse and dining; it's also home to the British Columbia Golf Museum (⇨ *Exploring chapter*). Greens fees are C$65 to C$75. ⊠ *5185 University Blvd., Point Grey* ☎ *604/224–1818* ⊕ *www.universitygolf.com.*

Westwood Plateau Golf and Country Club. Westwood is a well-manicured, 18-hole, par-72 course located just east of the city; it's closed November through March. The greens fee, which includes a cart, is C$169. The club also has a restaurant open seasonally. The 9-hole **Academy Course** nearby (☎ *604/941–4236*) is open year-round. ⊠ *3251 Plateau Blvd., Coquitlam* ☎ *604/552–0777 or 800/580–0785* ⊕ *www.westwoodplateaugolf.com.*

HEALTH, FITNESS, AND YOGA

Vancouver is on a health-and-wellness kick. Gyms, both public (operated by the Vancouver Park Board) and private, are well patronized. There are various martial arts, yoga, and Pilates classes offered around the city. If you're jonesing for a fitness fix, you shouldn't have trouble finding something to suit your fancy.

Bentall Centre Athletic Club. The Bentall Centre specializes in squash and also has racquetball courts and weight and cardio gyms; aerobics and yoga classes are given as well. The drop-in fee is C$15. ⊠ *1055*

Sea 'n' Ski

Given the proximity of water to mountain or bike path to swimming pool, and the ease of getting around by bike, bus, car, ferry, or even in-line skates, it's definitely possible to undertake two or more outdoor activities in a single day. Cross-trainers, this is the place for you.

If you're going to multitask, though, it's a good idea to plan ahead, and if you need to rent equipment, do so in advance. In the interest of making the most of your time, and ensuring your safety, we advise downloading maps and other descriptive information you may need. If you're venturing off the beaten path, be sure you're dressed suitably, have emergency food and gear, and leave notification of where you're headed and when you'll return.

And you're off. The possibilities are almost endless but here are some pointers for combining activities:

Kayaking in False Creek: The waters are usually tranquil in early morning so it's a good time to savor the pleasures of traveling at sea level.

Jogging around Stanley Park: Early-morning joggers have the seawall pretty much to themselves.

Swimming in Kitsilano Pool: Early morning is considered by many to be the best time to hit the lanes at Kits Pool.

Cycling the Greenway: By midmorning, all but the city's major arterial streets should be relatively calm. This may be the time to cycle the network of bicycle routes.

Fishing or wildlife watching: In all but the worst weather, you can rent a boat for a few hours spent in pursuit of a salmon, or join a tour in search of whales, sea lions, or eagles.

Tennis or beach volleyball: Late afternoon is a good time to head to Kitsilano Beach for a volleyball game, or to Stanley Park for a game of tennis.

Golf at Fraserview: A warm summer evening is the ideal time to golf at the most celebrated of the city's three public golf courses—all of which lie on the city's south-facing slope.

Night skiing at Grouse: On a crisp winter night, there's no better place to be than on the slopes of Grouse Mountain. The canopy of stars will glitter, while below, the city dazzles.

Dunsmuir St., lower plaza, Downtown ☎604/689–4424 ⊕ www.bentallcentreathleticclub.com.

Coal Harbour Community Centre. Operated by the Vancouver Park Board, this ultramodern facility on the Coal Harbour seawall, conveniently close to downtown hotels, has a fitness center with drop-in classes. ✉ 480 Broughton St., West End ☎604/718–8222 ⊕ www.coalharbourcc.ca.

★ **Richmond Olympic Oval.** Richmond benefitted more from the Olympic Games than any other Vancouver municipality with the opening of a speed-skating oval along the Frasier River. The signature Olympics facility, with a gorgeous architectural design, contains six basketball courts, Olympic-sized ice rinks, a huge fitness center, and even an indoor rowing tank. The Oval is just a 15-minute walk from the Canada Line. Day passes cost C$12.50. ⊠ *6111 River Rd., Richmond,* ☎ *778/296–1400* ⊕ *www.richmondoval.ca.*

Semperviva. Based in Kitsilano, this major yoga operator runs four studios—the Sun Centre, the Sky Centre, the City Centre, and the Sea Centre: the last, in a former fish factory on Granville Island, overlooks False Creek. ⊠ *200–1333 Johnstone St., Granville Island* ☎ *604/739–2009* ⊕ *www.semperviva.com* ✉ *Drop-in fee C$16.*

Vancouver Olympic Centre. Every visitor to Canada should consider experiencing curling at least once—it's the country's actual national pastime. There's no better place to try this than at Hillcrest Park's curling center. Learn the lingo, order a beer, then push off the "hack" to toss the 42-pound rock from the hog line over the "pebbles" in hopes of at least a "biter" (it's harder than it looks!). There's also an aquatic center here. ⊠ *4575 Clancy Loranger Way, lower plaza, Riley Park* ☎ *604/873–7000* ⊕ *www.vancouver.ca/parks.*

YMCA. An entirely reconstructed YMCA opened in spring 2010, with the latest in fitness facilities, at its long-time downtown location. ⊠ *955 Burrard St.,* ☎ *604/689–9622* ⊕ *www.vanymca.org.*

YWCA. The Y has an ozone pool, a cardio room, two coed and one women-only weight rooms, a whirlpool, steam rooms, and aerobics, yoga, and Pilates classes. The day rate is C$16. ⊠ *535 Hornby St., Downtown* ☎ *604/895–5777* ⊕ *www.ywcavan.org.*

HIKING

With its expansive landscape of mountains, inlets, alpine lakes, and approachable glaciers, as well as low-lying rivers, hills, dikes, and meadows, southwestern British Columbia is a hiker's paradise. That said, areas and trails should be approached with physical ability and stamina in mind. The North Shore Mountains, for example, may appear benign, but this is a vast and rugged territory filled with natural pitfalls and occasionally hostile wildlife, and you should exercise great caution. The Baden-Powell Trail is a roughly 48-km (30-mi) trail only for the ablest hikers; it extends the entire length of the North Shore Mountains, from Horseshoe Bay to Deep Cove, passing through both Cypress Provincial Park and Mount Seymour Provincial Park. Every year, hikers wander off clearly marked trails, or outside well-posted public areas, with tragic results. If you're heading into the mountains, hike with a companion, pack warm clothes (even in summer), and extra food and water, and leave word of your route and the time you expect to return. Remember that weather can change quickly in the mountains. You can check for a weather forecast with **Environment Canada** (⊕ *weatheroffice.ec.gc.ca*).

In addition to the Mountain Equipment Co-op listed at the head of the chapter, there are several places around town for good books, maps, and advice. **International Travel Maps & Books** (⊠ *530 W. Broadway* ☎ *604/879–3621* ⊕ *www.itmb.com*) publishes its own maps, and is also the local distributor for the Canada Map Office, stocking federally made topographic maps and charts of the region. **Wanderlust** (⊠ *1929 W. 4th Ave., Kitsilano* ☎ *604/739–2182* ⊕ *www.wanderlustore.com*) is

The hike up Grouse Mountain is no easy feat, but the views from the top, and from Goat Mountain, slightly farther up, are breathtaking.

a major supplier of goods and gear for travelers, and has a well-stocked section of maps and guidebooks.

Fodor's Choice ★ **Capilano River Regional Park.** This small but spectacular park is where you'll find the Capilano River canyon, several old-growth fir trees approaching 61 meters (200 feet), a salmon hatchery open to the public, and the Cleveland Dam, as well as 26 km (16 mi) of hiking trails. It's at the end of Capilano Park Road, off Capilano Road, in North Vancouver. ☎ *604/224–5739.*

Cypress Provincial Park. This 3,012-hectare (7,442-acre) park sprawls above Howe Sound, embracing the Strachan, Black, and Hollyburn mountains. On a clear day you can see Mt. Baker (in Washington State) and Vancouver Island. While the park includes a commercial ski and biking area operated by Cypress Bowl Resorts, much of the terrain is a public hiking paradise (bikes are not permitted on hiking trails). This is backcountry, though, and only experienced hikers should attempt the more remote routes, including the Baden-Powell and Howe Sound Crest trails, which traverse this mountain region. Maps and route descriptions are available on the Web site. ⊠ *Cypress Bowl Rd., off Hwy. 1, West Vancouver* ⊕ *www.hellobc.com.*

★ **Grouse Mountain.** Vancouver's most famous, or infamous, hiking route, the Grind, is a 2.9-km (1.8-mi) climb straight up 2,500 vertical feet to the top of Grouse Mountain. Thousands do it annually, but climbers are advised to be in "excellent physical condition" T; it's not for children. The route is open daily, 6:30 AM to 7:30 PM, from spring through autumn (conditions permitting). Or you can take the Grouse Mountain Skyride (gondola) to the top; a round-trip ticket is C$32.95, one-way down is

C$5. Eco-walks are led along the paths accessed from the Skyride, and there are additional hiking trailsfrom this point, like the Goat Mountain Trail, which can take you even farther up. ⊠ *6400 Nancy Greene Way, North Vancouver* ☎ *604/980–9311 Grouse Mountain, 604/432–6200 Metro Vancouver (formerly GVRD)* ⊕ *www.grousemountain.com.*

Indian Arm Provincial Park. This somewhat-remote region of rugged forested mountains, alpine lakes, vigorous creeks, and idyllic waterfalls lies north of Burrard Inlet (just east of Vancouver) along an 18-km (11-mi) fjord called Indian Arm. While much of the activity is on the water—there's boating, kayaking, scuba diving, and fishing—there are also excellent hiking opportunities through old-growth forest. Most trails have substantial elevation gain, and are not for the novice. Downloadable maps are available at ⊕ *www.bcparks.ca.* The park is accessed by water in Indian Arm, or by road from Buntzen Lake in Port Moody. ⊙ *Seasonal.*

★ **Lighthouse Park.** This 75-hectare (185-acre) wilderness park wraps around Point Atkinson and its historic lighthouse (of the same name), where Howe Sound meets Burrard Inlet in the municipality of West Vancouver. A bank of soaring granite (popular for picnicking) shapes the foreshore, while the interior is an undulating terrain of mostly Douglas fir, rich undergrowth, birds, and other wildlife. Trails, from easy to challenging, wend throughout. A trail map is downloadable at the municipal Web site. ⊠ *Beacon La. off Marine Dr., West Vancouver* ⊕ *www.hellobc.com.*

Lower Seymour Conservation Reserve. This 5,668-hectare (14,000-acre) reserve includes 25 km (15.5 mi) of hiking trails, some steep and challenging. ⊠ *End of Lillooet Rd., North Vancouver* ☎ *604/432–6286.*

Mount Seymour Provincial Park. Located 30 minutes by car from downtown Vancouver, this historic wilderness park of 3,508 hectares (14,683 acres) provides 14 hiking trails of varying length and difficulty. Some climb into exposed mountainside, and warm clothing—and caution—are advised. They include access to the Baden-Powell Trail, which continues northwest to Horseshoe Bay. You can also hike 3.2 km (just under 2 mi) down to Deep Cove on Indian Arm. In winter, the trails are used for snowshoeing. Good downloadable maps are available on the Web site. ⊠ *Mount Seymour Rd. off Seymour Pkwy., North Vancouver* ⊕ *www.hellobc.com.*

Pacific Spirit Regional Park. A 763-hectare (1,185-acre) forest, Pacific Spirit is on the Point Grey peninsula on Vancouver's west side, close to the University of British Columbia. Open year-round, dawn to dusk, it includes 54 km (33 mi) of walking and hiking trails. Some provide access to beaches on Burrard Inlet and Georgia Strait. ⊠ *4915 W. 16th Ave., Point Grey* ☎ *604/224–5739* ⊕ *www.hellobc.com.*

Fodor's Choice **Stanley Park.** Stanley Park is well suited for moderate walking and
★ easy hiking. The most obvious and arguably most picturesque route is the 8.8-km (5.5-mi) seawall around its perimeter, but this 1,000-acre park also offers 27 km (16.7 mi) of interior trails through the coniferous forest, including a few small patches of original forest, or old growth. The interior paths are wide and well maintained; here you'll

experience something of the true rain forest and spot some of the birds and small mammals that inhabit it. An easy interior trail runs around Lost Lagoon, and a popular interior destination is Beaver Lake. You can download a trail map at the Park Board Web site. ⇨ *For more information see the Stanley Park listing in Exploring Vancouver, Chapter 2.* ☎ *604/257–8400.*

GUIDED HIKES Novice hikers and serious walkers can join guided trips or do self-guided walks of varying approach and difficulty. Grouse Mountain *(⇨ see above)* hosts several daily "eco-walks" along easy, meandering paths accessed from the top of the Skyride. Discussion of flora and fauna and a visit to the Refuge for Endangered Wildlife (grizzly bears) is included. They're free with admission to Grouse Mountain Skyride.

3

Heritage Walking Tours. The City of Vancouver provides detailed information on self-guided walking tours of Chinatown, Gastown, Yaletown, and Shaughnessy. ⊕ *www.city.vancouver.bc.ca/commsvcs/planning/heritage/walks/.*

Rockwood Adventures. This company gives guided walks of rain forest or coastal terrain including Lighthouse Park, Lynn Canyon and Capilano Canyon, and Bowen Island in Howe Sound (including a short flight). They also run walking tours of Vancouver's Chinatown. ☎ *604/980–7749 or 888/236–6606* ⊕ *www.rockwoodadventures.com.*

HOCKEY

The Canucks have sold out every game since 2004, though tickets can be purchased at legal resale outlets. Watching NHL hockey in a Canadian city is one of sport's greatest spectacles, so try and catch a game if possible. If you can't attend in person, head into any bar on game night, especially Saturdays ("Hockey Night" in Canada), as game nights light up the city's bars and restaurants.

The **Vancouver Canucks** play at **General Motors Place** (⊠ *800 Griffiths Way, Downtown* ☎ *604/899–7400*).

JOGGING

Vancouverites jog at any time of day, in almost any weather, and dozens of well-trodden routes go through the leafy streets of the city's west side; there is also the wider Greenways network of "calmed roads." The seawall around the downtown peninsula and False Creek, into Kitsilano, remains the most popular route, though the hilly byways of the North Shore are also popular with serious runners. Visiting runners staying downtown will be drawn to the 8.8-km (5.5-mi) route around Stanley Park, or the 4 km (2.5 mi) around Lost Lagoon.

Running Room. This Canadian-based business is a good source of advice and downloadable route maps. ⊠ *679 Denman St., West End* ☎ *604/684–9771* ⊠ *1578 W. Broadway, Central Vancouver* ☎ *604/879–9721* ⊕ *www.runningroom.com.*

SKIING AND SNOWBOARDING

The North Shore Mountains—from Howe Sound in the west to Indian Arm in the east—are made up of dozens of peaks. The most prominent are The Lions, twin granite "ears" visible from around the Lower Mainland. The highest is Brunswick Mountain at 1,788 meters (5,866 feet). Skiing is generally confined to the Cypress Group (Mt. Strachan and Hollyburn Mountain), Grouse Mountain, and Mt. Seymour; all three have excellent downhill and snowboarding facilities. While ski areas and trails are generally well marked, once you ski outside the boundaries you're entering rugged wilderness that can be distinctly unfriendly to humans. All mountain-goers are strongly advised to respect maps and signposts. All mountains also offer a full range of services, including eateries, rentals, and lessons. The ski season generally runs from early December through early spring. Cypress Provincial Park is a major cross-country skiing area.

CROSS-COUNTRY **Cypress Mountain.** This private operator within Cypress Provincial Park maintains 19 km (10 mi) of cross-country or "Nordic" trails into the undulating, lake-dotted landscape of Hollyburn Mountain. There is a charge for their use. There are also 10 km (6 mi) dedicated to snowshoeing. ✉ *Cypress Bowl Rd., West Vancouver* ✛ *Exit 8 off Hwy. 1 westbound* ☎ *604/419–7669* ⊕ *www.cypressmountain.com.*

DOWNHILL SKIING AND SNOW-BOARDING While Whistler Resort, a two-hour drive from Vancouver, is the top-ranked ski destination in the region, the North Shore Mountains hold three excellent ski and snowboard areas. All have rentals, lessons, night skiing, and a variety of runs suitable for all skill levels. Grouse Mountain can be reached by TransLink buses. Cypress and Seymour each run shuttle buses from Lonsdale Quay and other North Shore stops.

Cypress Mountain. The most recent of three North Shore commercial ski destinations, Cypress is nonetheless well equipped, and was made even more so with the completion of freestyle skiing and snowboarding venues built for the 2010 Winter Olympics. Facilities include five quad or double chairs, 38 downhill runs, and a vertical drop of 1,750 feet. The mountain also has a snow-tubing area and snowshoe tours. ✉ *Cypress Bowl Rd., West Vancouver* ✛ *Exit 8 off Hwy. 1 westbound* ☎ *604/419–7669* ⊕ *www.cypressmountain.com.*

Grouse Mountain. Reached by gondola (with an entrance fee) from the upper reaches of North Vancouver, much of the Grouse Mountain resort inhabits a slope overlooking the city. While views are fine on a clear day, at night (the area is known for its night skiing) they're spectacular. Facilities include two quad chairs, 26 skiing and snowboarding runs, and several all-level freestyle-terrain parks. The vertical drop is 1,210 feet. There's a choice of upscale and casual dining in a good-looking stone-and-timber lodge. ✉ *6400 Nancy Greene Way, North Vancouver* ☎ *604/980–9311, 604/986–6262 snow report* ⊕ *www.grousemountain.com.*

Mount Seymour. Described as a full-service winter activity area, the Mount Seymour resort sprawls over 200 acres accessed from eastern North Vancouver. With three chairs for varying abilities; a beginner's rope tow, equipment rentals, and lessons; and toboggan and tubing runs, it's a popular destination for families. Snowboarding is particularly popular. The eateries aren't fancy. ✉ *1700 Mt. Seymour Rd., North Vancouver* ☎ *604/986–2261, 604/718–7771 snow report* ⊕ *www.mountseymour.com.*

WATER SPORTS

BOATING AND SAILING

With an almost limitless number and variety of waterways—from Indian Arm near Vancouver, up Howe Sound and the Sunshine Coast, across Georgia Strait to the Gulf Islands, and on to Vancouver Island, southwestern British Columbia is a boater's paradise. And much of this territory has easy access to marine and public services. One caution: this ocean territory is vast and complex; maritime maps are required. And one should always consult the Environment Canada marine forecasts (⊕ *www.weatheroffice.gc.ca*).

Blue Pacific Yacht Charters. This company rents motor- and sailboats for use between Vancouver Island and Seattle. ✉ *1519 Foreshore Walk, Granville Island* ☎ *604/682–2161 or 800/237–2392* ⊕ *www.bluepacific-charters.ca.*

Cooper Boating charters sailboats and cabin cruisers, with or without instructing skippers. ✉ *1620 Duranleau St., Granville Island* ☎ *604/ 687–4110 or 888/999–6419* ⊕ *www.cooperboating.com.*

CANOE-ING AND KAYAKING

Kayaking—seagoing and river kayaking—has become something of a lifestyle in Vancouver. While many sea kayakers start out (or remain) in False Creek, others venture into the open ocean and up and down the Pacific Coast. You can white-water kayak or canoe down the Capilano River and several other North Vancouver rivers. And paddling in a traditional, seagoing aboriginal-built canoe is an increasingly popular way to experience the maritime landscape.

Deep Cove Canoe and Kayak Rentals. Ocean-kayak rentals, guided trips, and lessons for kids and adults are all available at their North Shore base, from June to September. ✉ *2156 Banbury Rd., North Vancouver* ☎ *604/929–2268* ⊕ *www.deepcovekayak.com.*

Ecomarine Ocean Kayak Centre. Lessons and rentals are offered year-round from Granville Island, and from early May to early September at Jericho Beach and English Bay. ✉ *1668 Duranleau St., Granville Island* ☎ *604/689–7575 or 888/425–2925* ⊕ *www.ecomarine.com* ✉ *English Bay* ☎ *604/685–2925* ✉ *Jericho Beach* ☎ *604/222–3565.*

Lotus Land Tours. Kayaking tours in Indian Arm are run between May and October. The five-hour trip costs C$180 and includes a salmon barbecue lunch and hotel pickup. The company also hosts kayaking day trips in the Gulf Islands, including a floatplane flight back to Vancouver. Experience is not required. ☎ *604/684–4922 or 800/528–3531* ⊕ *www. VancouverNatureAdventures.com.*

Sea to Sky Kayak Center. These white-water specialists rent white-water, sea, and touring kayaks. They also provide instruction in sea kayaking and white-water kayaking on the Capilano and Seymour rivers, and offer introductory trips. ✉ *123 Charles St., North Vancouver* ☎ *604/ 983–6663* ⊕ *www.seatoskykayak.com.*

★ **Takaya Tours.** A trip with Takaya is a unique experience: you can paddle a 45-foot Salish oceangoing canoe while First Nations guides relay local legends, sing traditional songs, and point out ancient village sites. The two-hour tours leave from Cates Park in North Vancouver, and Belcarra Park in Port Moody. They also have trips up Indian Arm on motorized kayaks. Reservations are essential. ☎ *604/904–7410* ⊕ *www. takayatours.com.*

RIVER   Snowmelt from the coastal mountains, and broad rivers that run
RAFTING through the Pemberton Valley, north of Squamish, provide some of the best white-water rafting in British Columbia.

Canadian Outback Adventure Company. White-water rafting and scenic, family-oriented (not white-water) floats are offered on day trips from Vancouver. Transportation to and from Vancouver is available for an extra charge. ☎ *604/921–7250 or 800/565–8735* ⊕ *www.canadianout-back.com.*

Lotus Land Tours. This company runs river-rafting day trips from Vancouver to Whistler, including return transportation, guided rafting, and a barbecue lunch. ☎ *604/684–4922 or 800/528–3531* ⊕ *www. VancouverNatureAdventures.com.*

WINDSURFING The winds aren't heavy on English Bay, making it a perfect place for learning to windsurf. If you're looking for more challenging high-wind conditions, you have to travel north to Squamish.

Windsure Windsurfing School. Sailboard rentals and lessons are available between May and September at Jericho Beach, in Kitsilano. ☎ *604/224–0615* ⊕ *www.windsure.com.*

4

Vancouver Shops and Spas

WORD OF MOUTH

"Granville Island . . . the public market offers salmon, crab, and other seafood specialities, and many other specialty food items. I bought smoked salmon to bring home for Christmas gifts and a few bites of different types of smoked salmon and crab for a snack. There are many other types of gift shops there, too."

—jrpfeiffer

VANCOUVER SHOPS AND SPAS PLANNER

What to Bring Home

Uniquely Vancouver souvenirs include:

- **First Nations artwork**

- **Salmon,** smoked and vacuum-packed for travel

- **One-of-a-kind fashions** from emerging local designers

- **Anything from Roots**

- **Photos** (or photo books) of the city's spectacular nature landscape

The Tax Bite

A new tax replacing the 7% Provincial Sales Tax (PST) and 5% Goods and Services Tax (GST) has been proposed: the HST (Harmonized Sales Tax) of 12% will take effect in July 2010 if all goes smoothly, but it's the same 12%.

Most Intriguing Shops and Spas

Aberdeen Centre. A sparkly mall offering a good introduction to Vancouver's Asian shopping experience, including great restaurants and a Japanese $2 store.

Barbara-Jo's Books to Cooks. Featuring local and Canadian chefs and cuisine, this well-stocked cookbook shop also hosts culinary events and classes.

Les Amis du Fromage. Where cheese lovers go to swoon, sample, and stock up.

Miraj. The first of its kind in North America, this hammam and spa sets the exotic standard for luxury steams.

Portobello West Market. Emerging local designers with diverse arts, crafts, and fashion ideas hawk their distinctive wares at this festive once-a-month event (the last Sunday of the month) in a converted locomotive-maintenance building.

Robert Held Glass Studio. The source of world-renowned glassware. You can watch the glassblowers at work, too.

Top Shopping Experiences

Granville Island. From artist studios to a jam-packed food market, everything about Granville Island encourages browsing.

Hill's Native Art. Aboriginal art, from chintzy dime-a-dozen keepsake totem poles to real-McCoy treasures for serious collectors.

Holt Renfrew. Vancouver's most sophisticated, all-under-one-roof shopping experience, including deluxe spa services, a personal shopping concierge, and a martini rooftop lounge.

Store Hours

Store hours vary but are generally 10–6 Monday, Tuesday, Wednesday, and Saturday; 10–9 Thursday and Friday; and 11–5 or 11–6 Sunday. In Gastown, along Main Street, and on Commercial Drive, many shops don't open until 11 or noon.

Updated by
Carolyn B.
Heller

4

Unlike many cities where suburban malls have taken over, Vancouver is full of individual boutiques and specialty shops. Art galleries, ethnic markets, gourmet-food shops, and high-fashion outlets abound, and both Asian and First Nations influences in crafts, home furnishings, and foods are quite prevalent.

Vancouver has a community of budding fashion designers whose creative clothes and accessories populate the boutiques in the Gastown, Cambie Village, and Main Street/Mt. Pleasant neighborhoods. The monthly Portobello West Market is also an exciting showcase for emerging local designers.

Of course, Vancouver does have many of the same chain stores that you can find across North America, primarily downtown on Robson Street and in the malls. "Mall" doesn't just mean the Gap and Abercrombie, though, particularly in suburban Richmond where shopping destinations cater to an upscale Asian community. If you're not headed to Hong Kong, Beijing, or Tokyo, Richmond could be the next best thing.

In the art scene, look for First Nations and other aboriginal art, from souvenir trinkets to stellar, quality, contemporary designs; many galleries showcasing First Nations artists are in Gastown. Area artisans also create a variety of fine crafts, exhibiting and selling their wares at the Granville Island galleries.

Food—especially local seafood (available smoked and packed to travel), cheeses from British Columbia and across Canada, and even locally made chocolates, jams, and other goodies—make tasty souvenirs (or delicious picnic fare along the way). B.C. also has a rapidly maturing wine industry and local shops give advice about the region's offerings (and tastings, too). Just note the restrictions about taking alcohol back into your home country before you stock up.

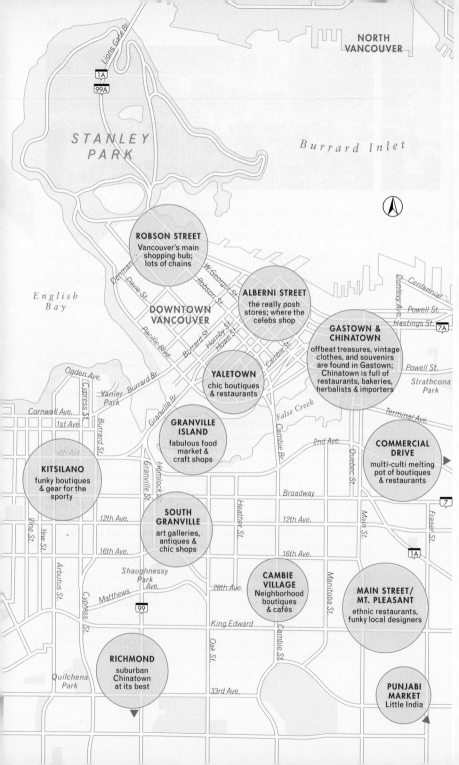

NORTH VANCOUVER

Burrard Inlet

STANLEY PARK

English Bay

ROBSON STREET
Vancouver's main shopping hub; lots of chains

ALBERNI STREET
the really posh stores; where the celebs shop

DOWNTOWN VANCOUVER

GASTOWN & CHINATOWN
offbeat treasures, vintage clothes, and souvenirs are found in Gastown; Chinatown is full of restaurants, bakeries, herbalists & importers

YALETOWN
chic boutiques & restaurants

GRANVILLE ISLAND
fabulous food market & craft shops

COMMERCIAL DRIVE
multi-culti melting pot of boutiques & restaurants

KITSILANO
funky boutiques & gear for the sporty

SOUTH GRANVILLE
art galleries, antiques & chic shops

CAMBIE VILLAGE
Neighborhood boutiques & cafés

MAIN STREET/ MT. PLEASANT
ethnic restaurants, funky local designers

RICHMOND
suburban Chinatown at its best

PUNJABI MARKET
Little India

Lions Gate Br.
1A 99A

Denman St.
Davie St.
W. Georgia St.
Robson St.
Pacific Blvd.
Burrard St.
Hornby St.
Howe St.
Cambie St.

Ogden Ave.
Cypress St.
Vanier Park
Burrard Br.
Cornwall Ave.
1st Ave.
Granville Br.
False Creek
Cambie Br.
2nd Ave.
Quebec St.

Dunlevy Ave.
Centennial
Powell St.
Hastings St. 7A
Powell St.
Strathcona Park
Terminal Ave.

4th Ave.
Burrard St.
Granville St.
Hemlock St.
12th Ave.
16th Ave.
Heather St.
Broadway
12th Ave.
16th Ave.
Main St.
7
1A

Vine St.
Yew St.
Arbutus St.
Cypress St.
Matthews
Shaughnessy Park Ave.
28th Ave.
King Edward
Oak St.
Cambie St.
Manitoba St.
33rd Ave.
Fraser St.

Quilchena Park
99

SHOPPING NEIGHBORHOODS

ROBSON STREET

Robson Street, particularly the blocks between Burrard and Bute streets, is the city's main fashion-shopping and people-watching artery. The Gap and Banana Republic have their flagship stores here, as do Canadian fashion outlets Club Monaco and Roots. Souvenir shops, shoe stores, and cafés fill the gaps. West of Bute, the shops cater to the thousands of Japanese and Korean students in town to study English: Asian food shops, video outlets, and cheap noodle bars abound.

ALBERNI STREET

One block north of Robson, Alberni Street at Burrard is geared to higher-income shoppers, with names such as Tiffany & Co., Louis Vuitton, Gucci, Coach, Hermès, and Betsey Johnson.

GASTOWN AND CHINATOWN

A hip crowd—restaurateurs, advertising gurus, photographers, and other creative types—have settled into **Gastown**, so the boutiques have gotten cooler. Look for locally designed and one-of-a-kind clothing and accessories, First Nations art, as well as souvenirs—both kitschy and expensive. Bustling **Chinatown**—centered on Pender and Main streets— is full of Chinese bakeries, restaurants, herbalists, tea merchants, and import shops.

YALETOWN

Frequently described as Vancouver's SoHo, this neighborhood on the north bank of False Creek is home to boutiques, home furnishings stores, and restaurants—many in converted warehouses—that cater to a trendy, moneyed crowd.

GRANVILLE ISLAND

On the south side of False Creek, **Granville Island** has a lively food market and a wealth of galleries, crafts shops, and artisans' studios. It gets so busy, especially on summer weekends, that the crowds can detract from the pleasure of the place; you're best off getting there before 11 AM.

SOUTH GRANVILLE

About two dozen high-end art galleries, antiques shops, and Oriental-rug emporiums are packed between 5th and 15th avenues on Granville Street, in an area known as **Gallery Row**. Granville Street between Broadway and 16th Avenue is known as **Granville Rise**, and it's lined with chic fashion, home-decor, and specialty-food shops.

KITSILANO

West 4th Avenue, between Burrard and Balsam, is the main shopping strip in funky Kitsilano. There are clothing and shoe boutiques, as well as housewares and gift shops. Just east of Burrard, several stores sell ski and snowboard gear.

CAMBIE VILLAGE

Revitalized after the opening of the Canada Line, which runs under Cambie Street, the **Cambie Village** district has a small collection of independent boutiques and cafés. Most shops are on Cambie between 18th and 20th avenues; the closest Canada Line stop is King Edward. Farther

MADE IN VANCOUVER

Vancouver doesn't just produce over-priced lattes and undersized condos. The city's creative denizens have designed a range of products from shoes to yoga wear:

Happy Planet Juices: Vancouverites have not only embraced this local company's mission to "turn the planet on to 100% organic juices," in 2008 they elected company cofounder Gregor Robertson the city's mayor.

Holey Soles: A competitor of the ubiquitous Crocs, these popular, brightly colored, cloglike, rubber-compound shoes are made in the Vancouver area and sold at outdoor and garden shops around town.

John Fluevog: Yep, those outra-geous shoes took their first step in Vancouver.

Lululemon Athletica: The styl-ized "A" insignia is as recognizable to yoga enthusiasts as the Nike "swoosh" is to sports fans.

Rocky Mountain Bicycles: B.C. invented the "free-riding" or "north shore" (from the North Shore Moun-tains) style of riding that's taken over the sport, and Rocky Mountain makes the steeds on which the style was pioneered.

north on Cambie, near the Broadway/City Hall station, is a collec-tion of big box stores, including Whole Foods, Best Buy, Winners, and Home Depot.

MAIN STREET/MT. PLEASANT

Main Street, between 20th and 30th avenues, is a funky, up-and-coming neighborhood, rich with ethnic restaurants and antiques, collectibles, and vintage-fashion shops. The main reason to explore here, though, is the growing number of eclectic boutiques that showcase local designers' creations. If distinctive yet economical fashion is your thing, you could easily spend a whole afternoon poking around these stores.

THE PUNJABI MARKET

In the **Punjabi Market** area, Vancouver's "Little India," curry houses, sweets shops, grocery stores, discount jewelers, and silk shops abound. This small community centers on Main Street between 48th and 51st avenues.

COMMERCIAL DRIVE

Guatemalan crafts, Italian shoes, and espresso bars with soccer matches broadcast live from Italy come together on **Commercial Drive,** between East 2nd Avenue and Venables Street, Vancouver's world-beat, offbeat melting pot.

RICHMOND

In suburban **Richmond,** south of downtown Vancouver, several large shopping malls—centered on and around No. 3 Road between Cambie Road and Granville Avenue—mix chain stores with small boutiques and eateries that cater to the area's upscale Asian residents. Aberdeen Centre could just as well be in Hong Kong. The Canada Line from downtown makes several stops in Richmond, convenient to the malls.

Yaletown has great boutiques for shopping during the day, and hip restaurants and bars (many with patios) for lounging in the evening.

DEPARTMENT STORES AND SHOPPING CENTERS

DEPARTMENT STORES

Many downtown department stores have migrated to shopping centers in the burbs where parking is free and easy and real estate more affordable. The Bay, descended from the historic Hudson's Bay Company, is one of the few mainstream department stores currently downtown.

The **Hudson's Bay Co.** A Canadian institution (even though it's now owned by Americans), The Bay was founded as part of the fur trade in the 17th century. A whole department sells the signature tri-color Bay blankets and other Canadiana. ⊠ *674 Granville St., at Georgia St., Downtown* ☎ *604/681–6211.*

Winners. This discount department store chain is heaven for bargain hunters. Among the regularly changing stock, you might unearth great deals on designer fashions, kids' clothes, housewares, and other paraphernalia. ⊠ *798 Granville St., at Robson, Downtown* ☎ *604/683– 1058.* ⊠ *491 W. 8th Ave.,Cambie* ☎ *604/879–3701.* ⊠ *Metropolis at Metrotown, 4700 Kingsway, Burnaby* ☎ *604/430–3457.*

SHOPPING CENTERS

In and around Vancouver are several shopping centers with an assortment of offerings.

★ **Aberdeen Centre.** First-rate Asian restaurants and cheap-and-cheerful food stalls, clothing stores stocking the latest Hong Kong styles, and Daiso—a Japanese bargain-hunters' paradise where most goods sell for just $2—make this swank mall a good introduction to Vancouver's

Asian shopping experience. Take the Canada Line south to Aberdeen station, about 20 minutes from downtown. ✉ *4151 Hazelbridge Way, Richmond* ☎ *604/270–1234.*

Metropolis at Metrotown. With 450 (give or take) stores—mostly North American chains—it's the province's largest shopping destination, easily reached via a 20-minute SkyTrain ride from downtown. Teens and serious shoppers alike flock to this sprawling mall; wear comfortable shoes. ✉ *4800 Kingsway, Burnaby* ☎ *604/438–3610.*

Oakridge Centre. With an airy skylighted atrium, Oakridge is one of the nicer malls to meander. There's a mix of trendy shops, midprice boutiques, and North American chains. It's a quick trip on the Canada Line from downtown: get off at the Oakridge-41st Avenue stop. ✉ *650 W. 41st Ave., at Cambie St., South Vancouver* ☎ *604/261–2511.*

Pacific Centre Mall. Filling three city blocks in the heart of downtown, this mall has mostly midprice, mainstream clothing shops, with some chicer pricier boutiques scattered throughout. There are several street-level entrances as well as access via Holt Renfrew, Sears, and the Vancouver City Centre Station—worth knowing about on rainy days. ✉ *700 W. Georgia St., Downtown* ☎ *604/688–7236.*

Sinclair Centre. Shops in and around this complex cater to sophisticated and pricey tastes with outposts such as Leone, Cartier, and Plaza Escada. ✉ *757 W. Hastings St., Downtown.*

SPECIALTY STORES

ANTIQUES, AUCTIONS, AND FLEA MARKETS

Key antiques hunting grounds are Gallery Row on Granville Street and along Main Street from 20th to 30th avenues.

DoDa Antiques. Concentrating on mid-20th-century jewelry, ceramics, glass, paintings, and prints, this old-timey treasure box is crammed full of intriguing finds. They stock First Nations art as well. ✉ *434 Richards St., Downtown* ☎ *604/602–0559.*

The Vancouver Flea Market. Housed in a "big red barn," the market's open every weekend and is only a five-minute walk from the Main Street SkyTrain station. You'll find all manner of treasures at all sorts of prices. ✉ *703 Terminal Ave., East Side* ☎ *604/685–0666.*

ART AND CRAFTS GALLERIES

DOWNTOWN A number of notable galleries are on the downtown peninsula.

Buschlen Mowatt. This downtown gallery is well-known for exhibiting works of contemporary Canadian and international artists. ✉ *1445 W. Georgia St., West End* ☎ *604/682–1234.*

★ **Coastal Peoples Fine Arts Gallery.** The gorgeous books and postcards make affordable souvenirs though you could well be tempted by the impressive collection of First Nations jewelry, ceremonial masks, prints, and carvings. ✉ *1024 Mainland St., Yaletown* ☎ *604/685–9298.* ✉ *312 Water St., Gastown* ☎ *604/684–9222*

Fodor'sChoice **Hill's Native Art.** This highly respected store has Vancouver's largest selection of First Nations art. If you think the main level is impressive, go
★

Inside the Coastal Peoples Fine Arts Gallery.

upstairs where the collector-quality stuff is. ✉ *165 Water St., Gastown* ☏ *604/685–4249.*

Inuit Gallery of Vancouver. In addition to quality Inuit art like the signature carvings in soapstone and antler, there's also an excellent collection of Northwest Coast Native art such as baskets, totems, bentwood boxes, and masks. ✉ *206 Cambie St., Gastown* ☏ *888/615–8399 or 604/688–7323.*

Marion Scott Gallery. Specializing in fine Inuit art from the Canadian North, gallery exhibits here include sculpture, prints, wall hangings, and drawings. ✉ *308 Water St., Gastown* ☏ *604/685–1934.*

Spirit Wrestler Gallery. With exhibits that include works of the Pacific Northwest First Nations, the Inuit of the Canadian Arctic, and the New Zealand Māori, this gallery showcases an intriguing comparison of cultural styles. ✉ *47 Water St., Gastown* ☏ *604/669–8813.*

GALLERY ROW   Gallery Row along Granville Street is home to about a dozen high-end contemporary-art galleries. Most are clustered between 5th Avenue and Broadway but the gallery district extends up to 15th Avenue.

Diane Farris Gallery. This high-profile gallery one block west of Granville Street often showcases new Canadian and international artists. ✉ *1590 W. 7th Ave., South Granville* ☏ *604/737–2629.*

Douglas Reynolds Gallery. In this collection of Northwest Coast First Nations art, particularly strong in woodwork and jewelry, some pieces date back to the 1800s, while others are strikingly contemporary. ✉ *2335 Granville St., South Granville* ☏ *604/731–9292.*

CLOSE UP

A Bit About—and How to Buy—Aboriginal Art

With 198 First Nations groups in British Columbia alone, it's easy to be mesmerized, even confused, by the range and diversity of the indigenous art you'll see. Different bands have traded materials, skills, and resources for centuries so that today it's often difficult to attribute any particular style to any one Nation. It's this blending, though, that has created such a rich cultural mosaic. That said, there are still some groups, such as the Haida and Coast Salish, who have strong identifiable traits.

Broadly speaking, First Nations art is a language of symbols, which come together to describe the legends and stories that link one community with another. And contrary to popular belief, although these symbols may share a similar meaning, they are by no means a common language: the Coast Salish, for example, view the hummingbird differently from how the Tsimshian Tribe do.

According to Rikki Kooy, whose Shuswap name is Spirit Elk Woman, there are two heartfelt ways many people purchase First Nations art. "The first is to fall in love with a region of British Columbia, and find the First Nations group that represents that area. The second is to fall in love with a piece for its calling." She goes on to explain that "Quality pieces have a flow. I call it a life." Rikki has been involved with retailing aboriginal art for more than 35 years and is an advisor to Aboriginal Tourism BC.

Once you've found yourself drawn to a particular piece, whether it's jewelry, a mask, or a print, there are three essential questions to consider in judging its integrity and authenticity.

1) Does the work or design have a title? Because First Nations art is highly symbolic, authentic pieces will be titled. Bear in mind that the title will usually allude to mythical lore, real-life stories, and/or the artist's ancestry.

2) Is the cultural group identified? Every piece holds a story, against which there is often a broader background of heritage, hierarchy, and geographic origin. For example, a Haida piece will likely have come from the Queen Charlottes, or have been made by a descendant from that region. By knowing the region, the nuances of the piece's symbolic language are more easily identified.

3) Is the artist identified, or better still, is there a background sheet available? First Nations peoples hold relationships in high esteem so dealers with integrity will have established a relationship with the artists they represent, and should have a background sheet on the artist and his heritage. This adds to the authenticity of the work, as well as giving you some background about the artist and his or her other works.

★ **Robert Held Art Glass.** At Canada's largest "hot glass" studio, located two blocks west of Granville Street, you can watch glassblowers in action, then browse the one-of-a-kind vases, paperweights, bowls, ornaments, and perfume bottles. Held's glass pieces have been exhibited at the Canadian Museum of Civilization in Ottawa and at galleries across North America. ✉ *2130 Pine St., between 5th and 6th Aves., South Granville* ☎ *604/737–0020.*

GRANVILLE ISLAND   Granville Island is a must-do destination for crafts aficionados. Stroll Railspur Alley (off Old Bridge Street), which is lined with working artists' studios; the Net Loft building opposite the Public Market also has several galleries. The "Artists & Artisans of Granville Island" brochure (available at shops around the island or online at ⊕ *www. granvilleislandartists.com*) has a complete listing of galleries and studios, but the following are some of our faves.

Circle Craft. This artists' co-op sells textiles, wood pieces, jewelry, ceramics, and glass works. ✉ *1–1666 Johnston St., Net Loft, Granville Island* ☎ *604/669–8021.*

Craft House. Run by the Crafts Council of B.C., this tiny house contains a veritable smorgasbord of works by local artisans. ✉ *1386 Cartwright St., Granville Island* ☎ *604/687–7270.*

Gallery of B.C. Ceramics. An impressive display of functional and decorative ceramics by local artists is for sale here. ✉ *1359 Cartwright St., Granville Island* ☎ *604/669–3906.*

GREATER VANCOUVER   **Khot-la-Cha Art Gallery & Gift Shop.** Located on the Capilano Reserve in North Vancouver, this longhouse-style gallery is a showcase for hand-crafted items made by members of the Squamish Indian Band, as well as other aboriginal artists in British Columbia and western Canada. You'll find ceremonial masks, hand-knit sweaters, moccasins, and jewelry made of silver, gold, porcupine quill, or bone. The store is owned by Nancy Nightingale, the daughter of Chief Simon Baker, whose traditional name, Khot-la-Cha, means "kind heart" in the Squamish language. ✉ *270 Whonoak St., North Vancouver* ☎ *604/987–3339.*

Lattimer Gallery. Stocking native arts and crafts in all price ranges, this shop is a short walk from Granville Island. ✉ *1590 W. 2nd Ave., False Creek* ☎ *604/732–4556.*

The **Museum of Anthropology Gift Shop.** They carry an excellent selection of Northwest Coast jewelry, carvings, and prints, as well as books on First Nations history and culture. Tip: pick up the museum's Guide

---

PORTOBELLO WEST

Modeled on London's Portobello Road, **Portobello West** is an art/fashion market showcasing emerging local designers—some are students, others are more established, but all sell unique, stylish wares. The event is held March–December on the last Sunday of the month, from noon to 6 PM. The venue—a converted locomotive-maintenance building—is about three-quarters of a mile from the Main Street SkyTrain station; catch the free shuttle at the corner of Station Street and Terminal Avenue. ✉ *1755 Cottrell St., East Side, at the Rocky Mountaineer Station* ⊕ *www.vancouver. portobellowest.com* ✉ *$2.*

4

No. 10, *A Guide to Buying Contemporary Northwest Coast Indian Arts* by Karen Duffek; though written in 1983, it's still a relevant and definitive guide for laypeople. ⊠ *6393 N.W. Marine Dr., University of British Columbia Campus, Point Grey* ☎ *604/822–3440.*

BOOKS

★ **Barbara-Jo's Books to Cooks.** Local-chef-turned-entrepreneur Barbara-Jo McIntosh spreads the good-food word with scores of cookbooks, including many by Vancouver- and B.C.-based chefs, as well as wine books, food-focused memoirs, and magazines. The store also hosts special events, recipe demos, and drop-in classes in its sparkling demonstration kitchen—they're a tasty way to explore local cuisine. The store's Web site, ⊕ *www.bookstocooks.com*, lists event schedules. ⊠ *1740 W. 2nd Ave., Kitsilano* ☎ *604/688–6755.*

Chapters. These chain outlets (most with a Starbucks attached) are the Canadian equivalent of Borders or Barnes & Noble, stocking a vast selection of popular books and CDs. Check out the special display tables for hot sellers, Canadian authors, and bargains. ⊠ *788 Robson St., Downtown* ☎ *604/682–4066* ⊠ *2505 Granville St., at Broadway, South Granville* ☎ *604/731–7822.* ⊠ *Metropolis at Metrotown, 4700 Kingsway, Burnaby* ☎ *604/431–0463.*

☪ **Kidsbooks.** Canada's largest selection of books for children, from tod-
★ dlers to teens, stocks the shelves here, and many of those shelves are kid-friendly—low, with plenty of reading nooks. ⊠ *3083 W. Broadway, Kitsilano* ☎ *604/738–5335.*

MacLeod's Books. One of the city's best antiquarian and used-book stores, this shop is a treasure trove of titles from mainstream to wildly eclectic. ⊠ *455 W. Pender St., Downtown* ☎ *604/681–7654.*

Sophia Books. This is the place to come for foreign-language books, magazines, and CDs. Even the staff is multilingual so you'll probably hear Japanese, French, Spanish, and English. ⊠ *450 W. Hastings St., Downtown* ☎ *604/684–0484.*

Wanderlust. For the travel-savvy, here's where to find thousands of travel books and maps, as well as luggage and travel accessories. ⊠ *1929 W. 4th Ave., Kitsilano* ☎ *604/739–2182.*

CLOTHES

CHILDREN'S **Dandelion Kids.** If you're shopping for style-conscious babies and kids
CLOTHING up to eight years old, check out the new, organic, and "recycled" duds. Fair-trade toys also fill the shelves. ⊠ *1206 Commercial Dr., East Side* ☎ *604/676–1862.*

Please Mum. With its range of comfortable, brightly colored clothing, this Vancouver-based, Canada-wide chain is known for its fun-to-mix-and-match separates that feature "grow touches"—they enable an item to grow with the child. ⊠ *2951 W. Broadway, Kitsilano* ☎ *604/732–4574* ⊠ *Oakridge Centre, 650 W. 41st Ave., South Vancouver* ☎ *604/261–5440* ⊠ *Metropolis at Metrotown, 4700 Kingsway, Burnaby* ☎ *604/430–1702.*

The Lululemon brand of yoga attire was founded in Vancouver in 1998.

Roots Kids. Synonymous with outdoorsy Canadian style, this Canadian company's signature casual wear is also available in children's sizes. ✉ *1153 Robson St., West End* ☎ *604/684–8801.*

West Coast casual is the predominant look in Vancouver, and the clothing stores reflect that, though you can also find chic designer outlets and shops selling more eclectic creations.

If you're looking for "made in Vancouver" fashions, head for Gastown or Main Street, as well as the trendy boutiques in Yaletown, where young, up-and-coming labels are sold at stores committed to giving Vancouver-based designers a leg up.

Barefoot Contessa. These cute shops mix creative looks with '40s-style glamour. Look for frilly feminine clothing (the homemade camisoles are in hot demand), jewelry, and bags—some by local designers—as well as vintage linens and decorative accessories. ✉ *3715 Main St., Main St./Mt. Pleasant* ☎ *604/879–1137* ✉ *1928 Commercial Dr., East Side* ☎ *604/255–9035.*

Dream Apparel & Articles for People. Come here to find a variety of wares by up-and-coming local designers. The creative selections target the hip twentysomething crowd. Under the same ownership, **Little Dream** (✉ *130–1666 Johnston St., Net Loft, Granville Island* ☎ *604/683–6930*) is a smaller version of this fashion-forward shop. ✉ *311 W. Cordova St., Gastown* ☎ *604/683–7326.*

Edie Hats. You name the hat and somewhere on the walls, rafters, shelves, or floor, you'll find it—fedoras, cloches, toques, sun hats, rain

Farmers' Markets

Vancouverites who are passionate about locally grown food flock to the city's weekly farmers' markets, which are also wonderful spots to assemble a picnic for the beach or track down a gourmet gift. Look for locally made cheeses, honeys, and jams, freshly baked breads, and homegrown raspberries, blueberries, or other seasonal fruits. Seasonal schedules can change so check ⊕ www.eatlocal.org to confirm.

■ West End Farmers' Market: Sat. 9 AM to 2 PM, mid-June to mid-Oct. (Nelson Park, 1100 block Comox St., West End)

■ Gastown Farmers' Market: Sun. 11 AM to 3 PM, mid-June to mid-Oct. (200 block Carrall St., between Water and Cordova Sts., Gastown)

■ Main Street Market: Wed. 3 to 7 PM, mid-June to mid-Oct. (Thornton Park, in front of the VIA Rail Station, near the Main St. SkyTrain Station)

■ Kitsilano Farmers' Market: Sun. 10 AM to 2 PM, mid-June to mid-Oct. (Kitsilano Community Centre, W. 10th Ave. and Larch St., Kitsilano)

■ Trout Lake Farmers' Market: Sat. 9 AM to 2 PM, mid-May to mid-Oct. (Trout Lake Community Centre, E. 15th Ave. and Victoria Dr., East Side)

■ UBC (University of British Columbia) Farm Market: Sat. 9 AM to 1 PM, June to mid-Oct. (6182 South Campus Rd., UBC campus, West Side)

4

---

hats, straw hats . . . Edie's has 'em all. ⊠ 4–1666 *Johnston St., Net Loft, Granville Island* ☎ 604/683–4280 or 800/750–2134.

Hazel & Co. While many Main Street shops target the young and hyper fashion conscious, this hip boutique appeals to youthful women of all ages with fashionable labels such as Mexx, Kensie, and their own in-house lines. They also carry cool clothes for moms-to-be. ⊠ 4280 *Main St., Main St./Mt. Pleasant* ☎ 604/730–8689.

Fodor's Choice ★ **Holt Renfrew.** High on the city's ritzy scale, Holts is a swanky showcase for international high fashion and accessories for men and women. Think Prada, Dolce & Gabbana, and other designer labels. ⊠ *Pacific Centre, 737 Dunsmuir St., Downtown* ☎ 604/681–3121.

★ **Leone.** Marble alcoves in an elegantly palatial store set the scene for men's and women's fashions by Jil Sander, Versace, Yves Saint Laurent, Rive Gauche, Dior, Miu Miu, and others. On the lower level is **L-2 Leone,** where you'll find edgier fashions and an Italian café. ⊠ 757 *W. Hastings St., Sinclair Centre, Downtown* ☎ 604/683–1133.

★ **Lululemon Athletica.** This is a real Vancouver success story: everyone from power-yoga devotees to soccer moms covet the fashionable, well-constructed workout wear with the stylized "A" insignia. The stores also provide free drop-in yoga classes; call or check ⊕ *www.lululemon. com* for details. ⊠ 1148 *Robson St., West End* ☎ 604/681–3118 ⊠ 2113 *W. 4th Ave., Kitsilano* ☎ 604/732–6111 ⊠ *Metropolis at Metrotown, 4800 Kingsway, Burnaby* ☎ 604/430–4659.

CLOSE UP

Top Spa Hurrah

Vancouver's spa scene is as diverse as its multicultural makeup and includes everything from exotic steam experiences to over-the-top indulgence. While many services give the nod to ancient wisdoms such as Ayurveda, you'll also find holistic spa and wellness destinations that incorporate elements of traditional Chinese medicine, Japanese Reiki, and New Age energy therapies, alongside medical aesthetics like Botox, microdermabrasion, and teeth whitening. As in many cities, hair salons often try to parlay "spa" into their mix to broaden their appeal, which usually means having to battle the noise and chemical smells of hairdressing to get to a backroom for your spa services. Ugh! Skip those; for authentic spa experiences, here are our top choices:

Absolute Spa at the Century. This expansive spa has an A-list of celebrity clients—Jennifer Lopez, Ethan Hawke, Gwyneth Paltrow, and Ben Affleck, to name a few. What makes this 15,000-square-foot spa really stand out, though, are all the extras that turn even a simple manicure into an experience: every treatment comes with a complimentary eucalyptus steam, a swim in the ozonated pool, a healthful snack (champagne and chocolate-coated strawberries are optional extras), and even a make-up touch-up to help you face the world of reality. Jet-lagged? The spa's several branches at Vancouver International Airport give antifatigue treatments and quick chair massages. Prefer to stay put? Absolute Mobile will come to you. ⊠ *1015 Burrard St., Downtown* 🕾 *604/684–2772.*

Absolute Spa at Hotel Vancouver. Although women enjoy the aura and treatments, this spa is really geared to men—with black-leather pedicure thrones, wide-screen TVs, video games, and computers to check on sports scores and stock prices. Robes and slippers are man-size and many treatments have a testosterone focus, with options like the "five o'clock buster" hot towel shave. ⊠ *900 W. Georgia St., Downtown* 🕾 *604/684–2772.*

BLO. Canada's first blow-dry bar specializes in catwalk-quality blowout styles for only C$31 in about 30 minutes. A visit to these funky pink-and-plastic outfitted lounges is a must-do for your do before a fancy dinner, or just because. They do extensions, too, and guys can get in on the act with Blo's "Blo Bro" service. ⊠ *1150 Hamilton St., Yaletown* 🕾 *604/909–9495.* ⊠ *791 W. Georgia St., at The Four Seasons HotelDowntown* 🕾 *604/609–5460*⊠ *1529 W. 14th Ave., South Granville* 🕾 *604/734–7599.*

Miraj. It's just about the most luxuriously authentic steam bath you'll get outside of Turkey. The entire experience feels at the periphery of the *Arabian Nights,* with Middle Eastern–inspired architecture and Jerusalem marble that stays cool to the touch as the temperature rises. A steam includes a light body scrub with black Moroccan soap and the option of a full body massage—highly recommended. Afterward, you get to curl up amongst the plethora of silk cushions where you're served Moroccan mint tea and a sweet cake. Snoozing is encouraged. ⊠ *1495 W. 6th Ave., South Granville* 🕾 *604/733–5151.*

Perfect Health Spa. Billed as a movie spa, you can watch your favorite chick flick on a 14-foot screen while having your nails done.

Locals love the space for group gatherings and private parties but there's a smaller cozier room in the back, complete with fireplace, that accommodates small groups of three or four people.Or you can opt for one of the color-therapy rooms, each themed to harmonize with one of the body's chakra (energy) centers. ⊠ *2525 Arbutus St., Kitsilano* ☎ *604/736–2111.*

Skoah. By specializing only in facials, Skoah has created a market niche for itself. There's no froufrou here, just top-quality skin care that puts the facial on a stratosphere unto itself. The contemporary design has a New York sassiness, and treatments are gender neutral. They'll even do foot and hand "facials." ⊠ *1011 Hamilton St., Yaletown* ☎ *604/642–0200.*

Spa Utopia. If you're looking for WOW, you can't beat this lavish, utopia-reaching spa with its ornamental columns, freestanding fountains, floor-to-ceiling windows, and waterfront views. There's a wide range of services but the massage therapies are especially enjoyable; practitioners are trained by the man who wrote the training manual on therapeutic spa massage. For the ultimate treat, book one of the hotel's spa suites and let the treatments come to you. ⊠ *999 Canada Pl., at Pan Pacific Hotel, Downtown* ☎ *604/641–1351.*

Spruce Body Lab. Urban and hip, sleekly designed, and gender neutral, Spruce is almost a medical spa since treatments such as Botox and acupuncture are on the menu in addition to regular spa services. Geo-Thermal Stone Therapy is one of the lab's signature treatments: it involves the placement of warm and cool stones on the body's different energy centers

as well as a full body massage— different from regular stone massages, and a much more dynamic experience. ⊠ *1128 Richards St., Yaletown* ☎ *604/683–3220.*

Vida Wellness Spa. Ayurvedic treatments, based on the 5,000-year-old Indian science of holistic wellness, are the specialty here, alongside regular services like facials and body wraps. Vida has made Ayurveda the central focus in its growing number of spas, and all the herbs, spices, and oils used in the Swedana, Shirodhara, and Abhyanga massages (to name a few) are customized to your particular body composition, or "dosha." Services include a complimentary steam. ⊠ *1088 Burrard St., at The Sheraton Wall Centre Hotel, Downtown* ☎ *604/682–8410 or 800/401–4018.* ⊠ *845 Burrard St., at The Sutton Place Hotel, Downtown* ☎ *604/682–8410 or 800/401–4018.* ⊠ *1601 Bayshore Dr., at the Westin Bayshore Hotel, West End* ☎ *604/682–3377*

Wedgewood Hotel Spa. What it lacks in size, it makes up for in intimacy. With only two treatment rooms (each large enough to convert to a couples suite), a spa service here is just like the Wedgewood Hotel itself: understated elegance with graceful attention to detail. Many services include unadvertised extras like a foot, hand, or scalp massage, and the complimentary steam room actually gets hot enough to soak the tension out of you. The spa carries Epicuren, a live-enzyme skin-care system of products favored by many dermatologists and cosmetic surgeons. The hotel also has an in-room spa program for guests. ⊠ *2nd floor–845 Hornby St., Downtown* ☎ *604/608–5340.*

4

One of a Few. The creative women's clothing here, from local and international makers, may not be one of a kind, but as the name of this funky little shop attests, you won't see the designs at mass-market retailers either. Next door, **Two of a Few** (⊠ *356 Water St., Gastown* ☎ *604/605–0630*), under the same ownership, carries both men's and women's lines. ⊠ *354 Water St., Gastown* ☎ *604/605–0685.*

Roots. For outdoorsy clothes that double as souvenirs (many sport maple-leaf logos), check out these Canadian-made sweatshirts, leather jackets, and other comfy casuals. ⊠ *1001 Robson St., West End* ☎ *604/683–4305* ⊠ *2665 Granville St., South Granville* ☎ *604/629–1300* ⊠ *Metropolis at Metrotown, 4700 Kingsway, Burnaby* ☎ *604/435–5554.*

> ### WORD OF MOUTH
>
> "For markets, Granville Island is where you'll want to be from the morning until 7PM. Granville Island Public Market is the most famous market in the city, with all kinds of food products. Outside of the market in the neighboring buildings are art studios, art galleries, craft shops, unique gift shops, as well as restaurants, waterfront walkways, boat rentals, etc. Really cool place to spend an afternoon."
> —Carmanah

Roots Outlet. You can pay top dollar downtown, but this factory outlet stocks good quality off-season and closeout items—at bargain prices. ⊠ *3695 Grandview Hwy., at Boundary Rd., East Side* ☎ *604/433–4337.*

Shop Cocoon. Independent designers can rent a rack, shelf, or wall space to showcase their work trade show–style in this small shop. Products change frequently and include ethically manufactured clothing, accessories, and jewelry. ⊠ *3345 Cambie St., Cambie* ☎ *778/232–8532.*

Tilley Endurables. Globe-trotters search out this practical, hard-wearing line of Canadian-made travel clothing: the Tilley Hat is an icon of seasoned travelers. ⊠ *2401 Granville St., South Granville* ☎ *604/732–4287.*

Twigg & Hottie. Local designers stock this outlet with one-of-a-kind creations ranging from the edgiest of Hollywood glam to chic street-wear funk. ⊠ *3671 Main St., Main St./Mt. Pleasant* ☎ *604/879–8595.*

VINTAGE CLOTHING

Changes. This friendly neighborhood storefront sells a mix of brand-new and good-quality secondhand items, all moderately priced. Also look for good-value jewelry by local and Canadian artists such as Kazumi and Brooklyn. It's a bit out of the way, but almost always worth the trip. ⊠ *4454 W. 10th Ave., Point Grey* ☎ *604/222–1505.*

Front and Company. Value-conscious fashionistas paw through the consignment and vintage clothing in this smart shop. There's a small section of designer samples and new items, as well as eclectic gifts. ⊠ *3772 Main St., Main St./Mt. Pleasant* ☎ *604/879–8431.*

Turnabout. The quality is so good that "used" is almost a misnomer at this long-established vintage-clothing store. The Granville Street location sells upscale women's wear; the Broadway branch sells more casual clothing, as well as men's clothes. ⊠ *3109 Granville St., South Granville* ☎ *604/734–5313* ⊠ *3112 W. Broadway, Kitsilano* ☎ *604/731–7762.*

A selection of goodies from Les Amis du Fromage.

FOOD

FOOD
MARKETS
Fodor's Choice
★

Granville Island Public Market. Locals and visitors alike crowd this indoor market that's part farm stand, part gourmet grocery, and part upscale food court. Stalls are packed with fresh produce, meats, just-caught fish, baked goods, and prepared foods from exotic cheeses and handmade fudge to frothy cappuccinos. If the sun is out, dine on your purchases out on the decks. At the **Salmon Shop** (☎ 604/669–3474), you can pick up fresh or smoked salmon vacuum-packed and wrapped for travel. For other local specialties (and great gifts for foodie friends), visit **Edible British Columbia** (☎ 604/662–3606), which sells jams, sauces, chocolates, and hundreds of other edible items from around the province. ✉ *1689 Johnston St., Granville Island* ☎ *604/666–5784.*

Lonsdale Quay. A short ride on the SeaBus from downtown (the best cruise value in town), this two-level indoor market is less frenzied than its Granville Island counterpart. Vendors sell prepared foods, seafood, and fresh produce as well as arts and crafts, kitchenware, and delicious pastries that should be enjoyed on the terrace with its views of the downtown skyline. ✉ *123 Carrie Cates Ct., North Vancouver* ☎ *604/985–6261.*

FOOD AND
CIGAR SHOPS

City Cigar. For cigar aficionados; Cuban cigars are legal and plentiful (although it's not legal to take them back into the United States). Is this why Tommy Lee Jones and Arnold Schwarzenegger stop here when they're in town? ✉ *888 W. 6th Ave., Fairview* ☎ *604/879–0208.*

★ **Les Amis du Fromage.** If you love cheese, don't miss the mind-boggling array of selections from B.C., the rest of Canada, France, and elsewhere at this shop of delicacies. The extremely knowledgeable mother-and-daughter owners, Alice and Allison Spurrell, and their staff encourage you to taste before you buy. Yum. ✉ *1752 W. 2nd Ave., Kitsilano* ☎ *604/732–4218.* ✉ *843 E. Hastings St.East Side* ☎ *604/253–4218*

Meinhardt Fine Foods. Pick up fixings for an elegant picnic or find a gift for a foodie friend at this sophisticated neighborhood groceteria. The same owners run a deli-style coffee shop next door to the Granville Street location, good for sandwiches, wraps, and pastries to eat in or take out. ✉ *3002 Granville St., South Granville* ☎ *604/732–4405.* ✉ *3151Arbutus St.Kitsilano* ☎ *604/732–7900*

T&T Supermarket. Check out this minichain of maxi-size Asian supermarkets for exotic produce, Chinese baked goods, and prepared foods. You can assemble an inexpensive lunch-to-go from the extensive hot food counter. ✉ *179 Keefer Pl., Chinatown* ☎ *604/899–8836* ✉ *2800 E. 1st Ave., at Renfrew, East Side* ☎ *604/254–9668* ✉ *Metropolis at Metrotown,4800 Kingsway, Burnaby* ☎ *604/436–4881* ✉ *8181 Cambie Rd., President Plaza, Richmond* ☎ *604/279–1818.*

Urban Fare. If you're a fan of Whole Foods, check out this local minichain; they're Vancouver's most stylish supermarkets. The expansive food displays are mouthwatering and come from all corners of the globe. ✉ *177 Davie St., Yaletown* ☎ *604/975–7550* ✉ *305 Bute St., Downtown* ☎ *604/669–5831* ✉ *1133 Alberni St., Downtown* ☎ *604/648–2716.*

PASTRY AND CHOCOLATE SHOPS

Chocolate Arts. Looking for a present for a chocolate lover? Check out the chocolates in First Nations motifs, specially designed by Robert Davidson, one of Canada's premier artists. ✉ *2037 W. 4th Ave., Kitsilano* ☎ *604/739–0475 or 877/739–0475.*

Ganache Patisserie. In true Parisian style, every delicious and decadent item here is a work of art. You can buy full cakes—say chocolate-banana cake or amaretto cheesecake—but a slice will also perk up your shopping day. ✉ *1262 Homer St., Yaletown* ☎ *604/899–1098.*

Purdy's. A chocolatier since 1907, Purdy's once made a liqueur-filled line, which was hawked to Americans during Prohibition. These days, Purdy's purple-foiled boxes of chocolate temptations are a popular gift. Outlets are scattered throughout the city. ✉ *Pacific Centre, 700 W. Georgia St., Downtown* ☎ *604/683–3467.*

WINE SHOPS

Liberty Wine Merchants. Selling wines from B.C. and around the world, this local minichain has helpful employees and convenient locations. ✉ *1289 Robson St., Downtown* ☎ *604/633–1922* ✉ *1660 Johnston St., Granville Island* ☎ *604/602–1120.* ✉ *4583 W. 10th Ave., Point Grey* ☎ *604/224–8050.*

CHINATOWN NIGHT MARKET

An Asian-style summer night market adds an entertaining dimension to your shopping excursions. This one's downtown and easy to get to.

Chinatown Night Market. Chinatown is at its liveliest when stalls set up shop selling food, T-shirts, and "do I really need this?" bits 'n bobs. It's open from mid-May to early September, 6:30 PM to 11 PM, Friday through Sunday. It's fun to wander. ✉ *Keefer St., between Columbia and Main Sts., Chinatown* ☎ *604/682–8998.*

Taylorwood Wines. To learn more about British Columbia wines, or to pick up a bottle (or a few), visit the knowledgeable staff at this Yaletown store that stocks only wines produced within the province. Weekly tastings let you try before you buy; check the Web site ⊕ *www. taylorwoodwines.com* for a schedule. ⊠ *1185 Mainland St., Yaletown* ☎ *604/408–9463.*

Viti Wine and Lager Store. What this diminutive shop at the Moda Hotel lacks in size, it makes up in quality, furnishing a strong selection of wines, beers, and liquors, with an emphasis on regional products. Wine tastings are held Thursdays; beer or whiskey tastings are held regularly on Fridays. ⊠ *900 Seymour St., Downtown* ☎ *604/683–3806.*

JEWELRY

Vancouver's leading jewelry shops are clustered along West Hastings Street. If you're looking for distinctive, locally made creations, browse the South Granville or Main Street neighborhoods.

Birks. Vancouver's link in this Canada-wide chain of high-end jewelers—a national institution since 1879—is in a neoclassical former bank building. An impressive staircase connects the main level to the mezzanine floor—descending, it feels as if you're royalty. ⊠ *698 W. Hastings St., Downtown* ☎ *604/669–3333.*

OhKuol. Environmentally friendly? Check. Locally made? Check. Funky chic and eminently wearable? Check and check. This lovely "wearable art" shop carries jewelry and other pieces made by Canadian artists, many of whom create their works from recycled materials. ⊠ *2439 Granville St., South Granville* ☎ *604/732–6600.*

Palladio. This is one of the city's most chic jewelers; expect to find high-fashion pieces in gold and platinum, top-name timepieces, and distinguished accessories. ⊠ *855 W. Hastings St., Downtown* ☎ *604/ 685–3885.*

HOUSEWARES

Doctor Vigari Gallery. In keeping with its offbeat environs on "the Drive" (i.e., Commercial Drive), expect to see a wildly eclectic assortment of jewelry, crafts, paintings, and household items and furniture, most by B.C. artists. ⊠ *1312 Commercial Dr., Commercial Drive* ☎ *604/ 255–9513.*

Villeroy & Boch. The hand-painted bowls and exclusive-to-Vancouver plates from this store with an international name in design for dining and housewares, make quality souvenirs. ⊠ *420 Howe St., Downtown* ☎ *604/681–5881.*

Walrus. "A pleasant surprise" is the motto of this airy gallerylike shop, where you never quite know what you'll find—perhaps candle holders, jewelry, handcrafted purses, one-of-a-kind T-shirts, or original artwork. They stock a mix of local and international designs and often host small exhibitions. ⊠ *3408 Cambie St., Cambie* ☎ *604/874–9770.*

OUTDOOR EQUIPMENT

Outdoor-oriented Vancouver is a great place to pick up camping and hiking gear. There's a cluster of outdoor-equipment shops on West Broadway between Yukon and Manitoba streets, and there are several snowboard, skiing, and bicycle outlets on West 4th Avenue, just east of Burrard Street.

Coast Mountain Sports. Though they're sometimes a bit pricey, you can count on finding high-performance (and high-fashion) gear at these large sports shops. ⊠ *777 Dunsmuir St., Pacific Centre Mall, Downtown* ☎ *604/687–7668* ⊠ *1625 Chestnut St., Kitsilano* ☎ *604/731–6181* ⊠ *4700 Kingsway, Metropolis at Metrotown Centre, Burnaby* ☎ *604/434–9397.*

★ **Mountain Equipment Co-op.** The massive warehouse-style outlet is a local institution with a good selection of high-performance and midprice clothing and equipment for hiking, cycling, climbing, kayaking, traveling, and just hanging around outdoors. A onetime C$5 membership is required. ⊠ *130 W. Broadway, Fairview* ☎ *604/872–7858.*

Taiga. Vancouver-based Taiga sells popular waterproof cycling gear, as well as other outdoor clothing, sleeping bags, and tents. ⊠ *301 W. Broadway, Fairview* ☎ *604/875–8388.*

Three Vets. Near Cambie Street and Broadway, this army surplus–style store has budget-price family camping equipment, outdoor clothing, and boots. They also have a native art collection worth seeing. ⊠ *2200 Yukon St., Fairview* ☎ *604/872–5475.*

SHOES AND ACCESSORIES

Dayton Boot Company. These biker boots have a worldwide, cultlike following because they're enduringly good, and hip, too. Celebrities like Kurt Russell, Harry Connick Jr., Cindy Crawford, and Sharon Stone are wearers. ⊠ *2250 E. Hastings St., East Side* ☎ *604/253–6671.*

Gravity Pope. Foot fashionistas make tracks to this Kitsilano shop that's jam-packed with trendy choices, including Camper, Puma, Kenneth Cole, and other international brands for men and women. ⊠ *2205 W. 4th Ave., Kitsilano* ☎ *604/731–7673.*

John Fluevog. You might've seen these shops in New York and Los Angeles, but did you know the funky shoe shops were started by a Vancouverite? The Gastown location is worth a look for the store itself, with its striking glass façade and soaring ceilings. ⊠ *837 Granville St., Downtown* ☎ *604/688–2828.* ⊠ *65 Water St., Gastown* ☎ *604/688–6228.*

Kalena's. You'll find everything from traditional leather sandals to fanciful purple pumps; fine Italian shoes are the specialty, though, at this family-run store. ⊠ *1526 Commercial Dr., East Side* ☎ *604/255–3727.*

Umbrella Shop. The place to help you keep obsessively dry. ⊠ *1550 Anderson St., Granville Island* ☎ *604/697–0919.*

Vancouver Nightlife and the Arts

WORD OF MOUTH

"Yaletown is a 'scene' with lounges and restaurants . . . it comes alive at night."

—Carmanah

NIGHTLIFE AND THE ARTS PLANNER

Where To Get Information

For event information, pick up a copy of the free *Georgia Straight* (available at cafés and book-stores and street boxes around town) or look in the entertainment section of the *Vancouver Sun*: Thursday's paper has listings in the "Queue" section. Web-surf over to ⊕ *www.gayvan. com* and ⊕ *www.gayvancouver. net* for an insider's look at the gay-friendly scene.

Where To Get Tickets

Ticketmaster. Tickets for many venues can be booked by calling or visiting their Web site. ☎ *604/280–4444* ⊕ *www.tick-etmaster.ca.*

Tickets Tonight. Sells half-price day-of-the-event tickets and full-price advance tickets to the theater, concerts, festivals, and other performing-arts events in Vancouver. Located at the Vancouver Tourist Info Centre. ✉ *200 Burrard St., Downtown* ☎ *604/684–2787* ⊕ *www.ticketstonight.ca.*

What To Wear

During the day, the Vancouver dress code usually falls somewhere between the fleece-laden pragmatism of Seattle and the cosmopolitan flair of San Francisco or Toronto. The Asian cultural influence is obvious as well, and you'll see lots of short plaid skirts on young women and well-coiffed hair on most men. Especially during the drizzly winter days, people dress for comfort first—and you probably should, too—saving the snazzy for the summer months. But when it comes to nightlife, Vancouverites get serious, and they love to dress up, so expect to see clubs and lounges filled with contemporary designs on the women and lots of smartly dressed men. Many clubs maintain strict dress codes but it's your partying peers who will look askance should you break out the fleece for an evening of dancing in the many übercool lounges or even in the watering holes.

What Things Cost

Painting the town red is gonna cost you. Perhaps not as much as it would in New York, Paris, or London, but don't leave your credit cards at home. If you're hitting the clubs, expect to pay a cover charge of around C$15. To see a name band or DJ perform at a club, you'll need to buy tickets well in advance—and expect to pay anywhere from C$25 to C$60. A beer will set you back around C$5, while a glass of wine or cocktail can cost between C$9 and C$15. Don't forget the 10% liquor tax added to the price of any alcoholic beverage, whether you're ordering at a bar, club, or restaurant. Tuesday and Wednesday are your best bets for a cheap night out: the comedy clubs charge about C$5 and neighborhood bars, featuring live music, often don't charge a cover.

Festivals to Plan Your Trip Around

FEB.: The **Vancouver International Mountain Film Festival** is a great intro to the mountain and wilderness culture of Canada and the world. (☏ 604/990–1505 ⊕ www.vimff.org)

Vancouver has one of North America's largest **Chinese New Year** celebrations. (⊕ www.tourismvancouver.com)

MAR.: At the **Vancouver Playhouse International Wine Festival**, over 1,600 wines from 15 countries are served. (☏ 604/872–6622 ⊕ www.playhousewinefest.com)

APR.: More than 3,000 cherry trees bloom each April, and the **Vancouver Cherry Blossom Festival** marks the occasion with a variety of programs and a haiku invitational. (☏ 604/257–8120 ⊕ www.vcbf.ca)

MAY: The **Vancouver International Children's Festival** is a week of storytelling, puppetry, circus arts, music, theater, and more. (☏ 604/708–5655 ⊕ www.childrensfestival.ca)

JUNE–SEPT.: The **Bard on the Beach Shakespeare Festival** takes place on the waterfront in Vanier Park. (☏ 604/739–0559 or 877/739–0559 ⊕ www.bardonthebeach.org)

JULY: **Vancouver Pride Week** is a celebration of diversity with tea dances, cruises, and parties. (☏ 604/687–0955 ⊕ www.vancouverpride.com)

The **Vancouver Folk Music Festival** welcomes folk singers and storytellers for three days of performances and children's programs. (☏ 604/602–9798 ⊕ www.thefestival.bc.ca)

Canada Day, on July 1st, is confederation day, celebrated with music and dancing at Canada Place and with interactive games and displays at Granville Island.

AUG.: The **Vancouver Queer Film Festival** is an 11-day showcase of drama, comedy, documentaries, musicals, and parties. (☏ 604/844–1615 ⊕ www.outonscreen.com)

Musicfest Vancouver is two weeks of orchestral, chamber, choral, world music, opera, and jazz performances around the city. (☏ 604/688–1152 ⊕ www.musicfestvancouver.ca)

SEPT.: The **Vancouver International Comedy Festival** is a week of wild antics, short films, stand-up, and theater. (☏ 604/683–0883 ⊕ www.comedyfest.com)

The **Vancouver Fringe Festival** is an eclectic mix of more than 500 theatrical offerings. (☏ 604/257–0350 ⊕ www.vancouverfringe.com)

SEPT.–OCT.: The **Vancouver International Film Festival** draws more than 150,000 people to view films from more than 50 countries. (☏ 604/685–0260 ⊕ www.viff.org)

Hours

Don't expect New York City hours on a night out in Vancouver. Indeed, while the city's bars, pubs, and lounges are usually open seven nights a week, they do close at a respectable 1 AM. Dance clubs get lively at about 10 PM and, depending on the Vancouver Police Department's ever-changing regulations, stay open until 3 AM on weekends; many are closed on Sunday and Monday.

Best Bets

Best Bartender: Josh Pape, at the Diamond

Best Classic Cocktails: Market by Jean George, at Shangri La

Best Hipster Bar: Pourhouse

Best Patio: Watermark on Kits Beach

Best Sake: Tojo's

Updated by
Crai S. Bower

With easy access to the sea and mountains, it's no surprise that Vancouver is such an outdoorsy kind of town, but once the sun goes down, the city's dwellers trade in their kayaks, hiking shoes, and North Face Windbreakers for something decidedly more chic.

There's plenty to choose from in just about every neighborhood: hipster Gastown has usurped Yaletown for the coolest cluster of late-night establishments and is now the place to go for swanky clubs and trendy wine bars. The gay-friendly West End is all about bumpin' and grindin' in retro bars and clubs, while a posh crowd of glitterati flocks to Yaletown's brewpubs and stylish lounges. Meanwhile, Kitsilano (the Venice Beach of Vancouver) attracts a laid-back bunch who like to sip beer and frilly cocktails on cool bar patios with killer views, especially in the summer. And with its fair share of galleries, film festivals, cutting-edge theater, comedy, opera, and ballet, Vancouver (also known as Hollywood North) also has all manner of cultural stimuli that you might be looking for.

BARS, PUBS, AND LOUNGES

Whether you're in the mood for something chill and loungey or crowded and trendy, you don't have to look far to find your ideal bar in Vancouver. One word of caution: if you're headed to any of the more happening spots, dress to impress and prepare to wait in line, though doorman have been known to make magic happen for the right price.

Afterglow. Typically packed by 10 PM, this Yaletown lounge, tucked behind Glowbal restaurant, gets its radiance from the fuchsia lighting on pink-and-white brick walls (or maybe the fake tans and hair spray have something to do with it). It's a great place to lounge on comfy sofas, sip colorful martinis, and practice the art of see-and-be-seen. ⊠ 1079 Mainland St., Yaletown ☎ 604/602–0835.

Blue Water Café and Raw Bar. The patio at this Yaletown café fills up quickly with an after-work crowd during warm weather, but inside you can count on the cozy bar to take the chill out of winter. You'll find a dozen varieties of B.C. oysters paired expertly with one of the largest selections of local wines in the city. The insatiable should try one of several seafood towers accompanied by a cool concoction from the vast back bar. ⊠ *1095 Hamilton St., Yaletown* ☎ *604/688–8078.*

Bridges. This Vancouver landmark near the Public Market has the city's biggest marina-side deck and a cozy nautical-theme pub. ⊠ *1696 Duranleau St., Granville Island* ☎ *604/687–4400.*

★ **Chambar.** This restaurant-cum-lounge has great bartenders and character. The back dining room has views of False Creek while the bar is all exposed-brick walls, vibrant art, and soft lighting. Try the Luini's Madonna: Amaretto, rose water, and fresh citrus served over ice. ⊠ *562 Beatty St., Gastown* ☎ *604/879–7119.*

Chill Winston. Decked out with plush, black-leather sofas, exposed wood beams, warm lighting, and a view of Gastown's lively square, this restaurant and lounge attracts a well-heeled crowd of jet-setters and urban dwellers. ⊠ *3 Alexander St., Gastown* ☎ *604/288–9575.*

Fodor'sChoice ★ **The Diamond.** At the top of a narrow staircase above Maple Tree Square, in one of the city's oldest buildings, the Diamond merges speakeasy simplicity with lounge cool. The large windows open completely providing an ideal vantage point to observe the Square's impromptu street theater as you sip something special. And oh what cocktails; bartender and co-owner Josh Pape's passion for mixology flows over his room like a conductor before a symphony. You can choose among "boozy," "proper," or "delicate" options on the drinks menu. The Buck Buck Mule is a refreshing mix of gin, sherry, cucumber juice, cilantro, lime juice, and ginger beer; the Tequila Martinez features tequila, vermouth, Lillet, peach bitters, and an orange twist. ⊠ *6 Powell St., Gastown* ☎ *604/408–2891..*

Fountainhead Pub. With one of the largest street-side patios in downtown, you can do as the locals do here: sit back, down a few beers, and watch the passersby. ⊠ *1025 Davie St., West End* ☎ *604/687–2222.*

George Ultra Lounge. One of Vancouver's swankiest lounges, George's is dedicated to classic cocktails and the people who drink them. Think local glitterati, execs in Armani suits, and ladies of a certain age sporting Gucci bags. Their wine cellar ain't bad either. ⊠ *1137 Hamilton St., Yaletown* ☎ *604/628–5555.*

Irish Heather. Expect a mixed crowd of local hipsters and tourists enjoying properly poured pints of Guinness, and live Irish music. There's a restaurant upstairs and out back in an atmospheric coach house is the **Shebeen,** or whiskey house, where you can try any of about 130 whiskeys. Check out Sunday's Long Table Series to make forty or so new friends amid ales and slow-food delicacies. ⊠ *210 Carrall St., Gastown* ☎ *604/688–9779.*

Mill Marine Bistro. This waterfront pub and restaurant has one of the best views of the North Shore Mountains from its expansive patio. ⊠ *1199 W. Cordova St., Downtown* ☎ *604/687–6455.*

Fodor'sChoice ★ **Pourhouse.** Paying homage to the Klondike Gold Rush and Pioneer Square spirit, Pourhouse has quickly appeared on numerous local Top

Ten lists. Gold Fashioned, Centennial, and Prospector take libation lovers on a historical tour of the city's highlights, while Pork and Beans, Welsh Rarebit, and Carpet Bag Steak show what a little imagination and fresh ingredients can do to transform tried-and-true dining options. ✉ *162 Water St., Gastown* ☎ *604/568--7022.*

Sanafir. The sensual aura at this bi-level restaurant and lounge (the name is Arabic for "meeting place") is set by lavish draperies, handcrafted Egyptian urns, and plush low-slung seats. The small-plates menu features Asian, Mediterranean, and Indian treats perfect for sharing. Come with a bunch of friends and you can lounge like kings in the harem-style beds on the upper level—but it doesn't come cheap. ✉ *1026 Granville St., Downtown* ☎ *604/678–1049.*

Sand Bar. With a highly rated seafood restaurant, a wine bar, and dancing Wednesday to Saturday nights in its **Teredo Bar,** this venue has something for everyone. For dramatic views over False Creek, reserve a table on the rooftop patio. ✉ *1535 Johnson St., Granville Island* ☎ *604/669–9030.*

★ **Tojo's.** This is the place to spend big bucks on sushi so grab a coveted seat at the bar and sample a great selection of handcrafted sake. ✉ *202–777 W. Broadway, Fairview* ☎ *604/872–8050.*

★ **Watermark on Kits Beach.** No summer visit to Vancouver is complete without an afternoon spent sipping lovely B.C. whites at the Watermark patio as the sun sets over the beach volleyball matches and bathing beauties at Kits Beach. Winter storm watching is also exceptional here, though you may want to retreat behind the floor-to-ceiling windows and dip your spoon into the seafood chowder rather than sample some of the warmer weather "Beach Bites" like the cold seafood platter. ✉ *1305 Arbutus St., Kitsilano* ☎ *604/738--5487.*

The Whip Gallery. It's a bit out of the way but this lofty space with exposed brick and Douglas fir–beamed ceilings attracts a hip crowd (they wear a lot of black). There's a bar, atrium, and mezzanine with a DJ. Order what's on tap (Storm Brewing, R&B, Unibroue) or choose from one of seven-deadly-sin martinis. ✉ *209 East 6th Ave., at Main St., East Vancouver* ☎ *604/874–4687.*

BREWPUBS

There's no better place to hang with the locals than a brewpub. Regardless of the neighborhood, you'll find the after-work crowd dressed in everything from suits to jeans and T-shirts. Get comfortable at the bar and order some appetizers to accompany a seasonal house brew on tap such as Yaletown Brewing Company's Red Brick Bitter or Indian Arm Pale Ale, which are brewed on the premises.

Dix Barbecue and Brewery. Near Yaletown and B.C. Place Stadium, this relaxed friendly place has a fireplace, a long mahogany bar, and vats brewing a variety of ales and lagers. They serve a fine Southern-style barbecue, slow smoked in-house in an apple- or cherrywood smoker. Watch out for a testosterone-heavy crowd on hockey and hoops nights. ✉ *871 Beatty St., Downtown* ☎ *604/682–2739.*

Dockside Brewing Company. This popular local hangout has a seaside patio, casual Pacific Northwest restaurant, and house-brewed German-style beer. ⊠ *Granville Island Hotel, 1253 Johnston St., Granville Island* ☏ *604/685–7070.*

Steamworks. Home to a pub, restaurant, and coffee bar, this hipster and urban-professional hangout has great harbor views, delish food, and beer that's brewed traditionally, in small batches. ⊠ *375 Water St., Gastown* ☏ *604/689–2739.*

Yaletown Brewing Company. Based in a renovated warehouse with a glassed-in brewery turning out several tasty beers, this always-crowded pub has a lively singles'-scene pub, a patio, and a restaurant. ⊠ *1111 Mainland St., Yaletown* ☏ *604/688–0064.*

HOTEL BARS

The hotel bar continues to be a favorite haunt for discerning locals, and a great place to unwind for out-of-towners. And you never know if you might spot a rock star at Opus or one of the New York Rangers hockey players at the Four Seasons's YEW bar.

Fodor's Choice ★ **Market by Jean George, at Shangri La.** Besides boasting the best rainy-season patio (it's covered and heated) in Vancouver, the Shangri La's bar and restaurant became the city's hottest spot the instant it opened in 2009. ⊠ *1128 W. Georgia St., Downtown* ☏ *604/689–1120.*

Fodor's Choice ★ **Opus Bar.** Local hipsters, international jet-setters, and film industry types sip martinis and lounge on Jacobsen egg chairs and Eames stools at this happening destination, which doubles as the hotel's lobby. It's small, but it's still one of the hippest cocktail destinations in the city. ⊠ *350 Davie St., in the Opus Hotel, Yaletown* ☏ *604/642–0557.*

★ **YEW Bar at the Four Seasons.** The Four Seasons's signature restaurant and bar provides a diverse environment of glass, natural woods, and granite to reflect B.C.'s stunning natural environment. Happy hour attracts the executives and at other times you'll see Canucks fans before or after the game, or late night cappers eager to stretch out on the low-rise banquettes or cozy up to the raw bar. A sumptuous mood and menu, with more than 150 wines by the glass and a perpetually changing cocktail list have established YEW as the top hotel bar in the city. ⊠ *791 W. Georgia St., Downtown* ☏ *604/689–9333.*

WINE BARS

Vancouver's recent proliferation of wine bars parallels the evolution of the B.C. wine industry. Today's well-chosen wine lists accompany everything from simple cheese plates to zesty crab cakes. These listings are particularly notable; more wine bars are listed in the Where to Eat in Vancouver chapter.

Bin 942 Tapas Parlour. This cozy South Granville room dishes up Asian- and Latin-influenced small plates that pair well with the eclectic wine list. The sister restaurant, **Bin 941**, in raucous Davie Street, also has a small, albeit expertly selected, wine list but the scene is more chaotic and

DID YOU KNOW?

The Opus bar, with its handcrafted, top-of-the-line cocktails, is one of Vancouver's hippest and hottest venues. Celebrity sightings are not uncommon.

definitely louder. ⊠ *1521 W. Broadway, Downtown* ☎ *604/734–9421* ⊠ *941 Davie St., Downtown* ☎ *604/683–1246.*

★ **Salt Tasting Room.** This hip wine bar and charcuterie has communal tables, concrete floors, and a killer selection of local and international wines perfect for pairing with cured meats and artisanal cheeses. ⊠ *45 Blood Alley, Gastown* ☎ *604/633–1912.*

CASINOS

Vancouver has a few casinos; proceeds go to local charities and arts groups. No alcohol is served, and guests must be at least 19.

Edgewater Casino. This casino features 500 slot machines, a poker room, 48 table games, and a bistro. It's open 24/7. ⊠ *311–750 Pacific Blvd. S, Downtown* ☎ *877/688–3343 or 604/687–3343.*

Royal City Star Riverboat Casino. Picture this, if you will: a Mississippi riverboat moored on the Fraser River. Its five decks include 24 gaming tables, a poker room, 300 slot machines, two bars, a lounge, and a restaurant. It's open 10 AM–4 AM daily. Admission is free. ⊠ *788 Quayside Dr., Westminster Quay, New Westminster* ☎ *604/519–3660.*

COMEDY CLUBS

Great venues, and local up-and-comers as well as names from the international comedy circuit make for some serious sidesplitting entertainment.

Vancouver TheatreSports League. A hilarious improv troupe performs four nights a week to an enthusiastic crowd at the New Revue Stage on Granville Island. ⊠ *Granville Island* ☎ *604/738–7013.*

Yuk Yuk's. This is the place to go Tuesday to Saturday evenings to check out the city's best professional stand-up comedians and up-and-coming amateurs. ⊠ *1015 Burrard St., in the Century Plaza Hotel, Downtown* ☎ *604/696–9857.*

GAY NIGHTLIFE

The city's gay community is centered in two distinctive neighborhoods: the West End (⊕ *www.westendbia.com*), with its flashy bars and flamboyant shops on Davie Street, and the thriving lesbian community of Commercial Drive (⊕ *www.thedrive.ca*), where authentic Italian cafés, Greek delis, and chill restaurants set the come-as-you-are vibe.

1181. This addition to the gayborhood is all about stylish interior design—plush sofas, glass coffee tables, wood-paneled ceiling—and fancy cocktails (think caipirinhas and mojitos). It gets particularly crowded on Saturdays, when a DJ spins behind the bar. ⊠ *1181 Davie St., West End* ☎ *604/687–3991.*

Celebrities. A recent multimillion-dollar facelift brought the celeb status back to this gay hot spot, which features a scantily clad crowd bumping and grinding to Top 40 hits, hip-hop, and R & B on a huge dance

5

floor equipped with the latest in sound, lighting, and visuals. Men and women are welcome. ✉ *1022 Davie St., West End* ☎ *604/681–6180.*

The Davie Village Café. This cute little second-floor café, with its hard-wood floors and local artists' work hanging on the walls, is ideal for a quick drink or bite to eat. Live entertainment and communal dinners take place on the various theme nights. ✉ *201–1141 Davie St., West End* ☎ *604/288–1819.*

The Fountainhead Pub. You won't find anyone poring over Ayn Rand books at "The Head." Instead, this friendly local pub attracts gays, straights, and undecideds to their street-side patio, ideally placed for watching the parade of local boys strut their stuff on Davie Street. ✉ *1025 Davie St., West End* ☎ *604/687–2222.*

Lick. Vancouver's most popular lesbian dance bar sizzles as girls who like girls dance to kick-ass electronic, hip-hop, and drum-and-bass beats. A quiet chill-out area in front provides respite from the noise and heat. Two other dance clubs, **Honey** and **Lotus,** at the same site, are open to all. ✉ *455 Abbott St., Gastown* ☎ *604/685–7777.*

Numbers. This renovated veteran of the Davie Street strip features five levels of furious fun, from live music to karaoke and an amateur strip night on the first Monday of the month. ✉ *1042 Davie St., West End* ☎ *604/685–4077.*

Odyssey. Vancouver's naughtiest dance club has a men-only back door, go-go boys, and theme nights like Feather Boa, a dragstravaganza where anything goes. ✉ *1251 Howe St., West End* ☎ *604/689–5256.*

MUSIC

DANCE CLUBS A smartly dressed crowd flocks to dance and celebrity-spot at upscale, chilled-out, and loungey clubs around town. At many clubs it helps to know a local with connections to avoid long lines, but if you don't, dress smartly and hope for the best.

Caprice. R & B and Top 40 play to a Britney- and Paris-wannabe crowd at this two-level former movie theater with a restaurant and lounge. Tag along with a hooked-up local or expect to wait in line, like, forever. ✉ *967 Granville St., Downtown* ☎ *604/681–2114.*

Commodore Ballroom. This 1929 dance hall has been restored to its art deco glory, complete with massive sprung dance floor and state-of-the-art sound system. Live indie rock bands and renowned DJs play here most nights. ✉ *868 Granville St., Downtown* ☎ *604/739–7469.*

ginger 62. This dark, moody '60s-inspired lounge—with its plush carpets, comfy sofas, and black-and-white retro films projected on the wall—attracts a crowd of beautiful locals and the occasional VIP dressed to the nines. When internationally renowned DJs come to town, this is where they spin. Be prepared to spend at least an hour waiting in line before setting foot inside. ✉ *1219 Granville St., Downtown* ☎ *604/688–5494.*

The Modern. In a heritage building and equipped with top-notch sound and light systems, this addition to the Gastown club scene has a sleek

The Yale is one of Vancouver's top spots for live music.

modern (what did you expect?) vibe, including polished concrete floors, dark smoked glass, colored tiling, countless mirrors, and neon lights. House and guest DJs spin an eclectic mix of funk, rock, soul, and Top 40 hits to a mostly thirtysomething crowd. ⊠ *7 Alexander St., Gastown* ☎ *604/647–0121.*

Shine. This luminous postmodern spot draws an eclectic crowd of trendsetters and college kids to its '80s classics, dancehall, rap, and rock-and-roll nights. A red chill-out room in back is the perfect place to end a sweaty night on the dance floor. ⊠ *364 Water St., Gastown* ☎ *604/408–4321.*

FOLK   The folk music scene in Vancouver revolves mainly around the Folk Music Festival. If you're a fan, plan your visit around mid-July. All other times, check out the Rogue Folk Club for folk events and happenings around town.

Rogue Folk Club. This nonprofit organization presents folk and traditional Celtic concerts at various venues around town. ☎ *604/736–3022.*

Vancouver Folk Music Festival. One of the world's leading folk- and world-music events, this festival takes place at Jericho Beach Park in mid-July. ⊠ *Kitsilano* ☎ *604/602–9798.*

JAZZ AND   Vancouver is home to one of the most sophisticated and accessible jazz
BLUES   scenes in Canada, with lots of clubs, bars, and restaurants hosting local and international talent. **Coastal Jazz and Blues Society** has a hotline that details upcoming concerts and clubs. The society also runs the **Vancouver International Jazz Festival,** which lights up 40 venues around town every June. ☎ *604/872–5200* ⊕ *www.coastaljazz.ca.*

Cellar Restaurant and Jazz Club. This is the top venue for jazz in Vancouver and the club calendar features a who's who of the Canadian jazz scene. ⊠ *3611 W. Broadway, Kitsilano* ☎ *604/738–1959.*

O'Doul's Restaurant & Bar. In the Listel Vancouver hotel, the bar is all mahogany and sepia tones, drawing a mixed crowd of chic tourists and locals to listen to some of the best local jazz musicians play nightly. ⊠ *1300 Robson St., West End* ☎ *604/661–1400.*

ROCK AND BLUES
The local music scene pales in comparison to those in Portland or Seattle, but remember that some British Columbia rockers and singers, like Nickelback, Hot Hot Heat, and Nelly Furtado got their start at Vancouver's local clubs way before the MTV crowd got to see them with Carson Daly on TRL.

Backstage Lounge. Local bands of questionable talent perform Wednesday through Saturday nights. Hit or miss. ⊠ *1585 Johnston St., Granville Island* ☎ *604/687–1354.*

Railway Club. In the early evening, this spot attracts film and media types to its pub-style rooms; after 8 it becomes a venue for local bands. Technically it's a private social club, so patrons must sign in, but everyone of age is welcome. ⊠ *579 Dunsmuir St., Downtown* ☎ *604/681–1625.*

Vogue Theatre. A former art deco movie palace, the Vogue hosts a variety of concerts by local and visiting performers. ⊠ *918 Granville St., Downtown* ☎ *604/331–7909.*

Yale. Live bands perform most nights at Vancouver's most established rhythm-and-blues bar. ⊠ *1300 Granville St., Downtown* ☎ *604/ 681–9253.*

THE ARTS

From performing arts to theater, classical music, dance, and a thriving gallery scene, there's much for an art lover to choose from in Vancouver.

CLASSICAL MUSIC

With so much going on at different classical music venues around town, you can easily enjoy something different every day you're in town.

CHAMBER MUSIC AND SMALL ENSEMBLES
Early Music Vancouver. Medieval, Renaissance, baroque, and early classical music is performed on period instruments year-round. The society also hosts the Vancouver Early Music Programme and Festival from mid-July to mid-August at the University of British Columbia. ☎ *604/732–1610.*

Friends of Chamber Music. A diverse selection of ensembles performs as part of the "Friends." ☎ *No phone* ⊕ *www.friendsofchambermusic.ca.* **Vancouver Recital Society.** The society presents both emerging and well-known classical musicians in recital September–May at the Chan Centre for the Performing Arts, the Vancouver Playhouse, and the Orpheum Theatre. In summer, they host the Vancouver Chamber Music Festival. Check the Web site for venues. (☎ *604/602–0363* ⊕ *www.vanrecital.com*).

The Centre in Vancouver for Performing Arts showcases a wide variety of international shows, including Broadway musicals, dance productions, and opera.

OPERA **Vancouver Opera.** The city's opera company stages four productions a year, from October through May, at the Queen Elizabeth Theatre. ☎ *604/682–2871.*

ORCHESTRAS **Vancouver Symphony Orchestra.** The resident company at the **Orpheum Theatre** presents classical and popular music performances to a wide variety of audiences. ✉ *884 Granville St., Downtown* ☎ *604/876–3434.*

DANCE

A few of the many modern-dance companies in town are DanceArts Vancouver and New Performance Works; besides the Scotia Bank Dance Centre, the Firehall Arts Centre and the Vancouver East Cultural Centre are among their performance venues.

Ballet British Columbia. Innovative ballet and timeless classics by internationally acclaimed choreographers are presented by this company; most performances are at the Queen Elizabeth Theatre. ☎ *604/732–5003.*

Scotiabank Dance Centre. The hub of dance in British Columbia, this striking building with an art deco facade has performances, studio showings, and other types of events by national and international artists. ✉ *677 Davie St., Downtown* ☎ *604/606–6400.*

MOVIES

Known as Hollywood North, Vancouver supports indie movie theaters featuring first- and second-run, underground, experimental, alternative, and classic films. Tickets are half price on Tuesday at most chain-owned Vancouver movie theaters.

Fifth Avenue Cinemas. This small multiplex shows foreign and independent films. ✉ *2110 Burrard St., Kitsilano* ☎ *604/734–7469.*

Pacific Cinémathèque. The not-for-profit society is dedicated to all things celluloid, from exhibitions to film tours and independent and international features. ✉ *1131 Howe St., Downtown* ☎ *604/688–3456.*

Ridge Theatre. A long-established art-house cinema, the Ridge is popular with the artsy crowd. ✉ *3131 Arbutus St., Kitsilano* ☎ *604/738–6311.*

THEATER

Vancouver has a sophisticated theater scene featuring more than 30 local theater companies and 21 venues.

Arts Club Theatre Company. This company operates two theaters. The **Arts Club Granville Island Stage** (✉ *1585 Johnston St., Granville Island* ☎ *604/687–1644*) is an intimate venue and a good place to catch works by local playwrights. The **Stanley Industrial Alliance Stage** (✉ *2750 Granville St., West Side* ☎ *604/687–1644*) is a lavish, former movie palace staging works by such perennial favorites as William Shakespeare and Noël Coward. Both operate year-round.

Carousel Theatre. Children's theater is the key here, with performances at the **Waterfront Theatre** (✉ *1410 Cartwright St., Granville Island* ☎ *604/685–6217.*

Centre in Vancouver for Performing Arts. This large space attracts big international shows, from Broadway musicals to Chinese dance productions. ✉ *777 Homer St., Downtown* ☎ *604/602–0616.*

Chan Centre for the Performing Arts. There's a 1,200-seat concert hall, a theater, and a cinema in the vast performance space. ✉ *6265 Crescent Rd., UBC Campus, Point Grey* ☎ *604/822–2697.*

Firehall Arts Centre. Innovative theater and modern dance are showcased at this intimate, downtown East Side space. ✉ *280 E. Cordova St., Downtown East Side* ☎ *604/689–0926.*

Queen Elizabeth Theatre. This is a major venue for ballet, opera, and similar large-scale events. ✉ *600 Hamilton St., Downtown* ☎ *604/665–3050.*

Theatre Under the Stars. Family-friendly musicals like *The Sound of Music* and *Kiss Me Kate* are the draw at Malkin Bowl, an outdoor amphitheater in Stanley Park, during July and August. You can watch the show from the lawn, or from the Rose Garden Tea House as part of a dinner–theater package. ☎ *604/687–0174.*

Vancouver East Cultural Centre. This is a multipurpose performance space. ✉ *1895 Venables St., East Vancouver* ☎ *604/254–9578.*

Vancouver Playhouse. The leading venue in Vancouver for mainstream theater is in the same complex as the Queen Elizabeth Theatre. ✉ *649 Cambie St., Downtown* ☎ *604/665–3050.*

Vogue Theatre. This former movie palace hosts theater and live music events. ✉ *918 Granville St., Downtown* ☎ *604/331–7909.*

Vancouver
Where to Eat

WORD OF MOUTH

"I tried a new (to me at least) restaurant, Coast, which was excellent. I had their variation on the traditional Canadian dish: lobster poutine, and it was very good as were the fresh raw oysters. It's quite the scene, so definitely make reservations and go on the early side if you prefer a quieter experience."

—NWWanderer

VANCOUVER WHERE TO EAT PLANNER

Reservations

Except in cafés and casual eateries, reservations are always a good idea, particularly for weekend evenings.

Tipping and Taxes

A 15% tip is expected. A 5% Goods and Services Tax (GST) is levied on the food portion of restaurant bills and a 10% liquor tax is charged on wine, beer, and spirits.

What to Wear

Dining is informal. Neat casual dress is appropriate everywhere; nice jeans are fine, though you might want something dressier than sneakers in the evening.

Wine

Many restaurants serve excellent B.C. wines. Sometimes the most interesting wines are from small producers, so ask for recommendations.

Smoking

Smoking is prohibited by law in all Vancouver restaurants.

What's Special in Vancouver?

Vancouver has hundreds of restaurants but if you're looking for a uniquely Vancouver experience, remember that Pacific Northwest seafood is always a good choice, and many restaurants emphasize fresh seasonal produce, Canadian cheeses, and locally raised meats. Vancouver also has some of the best Asian food in North America.

Hours

Most restaurants that serve lunch are open from 11:30 until 2 or 2:30. Downtown spots that serve a business clientele may not open for lunch on weekends. Dinner is usually served from 5:30 until at least 10. Some dining rooms are open later on weekends, but in general, Vancouver isn't a late-night eating city. Some restaurants close on Sunday or Monday.

What It Costs

Vancouver's top tables can be as pricey as the best restaurants in major American cities. You can often dine more economically at some of the smaller but just-as-inventive bistros or by sharing small plates at one of the many tapas-style eateries. Some restaurants have reasonably priced prix-fixe menus, and at certain times of the year, including the midwinter Dine Out Vancouver promotion, even the top dining rooms offer these fixed-price options. Check the Tourism Vancouver Web site (⊕ *www.tourismvancouver. com*) for details. Family-style Asian restaurants and noodle shops are generally a good value year-round, and when the sun is shining, you can always pick up some cheese, bread, and fruit, and picnic at the beach.

WHAT IT COSTS IN CANADIAN DOLLARS					
	¢	$	$$	$$$	$$$$
AT DINNER	under C$8	C$8–C$12	C$13–C$20	C$21–C$30	over C$30

Prices are for an average main course or equivalent combination of smaller dishes, at dinner.

BEST BETS FOR VANCOUVER DINING

With so many restaurants, how will you decide where to eat? Fodor's writers and editors have chosen their favorites by price, cuisine, and experience:

Fodor's Choice ★

Blue Water Cafe, p. 137
C Restaurant, p. 140
Vij's, p. 157
West, p. 158

By Price

$$$$

Bishop's, p. 151
Le Crocodile, p. 144
Lumière, p. 154
Raincity Grill, p. 147
Tojo's, p. 157

$$$

Boneta, p. 137
Chambar, p. 140
Cibo Trattoria, p. 141
Cru, p. 151

$$

Campagnolo, p. 140
Maenam, p. 154

$

Go Fish, p. 152
Legendary Noodle, p. 146
Nuba, p. 146
Kintaro Ramen, p. 144
Vera's Burger Shack, p. 149

By Cuisine

CHINESE

Kirin Mandarin, p. 144
Kirin Seafood, p. 154
Sun Sui Wah Seafood Restaurant, p. 156
Sea Harbour Seafood, p. 131
Shiang Garden Seafood Restaurant, p. 156

FRENCH

Le Crocodile, p. 144
Le Gavroche, p. 144
Lumière, p. 154
Jules Bistro, p. 144
Mistral French Bistro, p. 154

INDIAN

Chutney Villa, p. 133
Rangoli, p. 156
Vij's, p. 157

ITALIAN

Campagnolo, p. 140
Cibo Trattoria, p. 141
CinCin, p. 141
Il Giardino di Umberto, p. 143

JAPANESE

Tojo's, p. 157
Kingyo, p. 135

MODERN CANADIAN

Bishop's, p. 151
Boneta, p. 137
Cru, p. 151
Raincity Grill, p. 147
West, p. 158

SEAFOOD

Blue Water Cafe, p. 137
C Restaurant, p. 140
Coast, p. 142
Sea Harbour Seafood, p. 131
Tojo's, p. 157

VEGETARIAN

Foundation Lounge, p. 152
The Naam, p. 155
Nuba, p. 146
Rangoli, p. 156
Vij's, p. 157

By Experience

ROMANTIC

Le Crocodile, p. 144
Lumière, p. 154
Il Giardino di Umberto, p. 143
Raincity Grill, p. 147

SIPPING AND GRAZING

Chambar, p. 140
Cobre, p. 142
Cru, p. 151
Salt Tasting Room, p. 147
Wild Rice, p. 148

DISTINCTIVELY VANCOUVER

Bin 941, p. 137
Hapa Izakaya, p. 142
Japa-Dog, p. 149
Maenam, p. 154
Vij's, p. 157

GREAT VIEW

C Restaurant, p. 140
Nu, p. 146
Raincity Grill, p. 147
Salmon House on the Hill, p. 156
The Teahouse in Stanley Park, p. 148

LOTS OF LOCALS

Campagnolo, p. 140
The Flying Tiger, p. 152
Rodney's Oyster House, p. 147
Stella's, p. 156
Two Chefs and a Table, p. 148

HOT SPOTS

Boneta, p. 137
Chambar, p. 140
Cibo Trattoria, p. 141
Coast, p. 142
db Bistro Moderne, p. 151

6

A SIDE TRIP TO CHINA—FOR DINNER

With one of the largest Asian populations of any city outside of Asia, metropolitan Vancouver has a wealth of opportunities for Asian-food lovers.

The area's Chinese food, in particular, ranks among the best in North America. There are still many Chinese restaurants, markets, and bakeries in Vancouver's city-center Chinatown—the "old" Chinatown near downtown—but Richmond, the suburban "new" Chinatown near the airport, is where interesting things are really happening, food-wise.

Richmond is full of shiny shopping malls and upscale Chinese restaurants that cater to the well-to-do Asian community and rival the best of Hong Kong, Shanghai, or Taipei. Also abundant are hole-in-the-wall noodle shops, modest storefront eateries, bakeries selling golden-baked pastries or freshly steamed buns, and grab-and-go food courts. And best of all for visitors, the Canada Line—which links downtown and Richmond in less than 30 minutes—is a direct line to Richmond's Chinese eateries.

EAT REGIONALLY

Richmond's Chinese restaurants often focus on a style of cooking, so while the menu may be wide-ranging, stick with regional specialties— delicate steamed fish in a Cantonese dining room, and a fiery stir-fry or hotpot in a Sichuan eatery. Some places even specialize in particular dishes: ask about popular choices or just look around: if everyone's eating crispy salt-and-pepper chicken, you should, too.

EATING ALONG THE CANADA LINE

Aberdeen Station: The glitzy Aberdeen Centre Mall houses several worthwhile restaurants.Casual and fun **Northern Delicacy** (✉ *4151 Hazelbridge Way, Aberdeen Centre, Richmond* ☎ *604/233–7050*) cooks up Northern-style small plates to young Asian hipsters.

North of Aberdeen Station, **Sea Harbour Seafood Restaurant** (✉ *3711 No. 3 Rd., Richmond* ☎ *604/232–0816*) serves first-rate Hong Kong–style seafood to well-heeled locals. Ask for whatever fish is freshest, and try the distinctive pork with chayote squash. Although the exterior is modest, the food and service are high-end; reservations are recommended.

Lansdowne Station: Get off at Lansdowne for **Little Sheep Hot Pot** (✉ *5300 No. 3 Rd., Lansdowne Centre, Richmond* ☎ *604/231– 8966*), a branch of a China-based hot-pot chain. You choose a variety of meats (lamb is their specialty), vegetables, and noodles to cook at your table in a bubbling cauldron of broth. Look for the "Mongolian hot pot" sign on the east side of Lansdowne Centre Mall.

Richmond-Brighouse Station: Shanghai River Restaurant (✉ *7831 Westminster Hwy., Richmond* ☎ *604/233–8885*) specializes in Shanghai-style fare, including handmade dumplings and noodles (you can watch the chefs at work in the open kitchen). Book in advance for this popular spot.

Chili hounds should track down **Chuan Xiang Ge Szechuan Restaurant** (✉ *8211 Westminster Hwy., Richmond* ☎ *604/821– 9922*), a modest eatery serving fiery Sichuan fare. The Chuan Xiang Ge-Style Preserved Ham with Tea-Tree Mushrooms is a delicious stir-fry of smoky bacon and dried mushrooms that pairs well with an order of garlicky sautéed greens.

Even more basic, but equally delicious, are the food stalls on the second floor of the **Richmond Public Market** (✉ *8260 Westminster Hwy., Richmond* ☎ *604/821–1888*), rewarding adventurous diners with authentic Asian street foods.

DIM SUM

Dim sum (Chinese small plates) is wildly popular in Richmond, particularly for weekend brunch. Most Richmond dim sum restaurants eschew the custom of food carts circling the room. Instead, after you order from a (bilingual) menu, dishes are brought hot from the kitchen directly to your table. Many dim sum spots are less crowded before 11 AM, though if you're with a group, reservations are recommended anytime. **Fisherman's Terrace** (✉ *4151 Hazelbridge Way, Aberdeen Centre, Richmond* ☎ *604/303–9739*), in Aberdeen Centre Mall, is a popular spot for traditional Hong Kong-style dim sum. South of Aberdeen Station, **Shiang Garden Seafood Restaurant** (✉ *4540 No. 3 Rd., Richmond* ☎ *604/273– 8858*) offers both classic and more contemporary dim sum dishes. **Empire Seafood Restaurant** (✉ *7997 Westminster Hwy., Richmond* ☎ *604/249– 0080*), a short walk from Richmond-Brighouse Station, is another good dim sum choice.

6

A PASSAGE TO INDIA

From modest curry houses to more upscale dining rooms, Vancouver's Indian restaurants reflect the increasingly varied nature of the city's South Asian community, offering regional specialties from across India.

The Punjabi Market neighborhood, at Main Street and 49th Avenue, is a long-established "Little India" that was populated largely by migrants from northwest India. While many newer Indo-Canadian immigrants have settled outside Vancouver, in Surrey and other suburbs, the Punjabi Market is still worth a visit for its jewelry stores, sari shops, and—naturally—restaurants. Two long-standing eateries, **All India Sweets & Restaurant** (✉ *6507 Main St.* ☎ *604/327–0891* ⊕ *www.allindiasweetsrestaurant.com*) and **Himalaya Restaurant** (✉ *6587 Main St.* ☎ *604/324–6514*), serve traditional Punjabi dishes and vast, well-priced buffets.

DIWALI

Vancouver in the fall means Diwali, the South Asian festival of lights celebrated by Hindus, Sikhs, and Jains around the world. The festival showcases Indian music and dance; vendors sell Indian food; and community centers offer Indian craft workshops in sari wrapping and henna application (⊕ *www.vandiwali.ca*). Restaurants and snack shops in the Punjabi Market district sell colorful holiday sweets.

AROUND VANCOUVER, AROUND INDIA

To explore the food of Indian regions other than the Punjab, you'll need to venture farther afield. There's no one neighborhood in Vancouver proper that will satisfy all your Indian cravings, but bus no. 19 between Stanley Park and Metrotown stops near all of the following restaurants.

For south Indian fare, with its *dosa* (rice and lentil pancakes), *idli* (steamed rice cakes), and seafood and coconut curries, try the comfortably classy **Chutney Villa** (✉ *147 E. Broadway, Main St./Mt. Pleasant* ☎ *604/872-2228* ⊕ *www.chutneyvilla.com*).

If you're a big dosa fan, it's worth the trek to **House of Dosas** (✉ *1391 Kingsway, East Side* ☎ *604/875-1283* ⊕ *www. houseofdosas.ca*), a modest spot where the specialty is massive—and massively tasty—versions of this South Indian classic.

Some members of Vancouver's Indian community have their roots in Africa, particularly Uganda, and this cultural mix has created additional dining options. At the cheerful **Jambo Grill** (✉ *3219 Kingsway, East Side* ☎ *604/433-5060* ⊕ *www. jambogrill.ca* ⊙ *Closed Mon.*), you can pair the first-rate tandoori chicken or spicy grilled ribs with addictive *mogo* (cassava fries), curries, or masala fish.

FINE DINING, INDIAN-STYLE

When Vikram Vij opened his eponymous restaurant in the mid-1990s, **Vij's** (see full listing for contact info) shook up the Vancouver food scene. This contemporary South Asian dining room that paired traditional flavors and techniques with local produce and ingredients was unique in Canada, and indeed in North America. Vij's is still going strong—waits of over an hour for a table at this no-reservations spot are routine—while Vij and his wife/business partner Meeru Dhalwala also run the more casual **Rangoli** (✉ *1488 W. 11th Ave., South Granville* ☎ *604/736-5711* ⊕ *www.vijsrangoli.ca.* next door.

WHERE INDIA MEETS CHINA

With Vancouver's large Indian and Chinese communities, perhaps it's no surprise to find food that fuses the fare of these two nations. Two restaurants on Vancouver's East Side serve Indian-style Chinese dishes, where the sweet, sour, and hot tastes of India and China come together. For many South Asians, this hybrid cuisine is comfort food, akin to the chop suey and ginger beef served at old-style Chinese-American or Chinese-Canadian eateries. At **Green Lettuce** (✉ *1949 Kingsway, East Side* ☎ *604/876-9883* ⊕ *www. greenlettucerestaurant.com* ⊙ *No lunch Sat.–Tues.*), you'll find *paneer* (cheese) in ginger sauce, chili chicken, Manchurian cauliflower, and crispy hot-and-spicy tofu. At the equally popular **Chili Pepper House** (✉ *3003 Kingsway, East Side* ☎ *604/431-8633*), the menu ranges from hot and sour soup to okra and potato curry to Hakka-style vegetable chow mein.

6

BEYOND THE SUSHI BAR

Vancouverites joke that they could eat sushi every day for months and never visit the same restaurant twice. And while sushi bars do seem as numerous as raindrops in January, Japanese food in Vancouver means far more than just *maki* and *nigiri*.

Ramen shops are one popular, moderately priced, Japanese option, and if you're thinking packaged instant noodles, think again. The lines out the door at long-standing favorite **Kintaro Ramen** (⊠ *788 Denman St., West End* ☎ *604/682–7568*)attest to the quality of its hearty, comforting noodle soups, despite the barebones setting. At nearby **Motomachi Shokudo** (⊠ *740 Denman St., West End* ☎ *604/609–0310*), the Japanese-style wooden furnishings have more flair and the menu offers more choices for patrons who don't eat pork; a specialty here is smoky charcoal ramen (it tastes better than it sounds!).

SIPPING SAKE

Sake (rice wine)—along with beer or green tea—is the drink of choice for Japanese meals, and most Japanese restaurants serve at least one or two varieties of sake; higher-end spots offer an array of sake types. Vancouver even has its own sake brewery. **Artisan Sake Maker** (⊠ *1339 Railspur Alley, Granville Island* ☎ *604/685–7253* ⊕ *www.artisansakemaker.com*) has tastings in their shop.

FOR JAPANESE SMALL PLATES, SAY "IZAKAYA"

Vancouverites have fallen hard for *izakayas* (Japanese tapas bars), which combine the casual west coast vibe with a wide range of intriguing, easy-to-share small plates. Some izakayas, like the food-forward **Kingyo** (⌧ *871 Denman St., West End* ☎ *604/608–1677* ⊕ *www.kingyo-izakaya.com*) and the two branches of **Hapa Izakaya** (*see full listing for contact info*), are stylish and lively, while others, such as the **Guu** minichain (⌧ *838 Thurlow St., West End* ☎ *604/685–8817* ⌧ *1698 Robson St., West End* ☎ *604/685–8678* ⌧ *375 Water St., Gastown* ☎ *604/685–8682* ⊕ *www.guu-izakaya.com*), are just plain fun. Most *izakaya* dishes are in the C$8–C$12 range, so you can afford to experiment.

You'll find a variation on the small-plates theme at the city's *yakitori* shops, which specialize in skewers of grilled meat, chicken, and veggies. Mix and match skewers to make a meal at one of the branches of **Zakkushi** (⌧ *823 Denman St., West End* ☎ *604/685–1136* ⌧ *1833 W. 4th Ave., Kitsilano* ☎ *604/730–9844* ⌧ *4075 Main St., Main St./Mt. Pleasant* ☎ *604/874–9455* ⊕ *www.zakkushi.com*).

SNACKS TO GO

En route to or from the airport, make a detour for yet another Japanese treat. From a truck in a Richmond parking lot, **Tenku Bakudanyaki** (⌧ *7100 Elmbridge Way, Richmond* ⊕ *www.bakudanyaki.com*) serves cooked-to-order, baseball-size *bakudanyaki* (fritters), stuffed full of squid, shrimp, octopus, and cabbage and squirted with Japanese mayonnaise. These savory snacks come neatly packaged in a white take-out carton—a convenient grab-and-fly treat.

AND SUSHI, TOO . . .

If it is sushi you're craving, Vancouver is happy to oblige. From haute Japanese dining rooms like **Tojo's** (⇨ *see full listing for contact info*), to the cheap-and-cheerful sushi bars on nearly every corner, the city offers plenty of options for raw fish fans.

Conveniently located in the Robson Street shopping district, **Tsunami Sushi** (⌧ *1025 Robson St., West End* ☎ *604/687–8744*), where the sushi floats past you on little boats at the sushi bar, is fun for the kids; just don't expect high-end fare. Sushi aficionados head for **Yoshi** (*see full listing for contact info*), a serene traditional dining room near Stanley Park, where the sushi and sashimi come with mountain views.

6

By Carolyn B. Heller

From inventive neighborhood bistros to glamorous down-town dining rooms to Asian restaurants that rival those in the capitals of Asia, Vancouver has a diverse array of gas-tronomic options.

Many cutting-edge establishments are perfecting Modern Canadian fare, which—at this end of the country—incorporates regional seafood (notably salmon and halibut) and locally grown produce. Vancouver is a hotbed of "localism," with many restaurants emphasizing the provenance of their ingredients and embracing products that hail from within a 100-mile-or-so radius of the city, or at least from within B.C.

With at least a third of the city's population of Asian heritage, it's no surprise that Asian eateries abound in Vancouver. From mom-and-pop noodle shops, curry houses, and corner sushi bars to elegant and upscale dining rooms, cuisine from China, Taiwan, Hong Kong, Japan, and India (and to a lesser extent, from Korea, Thailand, Vietnam, and Malaysia) can be found all over town. Look for restaurants emphasizing Chinese regional cuisine (particularly in the suburb of Richmond), contemporary Indian-influenced fare, and different styles of Japanese cooking, from casual ramen shops to lively *izakayas* (Japanese tapas bars) that serve an eclectic array of small plates. Even restaurants that are not specifically "Asian" have long adopted abundant Asian influences—your grilled salmon may be served with *gai lan* (Chinese broccoli), black rice, or a coconut-milk curry.

British Columbia's wine industry is enjoying great popularity, and many restaurants serve wines from the province's 150-plus wineries. Most B.C. wines come from the Okanagan Valley in the province's interior, but Vancouver Island is another main wine-producing area. Merlot, Pinot Noir, Pinot Gris, and Chardonnay are among the major varieties; also look for ice wine, a dessert wine made from grapes that are picked while they are frozen on the vines.

If you enjoy strolling to scope out your dining options downtown, try Robson Street for everything from upscale Italian dining rooms to cheap, friendly Asian cafés and noodle shops, or explore Denman and Davie streets for a variety of ethnic eats. Gastown, which used to serve up mainly mainstream tourist fare, now has many more creative dining spots. In Yaletown, Hamilton and Mainland streets are full of restaurants and upscale bars, many with outdoor terraces. In Kitsilano, West 4th Avenue between Burrard and Balsam streets has plenty of restaurant choices.

An intriguingly diverse food district is Main Street, particularly between King Edward and 33rd avenues. Farther on the East Side, Commercial Drive has a plethora of cafés, world-beat eateries, and other casual options.

DOWNTOWN VANCOUVER

Use the coordinate (✛ B2) at the end of each listing to locate a site on the corresponding map.

$$
ECLECTIC

✕ **Bin 941.** Part tapas restaurant, part up-tempo bar, this bustling, often noisy hole-in-the-wall claims to have launched Vancouver's small-plates trend. Among the adventurous snack-size dishes, you might find bison satay, crab cakes topped with burnt-orange chipotle sauce, or grilled lamb sirloin served with tomato salad and feta vinaigrette. Snack on one or two, or order a bunch and have a feast. The Bin is open until 2 AM (midnight on Sunday). Bin 942, a sister spot in Kitsilano, is a touch more subdued (⇨ *Dining, Greater Vancouver*). ⊠ *941 Davie St., Downtown* ☎ *604/683–1246* ⊕ *www.bin941.com* ⇴ *Reservations not accepted* ⊟ *MC, V* ⊘ *No lunch* ✛ *D4.*

$$$–$$$$
SEAFOOD
Fodor's Choice
★

✕ **Blue Water Cafe.** Executive chef Frank Pabst features both popular and lesser-known local seafood (including frequently overlooked varieties like mackerel or herring) at this fashionable restaurant. You might start with B.C. sardines stuffed with pine-nut *gremolata*, a pairing of Dungeness crab and flying squid, or a selection of raw oysters. Main dishes are seafood centric, too—perhaps white sturgeon grilled with wheat berries, capers, and peppery greens, or a Japanese-style seafood stew. Ask the staff to recommend wine pairings from the B.C.-focused list. You can dine in the warmly lit interior or outside on the former loading dock that's now a lovely terrace. ■TIP➜ The sushi chef turns out both classic and new creations—they're pricey but rank among the city's best. ⊠ *1095 Hamilton St., Yaletown* ☎ *604/688–8078* ⊕ *www.bluewatercafe.net* ⊟ *AE, DC, MC, V* ⊘ *No lunch* ✛ *E5.*

$$$
MODERN
CANADIAN

✕ **Boneta.** Some of the city's most innovative dishes—and drinks—grace the tables of this Gastown restaurant, named after co-owner Mark Brand's mother. The exposed-brick walls and high ceilings make the room feel like a downtown loft, as do the almost-too-cool-for-school cocktails, including the Tharseo (lemon-thyme-infused gin, sherry, apple juice, honey, and citrus) and the B.K. (gin, Campari, chamomile syrup, and grapefruit). Vancouver is buzzing about such creations as smoked bison carpaccio served with arugula salad and a quail egg; squid-ink farfalle pasta topped with sablefish, calamari, and a briny puttanesca sauce; and grilled tuna with lobster mushrooms and eggplant caviar—dishes that would make any foodie mother proud. And mama wouldn't say no to the Valrhona chocolate "bar" paired with honey-and-chili ice cream. ⊠ *1 W. Cordova St., Gastown* ☎ *604/684–1844* ⊕ *www.boneta.*

6

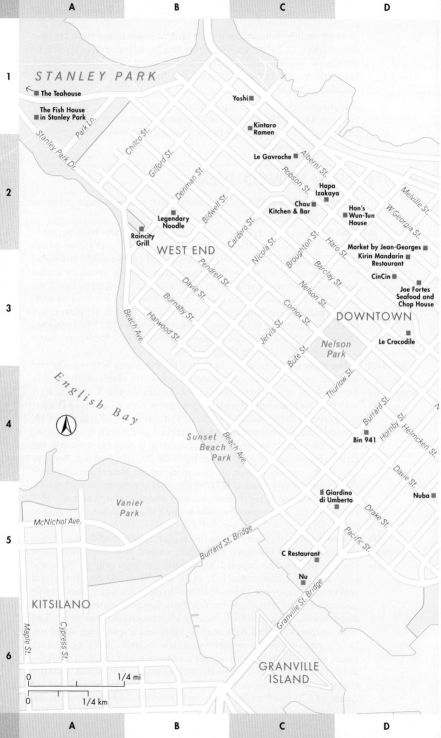

A **B** **C** **D**

1

STANLEY PARK

■ The Teahouse

The Fish House
■ in Stanley Park

Park Ln.

Yoshi ■

Kintaro
■ Ramen

Chilco St.

Le Gavroche ■

Alberni St.

Robson St.

Hapa
■ Izakaya

2

Gilford St.

Denman St.

Chau
Kitchen & Bar ■

Hon's
Wun-Tun
House

Melville St.

W. Georgia St.

Bidwell St.

■ Legendary
Noodle

Cardero St.

Nicola St.

Broughton St.

Haro St.

■ Market by Jean-Georges ■
Kirin Mandarin ■
Restaurant

■ Raincity
Grill

WEST END

Barclay St.

CinCin ■

Pendrell St.

Nelson St.

Joe Fortes ■
Seafood and
Chop House

3

Davie St.

Burnaby St.

Beach Ave.

Harwood St.

Cornox St.

Jervis St.

Bute St.

DOWNTOWN

Nelson
Park

Le Crocodile ■

Thurlow St.

English Bay

Burrard St.

Hornby St.

Helmcken St.

4

Sunset
Beach
Park

Beach Ave.

Bin 941 ■

Davie St.

Vanier
Park

Il Giardino
di Umberto ■

Nuba ■

McNichol Ave.

Drake St.

5

Burrard St. Bridge

Pacific St.

C Restaurant ■

Nu ■

KITSILANO

Maple St.

Cypress St.

Granville St. Bridge

GRANVILLE
ISLAND

6

0   1/4 mi

0   1/4 km

A **B** **C** **D**

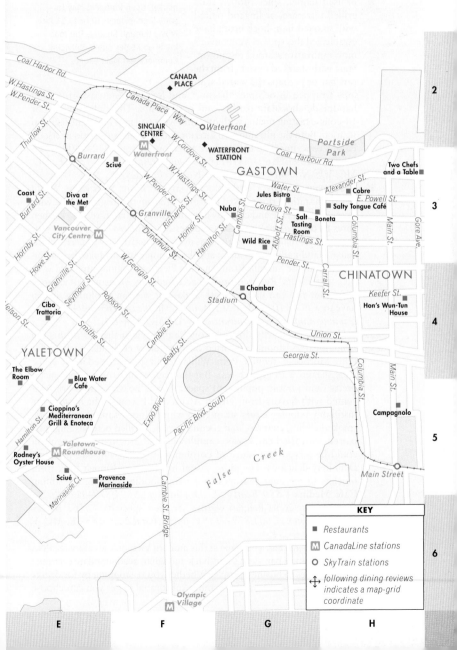

Where to Eat in Downtown Vancouver

1

Burrard Inlet

2

Coal Harbor Rd.

W. Hastings St.
W. Pender St.

Thurlow St.

Canada Place Way

CANADA PLACE

Waterfront

SINCLAIR CENTRE

Waterfront

W. Cordova St.

WATERFRONT STATION

Coal Harbour Rd.

Portside Park

Two Chefs and a Table

Burrard

Sciué

GASTOWN

Coast

Diva at the Met

Burrard St.

W. Pender St.

W. Hastings St.

Richards St.

Homer St.

Hamilton St.

Water St.

Alexander St.

Cobre

E. Powell St.

Granville

Granville St.

Dunsmuir St.

Jules Bistro

Nuba

Cordova St.

Abbott St.

Salty Tongue Café

Boneta

3

Hornby St.

Howe St.

Vancouver City Centre

Wild Rice

Salt Tasting Room

Hastings St.

Pender St.

Carrall St.

Columbia St.

Main St.

Gore Ave.

CHINATOWN

Nelson St.

Seymour St.

W. Georgia St.

Robson St.

Cambie St.

Chambar

Stadium

Keefer St.

Hon's Wun-Tun House

4

Cibo Trattoria

Smithe St.

Beatty St.

Union St.

Georgia St.

YALETOWN

The Elbow Room

Blue Water Cafe

Expo Blvd.

Columbia St.

Main St.

Campagnolo

5

Hamilton St.

Cioppino's Mediterranean Grill & Enoteca

Pacific Blvd. South

False Creek

Rodney's Oyster House

Yaletown-Roundhouse

Sciué

Provence Marinaside

Marinaside Ct.

Cambie St. Bridge

Main Street

KEY

■ *Restaurants*

Ⓜ *CanadaLine stations*

○ *SkyTrain stations*

✛ *following dining reviews indicates a map-grid coordinate*

6

Olympic Village

ca ⊟ *AE, MC, V* ⊘ *Closed Sun. No lunch* ⊕ *G3.*

$$$$
SEAFOOD
Fodor's Choice
★

✕ **C Restaurant.** Save your pennies, fish fans—dishes such as crispy trout served with oven-dried tomato and braised fennel, spice-rubbed tuna grilled ultrarare, or lingcod paired with smoked-ham-hock broth have established this spot as Vancouver's most innovative seafood restaurant. Start with shucked oysters from the raw bar or perhaps the seared scal-

CHINATOWN NIGHT MARKET

For interesting eats, check out the stalls at the Chinatown night market, open from mid-May to early September, 6:30 PM to 11 PM, Friday through Sunday. The market is on Keefer Street, between Columbia and Main streets.

lops wrapped in octopus "bacon," and finish with an assortment of handmade chocolate truffles and petits fours. The elaborate six- or 14-course tasting menus with optional wine pairings highlight regional seafood. Both the ultramodern interior and the waterside patio overlook False Creek, but dine before dark to enjoy the view. ⊠ *2–1600 Howe St., Downtown* ☎ *604/681–1164* ⊕ *www.crestaurant.com* ⊟ *AE, DC, MC, V* ⊘ *No lunch weekends or Nov.–Feb.* ⊕ *C5.*

$$
ITALIAN

✕ **Campagnolo.** On a dark block near the Main St./Science World SkyTrain station, this relaxed trattoria lights up the neighborhood with its welcoming vibe and casually contemporary Italian fare. The kitchen cures its own *salumi*, including soppressata, capicola, and various sausages—these make good starters, as do the addictive "crispy *ceci*" (chick peas). Handmade pastas and a small selection of mains take their inspiration from the Emiglia-Romagna and Piemonte regions, updated with B.C. ingredients. Reservations are accepted only for groups of eight or more, but you can unwind with a glass of wine in the lounge if you have to wait. ⊠ *1020 Main St., Main St./Mt. Pleasant* ☎ *604/484–6018* ⊕ *www.campagnolorestaurant.ca* ⊟ *AE, MC, V* ⊕ *H5.*

$$$
BELGIAN

✕ **Chambar.** A smartly dressed crowd hangs out at the bar of this hip Belgian eatery sipping imported beer or funky cocktails, such as the Poire Moroccan (tequila, Poire William, and spice-infused white grape juice shaken with egg whites). But the high-ceiling room is not just a pretty (and prettily populated) space. Classic Belgian dishes are reinvented with flavors from North Africa and beyond. The *moules* are justifiably popular, either steamed in white wine or sauced with exotic smoked chilies, cilantro, and coconut cream. Grilled octopus might be paired with fried chickpeas, cauliflower, and arugula, while venison could be served in a sauce of coronation grapes. Unusual, perhaps. Definitely delicious. For more casual breakfast and lunch fare, from omelets to *merguez* sausages to a daily noodle creation, try sibling **Café Medina** (*556 Beatty St., Downtown* ☎ *604/879–3114* ⊘ *No dinner*) next door; Belgian waffles are their specialty. ⊠ *562 Beatty St., Downtown* ☎ *604/879–7119* ⊕ *www.chambar.com* ⊟ *AE, MC, V* ⊘ *No lunch* ⊕ *G4.*

$–$$
VIETNAMESE

✕ **Chau Kitchen & Bar.** The scene at this modern Vietnamese eatery recalls a tropical cocktail bar, yet it's laid-back enough to accommodate everyone from families to businesspeople. Whether you're stopping by for drinks and snacks or settling in for a more substantial meal, you can choose from familiar traditional dishes— *pho* (noodle soup), spring rolls—or more adventurous creations, like the crisp watercress–and-jackfruit salad. There are intriguing cocktail options like Vietnamese mojitos or Beach Umbrella Margaritas (tequila, triple sec, cranberry juice,

and lime); the lemon-lime soda is a refreshing alternative. ✉ *1500 Robson St., West End* ☎ *604/682–8020* ⊕ *www.chaukitchenandbar.com* ▭ *MC, V* ✛ *C2.*

$$–$$$ ✕ **Cibo Trattoria.** Chef Neil Taylor cooked at London's River Café before
ITALIAN manning the stoves at this fine and funky trattoria. It's the space that's funky—a mix of original early-1900s architectural details, modern furnishings, and oversize pop art—while the updated Italian fare and solicitous service are nothing but fine. To start, consider the *ribollita* (a hearty soup of cannellini beans and kale) or perhaps the house-made mortadella with pickled asparagus. The pastas are made in-house, too, and could include potato gnocchi with Gorgonzola cheese or spaghetti with octopus and fresh cherry tomatoes. Still hungry? How about roasted pheasant with lentils and quince, or venison served with Sicilian-style caponata? The lengthy wine list emphasizes Italian labels, but B.C. is ably represented as well. For a lighter bite, join the local crowd at the adjacent **Uva Wine Bar** (☎ *604/632–9560* ⊕ *www.uvawinebar.ca*), which serves pastries, coffees, salads, and panini by day and Italian small bites, cheeses, and cured meats (with wines to match) until the wee hours. ✉ *900 Seymour St., in the Moda Hotel, Downtown* ☎ *604/602–9570* ⊕ *www.cibotrattoria.com* ▭ *MC, V* ⊗ *Closed Sun. No lunch* ✛ *E4.*

$$$–$$$$ ✕ **CinCin.** Gold walls, terra-cotta tiles, and the crowd-pleasing modern
ITALIAN Italian menu make this Tuscan-inspired restaurant appropriate for a business meal, a romantic tête-à-tête, or just a relaxing dinner after a long day. The heated terrace, shielded with greenery, feels a long way from busy Robson Street below. Inside, there's a lively scene around the hand-carved marble bar. The food, from the open kitchen and the wood-fire grill, oven, and rotisserie, changes seasonally, but might include arctic char with celeriac, smoked ricotta, and sunchoke risotto; beef short ribs braised in wine and served over polenta; and thin-crust wood-fired pizza. ✉ *1154 Robson St., upstairs, Downtown* ☎ *604/688–7338* ⊕ *www.cincin.net* ▭ *AE, DC, MC, V* ⊗ *No lunch* ✛ *D3.*

$$$–$$$$ ✕ **Cioppino's Mediterranean Grill & Enoteca.** Cioppino, a fragrant seafood
MEDITERRANEAN stew, is the signature dish at this lofty candlelit room. Chef Pino Posteraro impresses with homemade pastas and such Italian-Mediterranean dishes as Dover sole with fresh tomatoes and basil, and spit-roasted duck breast in a savory orange sauce. More rustic Italian fare, such as veal scaloppine and braised beef short ribs, is also on offer. In good weather, you can dine out on the street-side patio. ✉ *1133 Hamilton St., Yaletown* ☎ *604/688–7466* ⊕ *www.cioppinosyaletown.com* ▭ *AE, DC, MC, V* ⊗ *Closed Sun. No lunch* ✛ *E5.*

$$$–$$$$
SEAFOOD

✕ **Coast.** If your image of a fish house is lobster traps and buoys, toss that picture overboard when you cruise up to this see-and-be-seen seafood palace. Expect plenty of bling, from the shimmering lights to the sparkle-sporting patrons. What to eat? Why, seafood, of course—from oysters to sushi to fish-and-chips to any of the day's fresh catches, though they serve steak, too, if you must. While it contains a huge room, Coast frequently does a swimmingly good business, so reservations are recommended. ⊠ *1054 Alberni St., Downtown* ☎ *604/685–5010* ⊕ *www. coastrestaurant.ca* ⊟ *AE, DC, MC, V* ☻ *No lunch weekends* ✛ *E3.*

$–$$
NUEVO LATINO

✕ **Cobre.** Looking for a cool place to sip and nibble? *Bienvenidos!* Like many other restored Gastown properties, this loftlike space has the brick walls and wood-beamed ceilings that recall the district's earlier days. But what distinguishes Cobre from other trendy Vancouver dining rooms is its emphasis on fare from way south of the border. Taking its influences from across Latin America, the menu travels from ceviches to tacos to arepas to steak; the uniquely Vancouver twists come from the emphasis on local ingredients and on the small-plates-paired-with-cocktails style. ⊠ *52 Powell St., Gastown* ☎ *604/669–2396* ⊕ *www. cobrerestaurant.com* ⊟ *MC, V* ☻ *No lunch* ✛ *H3.*

$$$–$$$$
MODERN
CANADIAN

✕ **Diva at the Met.** Regional cuisine shines at this chic restaurant in the Metropolitan Hotel. The menu changes frequently but focuses on local seafood, produce, and wines: maybe a West Coast seafood chowder, salmon from the Queen Charlotte Islands matched with *farro* (a type of wheat) risotto and celeriac purée, or chicken with a potato-mushroom croquette. Choose a table at the back for an intimate evening, near the front or on the patio for a livelier scene. A light lounge menu is available all evening, and the after-theater crowd heads here for late-evening snacks and desserts. The suits come in at lunch or for the creative breakfasts. ⊠ *645 Howe St., Downtown* ☎ *604/602–7788* ⊕ *www. metropolitan.com/diva* ⊟ *AE, D, DC, MC, V* ✛ *E3.*

¢–$$
AMERICAN

✕ **The Elbow Room.** Known for the good-natured abuse the staff sometimes dishes out, this entertaining diner-style joint, where the lime-green walls are decorated with celebrity photos, is a Vancouver institution. Breakfast is served all day—the omelets are fluffy, the bacon is crisp, and the portions are generous—as well as burgers, sandwiches, and salads. ⊠ *560 Davie St., Downtown* ☎ *604/685–3628* ⊕ *www. theelbowroomcafe.com* ⌂ *Reservations not accepted* ⊟ *AE, MC, V* ☻ *No dinner* ✛ *E5.*

$$$–$$$$
SEAFOOD

✕ **The Fish House in Stanley Park.** This 1930s former sports pavilion with two verandas and a fireplace is surrounded by gardens, tucked between Stanley Park's tennis courts and putting green. Chef Karen Barnaby's food, including fresh oysters, grilled ahi tuna steak with a green-peppercorn sauce, and corn-husk-wrapped salmon with a maple glaze, is flavorful and unpretentious. Check the fresh sheet for the current day's catch. Traditional English afternoon tea is served between 2 and 4 daily. ⊠ *8901 Stanley Park Dr., Stanley Park* ☎ *604/681–7275 or 877/681–7275* ⊕ *www.fishhousestanleypark.com* ⊟ *AE, DC, MC, V* ✛ *A1.*

$–$$
JAPANESE

✕ **Hapa Izakaya.** *Izakayas* are Japanese pubs that serve tapas-style small plates designed for sharing, and they've sprouted up all over Vancouver. This sleek izakaya pub has two locations, both popular with

Izakaya are Japanese small plates, similar to Spanish tapas.

twenty- and thirtysomethings. Choose from the daily "fresh sheet," or sample other tasty tidbits, such as the mackerel (cooked table-side—with a blowtorch), udon noodles coated with briny cod roe, or the *ishi-yaki*, a Korean-style stone bowl filled with rice, pork, and vegetables. Sake or Japanese beer are the drinks of choice. If you're dining alone, sit at the counter facing the open kitchen to watch the action. The Robson branch is located city center; the Kitsilano branch is one block from Kits Beach. ⊠ *1479 Robson St., West End* ☎ *604/689–4272* ⊕ *www. hapaizakaya.com* ▭ *AE, MC, V* ⊘ *No lunch* ⊠ *1516 Yew St., Kitsilano* ☎ *604/738–4272* ▭ *AE, MC, V* ⊘ *No lunch* ✛ *C2.*

¢–$$ ✕ **Hon's Wun-Tun House.** This Vancouver minichain has been keeping
CHINESE residents and tourists in Chinese comfort food since the 1970s. You can find better Chinese food elsewhere, but Hon's locations are convenient and the prices are reasonable. The best bets on the 300-item menu are the dumplings and noodle dishes, any of the Chinese vegetables, and anything with barbecued meat. The Robson Street outlet has a separate kitchen for vegetarians and an army of fast-moving waitresses. The original Keefer Street location is in the heart of Chinatown. ⊠ *1339 Robson St., West End* ☎ *604/685–0871* ⊕ *www.hons.ca* ⌲ *Reservations not accepted* ▭ *MC, V* ✛ *D2* ⊠ *268 Keefer St., Chinatown* ☎ *604/688–0871* ⌲ *Reservations not accepted* ▭ *MC, V* ✛ *H4.*

$$$–$$$$ ✕ **Il Giardino di Umberto.** The vine-draped terrace or any of the four terra-
ITALIAN cotta-tiled rooms inside are inviting places to enjoy this long-established restaurateur's traditional Tuscan cuisine. A frequently changing menu includes a variety of pasta dishes, osso buco Milanese with saffron risotto, grilled salmon with saffron and fennel vinaigrette, and roast reindeer loin with a pink-peppercorn sauce. Dine here with someone

special. ⊠ *1382 Hornby St., Downtown* ☎ *604/669–2422* ⊕ *www. umberto.com* ▭ *AE, DC, MC, V* ☾ *Closed Sun. No lunch Sat.* ✛ *D5.*

$$$–$$$$
SEAFOOD

✕ **Joe Fortes Seafood and Chop House.** Named for a much-loved English Bay lifeguard, this lively brasserie just off Robson Street has a piano bar, a bistro, an oyster bar, and a delightful, covered rooftop patio. The menu is wide ranging, but steaks, chops, and generous portions of fresh seafood are the main draw. Try the cedar-planked salmon, the *cioppino* (a seafood stew), or the Seafood Tower on Ice—a lavish assortment that's meant to be shared. ⊠ *777 Thurlow St., Downtown* ☎ *604/669–1940* ⊕ *www.joefortes.ca* ▭ *AE, D, DC, MC, V* ✛ *D3.*

$$–$$$
FRENCH

✕ **Jules Bistro.** From garlicky escargots and steak frites to duck confit and crème caramel, traditional French bistro fare is alive and well at this buzzing Gastown spot. You won't find funky fusion creations or east-meets-west innovations—just the classic dishes you might see at a neighborhood bistro in Paris. It's cozy (some might say cramped), but that's part of the charm. Need a midafternoon pick-me-up? They serve light meals from 2:30 to 5:30. ⊠ *216 Abbott St., Gastown* ☎ *604/669–0033* ⊕ *www.julesbistro.ca* ▭ *AE, MC, V* ☾ *Closed Sun.* ✛ *G3.*

¢–$
JAPANESE

✕ **Kintaro Ramen.** If your only experience with ramen is instant noodles, get thee to this authentic Japanese soup joint. With thin, fresh egg noodles and homemade broth (it's a meat stock, so vegetarians are explicitly not invited), a bowl of noodle soup here is cheap, filling, and ever so tasty. Expect long lines, but you can use the waiting time to decide between lean or fatty pork and miso or soy stock: once you're inside the bare-bones storefront, the harried staff doesn't tolerate any dithering. ⊠ *788 Denman St., West End* ☎ *604/682–7568* ⌲ *Reservations not accepted* ▭ *No credit cards* ☾ *Closed Mon.* ✛ *C1.*

$$–$$$
CHINESE

✕ **Kirin Mandarin Restaurant.** A striking silver mural of a *kirin,* a mythical dragonlike creature, presides over this elegant two-tier restaurant. Specialties here are northern Chinese and Szechuan dishes, which tend to be richer and spicier than the Cantonese cuisine served at Kirin's other locations. If you're adventurous, start with the spicy jellyfish, redolent with sesame oil. Then try the Peking duck, or the kung pao lobster: sautéed lobster meat served with a deep-fried lobster claw. Dim sum is served daily. ⊠ *1166 Alberni St., 2nd fl., Downtown* ☎ *604/682–8833* ⊕ *www.kirinrestaurants.com* ▭ *AE, MC, V* ✛ *D3.*

$$$–$$$$
FRENCH

✕ **Le Crocodile.** Chefs prepare classic Alsatian-inspired food (such as the signature onion tart) at this long-established downtown restaurant. Despite the white-tablecloth sophistication, the golden yellow walls, café curtains, and burgundy banquettes keep things cozy. Favorite dishes include lobster with beurre blanc, veal medallions with morel sauce, and sautéed Dover sole. Many lunch options, including a black truffle omelet and a mixed grill of halibut, prawns, and wild salmon, are moderately priced. ⊠ *100–909 Burrard St., Downtown* ☎ *604/669–4298* ⊕ *www.lecrocodilerestaurant.com* ▭ *AE, DC, MC, V* ☾ *Closed Sun. No lunch Sat.* ✛ *D3.*

$$$–$$$$
FRENCH

✕ **Le Gavroche.** Classic French cuisine receives contemporary accents at this romantic restaurant, in an early-20th-century house tucked amid the downtown towers. Seafood entrées range from wild salmon paired with cabbage to smoked halibut served with braised leeks; meat options

DID YOU KNOW?

The Chinatown night market, on Keefer Street between Columbia and Main streets, is filled with stalls selling food, T-shirts, and all sorts of odds and ends.

include rich beef tenderloin and mustard-crusted rack of lamb. Vegetarian choices are always available. One of the few places with table-side service of steak tartare and Caesar salad, Le Gavroche also has a 5,000-label wine cellar. ⊠ *1616 Alberni St., West End* ☎ *604/685–3924* ⊕ *www. legavroche.ca* ⊟ *AE, DC, MC, V* ⊗ *No lunch weekends.* ⊹ *C2.*

¢–$
CHINESE

✕ **Legendary Noodle.** As you'd expect from the name, these compact storefronts specialize in noodles, and they're handmade here in the open kitchen. The choices are simple—noodles in soup or stir-fried—but you might also order a plate of garlicky pea shoots or a steamer of dumplings. The original Mount Pleasant location makes a convenient time-out if you're shopping the Main Street boutiques, while the West End branch is just a short stroll from English Bay. ⊠ *1074 Denman St., West End* ☎ *604/669–8551* ⊕ *www.legendarynoodle.ca* ⌿ *Reservations not accepted* ⊟ *MC, V* ⊠ *4191 Main St., Main St./Mt. Pleasant* ☎ *604/879–8758* ⊗ *Closed Tues.* ⊹ *B2.*

$$$–$$$$
MODERN
CANADIAN

✕ **Market by Jean-Georges.** Vancouver was all abuzz when celebrity chef Jean-Georges Vongerichten opened this contemporary dining room in the Shangri-La Hotel. While the globetrotting chef is rarely on-site, his signature Asian influences abound, as in the rice cracker–crusted tuna with a citrus-Sriracha (chili sauce) emulsion or the soy-glazed short ribs. These global flavors frequently garnish local ingredients; you might find Pacific halibut in a lemon-garlic broth or B.C.-raised venison sauced with cabrales (blue cheese) foam. If you don't fancy a full meal, you can dine lightly (and less expensively) on stylish salads or creative appetizers. Either way, you'll want to dress up a bit to match the sleek space. ⊠ *1115 Alberni St., Downtown* ☎ *604/695–1115* ⊕ *www.shangri-la. com* ⊟ *AE, DC, MC, V* ⊹ *D2.*

$$–$$$
MODERN
CANADIAN

✕ **Nu.** With its wall of windows overlooking False Creek, this contemporary dining room showcases lovely water views. The name is French for "naked," but that doesn't refer to the patrons' attire (which runs from smart-casual to business suits) or the room's furnishings (chic Euro style, from the funky bucket seats to the gilded brass ceiling). Instead, it represents the restaurant's philosophy of letting good-quality ingredients shine. You could linger over a cocktail and light bites, perhaps cute mini-burgers or a fried oyster paired with a beer "shooter," but don't overlook the more substantial dishes, which might include an elaborate cold seafood platter (heaping with salmon, tuna, spot prawns, mussels, and clams), a fricassée of cremini and oyster mushrooms served over linguine, or grilled bison with a green-peppercorn sauce. ⊠ *1661 Granville St., Yaletown* ☎ *604/646–4668* ⊕ *www.whatisnu.com* ⊟ *AE, MC, V* ⊹ *C5.*

¢–$$
MIDDLE EASTERN

✕ **Nuba.** You could make a meal of meze—appetizers like tabbouleh salad, *labneh* (spiced yogurt dip), or crispy cauliflower served with tahini sauce—at this cheap and cheerful duo of Lebanese restaurants. If you're looking for something heartier, try a plate of *mjadra*, a spicy mix of lentils and rice. They serve chicken kebabs, lamb *kafta* (patties), and other meat dishes, but most of the menu is vegetarian friendly. The Seymour Street branch is a quick-service café, while the larger Gastown location has a more extensive menu and, in the evenings, a more lounge-like vibe with occasional live music. ⊠ *1206 Seymour St., Downtown*

☎ 778/371–3266 ⊕ *www.nuba.ca* ⌂ *Reservations not accepted* ☰ *AE, MC, V* ✣ *D5* ✉ *207-B W. Hastings St., Gastown* ☎ *604/688–1655* ⌂ *Reservations not accepted* ☰ *AE, MC, V* ☉ *Closed Sun.* ✣ *G3.*

WORD OF MOUTH

"Raincity was a delight. We had the 100 Mile Tasting Menu which was excellent. The server was extremely knowledgeable and friendly." —StantonHyde

$$$-$$$$ ✕ **Provence Marinaside.** This airy, MEDITERRANEAN modern, Mediterranean-style eatery on Yaletown's waterfront presents French and Italian takes on seafood, including a delicious bouillabaisse and lush, garlicky wild prawns, though the rack of lamb and an extensive antipasti selection are also popular. The marina-view patio makes a sunny breakfast or lunch spot, and the take-out counter is a great place to put together a picnic. Under the same ownership, the **Provence Mediterranean Grill** (✉ *4473 W. 10th Ave., Point Grey* ☎ *604/222–1980*) serves a similar menu to West Side denizens. ✉ *1177 Marinaside Crescent, at foot of Davie St., Yaletown* ☎ *604/681–4144* ⊕ *www.provencevancouver.com* ☰ *AE, DC, MC, V* ✣ *E5.*

$$$-$$$$ ✕ **Raincity Grill.** One of the best places to try British Columbian food and MODERN wine is this lovely candlelit bistro overlooking English Bay. The menu CANADIAN changes regularly and relies almost completely on local and regional products, from salmon and shellfish to game and fresh organic vegetables. Vegetarian selections are always available, and the exclusively Pacific Northwest and Californian wine list has at least 40 choices by the glass. One popular alternative is the 100 Mile Tasting Menu—all ingredients in this multicourse dinner are sourced from within 100 mi of the restaurant. Another prix-fixe option, the early dinner (C$30), is a steal; it's served from 5 to 6 PM. Reservations are required for these prix-fixe dinners. ✉ *1193 Denman St., West End* ☎ *604/685–7337* ⊕ *www.raincitygrill.com* ☰ *AE, DC, MC, V* ✣ *B2.*

$-$$$ ✕ **Rodney's Oyster House.** This fishing-shack look-alike in Yaletown has SEAFOOD one of the widest selections of oysters in town (up to 18 varieties), from locally harvested to exotic Japanese *kumamotos*. You can pick your oysters individually—they're laid out on ice behind the bar—or try the clams, scallops, mussels, and other mollusks from the steamer kettles. Oyster lovers can also relax over martinis and appetizers in the attached Mermaid Room lounge. ✉ *1228 Hamilton St., Yaletown* ☎ *604/609–0080* ⊕ *www.rodneysoysterhouse.com* ☰ *AE, DC, MC, V* ☉ *Restaurant closed Sun., lounge closed Mon.–Wed. No lunch in lounge* ✣ *E5.*

$-$$ ✕ **Salt Tasting Room.** If your idea of a perfect lunch or light supper ECLECTIC revolves around fine cured meats, artisanal cheeses, and a glass of wine from a wide-ranging list, find your way to this sleek spare space in a decidedly unsleek Gastown lane. The restaurant has no kitchen and simply assembles its first-quality provisions, perhaps meaty *bunderfleisch* (cured beef), smoked pork chops, or B.C.-made Camembert, with accompanying condiments,

WORD OF MOUTH

"Salt Tasting Room…the place is a joy. In addition to the charcuterie choices, the toasted sandwich with a side soup and salad was excellent." —lvk

6

into artfully composed grazers' delights—more like an upscale picnic than a full meal. There's no sign out front, so look for the salt-shaker flag in Blood Alley, which is off Abbott Street, half a block south of Water Street. ⊠ *45 Blood Alley, Gastown* ☎ *604/633–1912* ⊕ *www. salttastingroom.com* ⊟ *AE, MC, V* ✛ *G3.*

¢–$$
CASUAL
✕ **Salty Tongue Café.** Tongues are always wagging at this deli-café's long communal table—a cheerful spot for a quick bite in Gastown. In the morning, you can pop in for coffee, muffins, or a full Irish breakfast (the Tongue is run by the Irish Heather, next door), while at midday, you can build your own sandwich or choose bangers-and-mash, quiche, or a pot-pie. ⊠ *212 Carrall St., Gastown* ☎ *604/688–9779* ⊕ *www.irishheather. com* ⌂ *Reservations not accepted* ⊟ *MC, V* ☽ *No dinner* ✛ *G3.*

$
CAFÉ
✕ **Sciué.** Inspired by the street foods of Rome, this cafeteria-style Italian bakery–café (pronounced "Shoe-eh") starts the day serving espresso and pastries, then moves to panini, soups, and pastas. One specialty is the *pane romano,* essentially a thick-crust pizza, sold by weight. There can be lines out the door at lunch, so try to visit early or late; the downtown location closes at 7 PM weeknights and 5 PM Saturdays, while the Yaletown branch keeps somewhat later hours: until 9 PM Monday through Saturday and until 7 PM Sundays. ⊠ *110–800 W. Pender St., Downtown* ☎ *604/602–7263* ⊕ *www.sciue.ca* ⌂ *Reservations not accepted* ⊟ *MC, V* ☽ *Closed Sun. No dinner Sat.* ✛ *E5* ⊠ *126 Davie St., Yaletown* ☎ *604/689–7263* ☽ *No dinner Sun.* ✛ *F3.*

$$$–$$$$
MODERN
CANADIAN
✕ **The Teahouse in Stanley Park.** The former officers' mess in Stanley Park is perfectly poised for watching sunsets over the water. The Pacific Northwest menu is not especially innovative, but it includes such specialties as beet-and-endive salad topped with warm goat cheese, and mushrooms stuffed with crab and mascarpone cheese, as well as seasonally changing treatments of B.C. salmon, halibut, and steak. In summer you can dine on the patio. ⊠ *7501 Stanley Park Dr., Ferguson Point, Stanley Park* ☎ *604/669–3281 or 800/280–9893* ⊕ *www.vancouverdine.com* ⊟ *AE, MC, V* ✛ *A1.*

$$$
MODERN
CANADIAN
✕ **Two Chefs and a Table.** Sometimes you have to go the extra mile for an excellent meal. To reach this storefront bistro, which glows like a beacon in the emerging Railtown neighborhood, you have to go the extra kilometer—it's about a half-mile east of the Gastown Steam Clock. There are fewer than 30 seats, including eight at the communal eponymous table (and yes, there are two chefs in the open kitchen). The menu is small, too, but the frequently changing selections, which might range from a classic coq au vin to grilled lamb with spiced-apple relish to salmon in a fire-roasted tomato broth, are all well executed. At lunch, they keep busy serving up pastas, burgers, and interesting sandwiches. Just the kind of place we'd want in our neighborhood. ⊠ *305 Alexander St., East Side* ☎ *778/233–1303* ⊕ *www.twochefsandatable.com* ⊟ *MC, V* ☽ *No dinner Mon.–Tues.* ✛ *H3.*

$–$$$
ECLECTIC
✕ **Wild Rice.** The look is decadent postmodern, with couches and a glowing aquamarine bar; the food, served in portions meant for sharing, borrows from China and across Asia but has a contemporary spin and an emphasis on local ingredients. You might find Chinese ravioli stuffed with a "sustainable Pacific fish" and sauced with green curry, B.C. halibut

CLOSE UP

Snack Attack

With sushi bars on every corner (or so it often seems), cafés all across the city, and plenty of burger joints, Vancouver has no shortage of places to grab a quick bite. Good "cheap eats" neighborhoods include the area around Granville and Seymour streets downtown, Robson Street near Denman in the West End, and Denman Street near Davie, a short walk from English Bay. Look for the following spots when you need to refuel.

Café Crêpe. Crêpes are a popular snack or light meal in Vancouver, and these petite cafés serve savory and sweet varieties.

Earl's. Big cheery rooms, upbeat music, chipper service, and a vast menu of burgers, salads, sandwiches, pastas, steaks, and vegetarian options make this local chain a favorite, especially for groups and families.

H-Mart. Need a *bulgogi* break while shopping downtown? This Korean supermarket, with a handy location at the corner of Robson and Seymour,

has a second-floor food court that cooks up inexpensive, made-to-order, and frequently spicy Korean fare.

Japa-Dog. Only in multi-culti Vancouver? Perhaps. But this Japanese hot dog stand has a loyal following, topping its bratwurst and wieners with teriyaki sauce, nori, and other Asian condiments. On sunny days, look for them at two Burrard Street locations: between Robson and Smithe and at the corner of West Pender.

Nat's Pizza. Serving New York–style wisecracks along with their Big Apple–inspired pies, this Vancouver icon is the place to go for a slice (or three). There are locations on Denman Street (in the West End) and on West Broadway (in Kitsilano).

Vera's Burger Shack. Local burger buffs sing the praises of this Vancouver minichain where the patties are loaded with a variety of contemporary condiments. If you're not into beef, opt for the veggie, turkey, or lamb varieties.

6

and soba noodles in a coconut-lemongrass broth, or locally raised tea-smoked duck with a galette of Asian pears. Cocktails that play on the menu's Asian flavors (such as the Lotus—lychee-infused vodka, lychee nectar, lime, and ginger ale) or an assortment of teas are the best drink choices. ⊠ *117 W. Pender St., Chinatown* ☎ *604/642–2882* ⊕ *www. wildricevancouver.com* ⊟ *MC, V* ⊗ *No lunch Sat.–Thurs.* ⊕ *G3.*

$$–$$$

JAPANESE

✕**Yoshi.** Sushi and sashimi are the specialties at this traditional Japanese restaurant, where picture windows face Stanley Park and the North Shore Mountains—try the fresh wild salmon, crab, or the special of the day. Interesting items come from the *robata* (grill), too, including meltingly tender black cod. The gracious staff is quick to refill your green tea or explain menu items. The restaurant is on the second floor, and in warm weather, you can dine on the terrace. With advance notice, you can order a *kaiseki* dinner, a classic meal with a prescribed sequence of small courses. ⊠ *689 Denman St., West End* ☎ *604/738–8226* ⊕ *www.yoshijapaneserestaurant.com* ⊟ *AE, DC, MC, V* ⊗ *No lunch weekends* ⊕ *C1.*

Fueled by Caffeine

"Fueled by Caffeine" is the slogan of a Vancouver-based minichain of coffeehouses, and it's also an apt description of the city. Although the Starbucks invasion is extensive, there are plenty of more colorful places—from sleek and modern to comfortably bohemian. You'll find the same variety of coffee drinks that you can get across North America, though some places refer to an "americano" (an espresso made with extra hot water) as a "canadiano." An increasing number of cafés provide free Wi-Fi, too.

Bean Around the World (✉ 1945 Cornwall Ave., Kitsilano ☎ 604/739–1069 ✉ 1002 Mainland St., Yaletown ☎ 604/685–9929 ✉ 4456 W. 10th Ave., Point Grey ☎ 604/222–1400 ✉ 2977 Granville St., S. Granville ☎ 604/731–9522 ✉ 3598 Main St., Main St./Mt. Pleasant ☎ 604/875–9199 ✉ 2528 Main St., Main St./Mt. Pleasant ☎ 604/873–8274), of the "Fueled by Caffeine" slogan, runs a number of comfortable coffeehouses around town. Granville Island has several coffee places, but only the **Blue Parrot Café** (✉ Granville Island Public Market, 1689 Johnston St., Granville Island ☎ 604/688–5127) provides sweeping views of False Creek. Some of Vancouver's best coffee is served at the several locales of **Caffè Artigiano** (✉ 1101 W. Pender, Downtown ☎ 604/685–5333 ✉ 763 Hornby, Downtown ☎ 604/694–7737 ✉ 740 W. Hastings St., Downtown ☎ 604/915–7200 ✉ 3036 W. Broadway, Kitsilano ☎ 604/734–3134), where the baristas have won prizes for their "Latte Art," making patterns in the froth. **Delaney's on Denman** (✉ 1105 Denman St., West End ☎ 604/662–3344) is a friendly, often crowded coffee bar near English Bay.

More than just a place to grab a cup of joe, **Raw Canvas** (✉ 1046 Hamilton St., Yaletown ☎ 604/687–1729) is a café and art gallery by day, wine bar and performance space by night.

Serious coffee drinkers head for Commercial Drive on the East Side. It's a bohemian 'hood full of spots to fuel a caffeine habit. With its marble-top tables and espresso drinks, **Caffe Calabria** (✉ 1745 Commercial Dr., East Side ☎ 604/253–7017) is one of many traditional Italian cafés along "The Drive." **Continental Coffee** (✉ 1806 Commercial Dr., East Side ☎ 604/255–0712) has a boho vibe and weekend lineups attest to first-rate coffee; the americano is particularly good. **Prado Café** (✉ 1938 Commercial Dr., East Side ☎ 604/255–5537) is industrial-chic, with gunmetal-gray chairs and blond-wood tables.

Vancouverites don't live by coffee alone: the contemporary city-center teahouse, **Muzi** (✉ 870 W. Cordova St., Downtown ☎ 604/689–3188) specializes in *matcha* (Japanese green tea), as well as other teas and herbal infusions. Tiny **O-Cha Tea Bar** (✉ 1116 Homer St., Yaletown ☎ 604/633–3929) serves 60 of its own blends, including rich, milky "Lat-Teas." At **T** (✉ 1568 W. Broadway, South Granville ☎ 604/730–8390), which sells a vast selection of teas and related paraphernalia, you can sample a cup in the serene, vaguely Japanese-style tearoom.

If you like your caffeine dark, rich, and chocolaty, don't miss **Chocoatl** (✉ 1127 Mainland St., Yaletown ☎ 604/676–9977). The shop is about as big as a bonbon and specializes in hot chocolate drinks.

GREATER VANCOUVER

Use the coordinate (✛ B2) at the end of each listing to locate a site on the corresponding map.

$$$–$$$$ ✕ **The Beach House at Dundarave Pier.** It's worth the drive over the Lions
MODERN Gate Bridge to West Vancouver for an evening meal or lunch at this
CANADIAN 1912 seaside house. Whether inside the terraced room or on the heated
beachside patio, most every table has views over Burrard Inlet and
Stanley Park. The Pacific Northwest menu changes seasonally but creates accessible takes on meat, poultry, and seafood, including halibut
or wild B.C. salmon. After your meal, you can take a stroll along the
pier or the seaside walkway. ✉ *150 25th St., off Marine Dr., West Vancouver* ☏ *604/922–1414* ⊕ *www.thebeachhouserestaurant.ca* ⊟ *AE, DC, MC, V* ✛ *A2.*

$–$$ ✕ **Bin 942.** High-energy murals and music keep things lively at this tiny
ECLECTIC tapas bar that stays open until 2 AM (midnight on Sunday). The real star
here, though, is the food. From the Kobe beef meatballs with black truffle sauce to the duck confit infused with Asian five-spice powder to the
kalamata olive hummus served with Navajo fry bread, the chef creates
some of the most eclectic small plates in town. Fun is also part of the
deal: the chocolate fruit "luv" fondue, for example, is designed for
two and comes with a paintbrush. Most of the excellent affordable
wines are available by the glass. ✉ *1521 W. Broadway, South Granville* ☏ *604/734–9421* ⊕ *www.bin941.com* ⌂ *Reservations not accepted* ⊟ *MC, V* ◷ *No lunch* ✛ *B3.*

$$$$ ✕ **Bishop's.** Before "local" and "seasonal" were all the rage, this highly
MODERN regarded room was serving West Coast cuisine with an emphasis on
CANADIAN organic regional produce. The menu changes regularly, but highlights
have included such starters as marinated Pacific sardines paired with
Barlotti beans, bacon, and tomatoes, and mains like Qualicum Bay scallops with potato confit, slow-roasted pork with rosemary gravy, and
locally raised beef tenderloin. All are expertly presented and impeccably
served with suggestions from Bishop's extensive local wine list. The
split-level room displays elaborate flower arrangements and selections
from owner John Bishop's art collection. ✉ *2183 W. 4th Ave., Kitsilano* ☏ *604/738–2025* ⊕ *www.bishopsonline.com* ⊟ *AE, DC, MC, V* ◷ *Closed 1st wk in Jan. No lunch* ✛ *A2.*

$–$$$ ✕ **Cru.** "Small plates and big glasses" is the motto at this stylish tapas-
MODERN and wine-focused restaurant, with romantic low lighting. More than
CANADIAN 35 wines by the glass (plus more by the bottle) complement the inventive designed-to-share dishes. There's a wonderfully crispy duck confit served with späetzle goat-cheese hash and a warm bacon dressing,
hearty wine-braised short ribs matched with macaroni-and-cheese, and
an assortment of cheeses from B.C., Québec, and beyond. Save room for
dessert, perhaps the chocolate truffle with peanut butter–mascarpone
mousse, or the goat-cheese cake with stewed fruits. ✉ *1459 W. Broadway, South Granville* ☏ *604/677–4111* ⊕ *www.cru.ca* ⊟ *AE, MC, V* ◷ *No lunch* ✛ *B3.*

$$–$$$ ✕ **db Bistro Moderne.** Under the same ownership as Lumière, this fashionable bistro next door is also run by celeb chef Daniel Boulud. Many of
FRENCH

6

the chef's New York dishes appear here, including the famous burger with black truffles, but the modern French-bistro fare gets a local angle, with grilled wild salmon and Fraser Valley pork chops paired with snap peas. On a sunny day the patio is a popular lunch or brunch destination. ⊠ *2551 W. Broadway, Kitsilano* ☎ *604/739–7115* ⊕ *www.dbbistro.ca* ⊟ *AE, DC, MC, V* ⊘ *No lunch Mon.* ✢ *B1.*

$–$$
ASIAN
✕ **The Flying Tiger.** Inspired by the street foods of Asia, this laid-back lounge has a menu that roams from the Philippines to Thailand to Singapore and beyond. Start with a creative cocktail, perhaps the Bengal Breeze (rum, mint, coconut syrup, and fresh lime juice), or a glass of B.C. wine, and sample a range of small plates, including crisp *panko*-crusted squid, petite pancakes heaped with duck confit and fresh herbs, or smoked B.C. sablefish paired with green-papaya salad. It's a fun place to come with a group, but solos are welcome, too. ⊠ *2958 West 4th Ave., Kitsilano* ☎ *604/737–7529* ⊕ *www.theflyingtiger.ca* ⊟ *AE, MC, V* ⊘ *No lunch* ✢ *A1.*

¢–$
VEGETARIAN
✕ **Foundation Lounge.** The interior at this East Side vegetarian joint—mismatched Formica tables, 1950s-style vinyl chairs, a cinder-block bar—may not win design prizes, and the service can be rather laid-back, but the bohemian vibe is friendly and the meat-free fare is tasty. Try the satay salad—mixed greens, tofu, and broccoli topped with a warm, tangy peanut sauce—or opt for a hearty veggie burger or the tofu-and-mango scramble. This storefront restaurant is hopping from midday until 1 AM. ⊠ *2301 Main St., Main St./Mt. Pleasant* ☎ *604/708–0881* ⊟ *MC, V* ✢ *B5.*

$–$$
SEAFOOD
✕ **Go Fish.** If the weather's fine, head for this seafood stand on the docks near Granville Island. It's owned by Gord Martin, of Bin 941/942 fame, so it's not your ordinary chippie. The menu is short—highlights include fish-and-chips, grilled salmon or tuna sandwiches, and fish tacos—but the quality is first-rate. It's hugely popular, and on sunny summer days, the waits can be maddening, so try to avoid the busiest times: noon to 2 PM and 5 PM to closing (which is at dusk). Since there are just a few (outdoor) tables, be prepared to take your food to go. To get here, walk along the waterfront path from Granville Island; by car, drive east from Burrard Street on 1st Avenue until it ends at the docks. ⊠ *1505 W. 1st Ave., Fisherman's Wharf, Kitsilano* ☎ *604/730–5039* ⊕ *www.bin941.com* ⊟ *MC, V* ⊘ *Closed Mon. No dinner* ✢ *A3.*

$–$$
ETHIOPIAN
✕ **Harambe.** The name means "working together" in Swahili, and the family that owns this welcoming restaurant works together to introduce guests to Ethiopia's traditional fare. Savory stews are served atop platter-size pancakes of *injera*, a tangy, almost spongy flatbread that becomes your utensil—you scoop up the stew with pieces of the bread. Order a combination platter to sample a range of flavors; the vegetarian version, which includes spinach, lentils, peas, assorted vegetables, and salad, is

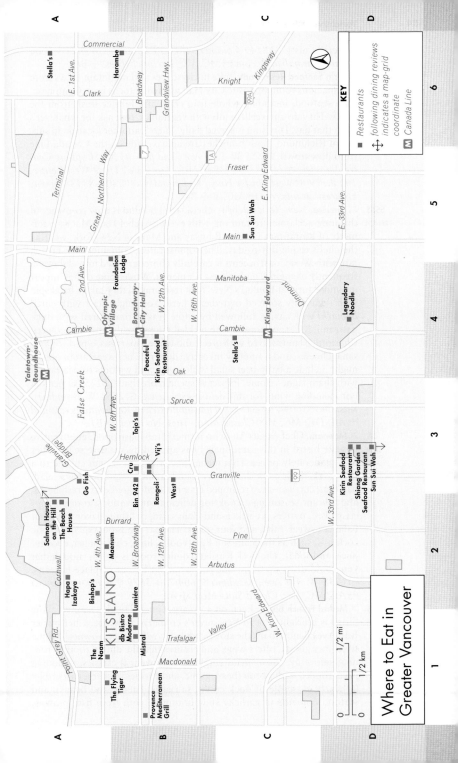

Where to Eat in Greater Vancouver

KEY

- ■ Restaurants
- ↔ following dining reviews indicates a map-grid coordinate
- Ⓜ Canada Line

Restaurants (by map position)

Row A
- Stella's
- Harambe

Row B
- Foundation Lodge
- Olympic Village Ⓜ
- Broadway–City Hall Ⓜ
- Tojo's
- Cru
- Bin 942
- Rangoli
- West
- Vij's
- Hemlock
- Go Fish
- Salmon House on the Hill
- The Beach House
- Maenam
- Hapa Izakaya
- Bishop's
- The Naam
- db Bistro Moderne
- Lumière
- Mistral
- The Flying Tiger
- Provence Mediterranean Grill

Row C
- Sun Sui Wah
- Main
- Peaceful
- Kirin Seafood Restaurant
- Stella's
- Kirin Seafood Restaurant
- Shiang Garden Seafood Restaurant
- Sun Sui Wah

Row D
- King Edward Ⓜ
- Legendary Noodle

Map labels

- Commercial
- E. 1st Ave.
- Clark
- E. Broadway
- Grandview Hwy.
- Knight
- Kingsway
- Fraser
- E. King Edward
- E. 33rd Ave.
- 99A
- 1A
- 7
- Main
- Manitoba
- W. 12th Ave.
- W. 16th Ave.
- Cambie
- 2nd Ave.
- Great Northern Way
- Terminal
- Yaletown–Roundhouse Ⓜ
- False Creek
- Granville Bridge
- W. 6th Ave.
- Spruce
- Oak
- Granville
- 99
- W. 33rd Ave.
- Pine
- Arbutus
- Valley
- W. King Edward
- Trafalgar
- Macdonald
- Burrard
- W. 4th Ave.
- W. Broadway
- W. 12th Ave.
- W. 16th Ave.
- Cornwall
- Point Grey Rd.
- KITSILANO
- Dumont

Scale: 1/2 mi / 1/2 km

especially tasty. ✉ *2149 Commercial Dr., East Side* ☎ *604/216–1060* ⊕ *www.harambecafe.com* ⊟ *MC, V* ✆ *No lunch Tues.* ✛ *B6.*

$$–$$$
CHINESE

✕**Kirin Seafood Restaurant.** Take in cityscapes and mountain views from this spacious room opposite City Hall where the focus is on Cantonese-style seafood, including whole fish, crab, and lobster fresh from the tanks. They do an excellent job with vegetables, too; ask for whatever's fresh that day. Dim sum is served daily. There's another location in suburban Richmond. Both branches are an easy ride on the Canada Line from downtown. ✉ *555 W. 12th Ave., 2nd fl., City Sq. Shopping Centre, Fairview* ☎ *604/879–8038* ⊟ *MC, V* ✛ *D3* ✉ *Three West Centre, 2nd fl., 7900 Westminster Hwy., Richmond* ☎ *604/303–8833* ⊕ *www.kirinrestaurants.com* ⊟ *MC, V* ✛ *B4.*

$$$$
FRENCH

✕**Lumière.** New York celebrity-chef Daniel Boulud is now co-owner of this long-acclaimed restaurant, with executive chef Dale MacKay, formerly of Restaurant Gordon Ramsay and Maze in New York, wearing the chef's toque day-to-day. The sophisticated, contemporary French fare with West Coast accents is carefully choreographed into elaborate, frequently changing, multicourse set menus. While some dishes appear in similar form at Boulud's New York restaurants, they take a local spin with regionally sourced ingredients here. You might start with cured *hamachi* with caviar, followed by a foie gras terrine paired with duck pastrami, B.C. spot prawns with pickled ramps, halibut from the Queen Charlotte Islands served with green and white asparagus, a plate of artisanal cheeses, and a suitably inventive dessert. Their vegetarian option might include a baby-beet salad with greens and walnuts or pea ravioli with champagne velouté. Expect to spend more than C$125 per person, not including wine, for this deluxe experience. ✉ *2551 W. Broadway, Kitsilano* ☎ *604/739–8185* ⊕ *www.lumiere.ca* ✍ *Reservations essential* ⊟ *AE, DC, MC, V* ✆ *Closed Mon.–Tues. No lunch* ✛ *B1.*

$$
THAI

✕**Maenam.** Chef Angus An (who formerly ran Gastropod, an inventive upscale bistro in this same space) has applied his creative sensibilities to a moderately priced Thai menu that brings this Asian cuisine to a new level. While some dishes may sound familiar—green papaya salad, pad thai, curries—they're amped up with local ingredients, fresh herbs, and vibrant seasonings. Look for delicious innovations, too: perhaps crispy B.C. oysters, a chicken-and-clam salad, or "three flavor fish" that balances sweet, salty, and sour tastes. The bar sends out equally exotic cocktails, such as the Siam Sun Ray (vodka, lime, chili, ginger, coconut juice, and soda). The sleek Kitsilano dining room is stylish enough that you could dress up a bit, but you wouldn't be out of place in jeans. ✉ *1938 W. 4th Ave., Kitsilano* ☎ *604/730–5579* ⊕ *www.maenam.ca* ⊟ *AE, MC, V* ✆ *Closed Sun.–Mon.* ✛ *A2.*

$$–$$$
FRENCH

✕**Mistral French Bistro.** Even on a dreary winter day, this sunny-yellow bistro is a bright spot in Vancouver's culinary landscape. Chef-owner Jean-Yves Benoît mans the stoves, while his wife (and co-owner) Minna welcomes guests, offers wine, and ensures that the dining room is running smoothly. Their menu emphasizes Provençal classics, including pasta topped with *pistou* (basil, garlic, and Parmesan cheese), *cassoulet* (a hearty casserole of duck confit, sausages, bacon, and beans), and seafood *bourride* (a garlicky stew brimming with fresh fish, prawns,

KEBAB QUEST

Among the many ethnic groups that have settled in greater Vancouver is a large Persian community, centered on the North Shore. Wander along North Vancouver's Lonsdale Avenue between 13th and 19th streets, and you can catch glimpses of Persian culture—and sample Persian tastes.

Start at Yaas Bazaar (⊠ *1860 Lonsdale Ave., North Vancouver* ☎ *604/990–9006* ⊕ *www.yaas.ca*), part grocery store and part good-value cafeteria, where you can pick up olives, feta cheese, and chewy sesame-topped breads for a picnic, or lunch on savory kebabs, stews, or one of the daily specials.

Looking for sweets? Head to Golestan Bakery (⊠ *1554 Lonsdale Ave., North Vancouver* ☎ *604/990–7767*), where the Persian pastries

include rosewater-scented baklava. At Ayoub's Dried Fruits and Nuts (⊠ *1332 Lonsdale Ave., North Vancouver* ☎ *604/982–9682* ⊕ *www. ayoubsdriedfruitsandnuts.com*), the freshly roasted pistachios, almonds, and watermelon seeds make good snacks, too.

For a sit-down Persian dining experience, venture out of the Lonsdale area. At locally popular Kashkool (⊠ *222 Pemberton Ave., North Vancouver* ☎ *604/904–3904*), the specialty is hearty stews, such as *fesenjan* (seasoned with saffron, walnuts, and pomegranate) or *gheymeh* (with split peas, crispy potatoes, and dried lime). Another good choice is Shalizar (⊠ *1863 Marine Dr., West Vancouver* ☎ *604/921–9500* ⊕ *www. shalizar.ca*), where stews, kebabs, and salads are also on the menu.

and scallops). The lunch menu includes soups and salads along with more substantial fare—the better to keep the rain at bay. ⊠ *2585 W. Broadway, Kitsilano* ☎ *604/733–0046* ⊕ *www.mistralbistro.ca* ▭ *AE, MC, V* ☻ *Closed Sun. and Mon.* ✢ *B1.*

$-$$ ✕ **The Naam.** Vancouverites have a love-hate relationship with the city's
VEGETARIAN oldest natural-foods eatery. Some go gaga for the famous baked fries with miso gravy and pack the wooden tables for the Thai noodle dishes, burritos, enchiladas, wicked chocolate desserts, and fresh-squeezed juices, while others grumble that this aging hippie is past its prime. Still, live blues, folk, and jazz most evenings keep things homey, and if you need to satisfy a late-night craving for a veggie burger, rest easy—the Naam is open 24 hours. Reservations are accepted only for groups of six or more and only between Monday and Thursday. ⊠ *2724 W. 4th Ave., Kitsilano* ☎ *604/738–7151* ⊕ *www.thenaam.com* ▭ *AE, DC, MC, V* ✢ *A1.*

$-$$ ✕ **Peaceful Restaurant.** Hop on the Canada Line to the Broadway/City
CHINESE Hall station to reach this modest and, yes, relatively peaceful, storefront eatery. Northern Chinese dishes are the specialty here, particularly the hand-pulled noodles that the cooks knead and stretch in the open kitchen. Other good choices are the mustard-seed vegetable salad (crisp shredded vegetables fired up with hot mustard), Szechuan green beans, cumin-scented lamb, and any of the dumplings; vegetarians also have plenty of options. They'll make more Westernized dishes, too, if beef with broccoli or kung pao chicken are your thing, but the helpful staff

are happy to guide you to more authentic Mandarin fare. ✉ *532 W. Broadway, Cambie* ☎ *604/879–9878* ⊕ *www.peacefulrestaurant.com* ☰ *MC, V* ✢ *B4.*

$$
INDIAN
✗ **Rangoli.** Next door to Vij's, and under the same ownership, this storefront bistro serves similarly innovative Indian fare in a much more relaxed environment. Nab a table on the sidewalk or in the small but modern interior space, and sample grilled chicken marinated in tamarind and yogurt; Indian-scented pulled pork served with sautéed greens; or a curry of portobello mushrooms and red peppers paired with a beet salad. Wash it all down with ginger lemonade or a mango *lassi.* ✉ *1488 W. 11th Ave., South Granville* ☎ *604/736–5711* ⊕ *www.vijsrangoli.ca* ⌦ *Reservations not accepted* ☰ *MC, V* ✢ *B3.*

$$$–$$$$
SEAFOOD
✗ **Salmon House on the Hill.** Perched halfway up a mountain, this restaurant has stunning water and city views by day and expansive vistas of city lights by night. It's best known for its alder-grilled salmon, though the grilled oysters, British Columbia prawns, and selections from the "Uniquely B.C." menu—three courses with ingredients locally sourced—are also tempting (you can opt for companion pairings of B.C. wines as well). The Northwest Coast First Nations–theme interior is tastefully done, though it can hardly compete with what's outside the windows. The Salmon House is about 30 minutes from Vancouver by car (depending on traffic). Go over the Lions Gate Bridge, follow the signs to Highway 1 west, then take the Folkestone Way exit off Highway 1. ✉ *2229 Folkestone Way, West Vancouver* ☎ *604/926–3212* ⊕ *www. salmonhouse.com* ☰ *AE, DC, MC, V* ⊘ *No lunch weekdays* ✢ *A2.*

$–$$
CHINESE
✗ **Shiang Garden Seafood Restaurant.** Dim sum aficionados make the trek to this upscale Cantonese restaurant in suburban Richmond for some of the tastiest tidbits in town. Order from the menu (there are no carts circling the dining rooms), or just point at what the other tables are having. In the evenings, Hong Kong–style seafood is the specialty. The multilevel restaurant, which is popular with Asian families, is in a shopping plaza, set back from No. 3 Road at Leslie Road. ✉ *4540 No. 3 Rd., Richmond* ☎ *604/273–8858* ☰ *DC, MC, V* ✢ *D3.*

$–$$
ECLECTIC
✗ **Stella's.** If you're looking for a bite and a brew while browsing Commercial Drive or Cambie Street, join the locals at these comfortable hangouts. Belgian beers are featured, so check the "fresh sheet" for current offerings. At the Commercial Drive location, the tapas-style menu of eclectic small plates rambles the world, from fried tofu with a sweet soy-*sambal* sauce, to achiote-rubbed steak tacos, or Belgian *poutine* (fried potatoes with cheese curds and gravy). At the Cambie branch, the offerings fall into more conventional starter-main-dessert classifications and focus on regional ingredients. At midday, both kitchens turn out less-exotic-but-still-worthy sandwiches and salads. ✉ *1191 Commercial Dr., East Side* ☎ *604/254–2437* ⊕ *www.stellasbeer.com* ☰ *MC, V* ✢ *C4* ✉ *3305 Cambie St., Cambie* ☎ *604/874–6900* ✢ *A6.*

$$–$$$
CHINESE
✗ **Sun Sui Wah Seafood Restaurant.** This bustling Cantonese restaurant with locations on the East Side and in suburban Richmond is best known for its excellent dim sum (served 10–3 daily), which ranges from traditional handmade dumplings to some highly adventurous fare. Dinner specialties include roasted squab marinated in the restaurant's secret

Chefs prepare regional Canadian cuisine at the popular restaurant West.

spice blend and king crab plucked live from the tanks, then steamed with garlic. ⊠ *3888 Main St., Main St./Mt. Pleasant* ☎ *604/872–8822 or 866/872–8822* ⊕ *www.sunsuiwah.com* ▭ *AE, DC, MC, V* ⊕ *D3* ⊠ *4940 No. 3 Rd., Richmond* ☎ *604/273–8208 or 866/683–8208* ⊕ *www.sunsuiwah.com* ▭ *AE, DC, MC, V* ⊕ *C5.*

$$$–$$$$ ✕ **Tojo's.** Hidekazu Tojo is a sushi-making legend in Vancouver, with
JAPANESE   thousands of special preparations stored in his creative mind. In this strikingly modern, high-ceilinged space, complete with a separate sake lounge, the prime perch is at Tojo's sushi bar, a convivial ringside seat for watching the creation of edible art. The best way to experience Tojo's creativity is to reserve a spot at the sushi bar and order *omakase* (chef's choice); chef Tojo will keep offering you wildly more adventurous fare, both raw and cooked, until you cry uncle. Budget a minimum of C$60 per person (before drinks) for the omakase option; tabs topping C$110 per person are routine. ⊠ *1133 W. Broadway, Fairview* ☎ *604/872–8050* ⊕ *www.tojos.com* ⌁ *Reservations essential* ▭ *AE, DC, MC, V* ☉ *Closed Sun. No lunch* ⊕ *B3.*

$$$ ✕ **Vij's.** At Vancouver's most innovative Indian restaurant, genial pro-
INDIAN   prietor Vikram Vij and his wife and business partner Meeru Dhalwala
Fodor's Choice   use local ingredients to create exciting takes on South Asian cuisine.
★   Dishes such as lamb "popsicles" in a creamy fenugreek-scented curry, or B.C. spot prawns and halibut with black chickpeas, are far from traditional but are spiced beautifully. If you're adventurous, start with the cricket *paranta*, a spicy flatbread made from, yes, ground crickets. Mr. Vij circulates through the room, which is decorated with Indian antiques and whimsical elephant-pattern lanterns, greeting guests and suggesting dishes or cocktail pairings. Expect to cool your heels at the

bar sipping chai or a cold beer while you wait for a table (lineups of more than an hour are common), but if you like creative Indian fare, it's worth it. ⊠ *1480 W. 11th Ave., South Granville* ☎ *604/736–6664* ⊕ *www.vijs.ca* ⌂ *Reservations not accepted* ▤ *AE, DC, MC, V* ⊗ *No lunch* ✛ *B3.*

$$$$
MODERN
CANADIAN
Fodor'sChoice
★

✕ **West.** Contemporary regional cuisine is the theme at this chic restaurant, one of the city's most innovative dining rooms. Among the kitchen's creations are octopus, quinoa, and black tobiko salad; smoked sablefish with Tarbais beans and watermelon radishes; and sake-braised pork cheeks served with plum puree, broccolini, and späetzle. There's an extensive selection of cheeses and decadent desserts that might include a mascarpone–espresso cake or a frozen lime parfait served on a coconut macaroon with fresh strawberries. If you can't decide, opt for one of the elaborate multicourse tasting menus (C$89–C$98). Marble floors, high ceilings, and warm caramel leather set into red walls make the space feel simultaneously energetic and cozy. ⊠ *2881 Granville St., South Granville* ☎ *604/738–8938* ⊕ *www.westrestaurant.com* ▤ *AE, DC, MC, V* ⊗ *No lunch weekends* ✛ *B3.*

Vancouver
Where to Stay

WORD OF MOUTH

"One of the best things about the Sylvia is the location . . . and the service was always excellent. This is an old building so definitely expect quirks. The room was comfortable and clean and a good value for the money. We really enjoyed our stay and would highly recommend the Sylvia for anyone visiting Vancouver."

—laustic

VANCOUVER WHERE TO STAY PLANNER

Apartment Rentals

Although the trend toward self-catered apartment suites began long before the recent era of economic woe, it really struck gold in Vancouver with the 2010 Winter Olympics. Some agencies have minimum stays. Options sometimes include housekeeping services, satellite TV or Wi-Fi availability, and other options. The site ⊕ www.makeyourselfathome. com (☎ 604/874–7817) provides a terrific range of private homes and suites available for short-term rentals; this site is especially good for last-minute bookings. On the higher end of the spectrum, head for ⊕ www. dreamvacationrent.com and its many luxury condominiums and executive homes.

Complimentary Transportation

Some properties have complimentary bicycles, others extend free limo services to the theater, or pickups when you've shopped yourself into the ground. That can be extremely handy, depending on your priorities.

Check-In Times

Check-in/out times vary, but you can usually count on having to be out by noon or 11 AM and getting your key after 3 PM. If they're not running full, most hotels will extend checkout by an hour or two if asked nicely and, at the very least, will stow your bags (gratis) for an afternoon.

Hotel Features

Unless stated in the review, hotels are equipped with elevators, and all guest rooms have air-conditioning, TV, telephone, and private bathroom. Internet (meaning some form of high-speed dial-up) and wireless access are noted when available.

Extra Costs

Most hotels let children under 18 stay free in their parents' room, though you may be charged extra for more than two adults. Parking runs about C$25–C$30 per day at downtown hotels, and is usually free outside the downtown core. Watch out for phone and Internet charges, which can add up. You'll also be charged a 10% accommodations tax and a 5% Goods and Services Tax (GST).

WHAT IT COSTS IN CANADIAN DOLLARS					
	¢	$	$$	$$$	$$$$
FOR TWO PEOPLE	under C$75	C$75–C$125	C$126–C$175	C$176–C$250	over C$250

Prices are for a standard double room in high season, excluding 10% room tax and 5% GST.

BEST BETS FOR VANCOUVER LODGING

Fodor's offers a selective listing of quality lodging experiences in every price range, from the city's best budget beds to its most sophisticated luxury hotels. Here, we've compiled our top recommendations by price and experience. The very best properties—in other words, those that provide a particularly remarkable experience in their price range—are designated in the listings with the Fodor's Choice logo.

Fodor's Choice ★

L'Hermitage Hotel, p. 168

Opus Hotel, p. 179

Sylvia Hotel, p. 177

Wedgewood Hotel & Spa, p. 173

By Price

$$$$

Fairmont Pacific Rim, p. 164

Pan Pacific Hotel, p. 169

Shangri-la Hotel, p. 171

Wedgewood Hotel & Spa, p. 173

Westin Bayshore Resort and Marina, p. 177

$$$

Barclay House in the West End, p. 174

$$

Sylvia Hotel, p. 177

The Victorian Hotel, p. 173

By Experience

FOR FAMILIES

Lord Stanley Suites on the Park, p. 176

Pacific Palisades Hotel, p. 176

Renaissance Vancouver Hotel Harbourside, p. 171

MOST CENTRAL

Fairmont Hotel Vancouver, p. 163

Four Seasons, p. 164

Wedgewood Hotel & Spa, p. 173

BEST HISTORIC CONVERSION

St. Regis Hotel, p. 172

MOST DOG-FRIENDLY

Fairmont Hotel Vancouver, p. 163

Fairmont Waterfront, p. 164

Opus Hotel, p. 179

Pacific Palisades Hotel, p. 176

Sheraton Vancouver Wall Centre, p. 171

MOST ROMANTIC

Barclay House in the West End, p. 174

Wedgewood Hotel & Spa, p. 173

HIPPEST 'N HOTTEST

L'Hermitage Hotel, p. 168

Loden Hotel, p. 168

Opus Hotel, p. 179

St. Regis Hotel, p. 172

BEST SPA

Century Plaza Hotel & Spa (Spa at the Century), p. 163

Pan Pacific Hotel (Spa Utopia), p. 169

Shangri-la Hotel (Chi Spa), p. 171

Sheraton Vancouver Wall Centre (Vida Spa), p. 171

BEST B&B

Granville House B&B, p. 179

7

By Chris
McBeath

Although Vancouver is a pretty compact city, each area has a distinct character and accommodation options. From uber-hip boutique hotels to heritage bed-and-breakfasts to sharp-angled glass-and-mirror towers, there are lodging choices for every style and neighborhood, whether it's the center of fashionista shopping, gracious tree-lined boulevards near Stanley Park, or the pulsing heart of the city's core.

Although the 2010 Winter Olympics spurred enough construction to change the face of Vancouver in just a handful of years, the city has managed to retain, and make the most of, some of its defining characteristics. For example, Vancouver is an extremely outdoorsy community, so hotel amenities can sometimes include free bicycles and free ski storage, and many hotel concierges can put you in contact with hiking and running groups who welcome visitors.

The city is also extremely pet friendly, especially when it comes to dogs, as evidenced by the number of dog-friendly services in hotels and around town—specialty dog delis (we're talking all-natural dog cookies, not hot dogs), doggie beaches (Ambleside in West Vancouver being the top one), special dog stay overs (⊕ *www.petsinthecity.ca*), and the packs of dogs you'll see parked outside a Starbucks while the professional walker grabs a java. Not only can you bring your pet with you to many of these properties, some even let you borrow *their* dog for a walk (check out the Fairmont Hotel Vancouver, for instance).

The local penchant for living a healthy lifestyle has also given rise to some top-quality spas, the scope of which reflects the cultural mosaic of the city: services covering the spectrum of indigenous practices from, say, Hawaiian Lomi Lomi to therapies incorporating Traditional Chinese Medicine, European treatments, and everything in between. In the hotel industry, it's become a question of "have a spa or lose a guest," and Vancouver hotels have certainly risen to the challenge.

Hotels with a water view are coveted and book up well in advance, as do some of the heritage B&Bs you'll find in the more fashionable neighborhoods, like the West End.

DOWNTOWN

Use the coordinate (✛ B2) at the end of each listing to locate a site on the corresponding map.

$$$–$$$$ 🏨 **Century Plaza Hotel & Spa.** Full kitchens and an indoor pool make this 30-story downtown high-rise a good family choice. The contemporary marble-tile lobby doesn't convey much warmth, and the predominantly taupe and mushroom tones are rather bland. All the amenities are here, though, including a highly rated full-service spa with lots of value-added facilities like steam rooms and an ozonated pool. The pricier one-bedroom suites are enlivened with French doors and spa-like bathrooms. Corner suites have balconies, and north-facing rooms above the seventh floor have mountain and ocean views. The hotel is also home to Yuk Yuks comedy club, and on most Friday and Saturday nights the restaurant clears some of the hardwood floors for dancing to DJ music. **Pros:** the spa; on-site entertainment; large rooms. **Cons:** an average-quality hotel trying to be a bit grand. ✉ *1015 Burrard St., Downtown* 🕾 *604/687–0575 or 800/663–1818* ⊕ *www.century-plaza. com* ⤳ *135 rooms, 135 suites* ⚒ *In-room: Kitchen (some), refrigerator, DVD (some), Wi-Fi (some). In-hotel: Restaurant, bar, pool, spa, laundry facilities, laundry service, Internet terminal, Wi-Fi, parking (paid), some pets allowed* ▤ *AE, DC, MC, V* ✛ *D4.*

$$$–$$$$ 🏨 **Delta Vancouver Suites.** Attached to a conference center, this business-oriented, all-suites hotel exudes a New York–modern, almost art deco, chic. The striking marble-and-cherrywood lobby soars three stories high. Although the suites aren't large, the minimalist blond furnishings, efficient layout—work stations are ergonomically designed—and floor-to-ceiling windows in most rooms create a sense of space. In-room spa services are offered, helping to make up for the lack of an on-site spa. The hotel's restaurant, Manhattan ($–$$$), is away from the madding crowd. **Pros:** central location; great restaurant; windows that actually open. **Cons:** one-way roads make getting here by car a bit of a headache. ✉ *550 W. Hastings St., vehicle entrance on Seymour St., Downtown* 🕾 *604/689–8188* ⊕ *www.deltavancouversuites.ca* ⤳ *225 suites* ⚒ *In-room: Refrigerator, Wi-Fi (some). In-hotel: Restaurant, room service, bar, pool, gym, laundry service, Wi-Fi, parking (paid), some pets allowed* ▤ *AE, D, DC, MC, V* ✛ *F3.*

$$$$ 🏨 **Fairmont Hotel Vancouver.** The copper roof of this 1939 château-style hotel dominates Vancouver's skyline, and the hotel itself is considered the city's gracious grande dame, redone to its original elegance. Guest rooms vary in size, but even the standard rooms have an aura of prestige, with high ceilings, lush draperies, and 19th-century-style mahogany furniture. Two friendly dogs (Mavis and Boe) are on hand for petting and walking, and the full-service spa here was Canada's first to cater to men, with big-screen TVs, Wi-Fi, and black-leather pedicure chairs; women are welcome, though. **Pros:** the male-oriented spa; great location for shopping; the architecture. **Cons:** diversity of "standard" room sizes can be irritating if you're expecting a room similar to the one you stayed in before. ✉ *900 W. Georgia St., Downtown* 🕾 *604/684–3131* ⊕ *www.fairmont.com/hotelvancouver* ⤳ *556 rooms, 37 suites* ⚒ *In-*

room: Refrigerator (some), Internet. In-hotel: 2 restaurants, room service, bar, pool, gym, spa, laundry service, Wi-Fi, parking (paid), some pets allowed ⊟ *AE, D, DC, MC, V* ✛ *E3.*

$$$$ ☷ **Fairmont Pacific Rim.** This third Fairmont hotel in Vancouver proper (a fourth Fairmont is at the Vancouver International Airport) is slated to be open by early 2010. Set right on the downtown waterfront, the 47-story tower represents the chain's first foray into the condominium-hotel format. The multimillion-dollar units embody extravagance, with their lavish views, swank design, tall windows, and plush amenities that include a signature Willow Stream spa, use of a private yacht, and chauffeur services. As of this writing, every indicator points to a rockin' product. **Pros:** location; we expect the usual high quality of Fairmont properties. **Cons:** pricey. ✉ *1038 Canada Pl., Downtown* ☏ *604/895–0612* ⊕ *www.fairmont.com/pacificrim* ⤳ *37 suites, 340 rooms* ♿ *In-room: Safe, refrigerator, Internet. In-hotel: Restaurant, room service, bar, pool, gym, laundry service, Wi-Fi, parking (paid), some pets allowed* ⊟ *AE, DC, MC, V* ✛ *F2.*

$$$$ ☷ **Fairmont Waterfront.** This luxuriously modern 23-story hotel is across the street from the Convention and Exhibition Centre and the Canada Place cruise-ship terminal, but it's the floor-to-ceiling windows with ocean, park, and mountain views in most guest rooms that really make this hotel special. Adorned with blond-wood furniture and contemporary Canadian artwork, each room also has a window that opens. Elevator waits can be frustrating so consider asking for a room on a lower floor, though you'll be sacrificing a view for this minor convenience. Next to the mountain-view pool is a rooftop herb garden—an aromatic retreat open to guests that includes a number of beehives, which are harvested on Friday afternoons (the honey is used in ganache truffles and honey-basil cocktails). The hotel's canine ambassador, Holly, is usually available for petting, pampering, and taking for strolls. **Pros:** harbor views; proximity to cruise-ship terminal; the lovely terraced pool near the patio herb garden; fresh honey products. **Cons:** long elevator queues; the seemingly always-busy lobby lounge; the garden patio if you're at all bee phobic. ✉ *900 Canada Pl. Way, Downtown* ☏ *604/691–1991* ⊕ *www.fairmont.com/waterfront* ⤳ *489 rooms, 29 suites* ♿ *In-room: Safe (some), kitchen (some), refrigerator, Internet. In-hotel: Restaurant, room service, bar, pool, gym, laundry service, Wi-Fi, parking (paid), some pets allowed* ⊟ *AE, D, DC, MC, V* ✛ *F2.*

$$$$ ☷ **Four Seasons.** Although this 29-story downtown luxury hotel is famous for pampering guests, recent upgrades to the registration area are rather bland. Gone are the oversized fresh flowers that once stated "elegant arrival". The focus now seems to be the hotel's Yew restaurant, a lively bistro-style affair that's partially hidden behind a large slatted wall so guests don't perceive any spillover buzz or excitement. Standard rooms, with understated color schemes, marble bathroom fixtures, and tall windows with city views, are spacious and traditionally furnished, as are the even more spacious corner rooms with sitting areas. Service is top-notch. **Pros:** premier location for shopping; Four Seasons service standards. **Cons:** no on-site spa. ✉ *791 W. Georgia St., vehicle entrance on Howe St., Downtown* ☏ *604/689–9333* ⊕ *www.fourseasons.com*

WHERE SHOULD I STAY?

	Vibe	Pros	Cons
Downtown (Robson to the Waterfront)	Central commercial/financial district hotels are mostly mid- to high-end, catering to tourists and business travelers. Low- to midprice hotels are on Granville Street, south of Robson.	Within walking distance of nearly all downtown sights and handy to the Canada Place cruise-ship terminal.	A little dull come evening as few people live in the area, but Granville Street, south of Robson, is lined with bars, clubs, and movie theaters.
West End/ Stanley Park	A lovely tree-filled, gay-friendly residential neighborhood close to downtown. Hotels in all price ranges are on the main arteries; historic hotels and B&Bs are on the side streets.	A pleasant alternative to the central business district. The beach at English Bay is the West End's hot spot for people-watching and casual dining.	Could be too quiet for some folks.
West Side	A combination of neighborhoods from tony Kerrisdale, to old-money Shaughnessy, to gentrified (partially hippie) Kitsilano, as well as Granville Island, and Point Grey.	Handy to beaches, the University of British Columbia campus, parks and gardens, and close to great shopping along West 4th Avenue and South Granville.	You may feel "out of the action" since these are residential areas. Although bus transit is excellent, having a car makes navigation easier.
Yaletown	Also on the downtown peninsula, this is where urban chic translates into New York–style loft apartments, beneath which lie trendy restaurants and boutique shops.	Lots of hip shopping and restaurants nearby, and a short ferry ride to Granville Island.	Sidewalks can be noisy; this is one of the most densely populated, high-rise areas of the city.

7

🛏 *306 rooms, 66 suites* ⌂ *In-room: Safe, refrigerator, Internet. In-hotel: Restaurant, room service, bar, pool, gym, laundry service, Wi-Fi, parking (paid), some pets allowed* ▭ *AE, DC, MC, V* ⊕ *E3.*

$$$$ ▦ **Hotel Le Soleil.** The staff at this classy, business-district boutique hotel prides itself on attentive personal service. The golden color scheme and intimate fireplace in the neoclassical lobby and the vibrant gold-and-crimson fabrics in the guest rooms—most are small suites—radiate warmth. Luxurious touches abound, such as 300-thread-count Egyptian cotton sheets and marble bathrooms. The Copper Chimney restaurant adds a New York–inspired bistro flair. Two penthouse suites have 24-foot ceilings and wraparound terraces. The hotel doesn't have a pool or fitness facilities, but you have access to the extensive facilities at the YWCA next door for a fee. **Pros:** chic; romantic; central location. **Cons:** no on-site spa or health club. ✉ *567 Hornby St., Downtown* ☎ *604/632–3000 or 877/632–3030* ⊕ *www.hotellesoleil.com* 🛏 *10 rooms, 109 suites* ⌂ *In-room: Safe, refrigerator, Wi-Fi. In-hotel: Restaurant, room service, bar, laundry service, Wi-Fi, parking (paid), some pets allowed* ▭ *AE, DC, MC, V* ⊕ *F2.*

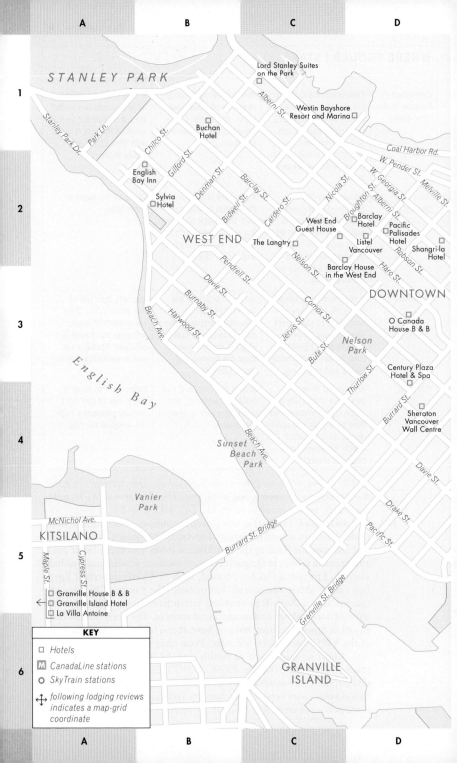

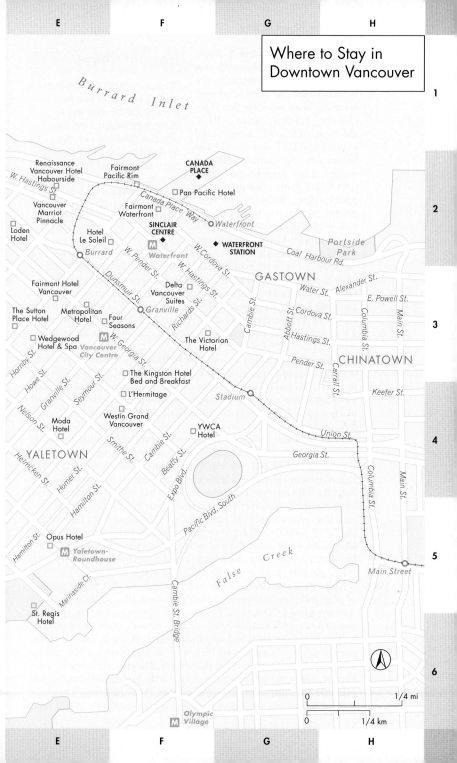

Where to Stay in Downtown Vancouver

Burrard Inlet

CANADA PLACE

Renaissance Vancouver Hotel Habourside
Fairmont Pacific Rim
Pan Pacific Hotel

W. Hastings St.

Vancouver Marriot Pinnacle

Loden Hotel

Fairmont Waterfront
Canada Place Way
Waterfront

Hotel Le Soleil

SINCLAIR CENTRE

Burrard

Waterfront

W. Pender St.
W. Cordova St.
WATERFRONT STATION

Coal Harbour Rd.

Portside Park

GASTOWN

Water St.
Alexander St.

Fairmont Hotel Vancouver

Dunsmuir St.

Delta Vancouver Suites

W. Hastings St.

Cordova St.
E. Powell St.

Columbia St.
Main St.

The Sutton Place Hotel

Metropolitan Hotel

Granville

Richards St.

Cambie St.

Abbott St.

Hastings St.

Four Seasons

W. Georgia St.

The Victorian Hotel

Pender St.

CHINATOWN

Carrall St.

Wedgewood Hotel & Spa

Vancouver City Centre

Hornby St.
Howe St.
Granville St.
Seymour St.

The Kingston Hotel Bed and Breakfast

L'Hermitage

Stadium

Keefer St.

Nelson St.

Moda Hotel

Westin Grand Vancouver

Smithe St.

Cambie St.

YWCA Hotel

Union St.

Columbia St.

Main St.

YALETOWN

Helmcken St.
Homer St.
Hamilton St.

Beatty St.

Expo Blvd.

Georgia St.

Opus Hotel

Hamilton St.

Yaletown-Roundhouse

Marinaside Ct.

Pacific Blvd. South

False Creek

Main Street

St. Regis Hotel

Cambie St. Bridge

Olympic Village

| 0 | | 1/4 mi |
| 0 | | 1/4 km |

$–$$ 🛏 **The Kingston Hotel Bed & Breakfast.** Convenient to shopping and the entertainment district, the family-owned and family-operated Kingston is an old-style four-story elevator building (circa 1910), the type of establishment you'd expect to find in Europe. Small and immaculate, the spartan rooms are decorated in a contemporary style, with flower-pattern bedspreads and pastel colors. Some rooms have private bathrooms; others have a sink in the room and share a bath down the hall. North-facing rooms

overlook a restaurant and bar–patio next door. That's not an issue in wet winter, but in summer the burble of bar talk below might disturb early-to-bed types. **Pros:** great location for the price; Continental breakfast included. **Cons:** some shared bathrooms; limited amenities. ⊠ *757 Richards St., Downtown* 🕿 *604/684–9024 or 888/713–3304* ⊕ *www.kingstonhotelvancouver.com* 🗗 *52 rooms, 13 with bath* 🛁 *In-room: No TV (some), Wi-Fi. In-hotel: Restaurant, bar, laundry facilities, Wi-Fi* 🖃 *AE, MC, V* ⫻ *CP* ✛ *F3.*

$$$–$$$$ 🛏 **L'Hermitage Hotel.** Get beyond the marble floors, silk-velvet fabric
Fodor's Choice walls, and gold-cushion benches in the lobby and you'll discover a
★ warm residential character to this mixed-use condo-boutique hotel. The studio, one-, and two-bedroom suites come with kitchenettes and in some cases fireplaces; faux-leather wall coverings convey an organic feel, and the oversized mirrors from Paris add just the right amount of bling. East-side rooms overlook a pool and garden patio. Breakfast is available in the elegant L'Orangerie guest-only lounge, which leads to a small library and free Internet terminals. Ideally located in the Entertainment District, this is the choice for feeling chicly at home. The hotel has HD satellite. **Pros:** uptown hotel has refreshingly residential vibe; excellent concierge; weekly rates. **Cons:** lacks full-service restaurant (but near many great eateries). ⊠ *788 Richards St., Downtown* 🕿 *778/327–4100 or 888/855–1050* ⊕ *www.lhermitagevancouver.com* 🗗 *40 rooms, 20 suites* 🛁 *In-room: Safe, kitchen, refrigerator, Wi-Fi. In-hotel: Room service, pool, gym, laundry service, Internet terminal, Wi-Fi, parking (paid)* 🖃 *AE, D, DC, MC, V* ✛ *F4.*

$$$$ 🛏 **Loden Hotel.** An ultrasophisticated boutique inn that has all manner of plug-and-play amenities, including in-room iPod stations and TVs with oversized LCD screens. Floor-to-ceiling windows fill the spacious guest rooms with natural light—and if you slide open the bathroom half wall you can enjoy the views from the soaker tub. The Voya restaurant has an Asian-infused French menu and a retro 1940s design with lots of mirrors and crystal chandeliers. The glitter continues on the outside, where the reflective glass covering the building creates the illusion that it's constructed entirely of mirrors. **Pros:** the lounge's intimacy lends it to discreet rendezvous; side-of-center location is a real find.

Cons: limited spa services; dark lobby. ✉ *1177 Melville St., Downtown* ☎ *604/669–5060 or 877/225–6336* ⊕ *www.theloden.com* ⟿ *70 rooms, 7 suites* ⌂ *In-room: Safe, refrigerator, Wi-Fi. In-hotel: Restaurant, room service, bar, gym, spa, laundry service, Wi-Fi, parking (paid), some pets allowed* ☰ *AE, D, DC, MC, V* ⊹ *E2.*

$$$$ ⊓ **Metropolitan Hotel.** Two lions guard the entrance, and a striking antique gold-leaf temple carving graces the lobby of this full-service business-district hotel. The spacious rooms, all designed according to the principles of feng shui, are decorated in muted colors, and even the standard rooms have luxurious extras, such as cozy duvets and Italian-made Frette bathrobes. Executive king and business-class rooms have printers, fax machines, and ergometric chairs. Extensive fitness facilities include heated pool, squash court, steam room, and a putting green on a third-floor terrace. Although shops are right outside the door, use the Jaguar limo-service for rides to the theater or Stanley Park. The restaurant, Diva ($$$–$$$$), is one of the city's finest, with a wine list offering some 225 selections. **Pros:** top-notch restaurant. **Cons:** a bit pretentious. ✉ *645 Howe St., Downtown* ☎ *604/687–1122 or 800/667–2300* ⊕ *www.metropolitan.com* ⟿ *104 rooms, 18 suites* ⌂ *In-room: Safe, refrigerator, Internet. In-hotel: Restaurant, room service, bar, pool, gym, laundry service, Wi-Fi, parking (paid), some pets allowed* ☰ *AE, D, DC, MC, V* ⊹ *E3.*

$$–$$$ ⊓ **Moda Hotel.** Situated kitty-corner to the opulent Orpheum Theatre and a major office supplies outlet, it's easy to bypass this boutique hotel that celebrated its 100th anniversary in 2008. Renovations have restored and modernized some of the building's original architectural features—such as recessed ceilings, gold-painted sconces, and a 1920s-style black-and-white tile floor in the lobby. Rooms are minimalist, modern, and comfortable. Be sure to ask for the quieter back-of-house units overlooking a parking lot; the hotel sits on an intersection of two busy transit arteries that rumble into the early morning. The hotel's Uva restaurants doubles as a coffee bistro by date and a wine bar at night. **Pros:** good value for location; nicely renovated; discounted parking. **Cons:** noisy intersection; older building; limited guest services. ✉ *900 Seymour St., Downtown* ☎ *604/683–4251* ⊕ *www.modahotel.ca* ⟿ *57 rooms* ⌂ *In-room: Safe, Wi-Fi. In-hotel: Restaurant, bar, laundry service, parking (paid), some pets allowed* ☰ *AE, MC, V* ⊹ *E4.*

$$$$ ⊓ **Pan Pacific Hotel.** A centerpiece of waterfront Canada Place, the luxurious Pan Pacific shares a complex with the Vancouver Convention and Exhibition Centre and Vancouver's main cruise-ship terminal. Rooms are large and modern with maple wood throughout, Italian linens, and stunning ocean, mountain, or skyline views, all of which have been enjoyed by a star-studded list of royals, celebs, and well-heeled newsmakers. High-end suites, some with private steam room, sauna, or baby-grand piano, are popular with visiting VIPs. The 26-room Roman bath–themed Spa Utopia and Salon is sumptuous, and the health-and-fitness center is state-of-the-art. If you're staying over a Friday or Saturday night, Puccini and pasta were never as good as at the Italian Opera Buffet in the main dining room. The Five Sails Restaurant is quieter and more exclusive. **Pros:** the harbor views; it's only an elevator ride to the

The Ten Hippest Hotel Lounges

Sometimes it's tempting not to leave your hotel, especially when the weather's yuck. In Vancouver, though, you won't be relegated to a divey old place with soggy french fries: many of the hotel bars and lounges are appealing and some are worth the trip even if you're not staying right upstairs.

900 West Lounge at Fairmont Hotel Vancouver: The wine bar, soaring ceilings, and piano stylings set the stage for a romantic rendezvous.

Bacchus Piano Lounge at the Wedgewood: Its decadent opulence makes any occasion special.

Beyond at The Century Plaza: High style on a budget, including hand-crafted cocktails.

Diva Lounge at the Metropolitan: Small, elegant, and as much a Mecca for foodies as the restaurant itself.

Gerard Lounge at Sutton Place: The clubby scene and exceptional martinis have made it the city's top spot for Hollywood stars.

Herons at Fairmont Waterfront: Upmarket cosmopolitan comfort for international travelers hanging around the Canada Place complex.

O'Doul's Bar at the Listel Hotel: Hot jazz and cool cocktails in a New York–chic atmosphere.

Opus Bar at Opus Hotel: Mingle with gorgeous people over innovative cocktails and a tapas-style menu.

Sylvia's at Sylvia Hotel: A longtime favorite of locals and writers who scribe away in dark corners.

Terrace Bar at Four Seasons: Snazzy and indulgent with its fair share of low-key celebs and Armani-clad business travelers.

Voya at The Loden: Intimately urban and off the main thoroughfares, it's the perfect spot for a clandestine rendezvous.

cruise-ship terminal; the "go the extra mile" service attitude. **Cons:** the atrium is open to the convention center's main lobby, so the hotel foyer, lounge, and entrance fill with delegates bearing conference badges talking shop, nabbing the best seats in the house, and vying for taxis. ⊠ *999 Canada Pl., Downtown* ☎ *604/662–8111, 800/663–1515 in Canada, 800/937–1515 in U.S.* ⊕ *www.panpacific.com* ⤴ *465 rooms, 39 suites* ⌂ *In-room: Safe, kitchen (some), refrigerator, Wi-Fi. In-hotel: 2 restaurants, room service, bar, pool, gym, spa, laundry service, Wi-Fi, parking (paid), some pets allowed* ▤ *AE, DC, MC, V* ✛ *F2.*

$$$-$$$$ ☷ **Renaissance Vancouver Hotel Harbourside.** With a lobby of glass walls this business-district hotel takes full advantage of its view-filled waterfront location. And the op-art decor in lime, orange, and black adds even greater drama. Rooms are larger than average and have either step-out or full-size glassed-in balconies with city or (in the more expensive rooms) partial water and mountain views. There's an indoor pool, a health club, and direct access to a waterside park—take all this and combine it with the "kids under 12 eat free" policy, and you have a good choice for families in an ocean-side high-rise. **Pros:** at the outer edge of the financial district; waterfront views. **Cons:** it's a five-block walk to major shopping and within a half block of the convention center expansion and a waterfront walkway leading to Stanley Park. ✉ *1133 W. Hastings St., Downtown* ☎ *604/689–9211 or 800/905–8582* ⊕ *www.renaissancevancouver.com* ⤵ *434 rooms, 8 suites* ⌂ *In-room: Safe (some), Wi-Fi. In-hotel: Restaurant, bar, pool, gym, laundry service, Wi-Fi, parking (paid), some pets allowed* ▭ *AE, D, DC, MC, V* ✛ *E2.*

$$$$ ☷ **Shangri-la Hotel.** It's the tallest building in Vancouver—a 61-story tower of angled glass studded with gold squares that glint in the sunshine. Shangri-la relishes in over-the-top superlatives, and this is the upscale Asian brand's first hotel in North America. Soaring windows make spacious rooms feel even roomier, and a scheme of warm latte tones and dark-wood paneling captures a sleek contemporary Asian aesthetic. Such high-tech perks as bedside curtain controls and "do not disturb" doorbell indicators further establish the property's five-star credentials, as do the luxurious linens, cuddly robes, and bathroom LCD TVs. The Chi Spa provides wonderful Asian and European therapies. **Pros:** first-rate concierge service; stellar Chi Spa (the first of this brand in North America). **Cons:** public areas could be a shade more inviting; on the city's busiest thoroughfare (though still relatively peaceful). ✉ *1128 W. Georgia St., Downtown* ☎ *604/689–1120* ⊕ *www.shangri-la.com* ⤵ *81 rooms, 38 suites* ⌂ *In-room: Safe, refrigerator, DVD, Wi-Fi. In-hotel: Restaurant, room service, bar, gym, spa, laundry service, Wi-Fi, parking (paid)* ▭ *AE, D, DC, MC, V* ✛ *D2.*

$$$-$$$$ ☷ **Sheraton Vancouver Wall Centre.** These two ultramodern glass high-rises and their landscaped courtyard take up an entire city block. Rooms in both towers—the north tower was Vancouver's tallest building until the Shangri-la took the crown—have floor-to-ceiling windows with views of water, mountains, and city. The best views are above the 14th floor or in one of the corner rooms with two walls of glass. Rooms are chic and spacious with exceptionally comfortable beds and original (often local) artwork. The upbeat, modern public areas are decorated with bright colors and an eclectic variety of art (including the world's largest collection of African pygmy art). **Pros:** amazing metro Vancouver view from higher floors; intriguing Ayurvedic spa; doggy packages with dog bed and special treats. **Cons:** so modern that "cool" actually feels a bit cold; location in no-man's land between downtown and Yaletown. ✉ *1088 Burrard St., Downtown* ☎ *604/331–1000 or 800/663–9255* ⊕ *www. sheratonwallcentre.com* ⤵ *659 rooms, 64 suites* ⌂ *In-room: Safe, refrigerator, Wi-Fi. In-hotel: 2 restaurants, room service, bars, pool, gym, spa, laundry service, Wi-Fi, parking (paid), some pets allowed* ▭ *AE, DC, MC, V* ✛ *D4.*

7

Even if you're not staying at the luxurious Wedgewood hotel, their spa treatments are a wonderful escape.

$$$–$$$$ **St. Regis Hotel.** If you can live without a doorman and room service, the St. Regis might be for you. The 1916 building has been revamped into an upscale New York–inspired property. Rooms and suites come in various shapes, sizes, and configurations (sofa beds and adjoining doors are good family options) as befits the building's original architecture. All have king- or queen-size beds as well as a choice of en suite bathroom styles—some have only a shower, but make no mistake, the showers are first-class, as are the heated bathroom floors, plug-and-play gadget panels, and in-room safes that accommodate laptops. While there are no views, rates include full breakfast and other niceties such as bottled water and Internet access. In addition to a decent bistro–bar, the building houses a Starbucks as well as Gothams, one of the city's best steak houses. Guests can purchase an exclusive day-pass to the state-of-the-art health club on Granville Street (complimentary if you book a suite). **Pros:** hot location; choice of room styles; full breakfast and other gratis perks. **Cons:** no views; slow historic elevator sometimes make the stairs a faster option (you can view original artwork at every turn in the stairwell). ⊠ *602 Dunsmuir St., Downtown* ☏ *604/681–1135 or 800/770–7929* ⊕ *www.stregishotel.com* ⤻ *50 rooms, 15 suites* ⌂ *In-room: Refrigerator (some), Wi-Fi. In-hotel: Restaurant laundry service, Wi-Fi* ⊟ *AE, DC, MC, V* ⎟⎢ *CP* ✛ *E5.*

$$$–$$$$ **The Sutton Place Hotel.** More like an exclusive European guesthouse than a large modern hotel, this refined property has rooms furnished in a Parisian style with soft neutrals and lush fabrics, and service is gracious and attentive. The full spa has a wide menu. La Grande Résidence (part of Sutton Place), an apartment hotel available for stays of at least a week, is next door, at 855 Burrard. The Fleuri restaurant serves

Continental cuisine and is particularly noted for its late-night chocolate buffet. There's an on-site wine merchant that stocks more than 500 labels and a European-style bakery for French pastries and croissants. **Pros:** classy; terrific lounge bar for romantic trysts; the chocolate buffet is diet decadence; wonderful spa. **Cons:** the wide-open, nondescript corridor joining restaurant and lounge couldn't be further from the hotel's discrete style: in other words, your tryst better not be clandestine! ⊠ *845 Burrard St., Downtown* ☎ *604/682–5511 or 800/961–7555* ⊕ *www.suttonplace.com* ⇆ *350 rooms, 46 suites, 164 apartments* ⚘ *In-room: Safe, refrigerator, DVD, Wi-Fi. In-hotel: Restaurant, room service, bar, pool, gym, spa, laundry service, Wi-Fi, parking (paid), some pets allowed* ⊟ *AE, D, DC, MC, V* ✛ *E3.*

$$$$ ⊡ **Vancouver Marriott Pinnacle.** The soaring 50-foot-high atrium lobby makes a striking entrance to this 38-story hotel a few blocks from the cruise-ship terminal and central business district. Decorated in modern pale woods and neutral tones, each room has almost a full wall of windows showcasing expansive views of Burrard Inlet and the North Shore Mountains or the city skyline. The hotel's Show Case restaurant and bar ($$$) serves West Coast cuisine with global influences. The walls of windows in the restaurant and bar edge the outside sidewalk so you may feel part of the show—this is not the place for a romantic tête-à-tête. **Pros:** modern; in the financial district midway between major shopping and Stanley Park; great concierge. **Cons:** restaurant a bit pricey for what you get; rooms often not available until 4 PM. ⊠ *1128 W. Hastings St., Downtown* ☎ *604/684–1128 or 800/207–4150* ⊕ *www.vancouvermarriottpinnacle.com* ⇆ *424 rooms, 10 suites* ⚘ *In-room: Safe, refrigerator (some), Internet. In-hotel: Restaurant, room service, bar, pool, gym, laundry service, Wi-Fi, parking (paid), some pets allowed* ⊟ *AE, D, DC, MC, V* ✛ *E2.*

$$–$$$ ⊡ **The Victorian Hotel.** Budget hotels can be handsome, as in the gleaming hardwood floors, high ceilings, and chandeliers at this prettily restored 1898 European-style pension. This is one of Vancouver's best-value accommodations—guest rooms in the two connecting three-story buildings have down duvets, Oriental rugs atop hardwood floors, lush draperies, and period furniture; a few have bay windows or mountain views. Some of the private bathrooms are outfitted with marble tiles and granite countertops (though some have a shower and no tub). Even the shared baths are spotlessly clean and nicely appointed. With three queen beds, room #15 is a good choice for families. **Pros:** great location for the price; helpful staff; clean; comfortable. **Cons:** location near the "rummy part of town" a few blocks east. It's relatively safe (honest), but common sense says you would probably take a cab to the door after midnight rather than walk. ⊠ *514 Homer St., Downtown* ☎ *604/681–6369 or 877/681–6369* ⊕ *www.victorianhotel.ca* ⇆ *39 rooms, 18 with bath* ⚘ *In-room: Internet, refrigerator (some). In-hotel: Laundry service, Wi-Fi, parking (paid)* ⊟ *MC, V* ⧈ *CP* ✛ *E3.*

$$$$ ⊡ **Wedgewood Hotel & Spa.** The small lavish Wedgewood is a member of
Fodor's Choice the exclusive Relais & Châteaux Group, and is run by an owner who
★ cares fervently about her guests. The lobby and guest rooms display a flair for old-world Italian luster with original artwork and antiques

7

selected by the proprietor on her European travels. Guest rooms are capacious and each has a balcony. The four penthouse suites have fireplaces, luxury spa bathrooms, and private garden terraces. All the extra touches are here, too: afternoon ice delivery, dark-out drapes, robes, and a morning newspaper. The turndown service includes homemade cookies and bottled water. The sophisticated Bacchus restaurant and lounge ($$$–$$$$) is in the lobby; it's also a terrific stop for afternoon tea after shopping along Robson Street. The tiny but posh on-site spa is incredibly popular—book ahead for an appointment. **Pros:** personalized and attentive service; afternoon tea with finesse; great location close to top shops. **Cons:** small size means it books quickly. ✉ *845 Hornby St., Downtown* ☎ *604/689–7777 or 800/663–0666* ⊕ *www.wedgewoodhotel.com* ⤶ *41 rooms, 43 suites* ♿ *In-room: Safe, refrigerator, Wi-Fi. In-hotel: Restaurant, room service, bar, gym, spa, laundry facilities, laundry service, Wi-Fi, parking (paid)* ▭ *AE, D, DC, MC, V* ✛ *E3.*

WEST END

$-$$ ⊟ **Barclay Hotel.** A great location steps from the shops of Robson Street and low rates make this three-story former apartment building one of the city's best-value pension-style hotels. The guest rooms are clean, if basic, but the 1930s building, with its wide corridors, skylights, and mahogany staircase, has old-world charm. Most of the front rooms overlooking Robson Street have mountain views but back rooms are quieter. Because the hotel caters to bus tours, try to book in advance. **Pros:** location; spacious rooms. **Cons:** can be noisy; must book early. ✉ *1348 Robson St., West End* ☎ *604/688–8850* ⊕ *www.barclayhotel. com* ⤶ *76 rooms, 10 suites* ♿ *In-room: Refrigerator (some). In-hotel: Bar, laundry service, parking (paid)* ▭ *AE, D, DC, MC, V* ✛ *D2.*

$$$-$$$$ ⊟ **Barclay House in the West End.** Stained glass, antiques, and art nouveau fixtures decorate this comfortable 1904 heritage house a few blocks from downtown or Stanley Park; a fireplace, leather couch, and extensive DVD/CD library make it a cozy rainy-day hangout. All units (except the Mountain) have private sitting rooms; several have clawfoot tubs and a brass, mahogany, or canopy queen bed. The Mountain Room has its own little Juliette balcony. Peace is assured, as there are no adjoining walls between guest rooms and staff is exceptionally helpful. Breakfast is a generous Continental menu with one hot dish; if the weather's warm, ask to enjoy it under the garden gazebo. **Pros:** snazzy heritage upgrade; residential neighborhood; private, helpful staff. **Cons:** not wheelchair accessible: there are a number of stairs and no elevator. ✉ *1351 Barclay St., West End* ☎ *604/605–1351 or 800/971–1351* ⊕ *www.barclayhouse.com* ⤶ *6 rooms* ♿ *In-room: Refrigerator, DVD, Internet (some). In-hotel: Wi-Fi, parking (free), no kids under 10* ▭ *AE, MC, V* ⊚ *BP* ✛ *D2.*

$-$$ ⊟ **Buchan Hotel.** On a tree-lined residential street a block from Stanley Park, this 1926 pension-style hotel vies with the Sylvia Hotel as one of Vancouver's best values. Popular with cyclists thanks to its bike storage and low-traffic location, the Buchan also provides free coffee and tea, a lounge with a fireplace, and ski storage, but no elevator. Rooms are simple but comfortable, with old-fashioned radiators. Rooms without baths have hand basins. **Pros:** residential neighborhood; quiet; close proximity to beach and Stanley Park; airport shuttle a five-minute walk away. **Cons:** parking either has time limits or is expensive; some rooms share a bath; not wheelchair accessible. ⊠ *1906 Haro St., West End* ☎ *604/685–5354 or 800/668–6654* ⊕ *www.buchanhotel.com* ⇱ *60 rooms, 34 with bath* ♿ *In-room: No phone. In-hotel: Laundry facilities, parking (paid)* ⊟ *AE, DC, MC, V* ⊕ *B1.*

$$$–$$$$ 🏨 **English Bay Inn.** European antiques, stained-glass windows, and touches of Asian art furnish this 1930s Tudor-style house near Stanley Park. The inn has a a tiny Italianate garden out back. One suite winds up two levels and has its own fireplace. A lower-level suite has a private entrance, an antique four-poster bed, and its own kitchen and dining area. Port and sherry are served by the living-room fire each evening, and homemade scones are prepared daily for the four-course breakfasts. **Pros:** adult-oriented; finessed elegance; knowledgeable and effective concierge. **Cons:** one too many gilt-edged mirrors; diamond-paned leaded-glass windows are homey but also make rooms a bit dark. ⊠ *1968 Comox St., West End* ☎ *604/683–8002 or 866/683–8002* ⊕ *www.englishbayinn.com* ⇱ *4 rooms, 2 suites* ♿ *In-room: Wi-Fi. In-hotel: Laundry service, parking (free)* ⊟ *AE, DC, MC, V* ⧉ *BP* ⊕ *B2.*

$$$–$$$$ 🏨 **The Langtry.** Staying at this inconspicuous 1930 former apartment building near Robson Street and Stanley Park is about as near as you can get to feeling like a West End resident. Six apartment-size suites are furnished in a mix of modern and art deco styles with cathedral ceilings, inlaid-oak floors, and French doors. Each has a full kitchen, a dining area, and a feather bed. Maid service is an optional extra and rates include a free gym membership to a club on nearby Denman Street. **Pros:** feel like a Vancouver resident. **Cons:** in a quiet neighborhood, but the fire station across the road might disturb your sleep. ⊠ *968 Nicola St., West End* ☎ *604/687–7892* ⊕ *www.thelangtry.com* ⇱ *6 suites* ♿ *In-room: Kitchen, DVD, Wi-Fi. In-hotel: Laundry facilities, parking (free), some pets allowed* ⊟ *MC, V* ⊕ *C2.*

$$$–$$$$ 🏨 **Listel Vancouver.** Art and jazz come together in this in-the-groove hotel on Vancouver's most vibrant shopping street. Gallery-floor guest rooms and suites display original or limited-edition works by Canadian artists and celebrity photographers alongside pieces from France, England, the United States, and Japan. Rooms on the Museum floor are decorated with work from contemporary First Nations artists. Custom-made furniture in Gallery and Museum rooms complements the art. You can catch live jazz nightly at O'Doul's Restaurant & Bar downstairs. **Pros:** the art concept provides an eclectic insight into regional culture; there's quality (local) jazz on your doorstep; hotel is highly green conscious, including

behind-the-scenes features like solar heating innovations. **Cons:** it's a three-block walk from the designer-label area of Robson Street, which can feel like forever if you're laden down with purchases. ⊠ *1300 Robson St., West End* ☎ *604/684–8461 or 800/663–5491* ⊕ *www. listel-vancouver.com* ➾ *119 rooms, 10 suites* ⚲ *In-room: Refrigerator, Internet, Wi-Fi. In-hotel: Restaurant, room service, bar, gym, laundry service, parking (paid)* ☰ *AE, D, DC, MC, V* ✛ *D2.*

$$$–$$$$ ⬚ **Lord Stanley Suites on the Park.** These small, enticing, fully equipped high-rise suites are right at the edge of Stanley Park. Each has in-suite laundry, an office nook, a sitting room, and one or two bedrooms. Suites tend to be on the small side but are a good deal, considering they're self-catering; those overlooking busy Georgia Street have an enclosed sunroom; those backing onto quieter Alberni Street have balconies. You're also close to many restaurants on Denman Street, a block away. **Pros:** residential neighborhood; fabulous views; great longer-stay option. **Cons:** few facilities and common areas; furnishings are a bit plain. ⊠ *1889 Alberni St., West End* ☎ *604/688–9299 or 888/767–7829* ⊕ *www.lordstanley.com* ➾ *100 suites* ⚲ *In-room: Kitchen, DVD (some), Internet. In-hotel: Gym, laundry service, parking (paid)* ☰ *AE, DC, MC, V* �◐ *CP* ✛ *C1.*

$$$–$$$$ ⬚ **O Canada House B&B.** This beautifully restored 1897 Victorian within walking distance of downtown is where the first version of "O Canada," the national anthem, was written, in 1909. Each bedroom has late-Victorian antiques, and modern comforts such as bathrobes help make things homey. The top-floor room is enormous, with two king beds and a private sitting and dining area. A separate one-room coach house in the garden is a romantic option though it faces onto the back alley and is a bit cramped. Breakfast, served in the dining room, is a lavish affair. **Pros:** gracious service; fantastic breakfast; residential location. **Cons:** rooms on the small side (except the top floor); not wheelchair accessible. ⊠ *1114 Barclay St., West End* ☎ *604/688–0555 or 877/688–1114* ⊕ *www.ocanadahouse.com* ➾ *7 rooms* ⚲ *In-room: Refrigerator, DVD, Wi-Fi. In-hotel: Wi-Fi, parking (free), no kids under 12* ☰ *MC, V* �◐ *BP* ✛ *D3.*

$$$$ ⬚ **Pacific Palisades Hotel.** Bright citrus colors, abstract art, and geometric patterns come together to create a high-energy South Beach look at this apartment building turned trendy Robson Street hotel—it's part of the hip Kimpton Hotels brand. The cheerfulness extends to the spacious guest rooms and suites, where big balconies and wall-to-wall windows keep things light and airy. Head for the higher floors for sweeping water and mountain views. Fun is the idea here, from the playful design motifs to the minibars stocked with toys, the in-room yoga kits, and the free evening wine receptions. Pet sitting, Frisbees, dog cookies, and a pet-services directory are all on offer. You may walk the hotel's dog, Petey, and even ask for a goldfish in a bowl to keep you company during your stay! **Pros:** spacious rooms with only four suites per floor; playfully designed; free use of bikes. **Cons:** narrow corridors; location smack in the middle of noisy Robson. ⊠ *1277 Robson St., entrance at Jervis St., West End* ☎ *604/688–0461 or 800/663–1815* ⊕ *www. pacificpalisadeshotel.com* ➾ *76 rooms, 157 suites* ⚲ *In-room: Kitchen*

(some), refrigerator, Wi-Fi. In-hotel: Restaurant, room service, bar, pool, gym, spa, laundry facilities, laundry service, Wi-Fi, parking (paid), some pets allowed ⊟ *AE, D, DC, MC, V* ✦ *D2.*

$$–$$$
Fodor's Choice
★
▦ **Sylvia Hotel.** To stay at the Sylvia in June through August, you must book six months to a year ahead: this Virginia-creeper-covered 1912 building is popular because of its low rates and near-perfect location: about 25 feet from the beach on scenic English Bay, 200 feet from Stanley Park, and a 20-minute walk from Robson Street. The rooms and apartment-style suites vary from tiny to spacious. Many of the basic but comfortable rooms are large enough to sleep four and all have windows that open. The restaurant and bar are popular and its tenure on English Bay has made it a nostalgic haunt for Vancouverites. **Pros:** beachfront location; close to restaurants; a good place to mingle with the locals. **Cons:** older building; parking can be difficult if the lot is full; the 15-minute walk to the downtown core is slightly uphill. ⊠ *1154 Gilford St., West End* ☎ *604/681–9321* ⊕ *www.sylviahotel. com* ⤶ *97 rooms, 22 suites* ⚭ *In-room: Kitchen (some), Wi-Fi. In-hotel: Restaurant, room service, bar, laundry service, Internet terminal, parking (paid), some pets allowed* ⊟ *AE, DC, MC, V* ✦ *B2.*

$$–$$$$
▦ **West End Guest House.** This Victorian B&B, built in 1906, is painted the deep pink of the "Painted Lady" variety of sweet pea flower—and the guesthouse is just as adorable inside, with a gracious front parlor, cozy fireplace, and early 1900s furniture. Most of the handsome rooms are furnished with antiques; two larger rooms have gas fireplaces. All the bathrooms have been stylishly renovated. The inn is a two-minute walk from Robson Street and five minutes from Stanley Park. The owners also have a suite in a modern building next door; it's ideal for families and couples looking for weekly lets. **Pros:** great heritage interior; quiet residential location; free use of mountain bikes; private patio garden. **Cons:** furnishings a bit precious. ⊠ *1362 Haro St., West End* ☎ *604/681–2889 or 888/546–3327* ⊕ *www.westendguesthouse.com* ⤶ *8 rooms* ⚭ *In-room: DVD, Wi-Fi. In-hotel: Bicycles, Internet terminal, Wi-Fi, parking (free)* ⊟ *AE, D, DC, MC, V* ⊠ *BP* ✦ *C2.*

$$$$
▦ **Westin Bayshore Resort and Marina.** Perched on Coal Harbour beside Stanley Park, the Bayshore has a idyllic marina on its doorstep as well as impressive harbor and mountain views. Most rooms take full advantage of this, with floor-to-ceiling windows that open to a railing or a step-out balcony. Interiors are cheery and comfortable, with plush armchairs and comfortable beds. The only downtown resort hotel, the Bayshore is also rich with recreational facilities, including fishing charters, sightseeing cruises, and poolside yoga. Vancouver's Seawall Walk connects the resort to Stanley Park and the Vancouver Convention and Exhibition Centre. **Pros:** resort amenities within minutes of downtown; the doormen still dress up as Beefeaters; fabulous water views; Stanley Park your next-door neighbor; great waterside walkways. **Cons:** away from the downtown core; the posh conference space sees many business travelers, which might put families off, and vice versa; tower rooms are a fair walk from registration. ⊠ *1601 Bayshore Dr., off Cardero St., West End* ☎ *604/682–3377* ⊕ *www.westinbayshore.com* ⤶ *482 rooms, 28 suites* ⚭ *In-room: Safe, refrigerator, Wi-Fi. In-hotel: 2 restaurants,*

7

L'Hermitage

Opus

Sylvia

Wedgewood

room service, bar, pools, gym, laundry service, Wi-Fi, parking (paid), some pets allowed ⊟ *AE, D, DC, MC, V* ♢ *D1.*

WEST SIDE

$$$–$$$$ 🏠 **Granville House B&B.** At the edge of posh Shaughnessy, this Tudor-revival house is Vancouver's only five-star B&B, and it exudes a peaceful elegance that belies its address on one of Vancouver's busiest thoroughfares. Trade your shoes for plush slippers (provided) in the front hall and head to one of the five king-size rooms, each with a sitting area and appointed with luxurious linens, spa robes, and amenities made locally on Salt Spring Island. There's a self-serve refreshment and coffee bar in the inviting modern lounge; Continental breakfast includes one hot dish. **Pros:** on the main drag into and out of town; a bus ride away from excellent South Granville shopping; customized independent check-in style. **Cons:** Granville Street is quite busy; everything at this B&B is so pristine that you might feel hesitant to muss the linens! ⊠ *5050 Granville St., Shaughnessy* ☎ *604/307–2300* ⊕ *www.granvillebb.com* ⟲ *4 rooms* ⚭ *In-room: Refrigerator, Wi-Fi. In-hotel: Laundry service, Wi-Fi, parking (free)* ⊟ *AE, DC, MC, V* ⎅ *BP* ♢ *A5.*

$$$ 🏠 **Granville Island Hotel.** Granville Island is one of Vancouver's more entertaining neighborhoods, but unless you've moored up in a houseboat, the only overnight option is the Granville Island Hotel. The exterior of this offbeat water's-edge building is part Mission style, part industrial: the result is modern and sophisticated. Inside, most guest rooms have water views through full-length windows which get a bit grimy when the east wind kicks up a salty brine. Rooms on the top floor (the third) have small balconies. The corridor in the east wing has a quirky view: it overlooks vats brewing away for the fashionable brewpub and restaurant downstairs. It's a fun place to stay, but for such an iconic location and design, the '80s-style textiles and furnishings don't maximize the hotel's potential. The Penthouse isn't worth the extra expense. **Pros:** unique island location; creek views; boat transit to interesting disembarkation points. **Cons:** island gets crazy busy, especially on weekends. ⊠ *1253 Johnston St., Granville Island* ☎ *604/683–7373 or 800/663–1840* ⊕ *www.granvilleislandhotel.com* ⟲ *74 rooms, 8 suites* ⚭ *In-room: Refrigerator, Internet. In-hotel: Restaurant, room service, bar, bicycles, laundry service, parking (paid), some pets allowed* ⊟ *AE, D, DC, MC, V* ♢ *A5.*

7

YALETOWN

$$$$ 🏠 **Opus Hotel.** The design team had a good time with this boutique hotel,
Fodor's Choice   creating fictitious characters and designing rooms for each. Billy's room
★   is fun and offbeat, with pop art and lime-green accents. Dede's room has leopard skin, velveteen, and faux-fur accents, while Bob and Carol's place has softer edges and golden tones. Amenities are fun, too: look for mini-oxygen canisters in the bathrooms—a whiff'll clear your head if you have a hangover, and it'll stimulate blood flow for other pursuits. Most rooms have a full wall of windows, lots of natural light, and views

of the city or the Japanese garden in the courtyard. Two rooms have private access to the garden; seventh-floor rooms have balconies. Other perks include dog walking if you've brought Fido along, personal shopping, and free car service anywhere downtown. The brand-new Canada Line from the airport is steps away. **Pros:** the central Yaletown location, right by a rapid transit station; it's funky and hip; the lobby bar is a fashionable meeting spot. **Cons:** renovated heritage building has no views; surrounding neighborhood is mostly high-rises; trendy nightspots nearby can be noisy at night.

✉ *322 Davie St., Yaletown* ☎ *604/642–6787 or 866/642–6787* ⊕ *www.opushotel.com* ⟿ *85 rooms, 11 suites* ♿ *In-room: Safe, refrigerator, DVD (some), Wi-Fi. In-hotel: Restaurant, room service, bar, gym, bicycles, laundry service, Wi-Fi, parking (paid), some pets allowed* ▭ *AE, DC, MC, V* ✛ *E5.*

$$$–$$$$ 🛏 **Westin Grand Vancouver.** With its dramatic modern design and all-suites layout, the Westin Grand—at the edge of Yaletown—is one of Vancouver's more stylish hotels. Most of the compact studios and one-bedroom suites have floor-to-ceiling windows with skyline views. Corner suites are larger and half have small balconies; deluxe suites have marble baths. All units have deep soaker tubs and kitchenettes. The hotel is close to the main sports-and-entertainment district and to plenty of fashionable restaurants. **Pros:** you can walk to major theater and stadium events. **Cons:** escalator access to reception; smallish rooms. ✉ *433 Robson St., Downtown* ☎ *604/602–1999 or 888/680–9393* ⊕ *www.westingrandvancouver.com* ⟿ *23 rooms, 184 suites* ♿ *In-room: Safe, kitchen, refrigerator, Wi-Fi. In-hotel: Restaurant, room service, bar, pool, gym, spa, laundry service, Wi-Fi hotspot, parking (paid), some pets allowed* ▭ *AE, D, DC, MC, V* ✛ *F4.*

$–$$ 🛏 **YWCA Hotel.** A secure, modern high-rise in the heart of the entertainment district and steps from Yaletown, the YWCA has bright, comfortable rooms—a few big enough to sleep five. Some share a bath down the hall, some share a bath between two rooms, and others have private baths. TV lounges and shared kitchens are available for all guests, and rates include use of the YWCA adults-only pool and fitness facility, a 15-minute walk away at 535 Hornby Street. **Pros:** clean and friendly; access to high-quality fitness center; a terrific alternative to hostel accommodation. **Cons:** shared facilities. ✉ *733 Beatty St., Downtown* ☎ *604/895–5830 or 800/663–1424* ⊕ *www.ywcahotel.com* ⟿ *155 rooms, 40 with bath* ♿ *In-room: Refrigerator, no TV (some), Wi-Fi. In-hotel: Laundry facilities, Internet terminal, Wi-Fi, parking (paid)* ▭ *AE, MC, V* ✛ *F4.*

Victoria and Vancouver Island Side Trips

WORD OF MOUTH

"Butchart Gardens in the evening was amazing. We went about 4pm, plenty of time to see the gardens in daylight, eat dinner there, then explore the illuminated gardens, which are open until 10pm. In Victoria, we particularly like Fisherman's Wharf with its quirky little houseboats, harbour seals and fish and chips!"

—Maria_H

VICTORIA AND VANCOUVER ISLAND SIDE TRIPS

TOP REASONS TO GO

★ **The Journey here:** Yup, getting here is one of the best things about Victoria. Whether by ferry meandering past the Gulf or San Juan islands, by floatplane (try to travel at least one leg this way), or on a whale-watching boat, just getting to Victoria from the mainland is a memorable experience.

★ **Spend an afternoon at the Butchart Gardens:** A million and a half visitors can't be wrong—these lavish gardens north of town truly live up to the hype.

★ **Tour the Royal British Columbia Museum:** One of Canada's best regional museums warrants repeat visits just to take in the myriad displays and exhibits.

★ **Embark on a whale-watching cruise:** It's an amazing way to view these magnificent animals in the wild.

★ **Traverse the Inner Harbour via a Ferry Boat:** The tiny foot-passenger ferries zipping across the Inner Harbour afford passengers a whole new perspective of the city center.

1 Downtown. Most of Victoria's shopping and sightseeing are in and around the Inner Harbour and a few blocks north, along Government Street up to Chinatown. The lovely residential areas of James Bay and Vic West, both within walking distance, also fall within downtown.

2 Oak Bay, Rockland, and Fairfield. The winding tree-lined streets of Victoria's oldest residential districts are home to gardens, mansions, and the extremely British-feeling Oak Bay Village. All of these areas take in expansive and stunning ocean and mountain views.

3 Sidney and the Saanich Peninsula. The B.C. and Washington State ferry terminals and the airport lie along this bucolic peninsula north of town, which is also home to the Butchart Gardens, an emerging wine region, several beaches, and the pleasant town of Sidney, with its many bookshops.

4 The West Shore and the Malahat. Wilderness parks, viewpoints, and historic sites—including Hatley Castle and Fort Rodd Hill—encourage exploration of these western Victoria suburbs.

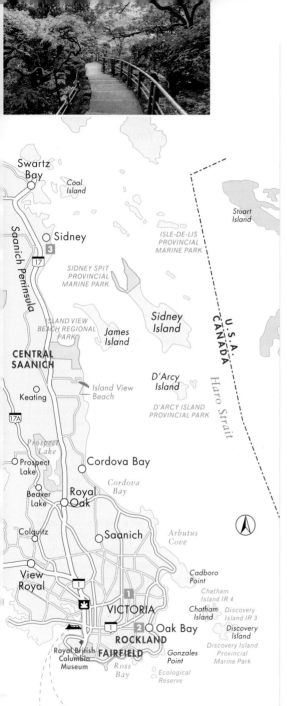

British Columbia

GETTING ORIENTED

Victoria's iconic build-
ings are clustered around
the Inner Harbour. To the
south, Beacon Hill Park
and James Bay extend to
Dallas Road, which runs
along the shore of Juan
de Fuca Strait. A short
walk north along the shop-
lined Government Street
leads to historic Bastion
Square, Market Square,
and Chinatown—which
are sometimes collectively
called Old Town. From
here, the Johnson Street
Bridge, which separates
the Inner Harbour from the
Upper Harbour, leads to
the waterfront walkways
of Vic West. About a mile
east of downtown are the
gardens and mansions of
Rockland, Fairfield, and
Oak Bay, the city's older
residential districts. Running
parallel to Government
Street are Blanshard
Street, which becomes
Highway 17 and leads to
the Saanich Peninsula, and
Douglas Street, which leads
to Highway 1 and the
rest of Vancouver Island.

8

VICTORIA AND VANCOUVER ISLAND SIDE TRIPS PLANNER

Visitor Information	Making the Most of Your Time

Visitor Information

Tourist Information Galiano Island Travel InfoCentre (📞 250/539–2233 ⊕ www. galianoisland.com). Hello BC (📞 800/435–5622 ⊕ www. hellobc.com). Salt Spring Island Visitor Information Centre (📞 250/537–5252 or 866/216–2936 ⊕ www. saltspringtoday.com). Sooke Region Museum and Visitor InfoCentre (📞 250/642–6351 or 866/888–4748 ⊕ www. sookeregionmuseum.com). Tourism Cowichan (📞 888/303–3337 ⊕ www. visit.cowichan.bc.ca). Tourism Vancouver Island (📞 250/754–3500 or 888/655–3483 ⊕ www.vancouverisland. travel). Tourism Victoria Visitor InfoCentre (✉ 812 Wharf St.V8W 1T3 📞 250/953–2033 or 800/663–3883 ⊕ www. tourismvictoria.com).

Making the Most of Your Time

You can see most of the sights in Downtown Victoria's compact core in a day, although there's enough to see at the main museums to easily fill two days. Many key sights, including the Royal BC Museum and the Parliament Buildings, are open on some summer evenings as well. You can save time by prebooking tea at the Empress Hotel and buying tickets to the Royal British Columbia Museum online.

You should also save at least half a day or a full evening to visit the Butchart Gardens. The least busy times are first thing in the morning, or on weekdays in the late afternoon and early evening; the busiest but most entertaining time is during the Saturday evening fireworks shows. If you have a car, you can make a day of it visiting the nearby town of Sidney and some of the Saanich Peninsula wineries.

An extra day allows for some time on the water, either on a whale-watching trip—it's fairly easy to spot orca in the area during summer—or on a Harbour Ferries tour, with stops for tea at Point Ellice House, a microbrew at Spinnakers' Brewpub, or fish-and-chips at Fisherman's Wharf. You can also explore the shoreline on foot, following all, or part, of the 7-mi (11-km) waterfront walkway.

With more time, you can explore some of the outlying neighborhoods; visit the Art Gallery of Greater Victoria, Craigdarroch Castle, or the delightful Abkhazi Gardens in the Oak Bay and Rockland areas; or head east to see Hatley Park and Fort Rodd Hill.

It rains often in Victoria, so if you get a fine day, set it aside for garden touring, whale-watching, kayaking, or cycling. Car-free bike paths run north to Sidney and east to Sooke.

If you're here for a while and, ideally, have a car (or really enjoy cycling), the wineries of the Cowichan Valley and the beaches past Sooke warrant a full day each—although it is possible to see both the West Coast and the Cowichan Valley in a one-day circle tour from Victoria. Salt Spring Island can be done as a day trip (market Saturdays are a highlight), though ferry schedules mean that the other islands usually require an overnight. Be warned, though: many people have planned day trips to the islands and ended up staying for years.

Local Cuisine

Wild salmon, locally made cheeses, Pacific oysters, organic vegetables, local microbrews, and even wines from the island's new farm-gate wineries (The B.C. government allows really small wineries to sell their wines "at the farm gate") are tastes to watch for. Vegetarians and vegans are well catered for in this health-conscious town, and seafood choices go well beyond traditional fish-and-chips. You may notice an Ocean Wise symbol on a growing number of menus: this indicates that the restaurant is committed to serving only sustainably harvested fish and seafood.

Some of the city's best casual (and not-so-casual) fare is served in pubs—particularly in brewpubs; most have an all-ages restaurant as well as an adults-only bar area.

Afternoon tea is a Victoria tradition, as is good coffee—despite the Starbucks invasion, there are plenty of fun and funky local caffeine purveyors around town.

What to bring home

In Victoria, as in the rest of B.C., the most popular souvenirs are First Nations arts and crafts, which you can pick up at shops, galleries, street markets, and—in some cases—directly from artists' studios. Look for silver jewelry and cedar boxes carved with traditional images and, especially around Duncan, the thick hand-knit sweaters made by the Cowichan people. B.C. wines, from wineshops in Victoria or directly from the wineries, make good souvenirs, too, as most are unavailable outside the province.

WHAT IT COSTS IN CANADIAN DOLLARS

	¢	$	$$	$$$	$$$$
Restaurants	under C$8	C$8–C$12	C$13–C$20	C$21–C$30	over C$30
Hotels	under C$75	C$75–C$125	C$126–C$175	C$176–C$250	over C$250

Restaurant prices are for a main course at dinner, not including 5% GST and 10% liquor tax. Hotel prices are for two people in a standard double room in high season, excluding 10% provincial accommodation tax, service charge, and 5% GST.

When to Go

Victoria has the warmest, mildest climate in Canada: snow is rare and flowers bloom in February. Summers are mild, too, rarely topping 75°F. If you're here for dining, shopping, and museums, winter is a perfectly nice time for a visit: it's gray and wet, and some minor attractions are closed, but hotel deals abound. If your focus is the outdoors—biking, hiking, gardens, and whale-watching—you need to come with everyone else, between May and October. That's when the streets come to life with crafts stalls, street entertainers, blooming gardens, and the inevitable tour buses. It's fun and busy but Victoria never gets unbearably crowded.

8

Festivals to plan your trip around

Victoria's top festivals take place in summer, when you're apt to encounter the best weather. For 10 nights in late June, international musicians perform during JazzFest International. Victoria's Inner Harbour becomes an outdoor concert venue in early August for Symphony Splash, when the Victoria Symphony plays a free concert from a barge moored in the middle of the harbor. August and September is the time for the Victoria Fringe Theatre Festival, during which you can feast from a vast menu of offbeat, original, and intriguing performances around town.

VICTORIA AND VANCOUVER ISLAND SIDE TRIPS PLANNER

Getting Here and Around

It's easy to visit Victoria without a car. Most sights, restaurants, and hotels are in the compact walkable core, with bikes, ferries, horse-drawn carriages, double-decker buses, step-on tour buses, taxis, and pedicabs on hand to fill the gaps. For sights outside the core—the Butchart Gardens, Hatley Castle, the Scenic Marine Drive—tour buses are your best bet. (See the Touring Victoria box for more info.)

Bike paths lace downtown and run along much of Victoria's waterfront, and long-haul car-free paths run to the ferry terminals as far west as Sooke. Most buses and ferries carry bikes.

By Train

The E&N Railiner, a small scenic train, runs once a day from Victoria to Courtenay on northern Vancouver Island. It stops almost everywhere en route, including Duncan and Chemainus in the Cowichan Valley. Reservations are recommended in summer.

Train Information VIA Rail (🕾 888/842-7245 ⊕ www. viarail.ca).

By Air

Victoria International Airport is 25 km (15 mi) north of downtown Victoria. The flight from Vancouver to Victoria takes about 25 minutes. To make the 30-minute drive from the airport to downtown, take Highway 17 south. A taxi is about C$55, plus tip. The Airporter bus service drops off passengers at most major hotels. The fare is C$18 one way. BC Transit buses no. 79 and 83 run just six times a day between the airport and downtown Victoria. The one-way fare is C$2.25.

There is floatplane service to Victoria's Inner Harbour in downtown Victoria with West Coast Air and Harbour Air. West Coast Air also flies from Whistler to downtown Victoria, May–September. Kenmore Air has daily floatplane service from May–September from Seattle to Victoria's Inner Harbour. Helijet has helicopter service from downtown Vancouver and Vancouver International Airport to downtown Victoria.

For the Gulf Islands, Harbour Air Seaplanes has regular service from downtown Vancouver to Salt Spring and Pender islands. Seair Seaplanes fly from Vancouver Airport to the Southern Gulf Islands. Saltspring Air flies from downtown Vancouver and Vancouver International Airport to the Southern Gulf Islands and to Maple Bay, near Duncan, in the Cowichan Valley. Kenmore Air has summer floatplane service from Seattle to the Gulf Islands. At press time, there was no scheduled floatplane service between Victoria and the Gulf Islands.

Contacts and Local Airlines Airporter (🕾 250/386-2525 or 877/386-2525 ⊕ www.victoriaairporter.com). **Harbour Air** (🕾 604/274-1277 or 800/665-0212 ⊕ www. harbour-air.com). **Helijet** (🕾 604/273-4688 or 800/665-4354 ⊕ www.helijet.com). **Horizon Air** (🕾 800/547-9308 ⊕ www.alaskaair.com). **Kenmore Air** (🕾 425/486-1257 or 866/435-9524 ⊕ www.kenmoreair.com). **Pacific Coastal Airlines** (🕾 250/655-6411 or 800/663-2872 ⊕ www. pacific-coastal.com). **Seair Seaplanes** (🕾 604/273-8900 or 800/447-3247 ⊕ www.seairseaplanes.com. **Saltspring Air** (🕾 250/537-9880 or 877/537-9880 ⊕ www. saltspringair.com). **West Coast Air** (🕾 604/606-6888 or 800/347-2222 ⊕ www.westcoastair.com).

By Boat and Ferry

From the B.C. Mainland

BC Ferries has daily service between Tsawwassen, about an hour south of Vancouver, and Swartz Bay, at the end of Highway 17 (the Patricia Bay Highway), about 30 minutes north of Victoria. Sailing time is about 1½ hours. Fares are C$13.50 per adult passenger and C$45 per vehicle each way. Vehicle reservations on Vancouver–Victoria and Nanaimo routes are optional and cost an additional C$15 to C$17.50. Foot passengers and cyclists don't need reservations.

BC Transit buses meet the ferries at both ends but if you're traveling without a car, it's easier to just take a Pacific Coach Lines bus. BC Ferries also sail from Horseshoe Bay, north of Vancouver, to Nanaimo, about two hours north of Victoria—convenient if you're traveling by car from Whistler or Vancouver's north shore to Vancouver Island.

An excellent option is combining four hours of whale-watching with travel between Vancouver and Victoria, offered by the Prince of Whales. The 74-passenger boat leaves Waterfront Station in downtown Vancouver daily at 9 AM and returns from the Butchart Gardens at 5:30 PM. One-way fares start at C$160.

Within Victoria

Victoria Harbour Ferries serve the Inner Harbour; stops include the Fairmont Empress, Chinatown, Point Ellice House, the Delta Victoria Ocean Pointe Resort, and Fisherman's Wharf. Fares start at C$4; multiple-trip and two-day passes are available. Boats make the rounds every 15 to 20 minutes, daily, March–October. The 45-minute harbor tours cost $20, and gorge cruises cost $25. At 10:45 AM on summer Sundays, the little ferries perform a water ballet set to classical music in the Inner Harbour.

*For details on Ferries to and around the Cowichan Valley and Gulf Islands, see the Side Trips section in this chapter.
*For Ferry service to/from Washington State, see the Travel Smart chapter.

Boat and Ferry Info BC Ferries (☎ 250/386–3431, 888/223–3779 in Canada ⊕ www.bcferries.com). **Queen of de Nile** (☎ Salt Spring Marina: 250/537–5810). **Prince of Whales** (☎ 888/383–4884 ⊕ www.princeofwhales. com). **Victoria Harbour Ferries** (☎ 250/708–0201 ⊕ www.victoriaharbourferry.com).

By Bus

Pacific Coach Lines has daily service between Vancouver and Victoria; the bus travels on the ferry.

BC Transit serves Victoria and around, including the Swartz Bay ferry terminal, Victoria International Airport, the Butchart Gardens, Sidney, and Sooke. Single-zone fare is C$2.25 (exact change); an all-day pass is C$7. Mid-June–August, Gray Line West's Butchart Gardens Express shuttle runs every 45 minutes from the bus depot behind the Fairmont Empress. Round-trip fare is C$47, including admission to the gardens; you can add a stop at Butterfly Gardens for C$12.

Bus Info BC Transit (☎ 250/382–6161 ⊕ www. bctransit.com). **Gray Line West** (☎ 250/388–6539 or 800/663–8390 ⊕ www. graylinewest.com). **Pacific Coach Lines** (☎ 604/662–7575 or 800/661–1725 ⊕ www.pacificcoach.com).

By Taxi

In Victoria, call Bluebird, Victoria Taxi, or Yellow Cabs. Salt Spring and Pender also have cab companies.

Contacts Bluebird Taxi (☎ 250/382–2222). **Pender Island Cab Company** (☎ 250/629–2222). **Salt Spring Silver Shadow Taxi** (☎ 250/537–3030). **Victoria Taxi** (☎ 250/383–7111). **Yellow Cabs** (☎ 250/381–2222).

8

Updated by Sue Kernaghan

Victoria, the capital of a province whose license plates brazenly label it "The Best Place on Earth," is a walkable, livable seaside town of fragrant gardens, waterfront paths, engaging museums, and beautifully restored 19th-century architecture. In summer, the Inner Harbour—Victoria's social and cultural center—buzzes with visiting yachts, horse-and-carriage rides, street entertainers, and excursion boats heading out to visit pods of friendly local whales. Yes, it might be a bit touristy, but Victoria's good looks, gracious pace, and manageable size are instantly beguiling, especially if you stand back to admire the mountains and ocean beyond.

At the southern tip of Vancouver Island, Victoria dips slightly below the 49th parallel. That puts it farther south than most of Canada, giving it the mildest climate in the country, with virtually no snow and less than half the rain of Vancouver.

The city's geography, or at least its place names, can cause confusion. Just to clarify: the city of Victoria is on Vancouver Island (not Victoria Island). The city of Vancouver is on the British Columbia mainland, not on Vancouver Island. At any rate, that upstart city of Vancouver didn't even exist in 1843 when Victoria, then called Fort Victoria, was founded as the westernmost trading post of the British-owned Hudson's Bay Company.

Victoria was the first European settlement on Vancouver Island, and in 1868, it became the capital of British Columbia. The British weren't here alone, of course. The local First Nations people—the Songhees, the Saanich, and the Sooke—had already lived in the areas for thousands of years before anyone else arrived. Their art and culture are visible throughout southern Vancouver Island. You can see this in private and public galleries, in the totems at Thunderbird Park, in the striking collections at the Royal British Columbia Museum, and at the Quw'utsun' Cultural and Conference Centre in nearby Duncan. Spanish explorers were the first foreigners to explore the area, although they left little more than place names (Galiano Island and Cordova Bay, for example). The thousands of Chinese immigrants drawn by the gold rushes of the late 19th century had a much greater impact, founding Canada's oldest Chinatown and adding an Asian influence that's still quite pronounced in Victoria's multicultural mix.

Despite its role as the provincial capital, Victoria was largely bypassed, economically, by Vancouver throughout the 20th century. This, as it turns out, was all to the good, helping to preserve Victoria's historic downtown and keeping the city free of skyscrapers and freeways. For much of the 20th century, Victoria was marketed to tourists as "The Most British City in Canada," and it still has more than its share of Anglo-themed pubs, tea shops, and double-decker buses. These days, however, Victorians prefer to celebrate their combined indigenous, Asian, and European heritage, and the city's stunning wilderness backdrop. Locals do often venture out for afternoon tea, but they're just as likely to nosh on dim sum or tapas. Decades-old shops sell imported linens and tweeds, but newer upstarts offer local designs in hemp and organic cotton. And let's not forget that fabric prevalent among locals: Gore-Tex. The outdoors are ever present here. You can hike, bike, kayak, sail, or whale-watch straight from the city center, and forests, beaches, offshore islands, and wilderness parklands lie just minutes away. A little farther afield, there's surfing near Sooke, wine touring in the Cowichan Valley, and kayaking among the Gulf Islands.

VICTORIA

Exploring Victoria is easy. A walk around downtown, starting with the museums and architectural sights of the Inner Harbour, followed by a stroll up Government Street to the historic areas of Chinatown and Old Town, covers most of the key attractions, though seeing every little interesting thing along the way could easily take two days. Passenger ferries dart across the Inner and Upper harbors to Point Ellice House and Fisherman's Wharf, while more attractions, including Craigdarroch Castle and the Art Gallery of Greater Victoria, lie about a mile east of downtown in the residential areas of Rockland and Oak Bay. Most visitors also make time for the Butchart Gardens, a stunning exhibition garden a 20-minute drive north on the Saanich Peninsula. Free time is also well spent strolling or biking through Beacon Hill Park and along the Dallas Road waterfront, heading out to such less-visited sights as Hatley Castle and Fort Rodd Hill, or checking out any of the area's beaches, wilderness parks, or wineries.

DOWNTOWN VICTORIA

Numbers in the text correspond to numbers in the margin and on the Downtown Victoria map.

TOP ATTRACTIONS

⓯ **Chinatown.** Chinese immigrants built much of the Canadian Pacific Railway in the 19th century, and their influence still marks the region. Victoria's Chinatown, founded in 1858, is the oldest and most intact such

CLOSE UP

Victoria Tours

AIR TOURS

Harbour Air Seaplanes has 20-minute flightseeing tours of Victoria and beyond, starting at C$99.

BOAT TOURS

The best way to see the sights of the Inner and Upper Harbour, and beyond, is by Victoria Harbour Ferries; 45- and 50-minute tours cost C$20 to C$25.

BUS TOURS

Gray Line West's double-decker buses tour downtown, Chinatown, Oak Bay, and Beacon Hill Park; Butchart Gardens tours and a Butchart Gardens Express shuttle are available. Big Bus has narrated tours on open-top and trolley-style buses, May–October; you can get on and off at any of the 22 stops. You can buy a C$35 ticket, good for 2 days, on board, but buy online and a third day's free.

CARRIAGE AND PEDICAB TOURS

Tally-Ho Sightseeing and Victoria Carriage Tours operate horse-drawn tours. Kabuki Kabs' narrated pedicab tours are C$1/min from the Empress Hotel.

FOOD AND WINE TOURS

Saturdays (May–October), Travel with Taste leads culinary tours of Victoria with a tea tasting, a wine tasting, and a chance to try artisanal delicacies; they also run day trips to the Cowichan Valley and Saanich Peninsula, and multiday trips to Sooke and Salt Spring Island. Vancouver Island Wine Tours will take you to the Cowichan Valley, Saanich Peninsula, and Salt Spring Island. Grand Wine Tours offers Cowichan Valley winery tours, with lunch. Friendly Organics run tours of organic farms and wineries. Gourmet Safaris has wineries, cheese makers, chocolate makers, and farms on their Salt Spring Island itineraries.

WALKING TOURS

The Architectural Institute of B.C. conducts walking tours of Victoria's historic neighborhoods for C$5 in July and August. Discover the Past Tours offers Ghostly Walks and Chinatown Tours. Victorian Garden Tours tours private and public gardens.

Info Architectural Institute of B.C. (☎ 800/667–0753 Ext. 333, 604/683–8588 Ext. 333 [Vancouver] ⊕ www.aibc.ca). **Big Bus Victoria** (☎ 250/389–2229 or 888/434–2229 ⊕ www.bigbusvictoria.ca). **Discover the Past Tours** (☎ 250/384–6698 ⊕ www.discoverthepast.com). **Friendly Organics** (☎ 250/655–4461 or 866/550–4461 ⊕ www.friendlyorganics.ca). **Grand Wine Tours** (☎ 250/881–1000 or 888/546–6736 ⊕ www.grandwinetours.com). **Gray Line West** (☎ 250/388–6539 or 800/663–8390 ⊕ www.graylinewest.com). **Harbour Air Seaplanes** (☎ 250/384–2215 or 800/665–0212 ⊕ www.harbour-air.com). **Island Gourmet Safaris** (☎ 250/537–4118 ⊕ www.islandgourmetsafaris.com). **Kabuki Kabs** (☎ 250/385–4243 ⊕ www.kabukikabs.com). **Tally-Ho Sightseeing** (☎ 250/514–9257 or 866/383–5067 ⊕ www.tallyhotours.com). **Travel With Taste** (☎ 250/385–1527 ⊕ www.travelwithtaste.com). **Vancouver Island Wine Tours** (☎ 250/661–8844 ⊕ www.vancouverislandwinetours.com). **Victoria Carriage Tours** (☎ 250/383–2207 or 877/663–2207 ⊕ www.victoriacarriage.com). **Victoria Harbour Ferries** (☎ 250/708–0201 ⊕ www.victoriaharbourferry.com). **Victorian Garden Tours** (☎ 250/380–2797 ⊕ www.victoriangardentours.com).

The grand Fairmont Empress hotel has a commanding position on Victoria's Inner Harbor.

district in Canada. If you enter from Government Street, you'll pass under the elaborate **Gate of Harmonious Interest,** made of Taiwanese ceramic tiles and decorative panels. Along Fisgard Street, merchants display paper lanterns and exotic produce. Mah-jongg, fan-tan, and dominoes were games of chance played on **Fan Tan Alley,** said to be the narrowest street in Canada. Once the gambling and opium center of Chinatown, it's now lined with offbeat shops, few of which sell authentic Chinese goods. Look for the alley on the south side of Fisgard Street between Nos. 545½ and 549½. At just two square blocks, Victoria's Chinatown is much smaller than Vancouver's and, though older, feels more sanitized. It's also more pleasant to stroll through as, unlike Vancouver's, it's not near a rough part of town. ⊠ *Fisgard St., between Government and Store Sts., Chinatown.*

⑨ Fairmont Empress. Opened in 1908 by the Canadian Pacific Railway, the ★ Empress is one of the grand château-style railroad hotels that grace many Canadian cities. Designed by Francis Rattenbury, who also designed the Parliament Buildings across the way, the Empress, with its solid Edwardian grandeur, has become a symbol of the city. The elements that made the hotel an attraction for travelers in the past—old-world architecture, ornate decor, and a commanding view of the Inner Harbour—are still here. Nonguests can stop by for afternoon tea (reservations are recommended; the dress code is smart casual), meet for a curry under the tiger skin in the Bengal Room, enjoy a treatment at the hotel's Willow Stream spa, browse the shops and galleries in the hotel's arcade, or sample the superb Pacific Northwest cuisine in the Empress Room restaurant. In summer, weather permitting, lunch, snacks, and

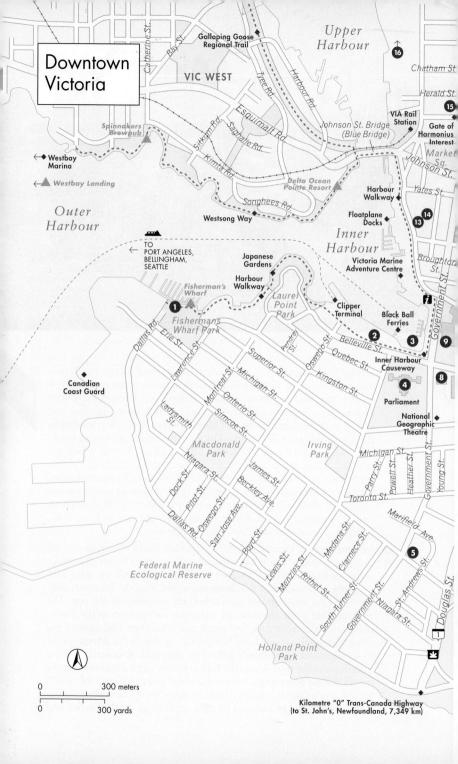

Downtown Victoria

VIC WEST

Upper Harbour

Galloping Goose Regional Trail

Bay St.
Catherine St.
Tree Rd.
Harbour Rd.

Chatham St.

16

Herald St.

15

Esquimalt Rd.

Sitkum Rd.
Saghalie Rd.

Johnson St. Bridge (Blue Bridge)

VIA Rail Station

Gate of Harmonius Interest

Market Sq.

Spinnakers Brewpub

Kimta Rd.

Johnson St.

Delta Ocean Pointe Resort

Harbour Walkway

Yates St.

← Westbay Marina

Songhees Rd.

Floatplane Docks

13   14

← Westbay Landing

Westsong Way

Outer Harbour

Westsong Way

Inner Harbour

Broughton St.

TO PORT ANGELES, BELLINGHAM, SEATTLE

Japanese Gardens

Victoria Marine Adventure Centre

Fisherman's Wharf

Harbour Walkway

Laurel Point Park

Clipper Terminal

Black Ball Ferries

Government St.

1

Fishermans Wharf Park

Dallas Rd.
Erie St.
Lawrence St.

Pendray St.
Oswego St.
Quebec St.

Belleville St.

2

Inner Harbour Causeway

3

9

i

Canadian Coast Guard

Superior St.
Montreal St.
Michigan St.
Ontario St.

Kingston St.

4

8

Simcoe St.

Parliament

Ladysmith St.

National Geographic Theatre

Macdonald Park

James St.
Beckley Ave.

Irving Park

Michigan St.
Parry St.
Powell St.
Heather St.
Government St.
Young St.

Niagara St.
Dock St.
Pilot St.
Oswego St.
San Jose Ave.
Boyd St.

Toronto St.

Dallas Rd.

Lewis St.
Menzies St.
Rithet St.
Medana St.
Clarence St.

Marifield Ave.

5

St. Andrews St.

Federal Marine Ecological Reserve

South Turner St.
Government St.
Niagara St.

Douglas St.

1

Holland Point Park

N

0 ——— 300 meters

0 ——— 300 yards

Kilometre "0" Trans-Canada Highway
(to St. John's, Newfoundland, 7,349 km)

Bastion Square **13**

Beacon Hill Park **6**

Chinatown **15**

Emily Carr House **5**

Fairmont Empress **9**

Fisherman's Wharf **1**

Legacy Art Gallery **12**

Maritime Museum of
British Columbia **14**

Miniature World **10**

Pacific Undersea Gardens **3**

Parliament Buildings **4**

Point Ellice House **16**

Royal British Columbia Museum **8**

Royal London Wax Museum **2**

St. Ann's Academy **7**

Victoria Bug Zoo **11**

KEY

🛈 Tourist information

🔱 Trans-Canada Hwy.

🚢 Ferry

- - - Pedestrian trail

▲ Harbour Ferries

CLOSE UP

Victoria Waterfront on Foot

You can walk most of the way around Victoria's waterfront from Westbay Marina on the Outer Harbour's north shore, to Ross Bay on the Strait of Juan de Fuca. The entire 11-km (7-mi) route takes several hours, but it passes many of the city's sights and great scenery. Waterfront pubs and cafés supply sustenance; ferries and buses offer transport as needed.

Begin with a ride on Harbour Ferries to Westbay Marina, the start of Westsong Way. This 4-km (2-mi) pedestrian path (no cyclists permitted) follows the waterfront past Vic West to the Johnson Street Bridge. The views across the harbor are rewarding, as is a stop at the waterfront Spinnakers Brewpub. Harbour Ferries stop at Spinnakers and at the Delta Ocean Pointe Resort, so you can choose to start from either point.

Once across the Johnson Street Bridge you can detour to Chinatown and Market Square or, to continue the walk, turn right to Yates Street, then right again down to the water (a Downtown Walk/Harbour Walkway sign shows the way). The route runs past floatplane docks and whale-watching outfitters (where a fish-tacos snack at Red Fish, Blue Fish—a waterfront take-out spot—may be in order) to the Inner Harbour Causeway. This ¼-mi waterfront walkway—busy all summer with street entertainers and crafts and snack vendors—curves

around the Inner Harbour from the Visitor Information Centre at the north end to the Royal London Wax Museum at the south end. It's only about a quarter mile around but could take a while if you stop to watch all the torch jugglers and caricature artists. The Fairmont Empress Hotel, the Royal BC Museum, and the Parliament Buildings are all here—just across the road from the water.

From the wax museum, detour along Belleville Street past the ferry terminals and pick the path up where it enters Laurel Point Park just past the Clipper terminal. From here, the route leads through Laurel Point Park (a pretty waterfront park) and past a marina to Fisherman's Wharf, where you can stop for fish-and-chips on the dock, or grab a ferry back downtown. To keep going, follow Dallas Road to the Ogden Point Cruise Ship terminal, where you can walk out on the breakwater for a view of the ships or grab a snack on the ocean-view deck of the Ogden Point Café.

You're now on the shore of Juan de Fuca Strait, where a footpath runs another 6 km (4 mi) along cliff tops past Beacon Hill Park to the historic cemetery at Ross Bay. Dog walkers, joggers and kite flyers are usually out in force on the grassy cliff top; stairways lead down to pebbly beaches. A hike north through Beacon Hill Park will get you back downtown.

cocktails are served on the Terrace Verandah overlooking the Inner Harbour. ⊠ *721 Government St., entrance at Belleville and Government, Downtown* ☎ *250/384–8111, 250/389–2727 tea reservations* ⊕ *www.fairmont.com/empress* ⊠ *Free, afternoon tea C$55.*

NEED A BREAK?

Good luck getting your sweet tooth past retro-looking Rogers' Chocolates Soda Shoppe (⊠ 801 Government St., Downtown ☎ 250/382–4249), where

staff from local candy maker Rogers whip up sundaes, shakes, and splits from their own brand of extra-rich ice cream.

❹ **Parliament Buildings.** Officially the British Columbia Provincial Legislative
★ Assembly Buildings, these massive stone structures are more popularly referred to as the Parliament Buildings. Designed by Francis Rattenbury (who also designed the Fairmont Empress Hotel) when he was just 25 years old, and completed in 1897, they dominate the Inner Harbour. Two statues flank the main entrance: one of Sir James Douglas (1803–77), who chose the site where Victoria was built, and the other of Sir Matthew Baille Begbie (1819–94), the man in charge of law and order during the gold rush era. Atop the central dome is a gilded statue of Captain George Vancouver (1757–98), the first European to sail around Vancouver Island. A statue of Queen Victoria (1819–1901) reigns over the front of the complex. More than 3,300 lights outline the buildings at night. The interior is lavishly done with stained-glass windows, gilt moldings, and historic photographs, and in summer actors play historic figures from B.C.'s past. When the legislature is in session, you can sit in the public gallery and watch British Columbia's democracy at work (custom has the opposing parties sitting 2½ sword lengths apart). Free, informative, 30- to 60-minute tours run every 20 to 30 minutes in summer and several times a day in the off-season (less frequently if school groups or private tours are coming through). Tours are obligatory on summer weekends (mid-May until Labor Day) and optional the rest of the time. ⊠ *501 Belleville St., Downtown* ☎ *250/387–3046* ⊕ *www.leg. bc.ca* ✆ *Free* ⊙ *Mid-May–early Sept., Mon.–Thurs. 9–5, Fri.–Sun. 9–7; early Sept.–mid-May, weekdays 9–4.*

❽ **Royal British Columbia Museum.** This excellent museum, one of Victoria's
ᗧ leading attractions, traces several thousand years of British Columbian
Fodor'sChoice history. Its First Peoples Gallery, home to a genuine Kwakwaka'wakw
★ big house and a dramatically displayed collection of masks and other artifacts, is especially strong. The Environmental History Gallery traces B.C.'s natural heritage, from prehistory to modern-day climate change, in realistic dioramas. An Ocean Station exhibit gets kids involved in running a Jules Verne–style submarine. In the Modern History Gallery, a replica of Captain Vancouver's HMS *Discovery* creaks convincingly, and a re-created frontier town comes to life with cobbled streets, silent movies, and the rumble of an arriving train. Also on-site is the National Geographic Theater showing a variety of IMAX films on a six-story-tall screen.

Optional one-hour tours, included in the admission price, run roughly twice a day in summer and less frequently in winter. Most focus on a particular gallery, though the 90-minute Highlights Tour touches on all galleries. Special exhibits, usually held between April and October, often attract crowds (and higher admission prices). Skip ticket lines by booking online.

The museum complex has several more interesting sights, beyond the expected gift shop and café. In front of the museum, at Government and Belleville streets, is the **Netherlands Centennial Carillon.** With 62 bells, it's the largest bell tower in Canada; the Westminster chimes ring

The Woolly Mammoth at the Royal British Columbia Museum.

out every hour, and free recitals are played most Sunday afternoons. Behind the main building, bordering Douglas Street, are the grassy lawns of **Thunderbird Park**, home to 10 totem poles (replicas of originals that are preserved in the museum) and Wawadit'la, a First Nations ceremonial big house. The house is not open to the public, but you can wander among the totems. Next door is **Helmcken House** (⊠ *10 Elliot St., Downtown* ⊘ *June to Labor Day, daily 12–4*), one of the oldest houses in B.C.; it was built in 1852 for pioneer doctor and statesman John Sebastian Helmcken. Inside are displays of the family's belongings, including the doctor's medical tools; admission is by donation. Next to Helmcken House is **St. Ann's School House.** Built in 1858, it's one of British Columbia's oldest schools (you can view the interior through the door). ⊠ *675 Belleville St., Downtown* ☎ *250/356–7226 or 888/447–7977; theater show times: 877/480–4887* ⊕ *www.royalbcmuseum.bc.ca* 🎟 *C$15, IMAX theater C$11, combination ticket C$23. Family rate (2 adults and 2 youths) C$37.50. Rates may be higher during special-exhibit periods* ⊘ *Museum: daily 9–5 (open until 10 PM most Fri. and Sat. early June–late Sept.). Theater: daily 10–8; call for show times.*

WORTH NOTING

13 **Bastion Square.** James Douglas, the former colonial governor for whom Douglas Street was named, chose this spot for the original Fort Victoria and Hudson's Bay Company trading post in 1843. Offices and restaurants occupy the old brick buildings, and in summer the square comes alive with street performers and crafts vendors. The former courthouse in the square now houses the Maritime Museum of British Columbia. ⊠ *Off Wharf St. at end of View St., Downtown.*

NEED A
BREAK?

You might be tempted to dismiss **Paradiso di Stelle** (✉ *10 Bastion Square, Downtown* ☎ *250/920–7266*), with its busy patio and prime Bastion Square location, as a bit of a tourist trap. True, it's popular, but service is quick and friendly, and the authentic Italian coffee, house-made gelato, paninis, and pastas are excellent. A water-view and people-watching table right in the action of Bastion Square is irresistible on a summer day.

❻ Beacon Hill Park. The southern lawns and waterfront path of this 154-acre park afford great views of the Olympic Mountains and the Strait of Juan de Fuca. There are ponds, jogging and walking paths, flowers and gardens, a petting zoo (open daily 10–5), and a cricket pitch. The park is also home to Mile Zero of the Trans-Canada Highway. Music plays in the band shell on summer evenings and, on Saturday nights in August, the Victoria Film Festival screens free movies here. ✉ *East of Douglas St., south of Southgate St., Downtown* ☎ *250/361–0600 City of Victoria Parks Division, 250/381–2532 children's farmyard, 250/389–0444 Victoria Film Festival* ⊕ *www.victoria.ca* ✆ *Free; Petting Zoo C$3.*

❺ Emily Carr House. One of Canada's most celebrated artists and a respected writer, Emily Carr (1871–1945) was born and raised in this extremely proper, wooden Victorian house before she abandoned her middle-class life to live in, and paint, the wilds of British Columbia. Carr's own descriptions, from her autobiography *Book of Small,* were used to restore the house. Catch, if you can, one of the days when an actress playing Carr tells stories of her life. Artwork on display includes work by modern-day B.C. artists and reproductions of Carr's work. You'll need to visit the Art Gallery of Greater Victoria or the Vancouver Art Gallery to see Carr originals. ✉ *207 Government St., James Bay* ☎ *250/383–5843* ⊕ *www.emilycarr.com* ✆ *C$6; C$10 for actress performances and other special events* ☉ *May–Sept., Tues.–Sat. 11–4; Oct.–Apr. by arrangement or during special events.*

❶ Fisherman's Wharf. Harbour Ferries stop at this fun nautical spot, just west of the Inner Harbour. Among the candy-color houseboats bobbing along the dock are several floating shacks selling ice cream, fish-and-chips, live crab, kayak tours, and tickets for whale-watching tours. One vendor, Grilligans, even has a paddle-through window to serve hungry kayakers; other booths sell fish to feed the harbor seals who often visit the quay. The busiest vendor is Barb's, an esteemed fish-and-chips spot. Farther along, past the floating gift shop, you can watch fishers unload their catches, and admire the various vessels, including a historic paddle wheeler, the SS *Beaver.* A shoreside park makes a nice picnic venue. ✉ *Corner of Superior and St. Lawrence Sts., Downtown* ☎ *250/708–0201 Victoria Harbour Ferries* ⊕ *www.victoriaharbourferry.com* ✆ *Wharf: free. Ferry: C$4* ☉ *Ferries run June–Aug., daily 9–9; Mar.–May, Sept., and Oct., daily 11–5.*

⓬ Legacy Art Gallery and Café. Rotating exhibits from the University of Victoria's vast art collection, as well as contemporary installations, are displayed in this airy downtown space. Shows in the 3,000-square-foot space comprise mostly Canadian works, including many by First Nations artists, but international painters are represented, too. The

8

gallery doubles as a quiet café, serving coffees, sandwiches, wraps, and baked goodies. ⊠ *630 Yates St., Downtown* ☎ *250/381–7670* ⊕ *www. legacygallery.ca* ⊠ *Free* ⊗ *Wed.–Sun. 10–5.*

⑭ **Maritime Museum of British Columbia.** The two floors of model ships, weap-
⊕ onry, ships' wheels, photographs, and figureheads at this museum, in Victoria's original courthouse, chronicle the province's seafaring history. Among the hand-built boats on display is the *Tilikum,* a dugout canoe that sailed from Victoria to England between 1901 and 1904. Kids can learn some scary tales about the pirates of the coast and even climb a crow's nest. On the third floor, the original 1888 vice-admiralty court-room looks ready for a court-martial. ⊠ *28 Bastion Sq., Downtown* ☎ *250/385–4222* ⊕ *www.mmbc.bc.ca* ⊠ *C$10* ⊗ *Daily 9:30–4:30.*

⑩ **Miniature World.** Children and model aficionados adore this charmingly
⊕ retro attraction, tucked into the Fairmont Empress Hotel. More than 85 miniature dioramas, including space, castle, fairy-tale scenes, and one of the world's largest model railways, are housed in kid-height glass cases, complete with recorded narration. The level of detail is impres-sive in the models, some of which date to the site's 1969 opening. Some of the models are animated and visitors can start and stop trains and turn dollhouse lights on and off with push buttons. Most people walk through in 30 minutes, but dollhouse collectors, model-train build-ers, and preschoolers can be absorbed for hours. ⊠ *649 Humboldt St., Downtown* ☎ *250/385–9731* ⊕ *www.miniatureworld.com* ⊠ *C$13* ⊗ *Mid-May–Labor Day, daily 9–9; rest of Sept. and early May, daily 9–7; Oct.–Apr., daily 9–5.*

❸ **Pacific Undersea Gardens.** If you want an up close look at a wolf eel
⊕ or an octopus, you might check out this underwater sea-life display, housed in and under a barge floating in the Inner Harbour. If you're at all claustrophobic, though, be warned: a dark staircase leads to a dark narrow tunnel 15 feet below water, where you can see local fish and other marine creatures darting about behind high windows. The U-shape tunnel opens to an underwater theater where a 20-minute narrated dive show, run roughly every hour in summer (less frequently in winter), gives everyone a chance to view the more interesting of the 5,000 or so creatures in the tanks. The biggest room of all is the above-water gift shop, which has a pretty good collection of nautical-theme toys. Regrettably, the site isn't wheelchair or stroller accessible, the windows are too high for small children to see (unless you pick them up), and the tunnel can get uncomfortably crowded, especially if a tour group is coming through. Tickets are good all day, though, so you can return later if need be. ⊠ *490 Belleville St., Downtown* ☎ *250/382–5717* ⊕ *www.pacificunderseagardens.com* ⊠ *C$9.75* ⊗ *July and Aug., daily 9–8; Sept.–June, daily 10–5.*

⑯ **Point Ellice House.** The O'Reilly family home, an 1861 Italianate cottage overlooking the Selkirk Waterway, has been restored to its original splendor, with the largest collection of Victorian furnishings in western Canada. Tea and fresh-baked goodies are served under an awning on the lawn. You can take a half-hour audio tour of the house (presented from a servant's point of view), stroll in the English country garden, or try your hand at croquet. Point Ellice House is only a few minutes' drive north of downtown, but it's in an industrial area, so it's more fun to come by sea. Victoria Harbour Ferries leave from a dock in front of the Fairmont Empress hotel; the sailing lasts about 15 minutes and takes in the sights of the harbor. ✉ *2616 Pleasant St., Downtown* ☎ *250/380–6506* ⊕ *www.pointellicehouse.ca* ✉ *C$6, C$23 including tea* ⊗ *Mid-May–mid-June and mid- to late Sept., Thurs.–Mon. 10–4 (tea daily 11–3, last tour 3:30); mid-June–mid-Sept., daily 11–5 (tea daily 11–3:30, last tour 4:30); Oct.–Apr. only open for special events.*

② **Royal London Wax Museum.** The 208 life-size wax figures on display here
☾ include plenty of royal and historic figures, as well as some grisly scenes in the (optional) Chamber of Horrors. The statues are technically well made, but more interesting is the grand colonnaded building they're housed in. Built in 1923 and designed by Francis Rattenbury (the architect behind the Empress Hotel and the Parliament Buildings), it was originally Victoria's steamship terminal and the first sight many visitors had of the city. ✉ *470 Belleville St., Downtown* ☎ *250/388–4461 or 877/929–3228* ⊕ *www.waxmuseum.bc.ca* ✉ *C$12* ⊗ *May–Aug., daily 9–9; Sept.–Apr., daily 9:30–5.*

⑦ **St. Ann's Academy National Historic Site.** This former convent and school, founded in 1858, played a central role in British Columbia's pioneer life. The academy's little chapel—the first Roman Catholic cathedral in Victoria—has been restored to look just as it did in the 1920s. The 6-acre grounds, with their fruit trees and herb and flower gardens, are also being restored as historic landscapes. ✉ *835 Humboldt St., Downtown* ☎ *250/953–8829* ⊕ *www.stannsacademy.com* ✉ *By donation* ⊗ *Gardens daily. Chapel mid-May–Aug., daily 10–4; Sept.–mid-May, Thurs.–Sun. 1–4.*

⑪ **Victoria Bug Zoo.** Local kids clamor to visit this offbeat minizoo, home to
☾ the largest live tropical insect collection in North America. You can even hold many of the 70 or so varieties, which include walking sticks, scorpions, millipedes, and a pharnacia—at 22 inches, the world's longest insect. The staff members know their bug lore and are happy to dispense scientific information. ✉ *631 Courtney St., Downtown* ☎ *250/384–2847* ⊕ *www.bugzoo.bc.ca* ✉ *C$8* ⊗ *Mid-June–early Sept., daily 10–6; early Sept.–mid-June, Mon.–Sat. 10–5, Sun. 11–5.*

OAK BAY, ROCKLAND, AND FAIRFIELD

The winding shady streets of Victoria's older residential areas—roughly bordered by Cook Street, Fort Street, and the seaside—are lined with beautifully preserved Victorian and Edwardian homes. These include many stunning old mansions now operating as bed-and-breakfasts, and Victoria's most elaborate folly: Craigdarroch Castle. With mansions come gardens, and several of the city's best are found here. Clusters of high-end shops include the extraordinarily British Oak Bay Village, described as a place "behind the Tweed Curtain" for its adherence to Tudor facades and tea shops. Among the lavish waterfront homes are plenty of public parks and beaches offering views across Juan de Fuca Strait to the Olympic Mountains of Washington State.

8

GETTING AROUND

A car or a bike is handy, but not essential, for exploring this area.

No wheels? Big Bus, Gray Line, and other tour companies offer Oak Bay and Marine Drive tours.

By public transit, take bus no. 11 or 14 from the corner of Fort and Douglas streets to Moss Street (for the Art Gallery of Greater Victoria), or to Joan Crescent (for Craigdarroch Castle). Government House is a few blocks south. The walk, about a mile past the antiques shops of Fort Street, is also interesting. To get to Oak Bay Village, take bus no. 2 (or bus 2A which continues to Willows Beach) from Johnson and Douglas streets downtown. If you're visiting the castle and gallery first, continue on the no. 11 and change to bus no. 2 at Oak Bay and Fort Street. Another useful route is bus no. 7: from Johnson and Douglas streets, it travels to Ross Bay Cemetery, Abkhazi Garden, and Oak Bay Village.

TOP ATTRACTIONS

★ **Abkhazi Garden.** Called "the garden that love built," this once-private garden is as fascinating for its history as for its innovative design. Seeds for the 1-acre residential garden were planted, figuratively, in Paris in the 1920s, when Englishwoman Peggy Pemberton-Carter met exiled Georgian Prince Nicholas Abkhazi. Separate World War II internment camps (his in Germany, hers near Shanghai) interrupted their romance, but they reunited and married in Victoria in 1946. They spent the next 40 years together cultivating their garden. Rescued from developers and now operated by the Land Conservancy of British Columbia, the Zen-like 1-acre site is recognized as one of Canada's most significant gardens and a leading example of West Coast horticultural design, resplendent with native Garry Oak trees, Japanese maples, and mature rhododendrons. The tearoom, in the sitting parlor of the modest, modernist home, serves lunch and afternoon tea. Watch for evening concerts in the garden. ✉ *1964 Fairfield Rd., Fairfield* ☎ *250/598–8096* ⊕ *www.conservancy.bc.ca* ✇ *C$10* ☾ *Mar.–Sept., Wed–Sun. 11–5.*

★ **Art Gallery of Greater Victoria.** Attached to an 1889 mansion, this modern building houses one of Canada's largest collections of Asian art. The Japanese garden between the buildings is home to the only authentic Shinto shrine in North America. The gallery, a few blocks west of Craigdarroch Castle, off Fort Street, displays a permanent exhibition of works by well-known Canadian artist Emily Carr and regularly changing exhibits of Asian and Western art. ✉ *1040 Moss St., Rockland* ☎ *250/384–4171* ⊕ *www.aggv.bc.ca* ✇ *C$12* ☾ *Mon.–Wed. and Fri.–Sat. 10–5, Thurs. 10–9, Sun. noon–5.*

★ **Craigdarroch Castle.** This resplendent mansion complete with turrets and Gothic rooflines was built as the home of one of British Columbia's wealthiest men, coal baron Robert Dunsmuir, who died in 1889, just a few months before the castle's completion. Now a museum depicting life in the late 1800s, the castle's 39 rooms have ornate Victorian furnishings, stained-glass windows, carved woodwork, and a beautifully restored painted ceiling in the drawing room. A winding staircase climbs four floors to a tower overlooking Victoria. Castles run in the family:

son James went on to build the even-more-lavish Hatley Castle just west of Victoria. Note that the castle is not wheelchair accessible and has no elevators. ⊠ *1050 Joan Crescent, Rockland* ☎ *250/592–5323* ⊕ *www.thecastle.ca* ☏ *C$12* ⊗ *Mid-June–early Sept., daily 9–7; early Sept.–mid-June, daily 10–4:30.*

WORTH NOTING

Government House Gardens. If you're in the area, you might take a stroll through the walled grounds and formal rose garden of Government House, the official residence of British Columbia's Lieutenant Governor, the Queen's representative in B.C. The stately, though modern, house itself isn't open to the public, though the 35 acres of gardens are. ⊠ *1401 Rockland Ave., Rockland* ☏ *Free* ⊗ *Daily dawn–dusk.*

Oak Bay Village. Described as the land "behind the tweed curtain," this self-consciously British area (with its own municipal hall) is home to such theme-y businesses as the Penny Farthing Pub and the Blethering Place tearoom, as well as plenty of sweet shops, bookshops, and antiques stores, most behind mock-Tudor facades. ⊠ *Along Oak Bay Ave. roughly between Foul Bay Rd. and Monterey Ave.* ⊕ *www.oakbayvillage.ca.*

Willows Beach Park. This neighborhood park has a nice sandy beach, a grassy park with a playground, and, this being Oak Bay, a teahouse. ⊠ *Along the Esplanade at the foot of Dalhousie St.*

SIDNEY AND THE SAANICH PENINSULA

30 km (18 mi) north of Victoria on Hwy. 17.

Home to the B.C. and Washington State ferry terminals as well as the Victoria International Airport, the Saanich Peninsula, with its rolling green hills and small family farms, is the first part of Vancouver Island that most visitors see. Although it's tempting to head straight for downtown Victoria, 25 minutes to the south, there are many reasons to linger here, including the Butchart Gardens, one of the province's leading attractions. Sidney's parklike waterfront, home to a brand-new aquarium and marine ecology center as well as cafés, restaurants, and a wheelchair-accessible waterfront path, is a launching point for kayakers, whale-watchers, and eco-tour boats heading out to explore the Gulf Islands National Park Reserve offshore.

GETTING HERE AND AROUND

To reach the area by car from downtown Victoria, follow the signs for the ferries straight up Highway 17, or take the Scenic Marine Drive starting at Dallas Road and following the coast north. It joins Highway 17 at Elk Lake (but take a map—even locals get lost traveling this way). Victoria transit buses serve the area, though not frequently. Bus tours to the Butchart Gardens run several times a day and many tours take in other sights in the area; several companies also offer winery tours. Gray Line West also runs a low-cost shuttle service to the Butchart Gardens and the Butterfly Gardens. Cyclists can take the Lochside Trail, which runs from Victoria to Sidney, detouring, perhaps, to some wineries along the way.

8

British Columbia Aviation Museum. Volunteers passionate about the history of flight have lovingly restored several dozen historic military and civilian airplanes, and even re-created a 19th-century flying machine at this museum near Victoria's International Airport. Pre-computer flight simulators, flight attendants' uniforms, a World War II–era aviation radio set (tapped into the action at the real airport next door), and memorials to Canadian military aviators are displayed in the museum hangar and tarmac outside. Volunteers conduct tours, which take about an hour. ⊠ *1910 Norseman Rd., Sidney* ☎ *250/655–3300* ⊕ *www.bcam. net* ☑ *C$7* ⊙ *May–Sept., daily 10–4; Oct.–Apr., daily 11–3.*

> **WORD OF MOUTH**
>
> "Butchart Gardens—beautiful place!! We took the Evening Illuminations tour with Gray Line and got to see the Gardens right before sunset and on into the late night.... Seeing the Gardens lit up at night was unique."
>
> —globetrotterxyz

The Butchart Gardens. This stunning 55-acre garden and National Historic Site has been drawing visitors since it was planted in a limestone quarry in 1904. Seven hundred varieties of flowers grow in the site's Japanese, Italian, rose, and sunken gardens. Highlights include the view over the ivy-draped and flower-filled former quarry, the dramatic 21-meter-high (70-foot-high) Ross Fountain, and the formal and intricate Italian garden, complete with a gelato stand. From mid-June to mid-September the gardens are illuminated at night with hundreds of hidden lights. In July and August, kids' entertainers perform Sunday through Friday afternoons; jazz, blues, and classical musicians play at an outdoor stage each evening; and fireworks draw crowds every Saturday night. The wheelchair- and stroller-accessible site is also home to a seed-and-gift shop, a plant identification center, two restaurants (one offering traditional afternoon tea), and a coffee shop; you can even call ahead for a picnic basket on fireworks nights. To avoid crowds, try to come at opening time, in the late afternoon or evening (except Saturday evenings, which also draw many visitors), or between September and June, when the gardens are still stunning. The grounds are especially magical at Christmas, with themed lighting and an ice rink. The gardens are about 20 minutes' drive north of downtown; parking is free and plentiful but fills up on fireworks Saturdays. You can get here by city bus 75 from Douglas Street downtown, but service is slow and infrequent. The Butchart Gardens Express Shuttle, run by Gray Line West, runs half-hourly service between downtown Victoria and the Butchart Gardens during peak season. Buses leave from the bus depot at 700 Douglas Street, behind the Fairmont Empress Hotel. The C$47 round-trip fare includes admission to the gardens. ⊠ *800 Benvenuto Ave., Brentwood Bay* ☎ *250/652–5256 or 866/652–4422. Gray Line West: 800/667–0882* ⊕ *www.butchartgardens.com* ☑ *Mid-June– late Sept. C$28, discounted rates rest of yr* ⊙ *Mid-June–Labor Day, daily 9 AM–10PM; Sept.–mid-June, daily 9 AM–dusk; call for exact times.*

The Centre of the Universe. You can enjoy great views of Victoria and the night sky through a 1.8-meter telescope, join astronomers and stargazers for summer-evening star parties, tour the observatory, or catch a planetarium show at this, the public face of the Dominion Astrophysical

Observatory. The hilltop site also offers great views over the surrounding countryside. ✉ *5071 W. Saanich Rd., Saanich* ☎ *250/363–8262* ⊕ *www.hia.nrc.gc.ca/cu* ✉ *C$9 before 7 PM, C$12 after 7 PM* ☉ *May–Sept., hours vary (call for times).*

☺ **Mount Douglas Regional Park.** A footpath and a road lead to a viewpoint at the 213-meter (758-foot) summit of Mt. Douglas, offering a 360-degree view of Victoria, the Saanich Peninsula, and the Malahat. On a clear day, you can even see the Gulf and San Juan islands and the mountains of Washington. The park, known locally as Mt. Doug, is also home to a long sandy beach, evergreen forests, hiking trails, and wildflower meadows. ✉ *Off Cedar Hill Rd., Saanich* ☎ *250/475–5522* ⊕ *www.gov.saanich.bc.ca* ✉ *Free.*

☺
★ **Shaw Ocean Discover Centre.** A simulated ride underwater in a deep-sea elevator is just the beginning of a visit to this fun and educational marine interpretive center, opened on Sidney's waterfront in 2009. Devoted entirely to the aquatic life and conservation needs of the Salish Sea—the waters south and east of Vancouver Island—the center displays local sea life, including luminous jellyfish, bright purple starfish, wolf eels, rockfish, and octopi, while hands-on activities, touch tanks, and knowledgeable volunteers inspire learning. Kids love the high-tech effects, including a floor projection that ripples when stepped on, streaming video, and a pop-up tank you can poke your head into. ✉ *9811 Seaport Pl., Sidney* ☎ *250/665–7511* ⊕ *www.oceandiscovery. ca* ✉ *$12* ☉ *Daily 10–5.*

Sidney Spit. In summer, a foot-passenger ferry makes the half-hour run to this long stretch of beach on Sidney Island, part of the Gulf Islands National Park Reserve. Hiking trails, picnic sites, and nonreservable campsites are also on the island. The ferry leaves several times a day from Beacon Wharf at the end of Beacon Avenue in Sidney. ☎ *250/655–4995 ferry information, 250/654–4000 park information* ⊕ *www.pc.gc. ca/gulf* ✉ *Ferry C$18, camping $13, park free* ☉ *Mid-May–June, weekends; July–early Sept., daily.*

8

NEED A
BREAK?

Not everyone loves ferry food. An option, if you're heading to or from a ferry at the Swartz Bay terminal, is to duck into the Stonehouse Pub (✉ 2215 Canoe Cove Rd. ☎ 778/426–1200) for a pint or a home-cooked meal. The tiny stone pub with garden looks like something you'd find in rural England. To find it, follow the signs for Canoe Cove Marina.

☺
★ **Victoria Butterfly Gardens.** Hundreds of butterflies—of 50 different species—flutter freely in an indoor tropical garden that's also home to orchids and carnivorous plants, koi, cockatoos, and flamingos. Twenty-minute guided tours run several times a day. The site is a popular stop en route to the Butchart Gardens, and children—and many adults—are entranced. The butterflies, which are bred for the center and not captured in the wild, are most active on sunny days. ✉ *1461 Benvenuto Ave., at the corner of West Saanich Rd. and Keating Cross Rd., Brentwood Bay* ☎ *250/652–3822 or 877/722–0272* ⊕ *www.butterflygardens. com* ✉ *C$12* ☉ *Mar., Apr., and early Sept.–Oct., daily 9:30–4:30; May–early Sept., daily 9–5:30; Nov.–Dec. and Feb., daily 9–4.*

THE WEST SHORE AND THE MALAHAT

West of downtown Victoria, along Highways 1 and 14, are the rapidly growing communities of View Royal, Colwood, the Highlands, Langford, and Metchosin, collectively known as the West Shore Communities. Although its rural nature is quickly giving way to suburban development, the area is worth a visit for its wilderness parks and national historic sites. Heading north, Highway 1 cuts through deep forests and over the 352-meter (1,155-foot) Malahat Summit on its way to the Cowichan Valley wine country. A viewpoint at the top, only accessible from the northbound lane, offers sweeping views over Finlayson Arm and the surrounding forested slopes.

🐾 **Fort Rodd Hill and Fisgard Lighthouse National Historic Sites of Canada.** The world's best-preserved coastal artillery fort (it dates to 1895) and Canada's oldest—and still operating—West Coast lighthouse occupy a parklike backdrop 14 km (8.4 mi) west of Victoria. You can walk through most of the buildings, including the lighthouse keeper's house, married quarters, guard houses, the delightfully named fortress-plotting room. Wandering deer, forest trails, and historic military hardware share the rolling seaside site, and the views from the gun emplacements over the entrance to Esquimalt Harbour are fabulous whether you're defending the city or having a picnic. To get there, take Highway 1A west to Ocean Boulevard. ✉ *603 Fort Rodd Hill Rd., off Ocean Blvd., West Shore* ☎ *250/478–5849* ⊕ *www.pc.gc.ca/fortroddhill* 🎟 *C$4* ⊙ *Mid-Feb.–Oct., daily 10–5:30; Nov.–mid-Feb., daily 9–4:30.*

Hatley Park National Historic Site of Canada. Built by James Dunsmuir, a

OFF THE
BEATEN
PATH

former premier of British Columbia and the son of Robert Dunsmuir (who built Craigdarroch Castle), this ivy-draped 40-room manor and its 565 acres of oceanfront grounds make up one of the finest intact Edwardian estates in Canada. Started in 1908 and built in just 18 months, the manor mixes Norman and Renaissance styles, which are meant to suggest a house that had stood for centuries. It's now part of the Royal Roads University campus, and the interior of the castle can be seen only by guided tour. The tours are informative, although almost none of the original furnishings—except a billiard table that was too big to remove—remain. You don't need to join a tour to see the beautifully preserved Italian, Japanese, and English rose gardens (though garden tours are occasionally available), or to see the small museum, which has artifacts from the Dunsmuir family and from the castle's days as a military college. To get there, take Highway 1A west from Victoria. Royal Roads University is on your left about half a mile past the turnoff to Fort Rodd Hill. ✉ *2005 Sooke Rd., Colwood, West Shore* ☎ *250/391–2666 or 866/241–0674* ⊕ *www.hatleypark.ca* 🎟 *Museum free, garden C$9.50, garden and 1-hr castle tour C$18* ⊙ *Museum daily 10–5. Castle May–Oct., daily 10–4; Nov.–Apr., call for times. Garden May–Oct., daily 10–5; Nov.–Apr., daily 10–4.*

🐾 **Goldstream Provincial Park.** Western red cedar, arbutus, eagles, bears, and three species of salmon thrive in this 288-hectare (711-acre) wilderness park just 16 km (10 mi) north of downtown Victoria. Picnic areas, easy riverside walks, challenging hikes, and camping draw visitors in

Hatley Park's 40-room castle is one of Canada's finest intact Edwardian estates; the gardens are quite spectacular, too.

summer. In winter, viewing stations are set up to watch thousands of bald eagles gather to feed on salmon. Covered, riverside picnic areas are close to the park entrance; park info and naturalists provide guidance at the visitor center, open 9–4:30 daily, a 10-minute walk from the parking lot. ⊠ *Hwy. 1* ⊕ *www.bcparks.ca* ◧ *C$3 per car.*

WHERE TO EAT

Victoria has a tremendous number and variety of restaurants for such a small city; this fact, and the glorious pantry that is Vancouver Island—think wild salmon and Pacific oysters, locally made cheese, and organic fruits and veggies—keeps prices down (at least compared to Vancouver) and standards up. Restaurants in the region are generally casual. Smoking is banned in all public places, including restaurant patios, in Greater Victoria, and on the Southern Gulf Islands. Victorians tend to dine early—restaurants get busy at 6, and many kitchens close by 9. Pubs, lounges, and the few open-late places mentioned here are your best option for an after-hours nosh.

DOWNTOWN

Use the coordinate (✛ B2) at the end of each listing to locate a site on the corresponding map.

$$$
CANADIAN
Fodor'sChoice
★

✕ **Aura.** One of Canada's top young chefs (Culinary Olympics star Brad Horen) meets the city's best waterfront patio at this chic eatery on the Inner Harbour's south shore. The seasonal-changing fare is locally sourced with Asian leanings: think wild local halibut and salmon; a "surf-and-turf" done with a sukiyaki-braised short rib, smoked scallops, and a maki roll; and a cellar full of hard-to-find Vancouver Island farm-gate wines. Sleek lines, warm colors, and water-view windows create a room that's both stylish and cozy. Live jazz plays Sundays. ✉ *680 Montreal St., at the Inn at Laurel Point, James Bay* ☎ *250/414–6739* ⊕ *www.aurarestaurant.ca* ▭ *AE, D, DC, MC, V* ⊹ *C4.*

$-$$
SEAFOOD
✕ **Barb's Place.** Funky Barb's, a tin-roofed take-out shack, floats on the quay at Fisherman's Wharf, west of the Inner Harbour off St. Lawrence Street. Halibut, salmon, oysters, mussels, crab, burgers, and chowder are all prepared fresh. The picnic tables on the wharf provide a front-row view of the brightly colored houseboats moored here, or you can carry your food to the grassy park nearby. Ferries sail to Fisherman's Wharf from the Inner Harbour. ✉ *Fisherman's Wharf, St. Lawrence St., Downtown* ☎ *250/384–6515* ▭ *AE, MC, V* ☯ *Closed Nov.–Feb.* ⊹ *B5.*

¢-$
CAFÉ
✕ **Blue Carrot Café.** Tucked off to the north side of Bastion Square in a historic building beside the Maritime Museum, this family-run spot with a few tables on the cobbles outside keeps local office workers fed with wholesome, mostly organic, omelet and eggs benedict breakfasts and affordable soup, sandwich, wrap, and burger lunches. The clubhouse sandwich and feta-avocado wraps are favorites, as are the yummy baked goods—all made by the owner herself. Local art lines the walls of the snug interior. ✉ *18B Bastion Sq., Downtown* ☎ *250/381–8722* ⌦ *Reservations not accepted* ▭ *MC, V* ☯ *No dinner. Closed Sun. Oct.– Mar.* ⊹ *E3.*

$$$-$$$$
SEAFOOD
✕ **Blue Crab Bar and Grill.** Fresh-daily seafood and expansive harbor views make this airy James Bay hotel restaurant a popular lunch and dinner spot. Signature dishes include a crab cake starter, a scallop-and-prawn sauté, and bouillabaisse in coconut green curry—but check the tempting daily specials on the blackboard. Desserts made in-house and a wine list highlighting British Columbia and Pacific Northwest wines round out the menu. The lounge area and patio, serving until 11PM nightly, has equally impressive views and a more casual menu. ✉ *Coast Harbourside Hotel and Marina, 146 Kingston St., Downtown* ☎ *250/480–1999* ⊕ *www.bluecrab.ca* ▭ *AE, D, MC, V* ⊹ *C5.*

$-$$$
FRENCH
✕ **Bon Rouge.** Craving a *croque madame* or a prawn crepe? Bouillabaisse, salade niçoise, or maybe just a really classy bacon-and-Gruyère cheeseburger? This casual bistro just off the Inner Harbour serves West Coast takes on French classics and has one of the city's nicest covered patios. Two inside rooms are done in high-energy red, white, and black; outside is a big shady space warmed by fireplaces, framed in greenery, and cooled with a wall fountain. There are sidewalk tables, too. The chef sources fare from nearby farms for the crepe-and-egg brunches, casual lunches, and romantic dinners. You can even buy fresh baguettes for a picnic to go. ✉ *611 Courtney St., Downtown* ☎ *250/220–8008* ⊕ *www.bonrouge.ca* ▭ *AE, MC,V* ⊹ *F4.*

$$-$$$
FRENCH
Fodor's Choice
★
✕ **Brasserie L'école.** French-country cooking shines at this informal Chinatown bistro, and the historic room—once a schoolhouse for the Chinese community—evokes a timeless brasserie, from the white linens and patina-rich fir floors to the chalkboards above the slate bar listing the day's oyster, mussel, and steak options. Sean Brennan, one of the city's

better-known chefs, works with local farmers and fishers to source the best seasonal, local, and organic ingredients. The menu changes daily but lists such classic bistro fare as duck confit, braised lamb shank, and trout with gnocchi. Be prepared for lines, though, as this 12-table spot does not take reservations. ⊠ *1715 Government St., Downtown* ☎ *250/475–6260* ⊕ *www.lecole.ca* ⌲ *Reservations not accepted* ▭ *AE, MC, V* ⊙ *Closed Sun. and Mon. No lunch* ✛ *F2.*

$$$
CANADIAN
Fodor's Choice
★

✕ **Cafe Brio.** "Charming, comfortable, and hip with walls of art—all backed by city's best chef and kitchen," is how one fodors.com user describes this bustling Italian villa–style room. The frequently changing menu highlights regional, organic fare; favorites include roast veal strip loin with crispy sweetbreads, butter-poached pheasant breast, local sablefish, albacore tuna, Cowichan Bay duck breast, and house-made charcuterie. Virtually everything, including the bread, pasta, and desserts, is made in-house—even the butter is hand churned. The 400-label wine list has a top selection of B.C. choices. ⊠ *944 Fort St., Downtown* ☎ *250/383–0009 or 866/270–5461* ▭ *AE, MC, V* ⊙ *No lunch* ✛ *H4.*

$$$
CANADIAN
★

✕ **Camille's.** Working closely with independent farmers, the chef at this long-established favorite concentrates on such locally sourced products as lamb, duck, and seafood; quail, venison, and ostrich often make an appearance, too. The menu is based on what's fresh, but might include lemon, ginger, and rock-prawn bisque; halibut with sea scallops and tiger prawns; or organic beef tenderloin. The five-course tasting menu, with optional wine matching, is popular. The wine cellar–like backdrop, on the lower floor of a historic building in Bastion Square, is candlelit and romantic, with exposed brick, local art, soft jazz and blues, and lots of intimate nooks and crannies. The wine list is well selected. ⊠ *45 Bastion Sq., Downtown* ☎ *250/381–3433* ⊕ *www.camillesrestaurant. com* ▭ *AE, MC, V* ⊙ *Closed Sun. and Mon. No lunch* ✛ *E3.*

$$–$$$
CANADIAN

✕ **Canoe Brewpub.** The lofty windows of this brick-lined power station–turned–brewpub open onto one of Victoria's best waterfront patios, overlooking the kayaking and ferry action on the gorge. The casual, locally sourced menu runs from such high-end pub snacks as halibut tacos and steamed edamame to steaks, burgers, Singapore noodles, thin-crust pizzas, and good old fish-and-chips. Choose from the adults-only brewpub or the all-ages restaurant—both have water-view patios. And try the beer—the Beaver Brown Ale, River Rock Bitter, and other signature creations are brewed on-site, the old-fashioned way. You can even see the vats from the pub. ⊠ *450 Swift St., Downtown* ☎ *250/361–1940* ⊕ *www.canoebrewpub.com* ⌲ *Reservations not accepted for patio or brewpub* ▭ *AE, DC, MC, V* ✛ *E2.*

$$$–$$$$
CANADIAN
★

✕ **Empress Room.** Candlelight dances beneath a carved mahogany ceiling at the Fairmont Empress hotel's flagship restaurant where one of the two gracious rooms has an expansive harbor view. The classically influenced, Pacific Northwest menu changes seasonally, but might feature appetizers such as seared local scallops or a selection of Vancouver Island oysters, and move to such mains as herb-dusted beef tenderloin; local wild salmon with Dungeness crab; or pan-roasted venison loin. Service is discreet and attentive, and there are more than 800 labels on the wine list. The Empress Room is also open for family-friendly

8

Cafe Brio is one of Victoria's premier dining destinations due to the top-notch regional food, an extensive wine list, and the casual and friendly ambience.

breakfasts. If the weather is fine, the summer-only Veranda serves lunch, cocktails, and early-evening snacks with Inner Harbour views. ⊠ *Fairmont Empress, 721 Government St., Downtown* ☎ *250/389–2727* ⊕ *www.fairmont.com/empress* ⌦ *Reservations not accepted for the Veranda* ▭ *AE, D, DC, MC, V* ✛ *E5*.

$$–$$$$ ✕ **Il Terrazzo.** A cute redbrick terrace edged with potted greenery and
ITALIAN warmed by fireplaces and overhead heaters makes Il Terrazzo—tucked
★ away off Waddington Alley near Market Square and not visible from the street—the locals' choice for romantic alfresco dining. The menu changes frequently, but starters might include spicy Italian sausages with braised fennel, or steamed mussels with sun-dried tomatoes and spicy banana peppers. Mains range from such traditional Northern Italian favorites as breaded scaloppini of pork tenderloin to a more local-leaning halibut with blackberries. Thin-crust pizzas come piping hot from the restaurant's open-flame stone oven. ⊠ *Johnson St., off Waddington Alley (½ block east of Wharf St., behind Willie's Bakery), Downtown* ☎ *250/361–0028* ⊕ *www.ilterrazzo.com* ▭ *AE, DC, MC, V* ⊙ *No lunch Sun. No lunch Sat. Oct.–May* ✛ *E3*.

$$ ✕ **J&J Won Ton Noodle House.** Lunchtime queues attest to the popularity
CHINESE of the fresh house-made noodles and wontons at this pan-Asian spot on antique row. The lines move fast, though, thanks to the efficient service. Szechuan and Shanghai specialties, from shrimp noodle soup to beef with hot-chili bean sauce, dominate the long menu, but Singapore-style noodles and Indonesian chow mein appear, too. The basic diner-style restaurant is low on character, but the crowds of locals and an open kitchen keep things buzzing. Reservations are accepted only for groups

of four or more. ✉ *1012 Fort St., Downtown* ☎ *250/383–0680* ⊕ *www. jjnoodlehouse.com* ▭ *MC, V* ⊘ *Closed Sun. and Mon.* ✛ *H4.*

$$$–$$$$
SEAFOOD

✕**Lure Seafood Restaurant and Bar.** Walls of windows embrace Inner Harbour views at the Delta Victoria Ocean Pointe Resort's flagship restaurant. Seafood-loving locals and hotel guests book window-side tables at sunset to watch the lights come on across the water: the large comfortable room with upholstered chairs and beige walls doesn't even try to compete with the view. The food puts on a good show, though, with elaborate presentations of locally sourced fare. Sooke trout, wild salmon, and B.C. halibut top a menu that also encompasses Cowichan Valley duck-and-herb–crusted rack of lamb. Breakfasts are highly rated, too. ✉ *45 Songhees Rd., Downtown* ☎ *250/360–5873* ⊕ *www. lurevictoria.com* ▭ *AE, DC, MC, V* ✛ *D3.*

$$$–$$$$
FRENCH
★

✕**Matisse.** The gracious owner greets each guest personally at this tiny gem of a traditional French restaurant where white linens, fresh flowers, and candlelight on the dozen or so tables set the stage for meals of such seasonally changing, well-executed bistro classics as vichyssoise, fillet bordelaise, or a fricassee of lobster, scallops, and prawns with black-truffle risotto. The primarily French wine list has plenty of affordable options and the bread pudding, crème brûlée, and housemade sorbets are much-loved finales. Piaf chansons on the speakers and Matisse originals on the wall add to the pleasing character. ✉ *512 Yates St., Downtown* ☎ *250/480–0883* ⊕ *www.restaurantmatisse.com* ▭ *AE, MC, V* ⊘ *No lunch. No dinner Mon. and Tues.* ✛ *E3.*

$–$$
CANADIAN
★

✕**Mo:Lé.** It's been called "fine dining for vegans," but this brick-lined Chinatown café has plenty of wholesome, organic, local fare for meat eaters, too. At breakfast, large helpings of free-range eggs, locally made sausages, and organic, spelt griddle cakes fuel a post-party, pre-yoga crowd. At lunch, locals might pop in for an avocado, dulse (seaweed), and sprout sandwich, a yam wrap, or an organic beef burger. The place is tiny, but the Habit coffee shop next door acts as a holding bar— the folks at Mo:Lé will let you know when your table's ready. ✉ *554 Pandora St., Downtown* ☎ *250/385–6653* ⊕ *www.molerestaurant.ca* ⌔ *Reservations not accepted* ▭ *MC, V* ⊘ *No dinner* ✛ *F2.*

$–$$
ASIAN
★

✕**The Noodle Box.** Noodles, whether Indonesian style with peanut sauce, thick Japanese udon in teriyaki, or Thai-style chow mein, are piled straight from steaming woks in the open kitchen to bowls or cardboard take-out boxes at this local answer to fast food. Malaysian, Singapore, and Cambodian-style curries tempt those who like it hot. The brick, rose, and lime walls keep things modern and high energy at the Douglas Street location near the Inner Harbour. The Fisgard Street outlet is a tiny hole-in-the-wall near Chinatown. ✉ *818 Douglas St., Downtown* ☎ *250/384–1314* ⌔ *Reservations not accepted* ▭ *AE, MC, V* ✛ *F4*✉ *626 Fisgard St., Downtown* ☎ *250/360–1312* ⌔ *Reservations not accepted* ▭ *AE, MC, V* ✛ *F2.*

$$–$$$
ITALIAN

✕**Pagliacci's.** Expect long lines at this lively New York–meets-Victoria trattoria where the tables are tightly packed to accommodate the crowds. Opened by Brooklyn's Siegel brothers in 1979, Pagliacci's is all showbiz, from the signed photos of the owners' movie-star friends plastering the walls to the live jazz playing several nights a week. The menu runs from the "Mae West" (finally a "veal" woman) to the Prawns Al Capone and includes about 20 pastas. Pag's is crowded, frenetic, and buckets of fun. ✉ *1001 Broad St., Downtown* ☎ *250/386–1662* ⊕ *www.pagliaccis.ca* ⌲ *Reservations not accepted* ▭ *AE, MC, V* ⊹ *F4.*

$–$$ ✕ **Re-Bar Modern Food.** Bright and casual, with lime-green walls and
VEGETARIAN a splashy Bollywood poster, this kid-friendly café in Bastion Square is *the* place for vegetarians in Victoria—but don't worry, the almond burgers, enchiladas, decadent baked goodies, and big breakfasts keep omnivores happy, too. Try the yam and pumpkin-seed quesadillas, the honey-glazed wild salmon, or the vegan Monk's Curry. An extensive selection of teas, fresh juices, and wheat-grass concoctions shares space on the drinks list with espresso, microbrews, and B.C. wines. ✉ *50 Bastion Sq., Downtown* ☎ *250/361–9223* ⊕ *www.rebarmodernfood.com* ▭ *AE, DC, MC, V* ☉ *No dinner Sun.* ⊹ *F3.*

$–$$ ✕ **Red Fish Blue Fish.** If you like your fish both yummy *and* ecologically
SEAFOOD friendly, look no further than this former shipping container on the pier at the foot of Broughton Street. From the soil-topped roof and biodegradable packaging to the sustainably harvested, local seafood, this waterfront take-out shop minimizes its ecological footprint. The chef offers a choice of local wild salmon, tuna, oysters, and scallops from the barbecue. Portuguese buns are baked daily for the seafood sandwiches, fish tacos come in grilled tortilla cones, and even plain old fish-and-chips are taken up a notch with a choice of wild salmon, halibut, or cod in tempura batter with hand-cut, thick fries. Be prepared for queues on sunny days. ✉ *1006 Wharf St., Downtown* ☎ *250/298–6877* ⊕ *www.redfish-bluefish.com* ⌲ *Reservations not accepted* ▭ *MC, V* ⊹ *E4.*

¢–$ ✕ **Sam's Deli.** For a quick pit stop while you're strolling the Inner Har-
CAFÉ bour, you can't beat this long-established, perpetually busy sandwich bar catercorner to the Tourist Information Office. Thick sandwiches, salads, big bowls of homemade soup, and lunch plate–size cookies come cheap, hearty, and cafeteria style. Breakfasts of egg-and-bagel sandwiches, fruit salad, and granola help fuel a day's sightseeing. High ceilings, wood booths, and historic photos give the interior—a former hotel lobby—a touch of atmosphere, and the patio seats are prime people-watching territory. ✉ *805 Government St., Downtown* ☎ *250/382–8424* ⊕ *www.samsdeli.com* ⌲ *Reservations not accepted* ▭ *AE, MC, V* ☉ *No dinner Nov.–Feb.* ⊹ *F4.*

$–$$ ✕ **Spinnakers Gastro Brewpub.** Victoria's longest menu of handcrafted
CANADIAN beer is just one reason to trek over the Johnson Street Bridge or hop a
★ Harbour Ferry to this Vic West waterfront pub. Canada's oldest licensed brewpub, Spinnakers relies almost exclusively on locally sourced ingredients for its top-notch casual fare. Opt for the pubby adults-only taproom, with its covered waterfront deck, double-sided fireplace, and wood-beam rooms; or dine in the all-ages waterfront restaurant. Either way you can enjoy such high-end pub grub as mussels steamed in ale, wild salmon fettuccine, or fish-and-chips with thick-cut fries. A take-away deli, bakery, and chocolatier is another place to try the house-made fare. ✉ *308 Catherine St., Downtown* ☎ *250/386–2739 or 877/838–2739* ⌲ *Reservations not accepted in the Taproom* ▭ *AE, MC, V* ⊹ *B2.*

Afternoon Tea in Victoria

Maybe it's the city's British heritage, but afternoon tea—a snack of tea, cakes, and sandwiches taken at about 4 PM, not to be confused with "high tea," a hot meal eaten at dinner-time—lives on in Victoria. The most authentic places are near the Inner Harbour and in the very British Oak Bay district, often described as being "behind the tweed curtain."

Victoria's most elaborate and most expensive afternoon tea is served, as it has been since 1908, in the ornate lobby of the **Fairmont Empress Hotel.** The tea is the hotel's own blend, and the cakes, scones, and crustless sandwiches are prepared by some of Victoria's finest pastry chefs. As you face the bill of C$55 per person in high season, remember that tea at the Empress is more than a snack; it was, historically, a way to keep civilization alive in this farthest outpost of the empire. Seatings start daily at noon. ⊠ *721 Government St., Downtown* ☎ *250/389–2727.*

Dripping with British memorabilia, **Blethering Place** serves a tea of scones, Devonshire cream, fruit, sandwiches, cakes, and tarts between 11 AM and 7:30 PM. English breakfasts and roast dinners are also available. ⊠ *2250 Oak Bay Ave., Oak Bay* ☎ *250/598–1413 or 888/598–1413.*

At tiny **Mela's Tearoom, an extension of** Winchester Galleries, an art dealer just east of the Inner Harbour, custom-blended teas, fruit salad, scones with jam and cream, and yummy chocolate ganache cake are served Tuesday–Saturday, noon–5, year-round. Organic coffee and European baked goods are available at the Viennese-style Café Mela, next door at 784 Humboldt Street.

⊠ *792 Humboldt St., Downtown* ☎ *250/382–8528.*

For a Pacific Rim twist on the tea tradition try the **Pacific Restaurant** in the Hotel Grand Pacific. There is a choice of teas and nibbles like spot-prawn brochettes, First Nations bannock with clotted cream and apple jam, and green tea–cured wild salmon lox. Tea is served 2–4:30 PM daily, for C$38 per person. ⊠ *463 Belleville St., Downtown* ☎ *250/380–4458.*

Everything, including the jam, is homemade for the Scottish-style teas served in the **White Heather Tea Room,** a lovely place with big windows. ⊠ *1885 Oak Bay Ave., Oak Bay* ☎ *250/595–8020.*

Several of Victoria's gardens and historic homes make atmospheric settings for tea. The sun-drenched living room of the **Abkhazi Garden,** at the Abkhazi home, is lovely for lunch and afternoon tea. ⊠ *1964 Fairfield Rd., Fairfield* ☎ *250/598–8096* ☺ *Mar.–Sept., Wed.–Sun. 11–5.*

The dining room at **The Butchart Gardens** serves traditional English afternoon tea, daily year-round. ⊠ *800 Benvenuto Ave., Brentwood Bay* ☎ *250/652–8222 or 866/652–4422.*

Wicker armchairs under an awning on the lawn of the Victorian **Point Ellice House** are a lovely setting for afternoon tea with home-baked goodies. Harbour Ferries from the Inner Harbour deliver you directly to the garden. ⊠ *2616 Pleasant St., Downtown* ☎ *250/380–6506* ⌑ *C$23 includes tea and admission to the cottage* ☺ *Mid-May–mid-June and mid-Sept.–late Sept. tea served Thurs.–Mon. 11–3; mid-June–mid-Sept tea daily 11–3:30.*

8

$-$$ ✕ **The Tapa Bar.** Chef-owner Danno
SPANISH Lee has re-created the fun and flavors of a Spanish tapas bar in this
little pedestrian-only lane off Government Street. Small flavorful
dishes run from simple-but-tasty
grilled vegetables to prawns in white

wine, spicy mussels, open-faced sandwiches, thin-crust pizzas, pastas, a
multitude of vegetarian options, and hearty soups. One specialty is the
Pollo Armanda: charbroiled boneless chicken with artichokes, sun-dried
tomatoes, capers, lemon, and white wine. Almond-stuffed dates are a
particular hit. Deep-yellow painted walls, exposed brick, distressed tile,
and lively artwork create a casual interior; the wrought-iron patio is a
choice spot on a sunny day. ■TIP➔ Just need a snack? Tapas are served
all afternoon and late into the evening. ✉ *620 Trounce Alley, Downtown*
☎ *250/383–0013* ▭ *AE, MC, V* ✢ *F3.*

¢-$ ✕ **Willie's Bakery & Cafe.** Housed in a handsome Victorian building near
CAFÉ Market Square, this bakery-café goes organic, free-range, and local in
its omelets, brioches, French toast, and homemade granola breakfasts
and its lunches of homemade soups, thick sandwiches, and tasty baked
treats. A brick patio with an outdoor fireplace is partially glassed in
so you can lunch alfresco even on chilly days. Willie's claims to be
the oldest bakery in British Columbia and bread is still baked in the
back room, just as it has been since 1887. ✉ *537 Johnson St., Downtown* ☎ *250/381–8414* ⊕ *www.williesbakery.com* ⬗ *Reservations not
accepted* ▭ *MC, V* ☾ *No dinner* ✢ *E3.*

$$-$$$ ✕ **Zambri's.** The downtown strip-mall surroundings might not impress,
ITALIAN but inside is a lively trattoria warmed by terra-cotta tiles, wood tables,
and an open kitchen producing traditional Italian dishes from local
organic ingredients. Lunch is busy and casual: order at the counter from
a daily changing roster of pastas and hot sandwiches. Dinner brings
table service and a menu of such hearty fare as *tagliolini* with crab ragù
and grappa, or roasted pork loin with salsa *pizzaiola* and polenta; a
nightly three-course tasting menu is also an option. ✉ *110–911 Yates
St., Downtown* ☎ *250/360–1171* ⊕ *www.zambris.ca* ⬗ *Reservations
not accepted* ▭ *AE, MC, V* ☾ *Closed Sun. and Mon.* ✢ *H3.*

OAK BAY AND ROCKLAND

$$-$$$ ✕ **The Marina Restaurant.** This large circular room with art deco rose-
SEAFOOD wood booths and a 180-degree view over the sailboats of the Oak Bay
Marina has a chef with a deft hand for seafood. Grills and pastas are
on the menu, but it's on daily specials, offering such local catches as
lingcod, trout, and wild salmon, served lightly sauced and teamed with
local organic vegetables, where things get interesting. Starters, such as
crab-and-halibut cheek-cakes or Salt Spring Island mussels, a lunch
menu of salads, pastas, and burgers, and an evening-only sushi bar
also favor local ingredients. An attached marina-side coffee bar makes
a handy stop on a seaside drive or cycle tour. ✉ *1327 Beach Dr., Oak
Bay* ☎ *250/598–8555* ▭ *AE, MC, V.*

$$$
CANADIAN
★

✕ **Paprika Bistro.** Local farmers, fishers, and winemakers provide most of the ingredients at this intimate neighborhood bistro, where the French- and Italian-inspired seasonal menus might include such starters as Cortes Island mussels and house-made charcuterie, followed by Cowichan Bay duck breast or just-caught local fish. Three small rooms with brocade booths and local art on paprika-and-lemon walls are warm, romantic, and informal. The cozy 80-seat restaurant is a local favorite. ⊠ *2524 Estevan Ave., Oak Bay and Rockland* ☎ *250/592–7424* ▭ *AE, MC, V* ⊘ *No lunch. Closed Sun. and Mon.*

SIDNEY AND THE SAANICH PENINSULA

$$–$$$$
CANADIAN

✕ **Brentwood SeaGrille & Pub.** Local seafood paired with wines from neighboring vineyards shine at this lofty ocean-view restaurant in the Brentwood Bay Lodge. Start, for example, with a Pacific spot-prawn salad, Dungeness crab cakes, or something from the sushi bar, then opt for Queen Charlotte halibut, roasted lingcod, butter-poached scallops, or Aleutian Islands sablefish. Beef, lamb, and poultry dishes appear as well, and a five-course tasting menu is often offered. Wood-burning fireplaces, two-story-high windows, and a wonderful array of Canadian art warm the interior; outside, a heated patio takes in views of Saanich Inlet. A more casual marina-view pub offers burgers, pizzas, and craft beers. ⊠ *849 Verdier Ave, Brentwood Bay* ☎ *250/544–5100* ▭ *AE, MC, V* ⊘ *No lunch in the SeaGrille restaurant.*

THE WEST SHORE AND THE MALAHAT

$$$$
CANADIAN
Fodor'sChoice
★

✕ **The Aerie.** Breathtaking views of Finlayson Arm and the Gulf Islands are the backdrop for some of Vancouver Island's finest meals at this resort restaurant, perched on a hillside north of Victoria. The chef relies almost exclusively on local organic ingredients and heritage produce varieties for his frequently changing breakfast, lunch, dinner, and multicourse tasting menus. Starters, for example, might be a warm-duck salad or local oysters, followed by such mains as arctic char, rack of lamb, or Pacific halibut. The cellar possesses many sought-after B.C. vintages. ⊠ *600 Ebedora Lane, off Hwy. 1, Malahat* ☎ *250/743–7115 or 800/518–1933* ▭ *AE, MC, V.*

8

$$–$$$
CANADIAN

✕ **Malahat Mountain Inn.** This roadhouse near the Malahat summit, about 30 minutes north of Victoria, doesn't look like much from the highway, but inside, the view over Finlayson Arm and the Gulf Islands is magnificent. The scenery is especially striking from the large outdoor deck, perched 600 feet (183 meters) over the Saanich Inlet. The lunch menu lists such casual fare as burgers, wraps, pastas, and hefty hot sandwiches; dinner brings straightforward pasta and meat dishes. If you can't tear yourself away from the scenery, consider a room at the 10-room inn next door; it's run by the same people ($$$–$$$$). ⊠ *265 Trans-Canada Hwy., Malahat* ☎ *250/478–1979* ⊕ *www.malahatmountaininn.ca* ▭ *AE, MC, V* ⊘ *Closed Mon. Oct.–May.*

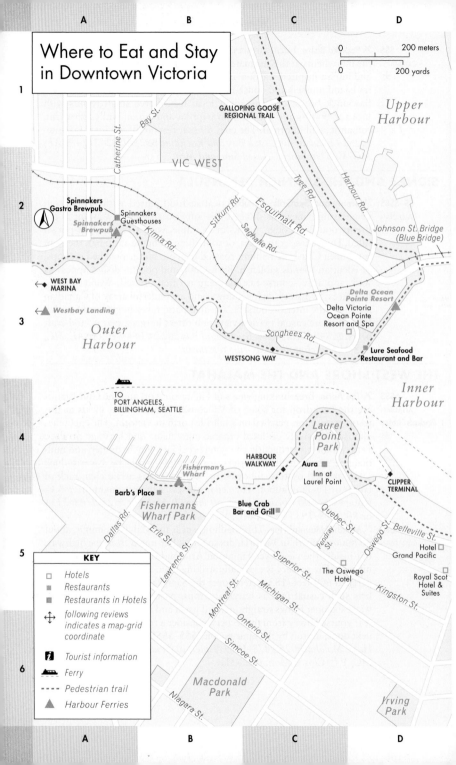

Where to Eat and Stay in Downtown Victoria

0 — 200 meters
0 — 200 yards

1

Upper Harbour

Bay St.

GALLOPING GOOSE REGIONAL TRAIL

VIC WEST

Catherine St.

Tyee Rd.

Harbour Rd.

2

Spinnakers Gastro Brewpub

Spinnakers Guesthouses

Spinnakers Brewpub

Sitkum Rd.

Esquimalt Rd.

Saghalie Rd.

Kimta Rd.

Johnson St. Bridge (Blue Bridge)

← WEST BAY MARINA

← ▲ Westbay Landing

Outer Harbour

Delta Ocean Pointe Resort

Delta Victoria Ocean Pointe Resort and Spa

3

Songhees Rd.

WESTSONG WAY

Lure Seafood Restaurant and Bar

TO PORT ANGELES, BILLINGHAM, SEATTLE

Inner Harbour

Laurel Point Park

4

Fisherman's Wharf

HARBOUR WALKWAY

Aura ■

Inn at Laurel Point

CLIPPER TERMINAL

Barb's Place

Fishermans Wharf Park

Blue Crab Bar and Grill ■

Quebec St.

Oswego St.

Belleville St.

Dallas Rd.

Erie St.

Lawrence St.

Pendray St.

Hotel □ Grand Pacific

5

KEY

□ Hotels
■ Restaurants
■ Restaurants in Hotels
⊕ following reviews indicates a map-grid coordinate

🛈 Tourist information
🚤 Ferry
--- Pedestrian trail
▲ Harbour Ferries

Superior St.

Montreal St.

Michigan St.

The Oswego Hotel

Royal Scot Hotel & Suites

Kingston St.

6

Ontario St.

Simcoe St.

Macdonald Park

Niagara St.

Irving Park

A   B   C   D

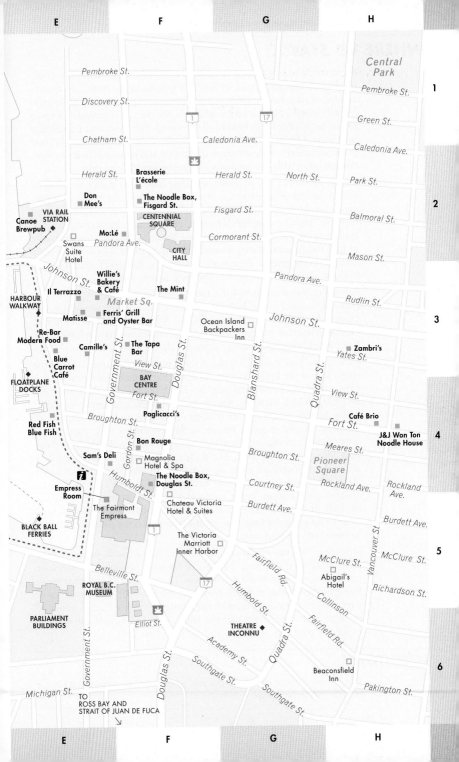

WHERE TO STAY

Victoria has a vast range of accommodation, with what seems like whole neighborhoods dedicated to hotels. Options range from city resorts and full-service business hotels to midpriced tour-group haunts, family-friendly motels, and backpacker hostels, but the city is especially known for its lavish B&Bs in beautifully restored Victorian and Edwardian mansions. Outlying areas, such as Sooke, Saanich, and the Malahat pride themselves on destination spa resorts and luxurious country inns, though affordable accommodation can be found there, too.

British Columbia law prohibits smoking inside any public building or within 20 feet of an entrance. As a result, all Victoria hotels are completely smoke-free, including on patios and balconies, and in public areas. Only the larger modern hotels have air-conditioning, but it rarely gets hot enough to need it. Advance reservations are always a good idea, especially in July and August. Watch for discounts of up to 50% in the off-season (roughly November to February); though even then you'll need to book, as many rooms fill with retirees escaping prairie winters.

Rooms in Victoria are levied a Goods and Services Tax (GST) of 5% plus a B.C. hotel tax of 10%. In addition, most downtown hotels also charge about C$15 per day for parking. Ask about phone and Internet charges (these can range from free to excessive) and have a look at the hotel breakfast menu; nearby cafés are almost always cheaper.

Downtown hotels are clustered in three main areas. James Bay, on the south side of the Inner Harbour near the Parliament Buildings, is basically a residential and hotel neighborhood. Bordered by the waterfront and Beacon Hill Park, the area is quiet at night and handy for sightseeing by day. It is, however, thin on restaurants and a bit of a hike to the main shopping areas. Hotels in the downtown core, particularly along Government and Douglas streets, are right in the thick of shopping, dining, and nightlife, but do get more traffic noise. You'll also see more of Victoria's growing homeless population in this area. Vic West, across the Johnson Street Bridge on the harbor's north shore, is another quiet option, but it's a good 15-minute walk or ferry ride to the bulk of shopping, dining, and sightseeing. Even so, you won't need a car to stay in any of these areas and, given parking charges, you may be better off without one.

Outside of downtown, Rockland and Oak Bay are lush, peaceful, tree-lined residential districts; the mile or so walk into town is pleasant, but you won't want to do it every day. The resorts and inns that we've listed further afield, in Saanich and on the Malahat are, for the most part, self-contained resorts with restaurants and spas. Each is about 30 minutes from downtown Victoria and you'll need a car if you want to make day trips into town.

DOWNTOWN

Use the coordinate (✣ B2) at the end of each listing to locate a site on the corresponding map.

$$$$ ⊡ **Abigail's Hotel.** A Tudor-style inn built in 1930, Abigail's is just three blocks from the Inner Harbour. The big sunny rooms are attractively and individually furnished in an English country style. Down comforters, whirlpool tubs, and wood-burning fireplaces in many rooms add to the luxurious aura, and the six large rooms in the Coach House building are especially lavish. A three-course breakfast is served at tables for two or on the patio; beer, wine, and complimentary appetizers are served each evening in the library. A spa-treatment room adds to the pampering. **Pros:** luxurious; atmospheric; and central. **Cons:** no pool or gym. ⊠ *906 McClure St., Downtown* ☎ *250/388–5363 or 800/561–6565* ⊕ *www.abigailshotel.com* ⇌ *23 rooms* ⌂ *In-room: DVD, Wi-Fi. In-hotel: Spa, laundry service, Internet terminal, Wi-Fi, parking (free), some pets allowed* ☰ *AE, MC, V* ⍨ *BP* ✛ *H5.*

$$–$$$$ ⊡ **Beaconsfield Inn.** This 1905 registered historic building four blocks
★   from the Inner Harbour is one of Victoria's most faithfully restored Edwardian mansions. Though the rooms and suites all have antique furniture, high ceilings, and period details, each also has a unique look; several rooms have jetted tubs or fireplaces, and one room even includes an Edwardian, wooden canopied tub. Three-course breakfasts and tea and sherry in the conservatory or around the library fire complete the English country-manor experience. In-room spa services are a nice touch, too. **Pros:** luxurious; kid-free. **Cons:** kids not permitted; several blocks from shopping and dining. ⊠ *998 Humboldt St., Downtown* ☎ *250/384–4044 or 888/884–4044* ⊕ *www.beaconsfieldinn.com* ⇌ *5 rooms, 4 suites* ⌂ *In-room: No a/c, Wi-Fi. In-hotel: Internet terminal, Wi-Fi, parking (free), no kids under 10* ☰ *AE, MC, V* ⍨ *BP* ✛ *H6.*

$$ ⊡ **Chateau Victoria Hotel & Suites.** Far-reaching views from the upper-floor suites and the 18th-floor restaurant are a plus at this good-value, centrally located, independent hotel where the entryway fountain and bright open lobby suggest a pricier place. Lower-floor standard rooms are small and plain but clean and well priced; suites are chicer, with full balconies, views, and an up-to-date, earth-tone color scheme. The upper-floor two-bedroom suites are huge and have private decks. A full range of in-room spa services is available and there's a bike storage room. **Pros:** free parking; free Internet; free local calls; great rates and location. **Cons:** standard rooms lack views. ⊠ *740 Burdett Ave., Downtown* ☎ *250/382–4221 or 800/663–5891* ⊕ *www.chateauvictoria.com* ⇌ *59 rooms, 118 suites* ⌂ *In-room: Safe, kitchen (some), refrigerator, Wi-Fi. In-hotel: 2 restaurants, room service, bars, pool, gym, laundry service, Internet terminal, Wi-Fi, parking (free), some pets allowed* ☰ *AE, D, DC, MC, V* ✛ *F5.*

$$$$ ⊡ **Delta Victoria Ocean Pointe Resort and Spa.** Across the Johnson Street Bridge from downtown Victoria, this waterfront property has all sorts of resort facilities, from tennis and squash courts to a popular spa, a 24-hour gym, and a waterfront walking path. Rooms, many with views of the Parliament Buildings across the water, are spacious and airy. Conferences do play a big role here, though kids are made welcome with check-in treats, discounted meals, and evening story time. The hotel's restaurant, Lure ($$$), offers fresh local seafood and expansive harbor views. **Pros:** water views; full range of facilities; free Internet; downtown

8

shuttle and harbor ferry service. **Cons:** not central; gets busy with conferences and groups. ⊠ *45 Songhees Rd., Downtown* ☎ *250/360–2999 or 800/667–4677* ⊕ *www.deltahotels.com/prov/p_british.html* ↩ *233 rooms, 6 suites* ♿ *In-room: Kitchen (some), refrigerator, Internet (some). In-hotel: Restaurant, room service, bar, tennis courts, pool, gym, spa, laundry service, Wi-Fi, parking (paid), some pets allowed* ⊟ *AE, D, DC, MC, V* ✛ *D3.*

$$$$ ⊞ **The Fairmont Empress.** A hundred years old in 2008, this ivy-draped harborside château and city landmark has aged gracefully, with top-notch service and sympathetically restored Edwardian furnishings. The 176 different room configurations include standard and harbor-view rooms with 11-foot ceilings. State-of-the-art gym equipment and an indoor pool are welcome touches. If you stay on the Fairmont Gold floor, you will enjoy a private lounge, a Continental breakfast, and evening snacks. The hotel is a tourist attraction, but a guests-only lobby separates hotel guests from the throng. **Pros:** central location; professional service; great spa and restaurant. **Cons:** small-to-average-size rooms and bathrooms; tourists in the public areas; pricey. ⊠ *721 Government St., Downtown* ☎ *250/384–8111 or 800/257–7544* ⊕ *www. fairmont.com/empress* ↩ *436 rooms, 41 suites* ♿ *In-room: No a/c (some), refrigerator, Internet. In-hotel: 2 restaurants, room service, bar, pool, gym, spa, laundry service, Internet terminal, Wi-Fi, parking (paid), some pets allowed* ⊟ *AE, D, DC, MC, V* ✛ *E5.*

$$$–$$$$ ⊞ **Hotel Grand Pacific.** The city's best health club (with yoga classes,
★ squash courts, and state-of-the-art equipment) and a prime Inner Harbour location appeal to savvy business and leisure regulars, including Seattleites stepping off the ferry across the street. Feng shui design elements apply throughout, lending a calm energy to the gleaming marble lobby. Rooms are large and surprisingly quiet, with deep soaker tubs, floor-to-ceiling windows, and a muted decor. Upper-floor rooms have views of the harbor, the Parliament Buildings, or mountains, which you can admire from your private balcony, big enough to sit out on. **Pros:** great health club; staffed business center; prime location; balconies and views. **Cons:** standard hotel décor; markup on local calls and Internet. ⊠ *463 Belleville St., Downtown* ☎ *250/386–0450 or 800/663–7550* ⊕ *www.hotelgrandpacific.com* ↩ *258 rooms, 46 suites* ♿ *In-room: Safe, refrigerator, DVD (some), Internet. In-hotel: 3 restaurants, room service, bar, pool, gym, spa, laundry service, Internet terminal, Wi-Fi, parking (paid), some pets allowed* ⊟ *AE, D, MC, V* ✛ *D5.*

$$$–$$$$ ⊞ **Inn at Laurel Point.** Set on a peninsula on the Inner Harbour's quiet
Fodor's Choice   south shore, this Asian-inspired hotel affords harbor views from every
★ room. A seaside Japanese garden, a resort's worth of facilities, and a museum-quality art collection make this freshly renovated, independent hotel a favorite among Victoria regulars. Rooms—especially in the Arthur Erickson–designed southern wing—are light and airy, with blond wood and Asian touches; all have balconies and some suites have large harbor-view decks. In-room spa services, free local calls and Internet, and an indoor pool are among the pluses. The restaurant is one of the city's best. **Pros:** views; quiet, parklike setting. **Cons:** 10-minute walk to downtown. ⊠ *680 Montreal St., Downtown* ☎ *250/386–8721 or*

800/663–7667 ⊕ www.laurelpoint.com ⇆ 135 rooms, 65 suites ⚄ In-room: Safe, refrigerator, Internet, Wi-Fi (some). In-hotel: Restaurant, room service, bar, pool, gym, laundry service, Internet terminal, Wi-Fi, parking (paid), some pets allowed ▭ AE, D, DC, MC, V ⊕ C4.

$$$$ 🏨 **Magnolia Hotel & Spa.** From the on-site spa to the valet parking, soaker tubs, sauna, and herb tea, the Magnolia, without actually saying so, caters beautifully to the female traveler—though the attention to detail, hop-to-it staff, and central location won't be lost on men either. Rooms are large, with tall windows, lots of natural light, rich colors, and good soundproofing; some have gas fireplaces. All the high-end details— duvets, turndown service, and newspapers at the door—are here, too. **Pros:** great location; friendly and helpful service; welcoming lobby with fireplace, tea, and coffee. **Cons:** no room service at breakfast; small fitness room and no on-site pool or hot tub though rates do include free passes to the nearby YM/YWCA. ✉ *623 Courtney St., Downtown* ☎ *250/381–0999 or 877/624–6654 ⊕ www.magnoliahotel.com ⇆ 64 rooms ⚄ In-room: Refrigerator, Wi-Fi. In-hotel: Restaurant, room service, bar, gym, spa, laundry service, Internet terminal, Wi-Fi, parking (paid), some pets allowed ▭ AE, D, MC, V ⫿⊙⫾ CP ⊕ F4.*

¢ 🏨 **Ocean Island Backpackers Inn.** The backpacker grapevine is full of
★ praise for this fun and friendly downtown hostel. Freshly renovated and impeccably managed by a thought-of-everything owner, the historic warren of a building houses 60 private rooms (three of which have private baths), several four- to six-bed dorms, secured entry, bike and bag storage, group day trips, heaps of travel information, a shared kitchen, and, best of all, an evening snack and beer lounge hopping with planned events. You can even borrow a guitar for open-mike night. ■**TIP→ Ask for a room away from the café if you want an early night.** Seniors and families mix well with the clean-cut young crowd, but ask, too, about the Ocean Island Suites ($), self-contained accommodations with kitchens in nearby James Bay. **Pros:** cheap, clean, and cheerful; loads of services; a great place to meet other travelers; $4 meals at the on-site café. **Cons:** shared bathrooms; private rooms are tiny; the few parking spaces go quickly. ✉ *791 Pandora Ave., Downtown* ☎ *250/385–1785 or 888/888–4180 ⊕ www.oceanisland.com ⇆ 9 4- to 6-bed dorms, 60 private rooms ⚄ In-room: No a/c, no phone, refrigerator (some), no TV, Wi-Fi. In-hotel: Restaurant, bar, laundry facilities, Internet terminal, parking (paid) ▭ AE, MC, V ⊕ G3.*

$$$ 🏨 **The Oswego Hotel.** Victoria's hip quotient increased a notch with the
★ opening of this chic all-suites hotel. Just in from the water in quiet-but-handy James Bay, the unassuming brick building is home to 80 sleek, modern suites. The look—black and white offset with soft neutrals, natural stone floors and countertops, and a wall of windows—is airy, modern, and comfortable with just a touch of West Coast. Full kitchens and balconies in most suites encourage hanging out. The inviting lobby and terrace doubles as a casual bistro ($$). **Pros:** stylish; comfortable; quiet; friendly staff; free local calls and Internet. **Cons:** Murphy beds in the studios; 10-minute walk to town center; no pool. ✉ *500 Oswego St., Downtown* ☎ *250/294–7500 or 877/767–9346 ⊕ www. oswegovictoria.com ⇆ 21 studios, 44 one-bedroom suites, 15 two-*

8

Inn at Laurel Point

Brentwood Bay Lodge & Spa

bedroom suites ☐ *In-room: No a/c, kitchen, Internet. In-hotel: Restaurant, bar, gym, laundry facilities, laundry service, Internet terminal, parking (paid), some pets allowed* ▭ *AE, MC, V* ⊕ *C5.*

$–$$ ☐ **Royal Scot Hotel & Suites.** Large suites, great rates, a handy location, and friendly staff keep families, seniors, and bus tours coming back to this well-run James Bay hotel—the games room, pool table, indoor pool, hot tub, laundry room, and even a small grocery store on-site make this an especially good choice. The interior is ordinary, but it's clean, freshly upholstered, and well maintained. The grounds, including a restaurant courtyard, are prettily landscaped with flower beds and hanging baskets, and a shuttle service saves the five-minute walk to the town center. **Pros:** great for kids; quiet neighborhood; free Internet and local calls. **Cons:** kids and tour groups. ✉ *425 Quebec St., Downtown* ☎ *250/388–5463 or 800/663–7515* ⊕ *www.royalscot.com* ☞ *30 rooms, 146 suites* ☐ *In-room: No a/c, safe, kitchen (some), refrigerator, Internet. In hotel: Restaurant, room service, bar, pool, gym, laundry facilities, laundry service, Internet terminal, Wi-Fi, parking (paid), some pets allowed* ▭ *AE, D, DC, MC, V* ⊕ *D5.*

$$$–$$$$ ☐ **Spinnakers Guesthouses.** Three houses make up the accommodations at this B&B, run by the owner of the popular Spinnakers Gastro Brewpub. The four Garden Suites, each with a separate bed and living room, are the nicest—and priciest. Surrounding an ivy-draped courtyard, each has a private entrance and is decorated with Asian antiques, Balinese teak butlers, and other objects gathered during the owner's world travels. Five rooms in the 1884 adults-only Heritage House are smaller (and less expensive) but nicely decorated with local art and English and Welsh antiques; most of these have fireplaces and double whirlpool tubs with rain showers. A one-bedroom bungalow has a private garden. Wherever you stay, you'll have a breakfast basket delivered in the morning. **Pros:** villa suites are beautiful; breakfast is delivered; free parking. **Cons:** 15-minute walk or five-minute drive to downtown; little else in the neighborhood (though a public market is planned for a site across the street) ✉ *308 Catherine St., Downtown* ☎ *250/386–2739 or 877/838–2739* ⊕ *www.spinnakers.com* ☞ *5 rooms, 4 suites, 1 cottage* ☐ *In-room: No a/c, kitchen (some), Wi-Fi. In-hotel: Restaurant, room service, bar, laundry service, Wi-Fi, parking (free), some pets allowed* ▭ *AE, MC, V* ⊺◯⏐ *CP* ⊕ *B2.*

$$$ ☐ **Swans Suite Hotel.** This 1913 former warehouse in Victoria's old town is one of the city's most enticing boutique hotels. The studios and one- and two-bedroom suites, all with full kitchens, are roomy, comfortable, and stylish with rich earth tones, exposed beams, and pieces from the late owner's extensive art collection. Many of the larger units have 11-foot ceilings, fireplaces, and loft bedrooms. Interior rooms have private courtyard-facing patios or balconies. More art—and nightly live music—fills the brewpub on the main floor. **Pros:** big; handsome suites with kitchens; great for families and groups; handy to shopping and restaurants. **Cons:** tiny lobby; pub noise on the lower floors; parking is off-site. ✉ *506 Pandora Ave., Downtown* ☎ *250/361–3310 or 800/668–7926* ⊕ *www.swanshotel.com* ☞ *30 suites* ☐ *In-room: No a/c, kitchen, DVD, Wi-Fi. In-hotel: Restaurant, room service, bar, laundry*

8

facilities, laundry service, Wi-Fi, parking (paid) ⊟ *AE, D, DC, MC, V* ⦿ *CP* ⊹ *E2.*

$$$$ 🏨 **Victoria Marriott Inner Harbour.** Film people, business travelers, and tourists like this central, modern, full-service hotel, just a block east of the Inner Harbour. The large, bright guest rooms have floor-to-ceiling windows, plush duvets, and marble bathroom floors; many have balconies. A large work desk, ergonomic chair, and free high-speed Internet and Wi-Fi make life easier for business travelers. The on-site Fire & Water Fish and Chophouse ($$$) is known for its prime rib. **Pros:** central location; great service; work-friendly rooms; indoor pool. **Cons:** local calls charged at C$1 each. ⊠ *728 Humboldt St., Downtown* ☎ *250/480–3800 or 877/333–8338* ⦿ *www.marriottvictoria.com* ➘ *228 rooms, 8 suites* ⅋ *In-room: Safe, refrigerator, Wi-Fi. In-hotel: Restaurant, room service, bar, pool, gym, laundry facilities, laundry service, Internet terminal, Wi-Fi, parking (paid), some pets allowed* ⊟ *AE, D, DC, MC, V* ⊹ *F5.*

OAK BAY AND ROCKLAND

$$$ 🏨 **Abbeymoore Manor Bed & Breakfast Inn.** This 1912 mansion has the
★ wide verandas, dark wainscoting, and high ceilings of its era but the attitude is informal, from the helpful hosts to the free snacks and coffee on tap all day. Two modern, one-bedroom suites on the ground floor have kitchens while five upper-level rooms charm with such period details as claw-foot tubs or four-poster king beds, and verandas or antique-tile fireplaces. The Penthouse Suite has a full kitchen and private entrance. Multicourse breakfasts are served family style or at tables for two in the sunroom or on the patio. In-room spa services include Thai massage. **Pros:** good value; friendly hosts; well staffed with excellent service. **Cons:** kids not permitted; a mile from the Inner Harbour; often booked in advance. ⊠ *1470 Rockland Ave., Rockland* ☎ *250/370–1470 or 888/801–1811* ⦿ *www.abbeymoore.com* ➘ *5 rooms, 3 suites* ⅋ *In-room: No a/c, no phone (some), kitchen (some), DVD (some), no TV (some), Wi-Fi. In-hotel: Internet terminal, parking (free), no kids under 12* ⊟ *MC, V* ⦿ *BP.*

$ 🏨 **Craigmyle Bed and Breakfast.** Affordable and historic, this four-story manor near Craigdarroch Castle has been a guesthouse since 1913. A large, welcoming common room is replete with Victoriana and original stained glass; a traditional English breakfast is served in the garden-view dining room. Rooms are cozy with floral bedspreads and wallpaper; all have private baths though in some cases the baths are across the hall. Two-room units and a guest kitchen appeal to families and single rooms are offered at a single rate. A one-bedroom suite has modern furnishings, a jetted tub, and a rain-forest shower; it's the only unit with a TV and kitchenette. **Pros:** affordable; atmospheric; family- and single-friendly. **Cons:** a bit removed from downtown; no elevator; parking lot isn't available during the daytime. ⊠ *1037 Craigdarroch Rd.* ☎ *250/595–5411 or 888/595–5411* ⦿ *www.BandBvictoria.com* ➘ *16 rooms, 1 suite* ⅋ *In-room: No a/c, no phone, no TV, Wi-Fi. In-hotel: Wi-Fi* ⊟ *AE, MC, V* ⦿ *BP.*

$$$–$$$$ ★ 🏨 **Fairholme Manor.** Original art, Viennese antiques, and dramatic furnishings shine in this lavish, 1885 Italianate mansion. Set in a parklike acre of gardens in the tree-lined Rockland district, the Fairholme has an open airy feel in its spacious, high-ceiling rooms. The suites are massive—generally about 900 square feet each—and most have a king bed, a view, and a fireplace. The Olympic Grand Suite has lush white sofas, a bay window, and a private ocean-view deck. In the lower-floor Fairholme room, the bathroom alone is big enough for a chaise lounge and palm tree next to the double-soaker tub. Small groups like the two-bedroom Rose Garden suite with its kitchen and private deck. Elaborate breakfasts—the hostess is a best-selling cookbook author—are served by the fireplace in the art-filled dining room, or at tables for two on the porch. **Pros:** peaceful setting; stunning decor; lavish breakfasts; welcoming hostess. **Cons:** a mile from downtown; no elevator. ⊠ *638 Rockland Pl., off Rockland Ave., Rockland* ☎ *250/598–3240 or 877/511–3322* ⊕ *www.fairholmemanor.com* ⬐ *1 room, 5 suites* ♿ *In-room: No a/c, kitchen (some), refrigerator (some), DVD, Wi-Fi. In-hotel: Laundry service, Wi-Fi, parking (free), no kids under 8* ⊟ *AE, MC, V* ⋈*BP.*

$$$–$$$$ 🏨 **Prior House Bed & Breakfast Inn.** Lush earth tones and brocade bed canopies, ocean-view balconies, wood-burning fireplaces, and down duvets are among the luxurious touches at this beautifully restored 1912 manor home where the Edwardian charm doesn't preclude such modern comforts as large-screen TVs and air-jet tubs. The rooms are big—starting at 750 square feet—all have private balconies or patios, and service standards are top-notch. Children and small pets are welcome in the lower-level Hobbit Garden Studios, which have private entrances and sleep four. Lavish breakfasts are served at tables for two in the dining room; breakfast in bed is always an option. **Pros:** luxurious; quiet; and rich in historic character. **Cons:** pricey; not central; no elevator. ⊠ *620 St. Charles St., Rockland* ☎ *250/592–8847 or 877/924–3300* ⊕ *www. priorhouse.com* ⬐ *3 rooms, 3 suites* ♿ *In-room: No a/c, refrigerator, DVD, Wi-Fi. In-hotel: Laundry service, Internet terminal, Wi-Fi, parking (free), some pets allowed* ⊟ *MC, V* ⋈*BP.*

$$$$ ★ 🏨 **Villa Marco Polo.** A classical European garden with a stone terrace, reflecting pool, and fountains is all part of the Tuscan-hideaway feel at this 1923 Italian Renaissance–style manor. Fireplaces, duvet-topped king beds, Persian carpets, and Italian art—along with pre-loaded iPods with docking stations—grace each of the four sumptuous rooms. The most romantic, though, are the Persia suite with its bed curtains and garden view, and the Zanzibar suite with its bay window and small balcony. The lavish four-course breakfast includes organic local produce; services at the on-site spa include Thai massage and mud-wraps. **Pros:** lots of comfy common areas; gracious hosts; full concierge services. **Cons:** a mile from downtown; no elevator. ⊠ *1524 Shasta Place, Rockland* ☎ *250/370–1524 or 877/601–1524* ⊕ *www.villamarcopolo. com* ⬐ *4 rooms* ♿ *In-room: No a/c, Wi-Fi. In hotel: Spa, laundry service, Internet terminal, Wi-Fi, parking (free), no kids under 12* ⊟ *AE, MC, V* ⋈*BP.*

8

SIDNEY AND THE SAANICH PENINSULA

$$$$

Fodor's Choice

★

⊡ **Brentwood Bay Lodge & Spa.** Every room has a private ocean-view patio or balcony at this adult-oriented boutique resort in a tiny seaside village. Handmade furniture, fireplaces, king beds topped with crisp Italian linens and sensuous black bedspreads, and original local art decorate each of the clean-lined, earth-toned rooms. Slate-lined bathrooms have jetted tubs and multihead showers, and shuttered windows bring ocean views to the tub. Handy to the Butchart Gardens (a five-minute hop on the resort's water taxi) and to local wineries, Brentwood Bay is known for the wine-based treatments at its lavish spa. The ocean-view restaurant and casual marine pub serve locally raised organic fare. Marine eco-cruises, kayak tours, and a dive center are among the many distractions. **Pros:** magnificent setting; great food; free Wi-Fi and calls across North America. **Cons:** pricey; 30-minute drive from downtown. ⊠ *849 Verdier Ave., Brentwood Bay* ☎ *250/544–2079 or 888/544–2079* ⊕ *www.brentwoodbaylodge.com* ⤵ *30 rooms, 3 suites* ⌂ *In-room: Safe, refrigerator, DVD, Wi-Fi. In-hotel: 2 restaurants, room service, bar, pool, gym, spa, diving, water sports, laundry facilities, laundry service, Internet terminal, Wi-Fi, parking (free)* ⊟ *AE, MC, V.*

$$–$$$$

★

⊡ **The Sidney Pier Hotel & Spa.** Stylish and ecologically friendly, this glass-and-stone boutique hotel on Sidney's parklike waterfront has helped put Sidney on the hipster radar. Rooms, done in chic black, crisp white, and sea-toned neutrals, with tall windows, rain-forest showers, and flat-screen TVs, range from excellent value ($$) non-view rooms to apartment-size suites with private ocean-view balconies. Sustainable local seafood is the focus at Haro's ($$$), the ocean-view restaurant. The marine theme continues from seaweed treatments at the spa to seashore walks with a resident marine biologist, and a marine concierge who'll set up whale-watching, kayaking, scuba diving, and more. **Pros:** views, style, and eco-cred; close to ferries and airport. **Cons:** 30 minutes from downtown, no pool. ⊠ *9805 Seaport Pl., Sidney* ☎ *250/655–9445 or 866/659–9445* ⊕ *www.sidneypier.com* ⤵ *46 rooms, 9 suites* ⌂ *In-room: Safe, kitchen (some), refrigerator, DVD, Internet. In hotel: 2 restaurants, room service, bar, gym, spa, laundry facilities, laundry service, Wi-Fi, parking (paid), some pets allowed* ⊟ *AE, DC, MC, V.*

THE WEST SHORE AND THE MALAHAT

$$$$

Fodor's Choice

★

⊡ **The Aerie.** Perched on 85 acres of hilltop 35 minutes north of Victoria, this Mediterranean-style villa complex has breathtaking views over Finlayson Arm and the Gulf Islands. Rooms in the three buildings vary, but all are lavish. Most provide a patio or balcony, and many have a fireplace and a whirlpool tub. Six large suites in the Villa Cielo, set 300 feet up the hill from the main resort, are especially lush, with rich fabrics, silk carpets, Brazilian cherry-wood floors, and sweeping views. The Aerie's restaurant is renowned; culinary tourists flock here for farm and winery tours, mushroom foraging trips, and private cooking classes. Ayurvedic and seaweed treatments are part of the extensive spa menu. **Pros:** wonderful views; great restaurant and spa; full range of facilities. **Cons:** 35 minutes from town; pricey; the bar is open only seasonally. ⊠ *600 Ebedora Lane, off Hwy. 1, West Shore and the Malahat* ☎ *250/743–7115 or 800/518–1933* ⊕ *www.aerie.bc.ca* ↴ *26 rooms, 7 suites* ♿ *In-room: Refrigerator, DVD, Wi-Fi. In-hotel: Restaurant, room service, bar, tennis court, gym, spa, laundry service, Internet terminal, parking (free), some pets allowed* ▭ *AE, MC, V* ☺ *Villa Cielo closed Nov.–Mar.*

$$$-$$$$ 🏨 **Westin Bear Mountain Golf Resort & Spa, Victoria.** Two Nicklaus Design golf courses are the draw at this resort community about 30 minutes northwest of the city center. Two hotel buildings, several restaurants, a spa, and an extensive health club (with beach volleyball, tennis, and a wintertime ice rink) form the core of this resort village. Rooms and suites in the Clubhouse and Fairway buildings are large, with slate bathroom floors, soft-green-and-gray earth tones, double-headed showers, large shared balconies, and a kitchen; suites have deep soaker tubs and fireplaces. **Pros:** great golf, spa, and health club; children's programs in summer. **Cons:** a car is essential; some construction still underway. ⊠ *1999 Country Club Way, West Shore and the Malahat* ☎ *250/391–7160 or 888/533–2327* ⊕ *www.bearmountain.ca* ↴ *78 rooms, 78 suites* ♿ *In-room: Safe, kitchen (some), refrigerator, DVD, Wi-Fi. In-hotel: 4 restaurants, room service, bar, 2 golf courses, tennis courts, pool, gym, spa, children's programs (ages 7–12), laundry service, Internet terminal, Wi-Fi, parking (free), some pets allowed* ▭ *AE, D, MC, V.*

NIGHTLIFE AND THE ARTS

For entertainment listings, pick up a free copy of **Monday Magazine** (it comes out every Thursday) or see the listings online at ⊕ *www. mondaymag.com.*

Tourism Victoria also has event listings, and you can buy tickets for many events at the **Visitor Information Centre** (⊠ *812 Wharf St.* ☎ *250/ 953–2033 or 800/663–3883* ⊕ *www.tourismvictoria.com*).

NIGHTLIFE

Victoria's nightlife is low-key and casual, with many wonderful pubs, but a limited choice of nightclubs. Pubs offer a casual vibe for lunch, dinner, or an afternoon pint, often with a view and an excellent selection of beer. The pubs listed here all serve food and many brew their own beer. Patrons must be 19 or older to enter a bar or pub in British Columbia, but many pubs have a separate restaurant section open to all ages. Several of Victoria's trendier restaurants double as lounges, offering cocktails and small plates well into the night. Dance clubs attract a young crowd and most close by 2 AM. A dress code (no jeans or sneakers) may be enforced, but otherwise, attire is casual. Smoking is not allowed in Victoria's pubs, bars, and nightclubs—this applies both indoors and on the patio.

BARS AND LOUNGES **Bengal Lounge.** Deep leather sofas and a Bengal tiger skin help to recreate the days of the British Raj at this iconic lounge in the Fairmont Empress Hotel. Martinis and a curry buffet are the draws through the week. On Friday and Saturday nights a jazz combo takes the stage.

✉ *721 Government St., Downtown* ☏ *250/384–8111* ⊕ *www.fairmont.com/empress.*

The Superior. Live, nightly acoustic blues and jazz and a small-plates menu of local organic fare attract a hip grown-up crowd to this café and nightspot near Fisherman's Wharf. ✉ *106 Superior St., James Bay* ☏ *250/380–9515* ⊕ *www.thesuperior.ca.*

Temple. Weekend DJs, martinis, and a trendy small-plates menu draw a fashionable late-evening crowd to this downtown restaurant, where a sandstone fireplace warms the cool modernist space. ✉ *525 Fort St., Downtown* ☏ *250/383–2313* ⊕ *www.thetemple.ca.*

Vista 18. You can take in lofty views of the city at this lounge on the 18th floor of the Chateau Victoria Hotel. ✉ *740 Burdett St., Downtown* ☏ *250/382–9258 www.vista18.com.*

DANCE CLUBS **Hermann's Jazz Club.** Dinner, dancing, and live jazz are on the menu at this venerable downtown restaurant and jazz club. ✉ *753 View St., Downtown* ☏ *250/388–9166* ⊕ *www.hermannsjazz.com.*

Lucky Bar. DJs, live bands, and a friendly crowd of locals make the most of Lucky's great sound system and dance floor. ✉ *517 Yates St., Downtown* ☏ *250/382–5825* ⊕ *www.luckybar.ca.*

Paparazzi Nightclub. Victoria's only gay club draws a mixed crowd with fun drag, karaoke, and club nights. ✉ *642 Johnson St., Downtown* ☏ *250/388–0505* ⊕ *www.prismlounge.com.*

Strathcona Hotel. This multifacility spot boasts a restaurant, a pub, a nightclub (Element—which often hosts live bands), and seven different bars, including a sports bar and a hillbilly-theme bar—not to mention beach volleyball played on the roof in summer. ✉ *919 Douglas St., Downtown* ☏ *250/383–7137* ⊕ *www.strathconahotel.com.*

PUBS **The Bard and Banker Public House.** This sumptuously decorated British-theme pub occupies a historic bank building on Victoria's main shopping street. ✉ *1022 Government St., Downtown* ☏ *250/953–9993* ⊕ *www.bardandbanker.com.*

Canoe Brewpub. One of Victoria's biggest and best pub patios overlooks the Gorge, the waterway just north of the Inner Harbour. Inside, the former power station has been stylishly redone, with high ceilings, exposed brick and beams, a wide range of in-house brews, top-notch bar snacks, and an all-ages restaurant. ✉ *450 Swift St., Downtown* ☏ *250/361–1940.*

Irish Times Pub. Stout on tap, live Celtic music nightly, and a menu of traditional and modern pub fare draw tourists and locals to this former bank building on Victoria's main shopping strip. ✉ *1200 Government St., Downtown* ☏ *250/383–7775* ⊕ *www.irishtimespub.ca.*

Spinnakers Gastro Brewpub. You can hop on an Inner Harbour Ferry to this local favorite on the Inner Harbour's north shore. Canada's first modern-day brewpub, it also has the city's longest menu of traditionally made, in-house brews. A covered waterfront deck, a double-sided fireplace, excellent pub grub, and an all-ages in-house restaurant make this a popular hangout. ✉ *308 Catherine St., Downtown* ☏ *250/386–2739* or *877/838–2739.*

Swans Brewpub. A stunning array of First Nations masks and other artworks hangs from the open rafters in this popular downtown brewpub, where jazz, blues, and swing bands play nightly. ⊠ *506 Pandora Ave., Downtown* ☎ *250/361–3310.*

THE ARTS

MUSIC **Summer in the Square.** Free jazz, classical, and folk concerts; cultural events; and more run all summer at Centennial Square, next to City Hall at Pandora and Douglas streets. Events start daily at noon. ☎ *250/361–0388* ⊕ *www.victoria.ca/residents/pdfs/centennial-square-spirit-of-summer.pdf.*

Victoria Jazz Society. Watch for music events hosted by this group, which also organizes the annual JazzFest International in late June. ☎ *250/388–4423* ⊕ *www.jazzvictoria.ca.*

Victoria Symphony. The Royal Theatre and the University Centre Farquhar Auditorium are the venues for regular season concerts. Watch, too, for **Symphony Splash** on the first Sunday in August, when the Victoria Symphony plays a free concert from a barge in the Inner Harbour. *Symphony Information:* ☎ *250/385–6515* ⊕ *www.victoriasymphony. ca.***Royal Theatre** ⊠ *805 Broughton St., Downtown* ☎ *250/386–6121 or 888/717–6121.* **University Centre Farquhar Auditorium** ⊠ *3800 Finnerty Rd., University of Victoria Campus* ☎ *250/721–8480.*

THEATER **The Belfry Theatre.** Housed in a former church, the Belfry has a resident company that specializes in contemporary Canadian dramas. ⊠ *1291 Gladstone Ave., Fernwood* ☎ *250/385–6815* ⊕ *www.belfry.bc.ca.*

Langham Court Theatre. One of Canada's oldest community theaters, the Langham Court stages the works of internationally known playwrights from September through June. ⊠ *805 Langham Ct., Rockland* ☎ *250/384–2142* ⊕ *www.langhamcourttheatre.bc.ca.*

McPherson Playhouse and the Royal Theatre. These two historic downtown theaters work together to host touring theater, dance, and musical performances. **Royal Theatre** ⊠ *805 Broughton St., Downtown.* **McPherson Playhouse** ⊠ *3 Centennial Sq., Downtown* ☎ *250/386–6121 or 888/717–6121* ⊕ *www.rmts.bc.ca.*

The Phoenix Theatre. University of Victoria theater students stage productions at this on-campus theater. ⊠ *3800 Finnerty Rd. University of Victoria Campus* ☎ *250/721–8000* ⊕ *www.phoenixtheatres.ca.*

Theatre Inconnu. Victoria's oldest alternative theater company, housed in a venue across the street from the Belfry Theatre, offers a range of performances at affordable ticket prices. ⊠ *1923 Fernwood Rd., Fernwood* ☎ *250/360–0234* ⊕ *www.theatreinconnu.com.*

Theatre SKAM. This alternative troupe stages shows through summer at such offbeat venues as the Galloping Goose Bike Path (the audience pedals from one performance to the next) and the back of a pickup truck in city parks. ☎ *250/386–7526* ⊕ *www.skam.ca.*

The Victoria Fringe Festival. Each August and September a vast menu of original and intriguing performances takes over several venues around

8

town; it's the last stop on a nationwide circuit of fringe-theater events attracting performers—and fans—from around the world. ☎ *250/383–2663* ⊕ *www.victoriafringe.com.*

SPORTS AND THE OUTDOORS

BEACHES

Cadboro Gyro Park. A sandy beach backed by a grassy park with a play area draws families to this sheltered bay, accessible via the Scenic Marine Drive. ✉ *Off Cadboro Bay Rd., Saanich.*

Cordova Bay. A long stretch of sand is the draw at this beach, just north of Mount Douglas Park on the Scenic Marine Drive. ✉ *Off Cordova Bay Rd., Saanich.*

★ **Juan de Fuca Provincial Park.** West of Sooke, this coastal wilderness park comprises a long string of beaches. Tossed with driftwood and backed with old-growth forest, these beaches are wild and magnificent with few services. China Beach has a vehicle-accessible campground, and Sombrio Beach attracts surfers. Botanical Beach, near Port Renfrew, has a wonderful array of sea life at low tide. ✉ *Off Hwy. 14, Sooke and the West Coast* ⊕ *www.env.gov.bc.ca/bcparks.*

Willows Beach. Close to downtown, this sandy family beach has a tearoom and a grassy, shaded play area. ✉ *At the foot of Dalhousie St., Oak Bay.*

Witty's Lagoon Regional Park. About 30 minutes west of downtown Victoria, near the community of Metchosin, this park is home to a sandy beach, forest, trails, marshlands, and a large lagoon—and home to 160 species of birds. There's also a nature house that presents interpretive programs. ✉ *Off Metchosin Rd., West Shore* ☎ *250/478–3344* ⊕ *www.crd.bc.ca/parks/wittys.*

BIKING

Victoria is a bike-friendly town with more bicycle commuters than any other city in Canada. Bike racks on city buses, bike lanes on downtown streets, and tolerant drivers all help, as do the city's three long-distance cycling routes, which mix car-free paths and low-traffic scenic routes.

BC Ferries will transport bikes for a nominal fee (just C\$2 from Vancouver). You can also rent bikes, bike trailers, and tandem bikes at several Victoria outlets for a few hours, a day, or a week. Helmets are required by law and are supplied with bike rentals.

BIKE ROUTES   **Cowichan Valley Trail.** A less-known rails-to-trails conversion is this 47-km (29-mi) multi-use path, part of the Trans-Canada trail, running from Shawnigan Lake to Cowichan Lake in the Cowichan Valley. ⊕ *www.trailsbc.ca.*

★ **Galloping Goose Regional Trail.** Following an old rail bed, this 55-km (33-mi) route officially starts at the Johnson Street Bridge downtown. The multi-use trail runs across old rail trestles and through forests to the town of Sooke, finishing at the abandoned gold-mining town of Leechtown. ☎250/478–3344 ⊕ www.crd.bc.ca/parks.

The Lochside Regional Trail. This fairly level, mostly car-free, 29-km (18-mi) route follows an old rail bed past farmland, wineries, and beaches from the ferry terminals at Swartz Bay and Sidney to downtown Victoria. It joins the Seaside Touring route at Cordova Bay and meets the Galloping Goose Trail just north of downtown Victoria. ☎250/478–3344 ⊕ www.crd.bc.ca/parks.

The Rotary Route. For an ambitious tour of southern Vancouver Island's back roads and bike trails, follow this 110-km (68-mi) signed route from Swartz Bay up to Nanaimo. ⊕ www.rotaryroute.org.

The Seaside Touring Route. Starting at Government and Belleville on the Inner Harbour, this 11-km (7-mi) route, marked with bright yellow signs, leads past Fisherman's Wharf and along the Dallas Road waterfront to Beacon Hill Park. It then follows the seashore to Cordova Bay, where it connects with Victoria's other two long-distance routes: the Lochside and Galloping Goose regional trails.

The Gulf Islands are also popular with cyclists. The scenery is wonderful, but the steep narrow roads and lack of dedicated bike paths can be frustrating.

BIKE RENTALS **Cycle BC Rentals.** Between May and October, you can rent bikes, kids'
AND TOURS bikes, and bike trailers at Cycle BC's Douglas Street outlet. The same company has motorcycles and scooters for rent at their Wharf Street location. ✉ 707 Douglas St., Downtown ☎250/380–2453 ✉ 950 Wharf St., Downtown ☎250/385–2453 or 866/380–2453 ⊕ www.cyclebc.ca.

CycleTreks. Besides renting bikes, this company also runs bike tours of Victoria, the Gulf Islands, and various parts of Vancouver Island, including a Cowichan Valley vineyard tour. They can also give you a ride to the start of Galloping Goose Trail or to the Butchart Gardens so you can pedal back. ✉ 1000 Wharf St. ☎250/386–2277 or 877/733–6722 ⊕ www.cycletreks.com.

8

GOLF

You can golf year-round in Victoria and southern Vancouver Island, and you almost have to, just to try all the courses. Victoria alone has several public golf courses, ranging from rolling sea-view fairways to challenging mountaintop sites. Southern Vancouver Island is home to the Vancouver Island Golf Trail, where you'll find 10 championship courses along a 250-km (150-mi) corridor. Golf Vancouver Island (☎888/465–3239 ⊕ www.golfvancouverisland.ca) has details.

Arbutus Ridge Golf Club. Mountain and ocean views from the course and the clubhouse are the draws at this challenging par-71 course, 40 minutes north of Victoria in the Cowichan Valley. ✉ 3515 Telegraph Rd., Cobble Hill ☎250/743–5000 ⊕ www.arbutusridgegolf.com.

★ **Bear Mountain Golf & Country Club.** Built near the top of a 335-meter (1,100-foot) mountain about 20 minutes north of Victoria, this is widely regarded as the island's most exciting course. Designed by Jack Nicklaus and his son Steve, the Mountain Course has an extra 19th

CLOSE UP

Victoria: Whale-watching

The thrill of seeing whales in the wild is, for many, one of the most enduring memories of a trip to Victoria. In summer (roughly April to October), about 85 orca, or killer whales (they're actually large dolphins, but that makes them no less exciting to see), reside in the Strait of Georgia between Vancouver and Victoria. They live in pods, and because their movements are fairly predictable, chances are high that you will see a pod on any given trip. Some operators claim sighting rates of 90%; others offer guaranteed sightings, meaning that you can repeat the tour free of charge until you spot a whale.

It's not unheard of to see whales from a BC Ferry en route to Victoria—but the ferries don't alter their routes to take advantage of whale-watching, so your best bet is to take a dedicated tour. A number of companies leave from Victoria's Inner Harbour, a few are based in Richmond (near Vancouver), and others leave from Sidney and Sooke, outside of Victoria.

Not all tours are alike, and the kind of boat you choose determines the kind of experience you're likely to have—though most companies have naturalists on board as guides, as well as hydrophones that, if you get close enough, allow you to listen to the whales singing and vocalizing.

Motor launches, which carry from 30 to more than 80 passengers, are comfortable, with washrooms, protection from the elements, and even snack-and-drink concessions. Seasickness isn't usually a problem in the sheltered waters near Victoria, but if you're not a good sailor, it's wise to wear a seasickness band or take antinausea medication. Ginger candy often works, too.

Zodiacs are open inflatable boats that carry about 12 passengers. They are smaller and more agile than cruisers and offer both an exciting ride bouncing over the waves and an eye-level view of the whales. Passengers are supplied with warm, waterproof survival suits. Zodiac tours are not recommended for people with back or neck problems, pregnant women, or small children.

Note that the kind of boat you choose does not affect how close you can get to the whales. For the safety of whales and humans, government and industry regulations require boats to stay at least 100 meters (328 feet) from the pods, though closer encounters are possible if whales approach a boat when its engine is off.

And, although the focus is on whales, you also have a good chance of spotting marine birds, Dall's porpoises, dolphins, seals, sea lions, and minke, gray, and humpback whales as well as other marine life. And, naturally, there's the scenery of forested islands and distant mountains.

There are dozens of whale-watching operators in the area. Some of the more established are:

Great Pacific Adventures offers year-round tours with both Zodiacs and covered vessels. Boats are equipped with hydrophones and all guides are marine biologists. In summer a three-hour tour starts at C$95. ✉ *1000 Wharf St.* ☎ *250/386–2277 or 877/733–6722* ⊕ *www. greatpacificadventures.com.*

Ocean Explorations conducts three-hour whale-watching trips in summer and two-hour marine tours in winter—all on hydrophone-equipped Zodiacs with qualified naturalists as guides. Summer trips start at C$95. ✉ *602 Broughton St.* ☎ *250/383–6722 or 888/442–6722* ⊕ *www. oceanexplorations.com.*

Prince of Whales is Victoria's biggest whale-watching company. They offer three-hour tours from Victoria on Zodiacs staffed by naturalists and equipped with hydrophones. Rates start at C$95.

Another option, and one worth planning a trip around, is the *Ocean Magic,* a 74-passenger cruiser staffed with naturalists that combines four hours of whale-watching with a trip from Vancouver to Victoria and includes a visit to the Butchart

Gardens. The cruiser leaves downtown Vancouver daily, June through September at 9 AM, arrives in Victoria's Inner Harbour in time for lunch, and returns for Vancouver from the Butchart Gardens at 5:30. Passengers can opt to stay in Victoria, or return by floatplane or ferry. Fares start at C$160 one-way. ✉ *812 Wharf St. (on the Inner Harbour Causeway)* ☎ *250/383–4884 or 888/383–4884* ⊕ *www.princeofwhales.com.*

Springtide Whale Tours is highly rated by visitors. They run tours on Zodiacs and on 61-foot motor yachts. Summer tours are three hours long, and the boats are equipped with hydrophones; guides are marine biologists. Rates are C$99. They're moving over the winter of 2009–10, so check the Web site for their new address. ✉ *Inner Harbor* ☎ *250/384–4444 or 800/470–3474* ⊕ *www. springtidecharters.com.*

Vancouver Island has two other whale-watching hot spots. Johnstone Strait, off Telegraph Cove on the island's northeast coast, has—in summer—one of the world's largest populations of orca and is an important center of whale research. Tofino and Ucluelet, on the island's west coast, draw whale-watchers every March and April when an estimated 20,000 Pacific gray whales cruise by on their annual migration.

8

hole built on a cliff ledge with striking views across the city. A second Nicklaus-designed layout, called the Valley Course, opened in 2009 at a slightly lower elevation. ✉ *1999 Country Club Way, off Millstream Rd. and Bear Mountain Pkwy., The West Shore* ☎ *250/744–2327 or 888/533–2327* ⊕ *www.bearmountain.ca.*

Olympic View Golf Club. The distant peaks of the Olympic Mountains are the backdrop to this bucolic par-72 course, home to two waterfalls and 12 lakes. The first B.C. course played by Tiger Woods, it's about 30 minutes' drive west of downtown Victoria in the suburb of Colwood. ✉ *643 Latoria Rd., off Veterans' Memorial Parkway, The West Shore* ☎ *250/474–3673 or 800/446–5322* ⊕ *www.olympicviewgolf.com.*

HIKING AND WALKING

Victoria is one of the most pedestrian-friendly cities in North America. Waterfront pathways make it possible to stroll virtually all around Victoria's waterfront. For some interesting self-guided walks around the city's historic areas, check out ⊕ *www.victoria.ca/tours* or pick up a free walking-tour map at the city's visitor information center. Though popular with cyclists, the area's long-distance paths are also great for long walks. For views and elevation, check out the trail networks in the area's many provincial and regional parks.

East Sooke Regional Park. This 3,500-acre park, 35 km (21) mi west of Victoria has more than 50 km (30 mi) of hiking trails, through forests and fields and along the rugged coastline.

Galloping Goose Regional Trail. An old railroad bed that's been reclaimed for walkers, cyclists, and equestrians, runs from downtown Victoria to just north of Sooke. It links with the Lochside Regional Trail to Sidney to create a continuous 100-km (62-mi) car-free route. ☎ *250/478–3344* ⊕ *www.crd.bc.ca/parks.*

Goldstream Provincial Park. This wilderness park, just 16 km (10 mi) north of town, has a vast network of trails, from wheelchair-accessible paths through ancient Douglas fir and cedar forests to challenging hikes to the view-blessed peak of Mt. Finlayson. Trails also lead to the 48-meter (157-foot) Niagara Falls. ✉ *Hwy. 1 at Finlayson Arm Rd., West Shore and the Malahat* ☎ *250/478–9414* ⊕ *www.env.gov.bc.ca/bcparks/* 🎫 *C$3 per car, per day.*

★ **Juan de Fuca Marine Trail.** This tough 47-km (30-mi) coastal hike begins at China Beach, near the village of Jordan River, about 48 km (29 mi) west of Victoria. There are three other trailheads, each with a parking lot, at Sombrio Beach, Parkinson Creek, and Botanical Beach (which is 5 km [3 mi] southeast of Port Renfrew), allowing hikers to tackle the trail in day-hike sections. ✉ *Off Hwy. 14, between Jordan River (southeast end) and Port Renfrew (northwest end)* ☎ *800/689–9025 camping reservations* ⊕ *www.env.gov.bc.ca/bcparks.*

Mount Douglas Regional Park. Trails through the forest to the 213-meter (758-foot) summit of Mt. Douglas reward hikers with a 360-degree view of Victoria, the Saanich Peninsula, and the mountains of Washington State. ⊠ *Off Cedar Hill Rd., Saanich* ☎ *250/475–5522* ⊕ *www. gov.saanich.bc.ca.*

Swan Lake Christmas Hill Nature Sanctuary. This sanctuary, with its 23-acre lake set in 150 acres of fields and wetlands, is just a few minutes from downtown Victoria. From the 2½-km (1½-mi) Lake Loop Trail and floating boardwalk, birders can spot a variety of waterfowl and nesting birds year-round. For great views of Victoria, take the 2½-km (1½-mi) round-trip hike to the top of Christmas Hill. The sanctuary's Nature House is open weekdays 8:30–4 and weekends noon–4. ⊠ *3873 Swan Lake Rd., Saanich* ☎ *250/479–0211* ⊕ *www.swanlake.bc.ca.*

KAYAKING

The Upper Harbour and the Gorge, the waterways just north of the Inner Harbour, are popular boating spots.

Island Boat Rentals. You can rent a kayak, canoe, motorboat, or rowboat at this outlet at the Canoe Marina, on the Upper Harbour, at the foot of Swift Street. ⊠ *450 Swift St.* ☎ *250/995–1661* ⊕ *www.greatpacific-adventures.com.*

Victoria Kayak. Setting out from the Harbour Air Adventure Centre on the Inner Harbour, this company provides 2½-hour tours to see seals, seal pups, and other marine life around Seal Island; it's a good tour for beginners. They rent kayaks, too. ⊠ *950 Wharf St.* ☎ *250/216–5646* ⊕ *www.victoriakayak.com.*

SCUBA DIVING

The waters off Vancouver Island have some of the best scuba diving in the world, with clear waters and rich marine life; visibility is best in winter. The Ogden Point Breakwater and Race Rocks Underwater Marine Park are popular spots close to town. In Brentwood Bay on the Saanich Peninsula are the Glass Sponge Gardens, a sea mountain covered with sponges that were thought to be extinct. Off Thetis Island, near Chemainus, in the Cowichan Valley, divers can explore a sunken 737 jetliner. Dive BC (⊕ *www.divebc.ca*) has details.

Ogden Point Dive Centre. Fills, rentals, guided dives, weekend charters, and a water-view café are all available at this PADI (Professional Association of Diving Instructors) dive center at the Ogden Point Breakwater near downtown Victoria. ⊠ *199 Dallas Rd., Downtown* ☎ *250/380–9119 or 888/701–1177* ⊕ *www.divevictoria.com.*

Rockfish Divers. This internationally accredited PADI dive outfitter, based at the Brentwood Bay Lodge & Spa on the Saanich Peninsula, offers charters, courses, and equipment rentals. ⊠ *849 Verdier Ave., Brentwood Bay* ☎ *250/889–7282, 250/544–2079, or 888/544–2079* ⊕ *www. brentwoodbaylodge.com.*

ZIP-TREKKING

A fast-growing sport, zip-trekking involves whizzing through the forest while attached to a cable or zip line.

8

Adrena Line Zipline Adventure Tours. About 40 minutes west of Victoria (behind the 17 Mile Pub on the road to Sooke), this adventure center has eight zip-line routes, ranging in length from 45 meters (150 feet) to 305 meters (1,000 feet), and two suspension bridges. It's open May to October, daily, and also offers night zipping. A shuttle bus runs twice daily from the Inner Harbour. ✉ *5128C Sooke Rd., Sooke* ☎ *250/642–1933 or 877/947–9145* ⊕

SHOPPING

Shopping in Victoria is easy: virtually everything is in the downtown area on or near Government Street stretching north from the Fairmont Empress hotel. Victoria stores specializing in English imports are plentiful, though Canadian-made goods are usually a better buy.

SHOPPING DISTRICTS AND MALLS

Antique Row. Fort Street between Blanshard and Cook streets is home to dozens of antiques, curio, and collectibles shops.

Chinatown. Exotic fruits and vegetables, toys, wicker fans, fabric slippers, and other Chinese imports fill the shops and the baskets set up in front of them along Fisgard Street. Fan Tan Alley, a narrow lane off Fisgard Street, has more nouveau-hippie goods, with an art gallery, a Nepalese import shop and a record store tucked in among its tiny storefronts.

The Design District. Wharf and Store streets, between Johnson and Fisgard, contains a cluster of Victoria's home decor shops. The two floors of import furnishings and lush fabrics at Chintz & Co. (1720 Store St.) are especially fun to browse through. ⊕ *www.victoriadesigndistrict.com.*

Fodor'sChoice ★ **Lower Johnson Street.** This row of candy-color Victorian shopfronts between Government and Store streets is Victoria's hub for independent fashion-designer boutiques. Storefronts—some closet size—are filled with local designers' wares, funky boutiques, and no fewer than three shops selling ecologically friendly clothes of hemp and organic cotton. ✉ *Johnson St. between Government and Store Sts., Downtown.*

Market Square. During the late 19th century, this three-level square, built like an old courtyard, originally provided everything a sailor, miner, or lumberjack could want. Restored to its original architectural character, it's now a pedestrian-only, café- and boutique-lined hangout. It's lined with independent shops selling toys, imports, gifts, souvenirs, jewelry, and local art. ✉ *560 Johnson St., Downtown* ☎ *250/386–2441.*

Trounce Alley. European designer boutiques and other high-end fashion outlets line this pedestrian-only lane north of View Street between Broad and Government streets. Sadly, a cheesy chamber-of-horrors attraction at the Government Street end spoils the Euro-chic mood.

Victoria Bay Centre. Downtown Victoria's main department store and mall has about 100 boutiques and restaurants. ✉ *1 Victoria Bay Centre, at Government and Fort Sts., Downtown* ☎ *250/952–5680.*

Fan Tan Alley, in Victoria's Chinatown, is said to be the narrowest street in Canada.

SPECIALTY STORES

Artina's. Canadian-made jewelry—all handmade, one-of-a-kind pieces—fills the display cases at this unique jewelry shop. ✉ *1002 Government St., Downtown* ☎ *250/386–7000 or 877/386–7700.*

Artisan Wine Shop. This offshoot of Okanagan winery Mission Hill Family Estate replicates a visit to the winery with a video show and tasting bar. The focus is Okanagan wine, but staff are knowledgeable about Vancouver Island producers as well. ✉ *1007 Government St., Downtown* ☎ *250/384–9994.*

Cowichan Trading Co. First Nations jewelry, art, moccasins, and Cowichan sweaters are the focus at this long-established outlet. ✉ *1328 Government St., Downtown* ☎ *250/383–0321.*

Hill's Native Art. Stock at this shop ranges from affordable souvenirs to original West Coast First Nations art. ✉ *1008 Government St., Downtown* ☎ *250/385–3911.*

Irish Linen Stores. Since 1917 this tiny shop has kept Victorians in fine linen, lace, and hand-embroidered items. ✉ *1019 Government St., Downtown* ☎ *250/383–6812.*

★ **Munro's Books.** This beautifully restored 1909 building houses one of Canada's prettiest bookstores. ✉ *1108 Government St., Downtown* ☎ *250/382–2464.*

★ **Rogers' Chocolates.** Rogers' has been making chocolates since 1885, and they're getting pretty good at it. Victoria creams are a local favorite and any of the goodies can be packed for travel. The current shop dates to 1903. ✉ *913 Government St., Downtown* ☎ *250/384–7021.*

Fodor's Choice
★ **Silk Road Aromatherapy & Tea Company & Spa.** For exotic teas (which you can sample at the tasting bar), aromatherapy remedies, and spa treatments (think green-tea facials), stop at this chic and multifaceted shop. ⊠ *1624 Government St., Downtown* ☎ *250/704–2688.*

STREET MARKETS

Victorians seem to relish any excuse to head outdoors, which may explain the recent boom in outdoor crafts, farmers', and other open-air markets around town.

Bastion Square Public Market. Crafts vendors and entertainers congregate in this historic square throughout the summer. On Thursdays and Fridays from June to September, local produce is for sale, with the stalls staffed by volunteer chefs. ⊠ *Bastion Square, off Government St., Downtown* ☎ *250/885–1387* ⊕ *www.bastionsquare.ca.*

James Bay Community Market. Organic food, local produce, crafts, and live music draw shoppers to this summer Saturday market just south of the Inner Harbour, behind the Parliament Buildings. ⊠ *Superior and Menzies Sts., Downtown* ☎ *250/381–5323* ⊕ *www.jamesbaymarket. com.*

Moss Street Market. "Make it, bake it, or grow it" is the rule for vendors at this street market, held 10 to 2 on summer Saturdays. ⊠ *Fairfield Rd., at Moss St., Fairfield* ☎ *250/361–1747* ⊕ *www.mossstreetmarket. com.*

Ship Point Night Market. Music and local crafts are spotlighted at this night market, held Friday and Saturday evenings in summer on the Inner Harbour. ⊠ *Ship Point Pier, Downtown* ☎ *250/413–6828* ⊕ *www. victoriaharbour.org.*

Sidney Thursday Night Market. More than 150 vendors of food, arts, crafts, and more take over the main street of this town, a 30-minute drive north of Victoria, each Thursday evening in summer. ⊠ *Along Beacon Ave., Sidney* ☎ *250/655–6433.*

SPAS

Since health, nature, and relaxing seem to be the major preoccupations in Victoria, it's not surprising that the city has enjoyed a boom in spas. Aesthetics are important, but natural healing, ancient practices, and the use of such local products as wine and seaweed are more the focus here. Local specialties include vinotherapy (applying the antioxidant properties of wine grapes externally, rather than internally).

The Aveda Institute. Vancouver Island's booming spa industry has to be staffed somehow, and this is where the technicians train. Supervised by pros, they offer budget-savvy clients everything from makeup touch-ups to hot-stone massages. Supervised student services top out at around C$60, or you can choose to have your treatment done by a professional. ⊠ *1402 Douglas St., Downtown* ☎ *250/386–7993* ⊕ *www. avedainstitutevictoria.ca.*

Haven Spa. Natural products and sea-themed treatments are highlights at this full-service spa at the Sidney Pier Hotel & Spa on the Saanich Peninsula. A pre-treatment steam room and post-treatment lounge add to the pampering. ⊠ *9805 Seaport Pl., Sidney* ☎ *250/655–9797* ⊕ *www. sidneypier.com.*

Le Spa Sereine. A custom-built pedicure room with fully reclining chairs and sunken basins is a draw at this independent downtown spa. Set in an atmospheric heritage building, it's also known for salt glows, hydrotherapy, reflexology, and Indian head massages. There's a hair salon on-site, too. ⊠ *1411 Government St., Downtown* ☎ *250/388–4419 or 866/388–4419* ⊕ *www.lespasereine.com.*

Silk Road Spa. Essential oils and organic skin- and body-care products are the draw at this serene Chinatown spa. The green-tea facial is especially popular. ⊠ *1624 Government St., Downtown* ☎ *250/704–2688* ⊕ *www.silkroadtea.com.*

The Spa at the Delta Victoria Ocean Pointe Resort. Organic skin-care products and harbor-view treatment rooms are among the draws at this popular hotel spa. Spa guests have access to the hotel's gym and pool, too. ⊠ *45 Songhees Rd., Downtown* ☎ *250/360–5938 or 800/575–8882* ⊕ *www.thespadeltavictoria.com.*

Spa at the Grand. Traditional Thai, Swedish, and deep-tissue massage as well as hair and beauty treatments are among the offerings at this intimate spa at the Grand Pacific Hotel. ⊠ *463 Belleville St., Downtown* ☎ *250/380–7862* ⊕ *www.hotelgrandpacific.com.*

Spa Magnolia. All-natural products and a hydrotherapy tub are the hallmark of this Aveda spa in the Magnolia Hotel. ⊠ *625 Courtney St., Downtown* ☎ *250/920–7721* ⊕ *www.spamagnolia.com.*

Willow Stream Spa at the Fairmont Empress Hotel. Victoria's most luxurious spa is actually a pretty good value, especially if you arrive, as suggested, an hour before your appointment to soak in the Hungarian mineral bath, sauna, and steam room—or order a bento-box lunch and make a day of it. ⊠ *633 Humboldt St., Downtown* ☎ *250/995–4650 or 866/854–7444* ⊕ *www.willowstream.com.*

SIDE TRIPS FROM VICTORIA

A few more days in the area gives you time to explore farther afield. Sooke and the Southwest Coast, the Cowichan Valley, or one of the Gulf Islands can make an easy day trip from Victoria, though any of them can warrant a weekend or longer for more serious exploration. These three regions around Victoria can be connected, so you don't have to retrace your steps.

How to choose? For wilderness beaches and forested hiking trails, take Highway 14 or cycle the Galloping Goose Trail to Sooke and the southwest coast. For food, wine, and First Nations culture, head north over the stunning Malahat drive to the Cowichan Valley. A great road trip? Take the Pacific Marine Circle Route around the two regions. Arts, crafts, kayaking, white-shell beaches, and a touch of neo-hippy island culture await those who visit Salt Spring, especially on market Saturdays (Salt Spring is also the only side trip manageable by public transport). You can truly get away from it all on the islands of Galiano, Mayne, or Pender. For families, the Cowichan Valley, with its Forest Discovery and raptor conservation centers, has the most obvious kid appeal, though all three destinations have beaches, forests, and cute farm animals. Be warned though: the long, winding Highway 14 past Sooke can be challenging for those prone to motion sickness.

GETTING HERE AND AROUND

The *Mill Bay Ferry*, a car ferry operated by BC Ferries, sails several times a day between Brentwood Bay on the Saanich Peninsula and Mill Bay in the Cowichan Valley. BC Ferries also sail several times a day from Swartz Bay, about 30 minutes north of downtown Victoria, to Salt Spring, Pender, Mayne, Galiano, and Saturna islands. Sailings to Salt Spring take 30 minutes. Sailings to the other islands take from 25 minutes to two hours, depending on the destination and number of stops. Reservations are not accepted on these routes. Salt Spring Island can also be reached from Crofton, about 20 minutes north of Duncan, in the Cowichan Valley. Twenty-minute sailings leave about once an hour. BC Ferries also sail to the Southern Gulf Islands (Galiano, Mayne, Pender, Saturna, and Salt Spring) from Tsawwassen, about an hour south of Vancouver. Vehicle reservations, at no extra charge, are recommended and are required on some sailings on these routes. If you're planning several sailings on BC Ferries, you may save some money with BC Ferries' SailPass, which offers multiple crossings for a set fare.

Gulf Islands Water Taxi runs passengers and bicycles between Salt Spring, Mayne, and Galiano islands on Saturdays in July and August. Between September and June, the taxis operate as school boats but will take other passengers when space permits. They run school days only (call for exact days) between Salt Spring, Mayne, Galiano, Saturna, and Pender. Fares are $C15 one-way or $25 round-trip. On Salt Spring Island the *Queen of de Nile* runs from Salt Spring Marina to Ganges town center at C$2 per trip.

Cowichan Valley Regional Transit, a separate BC Transit network, serves Duncan and the Cowichan Valley. Salt Spring Island has a small transit system serving the ferry terminals and the village of Ganges, but it doesn't meet every ferry, and doesn't run on Sundays. The other Gulf Islands don't have transit services.

ESSENTIALS

Bus Information BC Transit (*Cowichan Valley Regional Transit:* ☎ 250/746–9899. *Salt Spring Transit:* ☎ 250/537–6758 ⊕ www.bctransit.com).

Ferry Information BC Ferries (☎ 250/386–3431, 888/223–3779 in Canada ⊕ www.bcferries.com). **Gulf Islands Water Taxi** (☎ 250/537–2510 ⊕ members. unet.ca/~watertaxi).

SOOKE AND THE SOUTHWEST COAST

28 km (17 mi) west of Victoria on Hwy. 14.

The village of Sooke, on the shore of Juan de Fuca Strait, about a 30-minute drive west of Victoria, has two claims to fame: it's home to Sooke Harbour House, one of Canada's best-known country inns, and it's the last stop for gas and supplies before heading out to the beaches and hiking trails of the island's wild and scenic southwest coast.

From Sooke, the narrow and winding Highway 14 leads 80 km (48 mi) through birch and fir woods, with occasional sea views to Port Renfrew, a fishing village on the west coast. En route it passes Juan de Fuca Provincial Park, where trailheads lead to a series of forest-backed, driftwood-strewn beaches. The area is home to some excellent restaurants and high-end B&Bs, though other services are few.

To avoid retracing your steps to Victoria, you can follow the signs for the Pacific Marine Circle Route. This self-guided road trip follows Highway 14 from Victoria to Port Renfrew, where it takes a well-maintained back road through the forest to the village of Lake Cowichan. From here, Highway 18 leads to Highway 1 and back to Victoria. Driving time is about three hours, but watch your fuel gauge, as there are no gas stations between Sooke and Lake Cowichan and no services at all on the 55 km (30 mi) between Port Renfrew and Lake Cowichan.

GETTING HERE AND AROUND

Sooke is a 45-minute drive, mostly via Highway 14, west from Victoria, or a pleasant 3- to 4-hour cycle along the car-free Galloping Goose Trail. BC Transit also runs buses from downtown Victoria as far as the town of Sooke.

8

TOP ATTRACTIONS

★ Extending along the shore from Jordan River to near Port Renfrew, **Juan de Fuca Provincial Park** takes in several beaches, including China Beach, which has a campground; Sombrio Beach, a popular surfing spot; and Botanical Beach, with its amazing tidal pools. The **Juan de Fuca Marine Trail** is a tough 47-km (30-mi) hike running along the shore from China Beach, west of Jordan River, to Port Renfrew. Several trailheads along the way—at Sombrio Beach, Parkinson Creek, and Botanical Beach—allow day hikers to walk small stretches of it. ⊠ *Off Hwy. 14, between Jordan River (southeast end) and Port Renfrew (northwest end)* ☎ *800/689–9025 camping reservations* ⊕ *www.env.gov.bc.ca/bcparks for park information, www.discovercamping.ca for camping reservations* ⊉ *C$3 per car per day.*

WORTH NOTING

Logging roads from Port Renfrew lead to **Carmanah Walbran Provincial Park**, home to some of the world's largest spruce trees, some more than 800 years old, and ancient cedars over 1,000 years old. Walk-in wilderness camping is available; watch for logging trucks en route and bears once you're inside the park. ⊠ *Southwest of Lake Cowichan via logging roads* ⊕ *www.env.gov.bc.ca/bcparks.*

More than 3,500 acres of beaches, hiking trails, and wildflower-dotted meadows draw walkers to the **East Sooke Regional Park,** 7 km (4 mi) east of Sooke on the south side of Sooke Harbour.

French Beach Provincial Park comprises a sand-and-pebble beach, a campground, and seaside trails. The park lies 21 km (13 mi) west of Sooke. Whales like to feed in the area, and sometimes can be seen from shore. ⊠ *Hwy. 14* ☎ *800/689–9025 camping reservations* ⊕ *www.env. gov.bc.ca/bcparks for park information, www.discovercamping.ca for camping reservations* ⌑ *C$3 per car per day.*

Port Renfrew is a tiny fishing village 107 km (67 mi) from Victoria. At the end of Highway 14 you'll find the trail's end (or start) for hikers tackling the grueling West Coast Trail and the more accessible but still daunting Juan de Fuca Marine Trail. Salmon fishing is also a big reason for visiting the area. Resources include a general store, a pub, restaurants, a motel, B&Bs, beachside camping, and a range of rustic cabins. There's no garage in town, but gas is usually available at the marina (it's best to play it safe and fill up your tank before leaving Sooke). Botanical Beach, 5 km (3 mi) southeast of the village, is famous for the wealth of colorful marine life inhabiting its hundreds of tidal pools. From Port Renfrew, a 55-km (30-mi) mostly paved back road leads inland to Lake Cowichan in the Cowichan Valley. For visitor information, contact the Port Renfrew Recreation Centre at ☎ *250/647–0030.* For West Coast Trail info, contact the West Coast Trail Office at ☎ *250/647–5434.*

Locals and visitors come to cool off at **Sooke Potholes Provincial Park** (⊠ *End of Sooke River Rd., off Hwy. 14*), home to a series of natural swimming holes carved out of sandstone by the Sooke River.

Stop for information at the **Sooke Region Museum and Visitor Information Centre.** Watch for the red-and-white lighthouse lamp at the first traffic light as you arrive from Victoria. It sits in front of the Visitor Information Centre, which is also home to a small museum displaying local First Nations artifacts. ⊠ *2070 Phillips Rd., off Hwy. 14* ☎ *250/642–6351 or 866/888–4748* ⊕ *www.sookeregionmuseum.com* ⊙ *May–Oct., daily 9–5.*

West of the village, you'll reach **Whiffen Spit,** a natural breakwater about a mile long that makes a scenic walk with great bird-watching. It's at the end of Whiffen Spit Road.

WHERE TO EAT AND STAY

$$$

CANADIAN

★

✕ **Markus' Wharfside Restaurant.** Two art-filled rooms, one with a fireplace, and a small patio overlook Sooke Harbour from this former fisherman's cottage. The European-trained chef-owner makes the most of the local wild seafood and organic produce, much of it from the restaurant's own garden, with such made-from-scratch dishes as grilled scallops with cherry tomato, cucumber, and mint salsa; grilled lamb sirloin with peppered balsamic glaze; and the signature Tuscan-style seafood soup. ⊠ *1831 Maple Ave. S, Sooke* ☎ *250/642–3596* ⊕ *www. markuswharfsiderestaurant.com* ⊟ *MC, V* ⊙ *Closed Sun. and Mon. No lunch.*

$$$$ ✕ **Sooke Harbour House.** The relaxed, ocean-view dining room at this art-
CANADIAN filled lodge is the stage for some of the country's most innovative meals.
Fodor'sChoice The nightly four-course menus ($$$$) rely almost entirely on local pro-
★ visions, including seafood from nearby waters, traditional First Nations
foods, and about 200 varieties of herbs, vegetables, and edible flowers
from the inn's own organic garden. You can also book a Gastronomic
Adventure, which includes a visit with the chef and a multicourse tasting
menu. The 15,000-bottle wine cellar is exceptional—cellar tours run
nightly at 5:30 PM. ⊠ *1528 Whiffen Spit Rd., Sooke* ☎ *250/642–3421
or 800/889–9688* ⊕ *www.sookeharbourhouse.com* ⊟ *AE, MC, V* ⊘ *No
lunch. Call in Dec.–Feb., as there are some weekday closures.*

$$–$$$ 🏨 **Point No Point Resort.** About 25 km (15 mi) west of Sooke, this cabin
compound is known best for its little glassed-in restaurant ($$$),
perched high above the ocean and offering sweeping views across the
strait; binoculars at each table help with whale spotting while you dine.
The 24 cabins, overlooking a mile of private beach, Juan de Fuca Strait,
and the Olympic Mountains, are often booked well ahead by repeat
visitors. The one- and two-bedroom cabins—in single, duplex, and
quad units—range from the original 1952 log cabins to high-ceilinged
modern cottages. Every unit has a kitchen, a fireplace or woodstove, a
water view, and a deck; most have private water-view hot tubs. **Pros:**
remote and scenic; self-contained cottages assure privacy; good restau-
rant. **Cons:** remote; no phones or TVs. ⊠ *10829 West Coast Rd., Shirley*
☎ *250/646–2020* ⊕ *www.pointnopoint.com* ⤶ *24 cabins, 1 4-bedroom
house* ⌂ *In-room: No a/c, no phone, no TV. In-hotel: Restaurant, beach-
front, laundry service, some pets allowed* ⊟ *MC, V* ⊘ *Restaurant closed
for dinner Mon. and Tues., and on weekdays in Jan.*

$$$$ 🏨 **Sooke Harbour House.** Art, food, and gardens work together seam-
Fodor'sChoice lessly at one of Canada's best-loved country inns. Guest rooms, public
★ spaces, and even the outdoors are beautifully decorated with pieces
from the owners' vast art collection. Guest rooms in the 1929 ocean-
front inn, each with a fireplace and private balcony or patio are individ-
ually themed and exquisitely comfortable in an informal country-house
way. All the romantic requisites, from in-room spa services to breakfast
in bed, are offered. **Pros:** splendid and luxurious. **Cons:** expensive; no
pool. ⊠ *1528 Whiffen Spit Rd., Sooke* ☎ *250/642–3421 or 800/889–
9688* ⊕ *www.sookeharbourhouse.com* ⤶ *28 rooms* ⌂ *In-room: No
a/c, refrigerator, no TV, Wi-Fi. In-hotel: Restaurant, room service, spa,
beachfront, bicycles, laundry service, Internet terminal, Wi-Fi, parking
(free), some pets allowed* ⊟ *AE, MC, V* ⊘ *Closed Jan.* ⓘ◎ *BP.*

8

THE COWICHAN VALLEY

60 km (37 mi) north of Victoria on Trans-Canada Hwy., or Hwy. 1.

The Cowichan people were on to something when they called this fer-
tile valley north of Victoria "The Warm Land." The region, roughly
from Mill Bay to Ladysmith, is said to be blessed with the warmest
year-round temperatures and more hours of sunshine each year than
anywhere else in Canada. Home to a quarter of Vancouver Island's
productive farmland, and among the most artists per capita anywhere
else in the country, the Cowichan Valley has earned another moniker,

The Wine Islands

Thanks to a Mediterranean climate, rich soil, and loads of sunshine—not to mention dedicated winemakers and appreciative consumers—southern Vancouver Island is blossoming into one of North America's fastest-growing, if least known, wine regions. Cool-climate varietals—such as Pinot Noir, Ortega, and Pinot Gris—do well here, at a latitude equivalent to northern France, but it's not all about grapes: English-style craft cider, off-beat kiwi and blackberry wines, and traditionally made balsamic vinegar are also among the local special-ties. The region centers around the Cowichan Valley, a bucolic area about a 45-minute drive north of Victoria. Dubbed "The New Provence" for its proliferation of organic farms, winer-ies, restaurants, and specialist food producers, the valley is home to about a dozen wineries. More are on the Saanich Peninsula, about 20 minutes north of Victoria and, increasingly, dot-ted across the offshore Gulf Islands.

Touring is easy and wonderfully low-key: burgundy-and-white Wine Route signs, as well as maps available in local tourist offices, show the way. BC Ferries' Mill Bay Ferry links the Cow-ichan Valley to the Saanich Peninsula; ferries also connect both regions with Salt Spring Island, so you can tour the whole area without doubling back to Victoria.

Vancouver Island's wineries are, with a few exceptions, small, family-run, labor-of-love operations. Finding the wineries, hidden down winding coun-try lanes, tucked between farm stands and artists' studios, is part of the fun. Not all the wineries have enough staff to offer tours, but most offer tastings—it's always a good idea to call ahead. Some also serve lunch.

Speaking of restaurants, some of the area's best lunches are served on win-ery patios. Among them is **Merridale Ciderworks,** where cider is made in the traditional English way. Visitors can tour the cidery, taste the wares, and linger over lunches of local fare served on the orchard-view patio. There's also a day spa, with massages and pedicures given in an orchard-view yurt or a meadow-view gazebo. ⊠ *1230 Merridale Rd., Cobble Hill* ☎ *250/743–4293 or 800/998–9908* ⊕ *www.merridalecider.com.*

An outdoor bistro on a shady patio, serving lunch May–September, is a draw at Cowichan Valley's **Cherry Point Vineyards.** Owned by the Cowichan Tribes First Nation it pro-duces Pinot Noir, Pinot Blanc, Pinot Gris, Ortega, and a popular blackberry dessert wine. Free tours and tastings run daily in summer (call for hours in winter). ⊠ *840 Cherry Point Rd., Cobble Hill* ☎ *250/743–1272* ⊕ *www.cherrypointvineyards.com.*

Another local favorite is **Zanatta Win-ery,** which produces lovely Ortega, Pinot Grigio, and Damasco entirely from grapes grown on its own 30 acres. If you can, time a visit for an Italian-style lunch on the veranda of the winery's 1903 farmhouse. ⊠ *5039 Marshall Rd., Duncan* ☎ *250/748–2338* ⊕ *www.zanatta.ca.*

Over at the northern tip of the Saanich Peninsula, **Muse Winery** specializes in estate-grown Ortega and Pinot Gris varieties; a patio bistro serves lunch on summer weekends. ⊠ *11195 Chalet Rd., North Saanich* ☎ *250/656–2552* ⊕ *www.musewinery.ca* ☉ *Wed.–Mon. noon–5.*

The peninsula's most whimsical winery is the family-run **Marley Farm Winery.** The winemakers (distant relatives of the Reggae legend) produce Pinot Noir and Pinot Grigio, but are best known for their fruit wines, made from blackberries, raspberries, kiwi, and other sweet fruits. Sheep keep the 30-acre site weed-free, and kids are welcome at this family-friendly farm. ⊠ *1831 Mount Newton Cross Rd., Saanichton* ☎ *250/652–8677* ⊕ *www.marleyfarm.ca* ⊙ *May–Sept., daily 11–5; call for winter hours.*

Traditional ciders, made with apples grown on-site, are paired with local cheeses, preserves and other delectables at **Sea Cider Farm & Ciderhouse,** on the Saanich Peninsula. It's open year-round for tours and tastings. ⊠ *2487 Mount Saint Michael Rd. (off Central Saanich Rd.), Saanichton* ☎ *250/544–4824* ⊕ *www.seacider.ca* ⊙ *Wed.–Sun. 11–6.*

Salt Spring Island is also part of British Columbia's burgeoning wine country, with two wineries side by side on the main road between Fulford and Ganges, and a third just north of Ganges.

At **Garry Oaks Winery** production includes Pinot Gris, Pinot Noir, and a popular Bordeaux blend called Fetish. The winery is open for tastings daily in July and August (call ahead in the spring and fall); tours are offered by appointment. ⊠ *1880 Fulford-Ganges Rd.* ☎ *250/653–4687* ⊕ *www.garryoakswinery.com* ⊙ *Early Apr.–mid-June, Fri.–Sun. noon–5; mid-June–early Sept., daily noon–5; rest of year by appointment.*

Salt Spring Vineyards produces Pinot Gris, Pinot Noir, blackberry port, and more, almost entirely from island-grown fruit. Wine by the glass as well as local bread and cheese are available for picnics on the vineyard-view patio; there's a small B&B on-site. ⊠ *151 Lee Rd., off 1700 block Fulford-Ganges Rd.* ☎ *250/653–9463* ⊕ *www. saltspringvineyards.com.* ⊙ *Apr.–mid-June, weekends noon–5; mid-June–Aug., daily 11–5; Sept., Fri.–Sun. 11–4; Oct., Sat. noon–5; rest of year by appointment.*

Mistaken Identity. This organic vineyard and winery, opened in 2009 just north of Ganges, produces Pinot Gris, Pinot Rosé, and Gewürztraminer. The offbeat name was inspired by tasters who guessed the wine was from Europe, Australia, or anywhere but western Canada. ⊠ *164 Norton Rd.* ☎ *250/538–9463 or 877/918–2783* ⊕ *www.mistakenidentityvineyards.com* ⊙ *Late June–early Sept., Thurs.–Sun. 11–5; rest of year by appointment.*

FESTIVALS

Food festivals are a great way to enjoy the Wine Islands. **Taste: Victoria's Festival of Food and Wine** (⊕ *www.victoriataste.com*) brings a wealth of local food and wine producers, tastings, and events to Victoria in July.

In September watch for the **Vancouver Island Feast of Fields** (⊕ *www. ffcfprojects.ca/feast*), a culinary picnic and celebration of local food held on a local farm, and the **Cowichan Wine and Culinary Festival** (⊕ *wines. cowichan.net*), a two-day event celebrating Vancouver Island wine, food, music, and art.

8

"The New Provence," thanks to its wealth of wineries, small organic farms, and burgeoning local-food culture.

Highway 1 from Victoria cuts north-south through the valley, while winding side roads lead to studios, wineries, and roadside farm stands. Duncan, the valley's main town, is home to the Quw'utsun' Cultural and Conference Centre, one of B.C.'s leading First Nations cultural centers. Thirty minutes' drive north is Chemainus, a cute if touristy little town decorated with outdoor murals. Ladysmith, at the valley's north end, has a historic town center and a sandy ocean beach. About 10 minutes' drive south of Duncan are Cowichan Bay, a tiny fishing village with houses built on stilts over the water, and Cobble Hill, home to a cluster of wineries. Lake Cowichan and Shawnigan Lake draw campers, boaters, and summer cottagers. The Cowichan Valley Rail Trail, a long-distance foot-and-bike path, connects the two lakes.

GETTING HERE AND AROUND

There are three ways to get here from Victoria: make the hour's drive north on Highway 1 over the scenic Malahat Summit; take the Mill Bay Ferry from Brentwood Bay on the Saanich Peninsula; or book a ticket on the E&N Railiner, which runs once a day from Victoria's VIA Rail station and makes several Cowichan Valley stops, including Duncan and Chemainus. It's also possible to travel here via a back road from Port Renfrew, west of Sooke, following the Pacific Marine Circle Route.

COWICHAN BAY

Often called Cow Bay, this funky little town about 10 minutes' drive south of Duncan (take Cowichan Bay Road off Highway 1) is made up largely of houseboats and houses built on pilings over the water. Seafood restaurants, nautical shops, boat builders, kayaking outfitters, and B&Bs line the waterfront. Hilary's Cheese and True Grain Bread, side by side at 1737 and 1725 Cowichan Bay Road, draw foodies with their artisanal cheeses and organic baked goods, respectively. A few doors away, Arthur Vickers Gallery at the Shipyard displays the well-known artist's work in a historic shipyard space.

The **Cowichan Bay Maritime Centre** has interesting maritime paraphernalia, including historic dive suits and model boats, displayed along a pier, which is also a great place to take in views of the village and boats at harbor. You may also be able to watch boat builders and First Nations artists at work in the attached studio. ⊠ *1761 Cowichan Bay Rd.* ☎ *250/746–4955* ⊕ *www.classicboats.org* ✆ *Free* ☉ *Daily dawn–dusk.*

DUNCAN

Duncan, the largest town in the valley, is nicknamed the City of Totems for the more than 40 totem poles that dot the small community. Between May and September, free walking tours of the totems leave hourly from the south end of the train station building on Canada Avenue (contact the Duncan Business Improvement Area Society, at ☎ *250/715–1700*, for more information). On Saturdays from March to November the city square at the end of Craig Street hosts an outdoor market, where you can browse for local produce, crafts, and specialty foods. Duncan

The town of Duncan, in the Cowichan Valley, is nicknamed the City of Totems because there are more than 40 totem poles dotting the community.

is also home to the world's largest hockey stick—look for it on the outside wall of the Duncan arena on the west side of Highway 1 as you drive through town.

Kids and train enthusiasts adore riding the rails at the **British Columbia Forest Discovery Centre,** a 100-acre outdoor museum just north of Duncan. Pulled by a 1910 steam locomotive, a three-carriage train toots through the woods and over a trestle bridge across a lake, stopping at a picnic site and playground on the way. Forestry-related exhibits around the site include a 1930s-era logging camp, historic logging equipment, and indoor exhibits about the modern science of forestry. Interpretive trails through the forest lead to ancient trees, one dating back more than 500 years. During July and August, the steam train runs every half hour, daily, and guided walking tours of the site are also available. In May, June, and September, the train may be replaced with a gas locomotive. ⊠ *2892 Drinkwater Rd., Trans-Canada Hwy.* ☏ *250/715–1113 or 866/715–1113* ⊕ *www.discoveryforest.com* ✉ *C$14 including train ride* ⊗ *Early Sept.–mid-Oct. and mid-Apr.–May, Thurs.–Mon. 10–4:30; June–early Sept., daily 10–5; Dec., Fri–Sun 4–9.*

The **Cowichan Valley Museum** has local historic artifacts in a still-functioning 1912 train station. ⊠ *130 Canada Ave.* ☏ *250/746–6612* ⊕ *www. cowichanvalleymuseum.bc.ca* ✉ *C$2* ⊗ *June–Sept., Mon.–Sat. 10–4; Oct.–May, Wed.–Fri. 11–4; Sat. 1–4.*

At **Pacific Northwest Raptors,** a conservation center about 10 minutes northeast of Duncan, you can learn about the ecology of raptors, and see owls, hawks, falcons, and eagles in natural settings. Free-flying bird demonstrations are held each day (call for times); you can also join a trainer on a brief falconry or ecology course. ⊠ *1877 Herd Rd.V9L 5W4* ☎ *250/746–0372* ⊕ *www.pnwraptors.com* ☎ *C$12* ⊘ *Mid-Mar.– Oct., daily 11–4:30.*

☉ The **Quw'utsun' Cultural and Conference Centre** occupies a parklike location
★ on 6 acres of shady riverbank. This village of cedar longhouses is one of Canada's leading First Nations cultural and educational facilities. A 20-minute video in a longhouse-style theater introduces the history of the Cowichan people, B.C.'s largest aboriginal group, and a 30-minute walking tour reveals the legends behind the site's dozen totem poles. Crafts demonstrations and dance performances run occasionally during summer, and the many indigenous plants on-site are labeled with information about their traditional uses. The gift shop stocks, among other things, the hand-knit Cowichan sweaters that the area is known for, and the Riverwalk Café offers a rare opportunity to sample First Nations fare. ⊠ *200 Cowichan Way* ☎ *250/746–8119 or 877/746–8119* ⊕ *www.quwutsun.ca* ☎ *C$15* ⊘ *June–mid-Sept., Tues.–Sat. 10:30–3 (tours hourly 11–2).*

CHEMAINUS

Chemainus, 25 km (16 mi) north of Duncan, is known for the bold epic murals that decorate its townscape, as well as for its beautifully restored Victorian homes. Once dependent on the lumber industry, the small community began to revitalize itself in the early 1980s when its mill closed down. Since then the town has brought in international artists to paint a total of 40 murals depicting local historical events around town. Footprints on the sidewalk lead you on a self-guided tour of the murals. Tours by horse and carriage, replica-train rides, free outdoor concerts, a weekly night market, and plenty of B&Bs, cafés, and crafts shops all help pass the time here.

The **Chemainus Theatre** (⊠ *9737 Chemainus Rd.* ☎ *250/246–9820 or 800/565–7738*) presents family-oriented performances.

WHERE TO EAT AND STAY

$–$$ ✕ **La Pommeraie.** Neighboring farms supply much of the fare at this
CANADIAN   bistro, tucked down a country lane at Merridale Estate Cidery. The bistro, part of the gambrel-roofed cider house, showcases local art on whitewashed walls within, and orchard and forest views from the wide, covered veranda. You can match house-made ciders to your meal of, say, a local lamb-and-rosemary burger or a simple salad of mixed mushrooms and artichokes over organic greens. On Sundays, locals flock here for brick-oven pizza with live jazz playing in the background. ⊠ *1230 Merridale Rd., Cobble Hill* ☎ *250/743–4293 or 800/998–9908* ⊕ *www. merridalecider.com* ▭ *MC, V* ⊘ *No dinner Mon.–Thurs. Closed Jan.*

$$$ ✕ **The Masthead.** You know a chef cares about local food when his menu
CANADIAN   lists how far each ingredient has traveled to reach your plate. At this historic seaside roadhouse in Cowichan Bay, 5 mi is an *average sourcing distance* for the spot prawns, lamb, duck and venison, with the mussels, clams, and halibut not far behind. The poached Dungeness crab is from the bay just outside; the "Man Steak" rib eye and rack of lamb from nearby farms. The 1863 wood-paneled room offers sea views throughout, but waterside deck tables are favored by the loyal local clientele.

The long wine list includes several not even available at the vineyard. ✉ *1705 Cowichan Bay Rd., Cowichan Bay* ☎ *250/748–3714* ⊕ *www.themastheadrestaurant.com* ▭ *AE, MC, V* ⊗ *No lunch.*

$-$$

CANADIAN

✗ **Riverwalk Café.** This little riverside café, part of Duncan's Quw'utsun' Cultural and Conference Centre, offers a rare opportunity to try traditional B.C. First Nations fare. All meals start with warm fried bread with blackberry jam and salmon spread. From there, the menu offers both the familiar (salads, burgers, and fish-and-chips made with salmon) and the more unusual: venison in blackberry-mint sauce, elk escalope on baby spinach greens, or a slow-cooked stew of surf clams, salmon, halibut, and vegetables. For a treat, try the Me'Hwulp, a Salish afternoon tea for two, with candied salmon, blue-crab cakes, blackberry tarts, and more—all served on a cedar platter. A kids' menu and riverview patio in a parklike environment make this a pleasant family spot. ✉ *200 Cowichan Way, Duncan* ☎ *250/746–4370* ▭ *MC, V* ⊗ *No dinner. Closed Sun. and Mon. and mid-Sept.–May.*

$$-$$$

🏠 **Fairburn Farm Culinary Retreat & Guesthouse.** This 1896 manor on 130 pastoral acres is the centerpiece of a historic farm, Canada's first water-buffalo dairy, and a destination for lovers of terrific local food who gather here in summer for Saturday cooking classes and long Sunday lunches on the veranda. Overnight guests in the cozy but simply furnished meadow-view rooms are treated to an organic farm breakfast and, on Thursdays to Saturdays, dinners of homegrown fare. A 1930s workers' cottage sleeps five, though rates here don't include breakfast. **Pros:** wonderful farm-fresh food; peaceful rural surroundings. **Cons:** remote; the farm is at the end of a country road and some distance from town. ✉ *3310 Jackson Rd., Duncan* ☎ *250/746–4637* ⊕ *www.fairburnfarm.bc.ca* ↗ *6 rooms, 1 cottage* ⚐ *In-room: No a/c, no phone, kitchen (some) no TV, Wi-Fi (some). Closed mid-Oct–mid-Nov.* ▭ *MC, V* ⊖*BP.*

THE GULF ISLANDS

Of the hundreds of islands sprinkled across Georgia Strait between Vancouver Island and the mainland, the most popular and accessible are Galiano, Mayne, Pender, Saturna, and Salt Spring. A temperate climate, white-shell beaches, rolling pastures, and forests are common to all, but each island has a unique flavor. Though rustic, they're not undiscovered. Writers, artists, and craftspeople as well as weekend cottagers and retirees from Vancouver and Victoria take full advantage of them. Hotel reservations are a good idea in summer. Only Salt Spring has a town, but food and accommodation are available on all of the islands. Mayne, Saturna, and Pender contain sections of the Gulf Islands National Park Reserve (☎ *250/654–4000* ⊕ *www.gulfislandsnationalpark.com*), a land-and-marine park spread across several inhabited and uninhabited islands.

GETTING HERE AND AROUND

BC Ferries sail from Sidney, on the Saanich Peninsula, just north of Victoria, to all five of the islands, several times a day; these routes don't take reservations, so arrive early if you're taking a car—45 minutes to an hour early is a good rule of thumb in summer, half an hour in winter. Sailings range from half an hour to over an hour, depending on stops. Bikes, pets, and foot passengers are welcome. Ferries from the BC mainland leave from Tsawwassen, just south of Vancouver. On these routes, car reservations are highly recommended; for busier sailings, they're required. It's a three-hour journey from Tsawwassen to Salt Spring, less for the other islands.

Travel between the islands on BC Ferries is possible but generally requires an overnight stay at one of the islands. A fun, low-cost way to cruise the islands is to take one of BC Ferries' Gulf Islands Day Trips—traveling as foot passenger from Swartz Bay, around the islands and back, without disembarking. It's also possible to visit Mayne and Galiano from Salt Spring via water taxi, which doubles as the island school boat.

Salt Spring Island has the most frequent ferry service, and three terminals: ferries from Swartz Bay, near Victoria, arrive at Fulford Harbour, on the southern tip of the island, 20 miles from Ganges, the main town. Ferries from the BC mainland arrive at Long Harbour, on the island's east coast. Salt Spring also has BC Ferry service from the Cowichan Valley, with sailings every hour or so from Crofton, 20 minutes north of Duncan, to Vesuvius Bay on Salt Spring. A BC Transit minibus runs from all three ferry terminals to the town of Ganges, but it doesn't meet every ferry; check online schedules first. For a taxi on Salt Spring, call Silver Shadow Taxi.

Transport on the other islands is limited: Pender has the Pender Island Cab Company, and Galiano has the Daytripper Bus, which runs between the ferry terminal and Montague Harbour several times a day in summer. Most island accommodations collect guests from the ferry terminal if asked. Cycling is popular on the islands, despite the hilly terrain.

ESSENTIALS
Bus Info Daytripper Bus (☎ 250/539–5815).

Ferry Info BC Transit (⊕ www.bctransit.com/regions/ssi/?p=2.list).

Taxi Info Pender Island Cab Company (☎ 250/629–2222). **Silver Shadow Taxi** (☎ 250/537–3030).

Water Taxi Info (⊕ members.unet.ca/~watertaxi/).

SALT SPRING ISLAND
28 nautical mi from Swartz Bay (32 km [20 mi] north of Victoria), 22 nautical mi from Tsawwassen (39 km [24 mi] south of Vancouver).

With its wealth of studios, galleries, restaurants, and B&Bs, Salt Spring is the most developed, and most visited, of the Southern Gulf Islands. It's home to the only town in the archipelago (Ganges) and, although it can get busy on summer weekends, has not yet lost its relaxed rural feel. Outside of Ganges, the rolling landscape is home to small organic farms, wineries, forested hills, quiet white-shell beaches, and several swimming lakes.

What really sets Salt Spring apart is its status as a "little arts town." Island residents include hundreds of artists, writers, craftspeople, and musicians, many of whom open their studios to visitors.

To visit local artists in their studios, pick up a free **Studio Tour** map from the Visitor Information Centre in Ganges.

At Hastings House Country House Hotel near Ganges, A Sculpture Trail—with intriguing art installations in the woods—is open to the public.

At the south end of Salt Spring Island, where the ferries from Victoria arrive, is the tiny village of **Fulford**, which has a restaurant, and several offbeat boutiques.

Ferries from Crofton, on Vancouver Island, arrive on the west side of Salt Spring Island at **Vesuvius**, an even smaller community with a restaurant, a tiny grocery store–cum-café, a beach, and crafts studios.

Ganges, a seaside village about 30 km (18 mi) from the Fulford Ferry Terminal, is the main commercial center for Salt Spring Island. It has about a dozen art galleries and several restaurants, as well as the essentials: banks, gas stations, groceries, and a liquor store.

★ Locals and visitors flock to Ganges on summer Saturdays for the **Salt Spring Island Saturday Market** (☎ *250/537–4448* ⊕ *www.saltspringmarket. com*), held in Centennial Park every Saturday, April through October. Everything sold at this colorful outdoor market is made or grown on the island; the array and quality of crafts, food, and produce is dazzling.

Burgoyne Bay Provincial Park (✉ *Fulford-Ganges Rd. at Burgoyne Bay Rd.,* ⊕ *www.env.gov.bc.ca/bcparks*), just off the main road toward the southern end of the island.

Near the center of Salt Spring Island, Baynes Peak in **Mt. Maxwell Provincial Park** (✉ *Mt. Maxwell Rd., off Fulford–Ganges Rd.*) has spectacular views of south Salt Spring, Vancouver Island, and other Gulf Islands. The last portion of the drive is steep, winding, and unpaved.

☺ **Ruckle Provincial Park** (✉ *Beaver Point Rd.* ☎ *250/653–4115 or 877/559–*
★ *2115* ⊕ *www.env.gov.bc.ca/bcparks*) is the site of an 1872 homestead and extensive fields that are still being farmed. Several small sandy beaches and 8 km (5 mi) of trails winding through forests and along the coast make this one of the islands' most appealing parks. Walk-in campsites on a grassy seaside field, and eight drive-in campsites in the woods, are available on a first-come, first-served basis and fill quickly in summer.

WHERE TO EAT AND STAY

$–$$$
ITALIAN
✕ **Auntie Pesto's Café & Delicatessen.** Fresh local ingredients, house-made bread, and Mediterranean flavors keep regulars well fed at this family-run village center spot. Breakfast omelets, enjoyed with fruit salad and good coffee, lunches of homemade soup and grilled sandwiches (the Johnny B will feed a hungry teen, though some of the croissant versions are smallish), and Mediterranean-themed dinners of, say, sablefish, duck, or big plates of pasta make the bustling interior and marina-view deck busy all day. ✉ *2104–115 Fulford Ganges Rd., Ganges* ☎ *250/537–4181* ▭ *MC, V* ☺ *Closed Sun.*

$$–$$$
SEAFOOD
✕ **Calvin's Bistro.** Seafood—whether in the form of a wild salmon fillet, baby-shrimp linguine, or good old halibut-and-chips—tops the menu at

this comfortable marina-view bistro in Ganges. Locals also flock here for such Thai dishes as coconut prawns, spring rolls, and bouillabaisse in red coconut curry. A long list of lunchtime sandwiches and burgers includes local lamb, wild salmon, and even Wiener schnitzel. Inside booths are cozy, while the big patio has great harbor views. Friendly Swiss owners account for the homemade European desserts and welcoming service. ⊠ *133 Lower Ganges Rd., Ganges* ☎ *250/538–5551* ▭ *MC, V* ⊗ *Closed Mon., No lunch Sun. Closed Sun., Sept.–Apr.*

$$$–$$$$
SCANDINAVIAN
★

✕ **House Piccolo.** Piccolo Lyytikainen, the Finnish-born chef-owner of this tiny restaurant—in a village center heritage house—serves beautifully prepared and presented European cuisine. Creations include Scandinavian-influenced dishes such as B.C. venison with a juniper-and-rowanberry demi-glace and charbroiled fillet of beef with Gorgonzola sauce. For dessert the chocolate terrine Finlandia and vodka-moistened lingonberry crepes are hard to resist. The 250-item wine list includes many hard-to-find vintages. The indoor tables are cozy and candle-lighted; the outdoor patio is a pleasant summer dining spot. ⊠ *108 Hereford Ave., Ganges* ☎ *250/537–1844* ▭ *MC, V* ⊗ *No lunch; call ahead for winter hrs.*

$$–$$$
ECLECTIC

✕ **Rock Salt.** You can watch the ferry coming up the harbor from the sea-view windows of this Fulford Harbour local favorite. Wholesome, organic, and local goodies run from slow-baked ribs and lamb burgers to seafood curries, Asian hot pots, pad thai, and a much-loved yam quesadilla. Vegans are well catered for here, with yummy bean stews and lentil burgers, and the made-from-scratch breakfasts are worth getting up early for. If you must leave the island, the take-out counter offers provisions for your onward journey. ⊠ *2921 Fulford Ganges Rd., Fulford* ☎ *250/653–4833* ⊕ *www.rocksaltrestaurant.com* ▭ *MC, V.*

$$$$
Fodor's Choice
★

▦ **Hastings House Country House Hotel.** The centerpiece of this 22-acre seaside estate—with its gardens, meadows, and harbor views—is a 1939 country house, built in the style of an 11th-century Sussex manor. Guest quarters, which are in the manor, in renovated historic outbuildings, and in a newer addition overlooking Ganges Harbour, are decorated in an English-country style, with antiques, locally crafted woodwork, and fireplaces. The Post, a stand-alone two-room cottage, is a honeymoon favorite; the secluded three-bedroom Churchill Cottage has a kitchen and a private driveway. Four-course and à la carte dinners in the manor house ($$$$) serve local seafood and herbs and produce from the inn's gardens. **Pros:** wonderful food; top-notch service; historic character. **Cons:** no pool; some rooms overlook a pub next door; rates are high. ⊠ *160 Upper Ganges Rd., Ganges* ☎ *250/537–2362 or 800/661–9255* ⊕ *www.hastingshouse.com* ⏍ *3 rooms, 14 suites, 1 guesthouse* ♨ *In-room: No a/c (some), kitchen (some), refrigerator, Wi-Fi. In-hotel: Restaurant, bar, spa, bicycles, Internet terminal, Wi-Fi, parking (free), no kids under 16* ▭ *AE, MC, V* ⊗ *Closed mid-Nov.–mid-Mar.* ⏏❘ *BP.*

GALIANO ISLAND

Galiano, with its 26-km-long (16-mi-long), unbroken eastern shore and cove-dotted western coast is arguably the prettiest of these islands. It's certainly the best for hiking and mountain biking, with miles of trails through the Douglas fir and Garry Oak forest. Mt. Galiano and Bodega

Ridge are classic walks, with far-reaching views to the mainland. Most shops and services—including cash machines, gas pumps, galleries, and a bookstore—are clustered near the Sturdies Bay ferry terminal. A visitor information booth is just to your right as you leave the ferry. The **Daytripper Bus** runs between Sturdies Bay and Montague Harbour several times a day in July and August (☎ 250/539–5815).

For sustenance, check out **Sturdies Bay Bakery & Cafe** (☎ 250/539–2004)—a favorite local breakfast stop—and **Max & Moritz Spicy Island Food House** (☎ 250/539–5888), offering German and Indonesian takeout from a catering van at the ferry terminal.

You can rent a kayak, boat,m or moped at **Montague Harbour Marina** (✉ *Montague Rd., just east of park* ☎ *250/539–5733 marina, 250/539–2442 kayak rentals, 250/539–3443 moped and boat rentals*). The **Harbour Grill** (☎ *250/539–5733*) at the marina serves breakfast and lunch daily, and dinners Thursday through Sunday on its heated ocean-view deck. It's open May through September.

🖰 **Montague Harbour Provincial Marine Park** (✉ *Montague Park Rd., off*
★ *Montague Rd.* ☎ *800/689–9025 camping reservations* ⊕ *www.discovercamping.ca*) has walk-in and drive-in campsites and a long shell beach famed for its sunset views. C$3 per car per day.

NEED A BREAK? The Hummingbird Inn Pub (✉ *47 Sturdies Bay Rd.* ☎ *250/539–5472*) is a friendly local hangout, with live music on summer weekends. Also in summer, the pub runs a free shuttle bus to the Montague Harbour Marina and campsite.

WHERE TO STAY

Harbour Grill (☎ *250/539–5733*) at the marina serves breakfast and lunch daily, and dinners Thursday through Sunday on its heated ocean-view deck. It's open May through September.

$$$–$$$$
Fodor'sChoice
★

🖭 **Galiano Oceanfront Inn & Spa.** A yoga suite overlooking a meditation garden, seaside massage, an infrared sauna, and a mineral flotation bath are among the serenity-inducing highlights at this waterfront retreat on Sturdies Bay. Suites have full kitchens and big, covered sea-view balconies, each with a jetted tub, outdoor fireplace, and grill. Rooms have hidden Murphy-style massage tables; all are serene with clean lines, earth tones, water views, and local art. The oceanfront restaurant ($$$) has fine locally sourced fare to go with the view; summer brings wood-fired pizzas on a Tuscan-style patio. Hemp-seed rubs and wild blueberry–smoothie wraps are among the spa's innovative treatments. **Pros:** no car needed (the resort's golf cart can meet you at the ferry and eco-friendly "smart cars" can be rented at the resort); well-equipped suites encourage long stays; quiet and lovely environment. **Cons:** no morning room service; breakfast starts at 9. ✉ *134 Madrona Dr., Galiano Island* ☎ *250/539–3388 or 877/530–3939* ⊕ *www.galianoinn.com* ⤴ *10 rooms, 10 suites* ⌂ *In-room: No a/c, kitchen (some), refrigerator, DVD, Wi-Fi. In-hotel: Restaurant, room service, bar, spa, beachfront, laundry service, Wi-Fi, parking (free), some pets allowed, no-smoking rooms* ▭ *AE, MC, V* ⦿*BP for rooms only.*

8

Fresh crab is a delicacy around the Gulf Islands, especially in Ganges Harbour, on Salt Spring Island.

MAYNE ISLAND

The smallest of the Southern Gulf Islands, Mayne also has the most visible history. The buildings of Miners Bay, the island's tiny commercial center, date to the 1850s, when Mayne was a stopover for prospectors en route to the gold fields.

GETTING HERE AND AROUND

As the quietest and least hilly of the islands, Mayne is a good choice for cycle touring. **Mayne Island Bike and Kayaking** (☎ 250/539–2463) has rentals.

Plumper Pass Lockup (✉ *433 Fernhill Rd.* ☎ *No phone*) was built in 1896 as a jail but is now a minuscule museum (open July–Labor Day, Fri.–Mon. 10–2, free) chronicling the island's history.

You can also stop for a meal or a drink on the deck at the **Springwater Lodge** (✉ *400 Fernhill Rd., Miners Bay* ☎ *250/539–5521*), one of the province's oldest hotels. Active Pass Lighthouse, at the end of Georgina Point Road, is part of **Georgina Point Heritage Park.** Built in 1885, it still signals ships into the busy waterway. The grassy grounds are great for picnicking.

Bennett Bay Park, part of the Gulf Islands National Park Reserve, has walking trails and one of the island's most scenic beaches.

A 45-minute hike up **Mt. Parke** leads to the island's highest point and a stunning view of the mainland and other Gulf Islands.

On Saturdays, between July and mid-October, check out the **Farmer's Market** outside the Miners Bay Agricultural Hall. Open 10 to 1, it sells produce and crafts while local musicians entertain shoppers.

Built entirely by volunteers, the 1-acre **Japanese Garden** at Dinner Bay Park honors the island's early Japanese settlers. It's about 1 km (½ mi) south of the Village Bay ferry terminal. Admission is free.

WHERE TO STAY

$–$$ ★ ⊡ **Mayne Island Resort.** Overlooking Bennett Bay and just steps from Mayne Island's best-loved beach, this chic modern resort enjoys a prime waterfront location. Each of the one-bedroom cottages has French doors leading to a seafront patio or deck. Zinc-inlay tables, reclaimed hardwood floors, vaulted ceilings, leather headboards, and gas fireplaces are among the luxe touches. Lodge rooms are simpler but have great views, too. At press time, a spa, indoor pool, gym, and more cottages were planned. **Pros:** waterfront; stylish, private cottages. **Cons:** a steep drop to the water makes it unsuitable for small children; construction will be underway for some time. ⊠ *494 Arbutus Dr., Mayne Island* ☎ *250/539–3122 or 866/539–5399* ⊕ *www.mayneislandresort. com* ⤴ *18 cottages, 8 rooms* ⚲ *In-room: Kitchen (some), DVD (some), Wi-Fi. In-hotel: Restaurant, bar, beachfront, Wi-Fi, parking (free), some pets allowed.* ⊟ *AE, MC, V.*

PENDER ISLAND

Just a few miles north of the U.S. border, Pender is actually two islands: North Pender and South Pender, divided by a canal and linked by a one-lane bridge. Most of the population of about 2,000 cluster on North Pender, whereas South Pender is largely forested and undeveloped. There's no town on either island, but you can find groceries, gas, a bank, pharmacy, and liquor store at North Pender's Driftwood Centre. A farmers' market runs on summer Saturdays at Pender Island Community Hall and crafts shops, studios, and galleries are open throughout the islands. You can rent a bike or scooter rentals at Otter Bay Marina (250/629–3579), near the ferry terminal.

★ Both North Pender and South Pender host sections of the **Gulf Islands National Park Reserve** (☎ *250/654–4000* ⊕ *www.gulfislandsnationalpark. com*). On South Pender a steep trail leads to the 244-meter (800-foot) summit of **Mt. Norman,** with its expansive ocean and island views. Trails start at Ainslie Road, Canal Road, and the Beaumont section of the park. For an easy walk in the woods, visit the delightfully named Enchanted Forest Park on South Pender.

The Penders are blessed with beaches, boasting more than 30 public beach-access points.

The small pebble beach at **Gowlland Point Park,** at the end of Gowlland Point Road on South Pender, is one of the prettiest on the islands, with views across to Washington State.

The sandy beach at **Mortimer Spit** is a sheltered spot for swimming and kayaking; it's near the bridge linking the two islands.

A waterview café, an artisans' co-op, and views to Saturna and Mayne Islands are the draws at Hope Bay, a lovely cove on North Pender's eastern shore. ⊠ *4301 Bedwell Harbour Rd, North Pender Island.*

You can sample a glass of Pinot Noir or Rosé on the terrace at **Morning Bay Vineyard**, Pender's only winery. ⊠ *6621 Harbour Hill Dr., North*

8

Pender Island ☎ 250/629–8351 ⊕ www.morningbay.ca ⊘ Open for tastings May–early Sept., Wed.–Sun. 10–5; early Sept.–Apr., Fri.–Sun. noon–5; or by appointment. Tours by appointment.

Roesland, a historic cottage resort on North Pender, is part of the Gulf Islands National Park Reserve. An easy 15-minute walk leads out to a tiny islet, and a 1908 farmhouse on the site houses the Pender Islands Museum. ⊠ *2408 South Otter Bay Rd., North Pender Island ☎ 250/629–6935 ⊕ www.penderislandmuseum.org ⊘ Museum: Easter–mid-Oct., weekends 10–4.*

NEED A BREAK?
You can refuel before catching the ferry at the Stand (⊠ *Otter Bay Ferry terminal, end of Otter Bay Rd.* ☎ *250/629–3292*), a rustic take-out shack at the Otter Bay ferry terminal. The burgers—whether beef, venison, oyster, or veggie—are enormous, messy, and delicious.

WHERE TO STAY

$$$$
Fodor's Choice
★

Poets Cove Resort & Spa. One of the Gulf Islands' most luxurious developments fills a secluded cove on South Pender. A nautical-theme lodge and a scattering of two- and three-bedroom cottages overlook a marina and a forest-framed cove. All units have fireplaces, heated bathroom floors, and decks or balconies with stunning ocean views; cottages have private ocean-view hot tubs. The restaurant ($$$–$$$$) serves top-notch Pacific Northwest fare, and the lounge offers high-end pub meals. A waterfall tumbles over a steam grotto outside the lavish spa. Activities include whale-watching, vineyard tours, yoga classes, and kayak tours. **Pros:** great views; family-friendly and a full range of activities, including summer evening children's programs. **Cons:** twenty-minute drive from the ferry. ⊠ *9801 Spalding Rd., Pender Island ☎ 250/629–2100 or 888/512–7638 ⊕ www.poetscove.com ⤳ 22 rooms, 15 cottages, 9 villas ♿ In-room: No a/c, kitchen (some), refrigerator, DVD, Wi-Fi. In-hotel: Restaurant, bar, tennis court, pools, gym, spa, beachfront, water sports, bicycles, children's programs (ages 5–12), laundry facilities, Internet terminal, Wi-Fi, some pets allowed ⊟ AE, MC, V.*

Saturna Island. With just 300 residents, remote Saturna Island is taken up largely by a section of the Gulf Islands National Park Reserve and is a prime spot for hiking, kayaking, and beachcombing.

Said to be the only island whose population is campaigning for less ferry service, Saturna usually takes two ferries to reach. It has no bank or pharmacy but does have an ATM machine, pub, a general store, and winery—Saturna Island Family Estate Winery—where between May and October, you can lunch on a terrace overlooking the vineyards and the sea. ⊠ *8 Quarry Trail ☎ 250/539–3521 or 877/918–3388.*

Whistler, the Okanagan, Tofino and the Pacific Rim

WORD OF MOUTH

"The drive up the Sea to Sky highway is gorgeous and of course there are all sorts of outdoor activities available up at Whistler."
—NWWanderer

WELCOME TO WHISTLER, THE OKANAGAN, TOFINO AND THE PACIFIC RIM

TOP REASONS TO GO

★ **Ski Whistler and Blackcomb:** With over 8,000 acres of skiing terrain, combined with four seasons of adventure and a village full of amenities, this is North America's premier mountain resort.

★ **Getting to Whistler:** The Sea-to-Sky Highway, one of North America's most scenic highways, gets you from Vancouver to Whistler in about two hours.

★ **Sample Okanagan Wines:** You might not have heard of them yet but the wineries of the Okanagan Valley are producing some highly acclaimed wines; small batches mean they don't often make their way to U.S. wine stores.

★ **Storm watching in Tofino:** Though long considered one of B.C.'s most sublime summer environments, Tofino has managed to transform the hostile winter of Vancouver Island's west coast into both a surfing and storm-watching destination between November and March. The coast provides plenty of other coastal enticements during other seasons.

Map showing Vancouver Island and surrounding area, with scale 50 mi / 50 km. Locations include: Chilko Lake, Gold River, Comox, Port Alberni, Gibsons, Parksville, Strait of Georgia, Tofino, Nanaimo, Ucluelet, Barkley Sound, Duncan, Sidney, VANCOUVER ISLAND, Pacific Rim National Park, Neah Bay, VICTORIA, Strait of Juan de Fuca, Port Angeles, Pacific Ocean. Highway markers 19, 4, 3.

1 Whistler. Just 120 km (74 mi) north of Vancouver, Whistler is easy to get to, and the scenery on the way up will take your breath away. This alpine paradise holds thrills for skiers and nonskiers alike, all enhanced after the 2010 Winter Olympics. Attractions like the Squamish-Lil'Wat Centre represent lasting benefits of the Games.

2 The Okanagan Valley. Long known as the fruit-growing capital of Canada, the Okanagan has also become a significant wine-producing area. The Okanagan is about a five-hour drive from Vancouver. Within the Okanagan region, it's about 125 km (75 mi), or a two-hour drive, from Kelowna to Osoyoos.

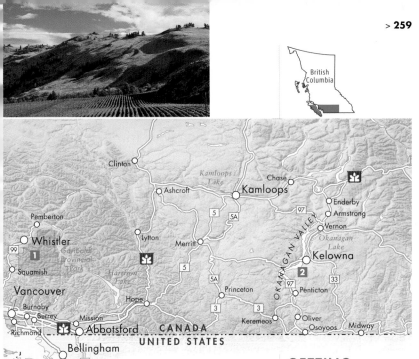

British Columbia

3 Tofino, Ucluelet, and the Pacific Rim. The stretch of open coast along the western edge of Vancouver Island makes in-season from out-of-season, as visitors come to watch the dramatic winter storms coming off the water. And the summers here sparkle. Tofino and Ucluelet are the tourism-oriented towns at either end of the Pacific Rim National Park Reserve.

GETTING ORIENTED

Each of these excursions can easily be combined with a few days in Vancouver or Victoria. Heading up to Whistler takes only a couple of hours but traveling by car to the Okanagan or Tofino requires more of a commitment. All three trips purvey gorgeous scenery and ample places to pause. Taking the BC Ferries to Nanaimo en route to Tofino offers an added bonus of vistas and adventure.

9

WHISTLER PLANNER

How Much Time Do I Need?

Whistler teems with partying Vancouverites, especially during the off-season. Three days provides plenty of time for zipping, skiing, biking, or whatever your alpine adventure of choice may be. Whistler's many festivals last from 4 to 10 days so check below, and the Whistler Tourism Web site, to find your celebration of choice, though everyday's a "happening" in this village.

Visitor Information

Contacts Tourism Whistler (🕾 800/944-7853, 604/664-5625 in Vancouver ⊕ www. whistler.com). **Whistler Activity and Information Center** (✉ 4010 Whistler Way 🕾 604/932-2394).

Festivals To Plan Your Trip Around

FEB.: Winterpride Whistler: The resort heats up for a week with naughty nightlife, fine dining, fabulous après-ski, and slope-side fun. (⊕ www.gaywhistler.com)

MAR.: Women's Week: What's a girl to do? Lots during this week of Snowboard and Ski camps, clinics, après-ski events, dancing, and offers just for gals. (⊕ www. whistlerblackcomb.com)

APR.: Telus World Ski & Snowboard Festival: This raucous end-of-the-season bash fills ten days with music, arts, and extreme sports. (⊕ www.whistler.com)

MAY: Whistler Wellness Week: Seminars, fitness demonstrations, products trials, and other events focus on health and wellness. (⊕ www.whistlerwellness.com)

JULY: Whistler Children's Art Festival: Whistler's Creekside hosts a fun-filled weekend for the entire family. (⊕ www. whistlerartscouncil.com)

AUG.: Kokanee Crankworx: This annual mountain-bike festival showcases the sport's boldest and most talented athletes as they whip down double black-diamond runs; there are also daily concerts a and huge downhill biking scene. (⊕ www.crankworx.com)

NOV.: Cornucopia: There's a little bit of everything at this annual festival for foodies and oenophiles. (⊕ www. whistlercornucopia.com)

DEC.: Whistler Film Festival: This annual celebration of film features world premieres from top directors, industry events, and parties, all with a Canadian focus. (⊕ www. whistlerfilmfestival.com)

WHAT IT COSTS IN CANADIAN DOLLARS

	¢	$	$$	$$$	$$$$
Restaurants	under C$8	C$8-C$12	C$13-C$20	C$21-C$30	over C$30
Hotels	under C$75	C$75-C$125	C$126-C$175	C$176-C$250	over C$250

Restaurant prices are for a main course at dinner, not including 5% GST and 10% liquor tax. Hotel prices are for two people in a standard double room in high season, excluding 10% provincial accommodation tax, service charge, and 5% GST.

Getting Here and Around

Just 120 km (75 mi) north of Vancouver on Highway 99 (Sea-to-Sky Highway), there are many ways to get to Whistler from Vancouver, depending on your budget. You won't need a car once you're here; even if you choose to stay outside the village, you can get around easily with public shuttles or taxis. The closest airport is Vancouver International Airport, about 120 km (74 mi) away.

By Bus: Perimeter Whistler Express has daily bus service to Whistler from Vancouver International Airport and from many Vancouver hotels (11 times a day in ski season, 7 times a day in summer). Fares start at C$65 one way; reservations are recommended. Greyhound Canada has service to Whistler from the downtown Vancouver depot and from Vancouver Airport.

By Car: Driving from Vancouver to Whistler takes approximately two hours along the scenic Sea-to-Sky Highway, (aka Highway 99). It's recommended to check weather conditions during the winter season.

By Helicopter: If you've got the money, travel in style: Glacier Air Tours has charter helicopter and airplane service between Whistler and the Vancouver International Airport or Vancouver Harbour for C$225 to C$3,000. West Coast Air connects Victoria and Whistler, June through September for C$288.

By Limo: LimoJet Gold runs limo service from Vancouver International Airport (YVR) to Whistler for C$295 per trip. Pearl International Limousine Service has stretch limos, sedans, 10-passenger vans, and excursion limos—all equipped with blankets, pillows, bottled water, and videos so you can enjoy the ride. Rates start at about C$300. Vancouver All-Terrain Adventures charters four-wheel drives from YVR or downtown Vancouver to Whistler. Vehicles travel in all weather and will stop for sightseeing. The cost starts at C$350 one way.

By Train: The Whistler Mountaineer is a three-hour, premier train journey from North Vancouver to Whistler. It's an "experience" train trip, providing passengers with commentary and refreshments while taking in the Sea-to-Sky's jaw-dropping scenery. Fares start at C$110 one-way.

Getting Around In Whistler

The Whistler and Valley Express (WAVE) transit system operates a free public-transit system within Whistler village, and paid public transit throughout the Valley and north to Pemberton.

For a cab in Whistler call Sea to Sky Taxi.

Transportation Contacts BC Transit (☎ 604/932–4020 ⊕ www.bctransit.com/regions/whi/?p=1.txt). **Sea to Sky Taxi** (☎ 604/932–3333).

Contacts Downtown Vancouver Depot (✉ 1150 Station St. ☎ No phone). **Greyhound Canada** (☎ 604/482–8747 or 800/661–8747 ⊕ www.greyhound.ca). **Blackcomb Helicopters** (☎ 604/938–1700 ⊕ www.blackcombhelicopters.com). **Glacier Air** (☎ 800/208–4421 ⊕ www.glacierair.com). **LimoJet Gold** (☎ 604/273–1331 or 800/278–8742 ⊕ www.limojetgold.com). **Ministry of Transportation** (⊕ www.drivebc.ca). **Pearl International Limousine Service** (☎ 604/732–7897 or 877/977–3275 ⊕ www.pearllimousine.com). **Perimeter Whistler Express** (☎ 604/266–5386 or 877/317–7788 ⊕ www.perimeterbus.com). **Vancouver All-Terrain Adventures** (☎ 604/984–2374 or 888/754–5601 ⊕ www.all-terrain.com). **West Coast Air** (☎ 800/347–2222 ⊕ www.westcoastair.com). **Whistler Mountaineer** (☎ 888/687–7245 ⊕ www.whistlermountaineer.com).

9

WHISTLER

Fodor's Choice *120 km (74 mi) north of Vancouver, 58 km (36 mi) north of Squamish.*
★

With two breathtaking mountains—Whistler and Blackcomb—enviable skiing conditions, championship golf
courses, more than 200 shops, 90 restaurants and bars,
an array of accommodations, spas, hiking trails, and what
experts consider the best mountain-bike park in the world,
it's no surprise that Whistler, located just 75 miles north of
Vancouver, consistently ranks as the top ski resort in North
America.

Back in the early 1960s Whistler's early visionaries designed the ski
resort as a car-free village with the 1968 Winter Olympics in mind,
though the Olympic vision didn't become manifest until Whistler
served as the host resort for the 2010 Winter Olympic Games. Whistler's already strong infrastructure received a boost with the widening
of Highway 99 and other upgrades. Whistler also added the Squamish-
Lil'Wat Centre, a gorgeous cultural focal point for these proud First
Nations who have occupied and explored this region of forests, fjords,
and mountains for millennia.

Whistler Resort, which includes Whistler and Blackcomb mountains,
has the largest ski area and two of the longest vertical drops on the
continent, as well as one of the world's most advanced lift systems.
But people who visit during any season will discover that there is more
to Whistler than snow. Indeed, today's Whistler is about much more
than skiing and snowboarding; each winter, people flow into Whistler
with no intention of riding a chairlift. They come for the many spas,
shops, and restaurants, and the varied nightlife. Four championship
golf courses, the world's largest downhill bike park, and hundreds of
miles of trails provide just a few of the shoulder season and summer

options. Visitors come to ride horses, go zip-lining across Fitzsimmons Valley, or take a helicopter ride to hike and have lunch on one of dozens of nearby glaciers.

The drive into the Coast Mountains from Vancouver is a stunning sampler of mainland British Columbia. You'll follow the Sea-to-Sky Highway (Highway 99) past fjordlike Howe Sound, the town of Squamish, and into Whistler Resort. Once you're in Whistler, though, anywhere you want to go within the resort is within a few minutes' walk, and parking lots ring the village (although as a hotel guest, you may have access to underground parking). The bases of Whistler and Blackcomb mountains are also just at the village edge. In fact, you can ski right to the door of the many slope-side hotels and condos, though you then miss the fun of the après-ski parade through the pedestrian-only village, a bold urban-design decision that has resulted in an incredibly accessible resort. Families take to the Village Stroll in search of COWS Ice Cream and its racks of novelty, bovine-themed T-shirts. Couples shop for engagement rings or the latest ROOTS styles. Skiers and snowboarders shuffle through the crowd, leaning their skis and boards against the buildings to dip into the vibrant après-ski scene on a dozen outdoor heated patios.

The Village warren continues to expand and Village North (or Marketplace) has all but been absorbed. The petit Upper Village—Blackcomb Mountain's base—remains somewhat isolated but a wonderful footpath connects the two areas. Whistler Creekside, located ten minutes south on Highway 99, is the latest shopping, dining, and real estate development.

Meanwhile, Whistler has also been building its identity as a progressive, livable city, with programs for accessible housing and strong schools, and launching an effort to be the greenest township on the planet. Though only 8% of the 100 square miles that comprise Whistler is designated for development, North America's premier four-season resort continues to grow, especially now that the world has visited during the 2010 Winter Games.

EXPLORING

Squamish-Lil'wat Centre. This joint cultural project was put together by the neighboring Squamish Nation and Lil'wat Nation to preserve their cultural traditions and to allow others to learn about them. The concrete, cedar, and fir structure melds the longhouse of the coastal Squamish people with the traditional Lil'wat pit house, and inside, visitors can discover artifacts from past and present. Carvings adorn the walls, and displays of art, artifacts, tools, and dugouts display the nuances of different coastal fishermen and hunters. The on-site café ($), which serves contemporary food with a First Nations twist—think Lil'wat venison chili, a "mountain hoagie" with bison salami and wild-boar prosciutto, or a "Caesar" salad of romaine and Parmesan with bannock croutons—is worth a visit itself. ⊠ *4584 Blackcomb Way, Whistler* ☎ *604/964–0990* ⊕ *www.slcc.ca* ⊠ *C$18* ⊙ *Daily 9:30–5.*

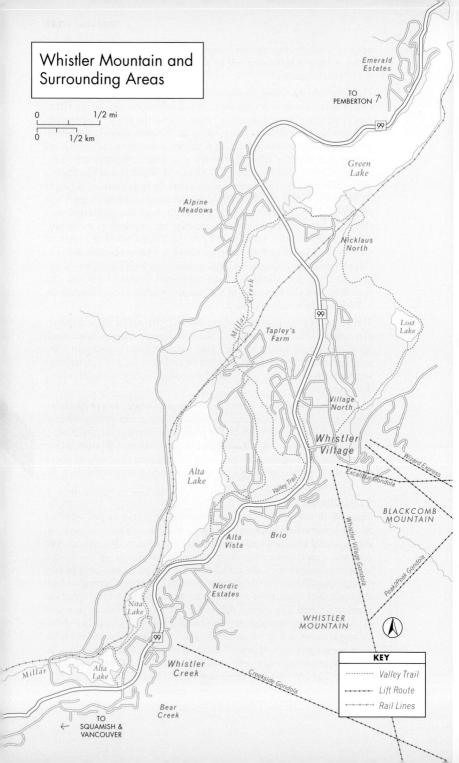

ON-MOUNTAIN EATING OPTIONS

Like the world's best ski resorts, Whistler has a great variety of on-mountain eating options. You'll find them all listed on the trail/resort map but these are the key ones to know about.

Both Whistler and Blackcomb have a day lodge, accessible from the gondola, with a cafeteria that serves an array of soup, sandwich, and hot food options. At the other end of the spectrum, there is fine dining at Christine's in Blackcomb's Rendez-vous day lodge and at Steep's in

Whistler's Roundhouse. Should you be moving about on one plank or two, don't miss Whistler's Harmony Hut and Blackcomb's Horstman Hut for spectacular views, chili, and other comfort foods. Blackcomb skier's in the know head to the Glacier Creek Lodge for a shorter lunch line. Summer travelers should defnitely check out the BBQ that flares up each weekend evening on the Roundhouse patio. Mountainside hikers and gondola passengers will find pastries at Harmony and lunches at Horstman during the summer.

WHERE TO EAT

When Vancouver's celebrity chefs decided to spread their wings and fly out of town, Whistler provided the logical destination. Today, some of the top ski-resort restaurants in the world take advantage of the growing locavore or "slow food" movement—as showcased during four months of Sunday farmers' markets and organic bounty—to provide diners with a surprising array of Northwest cuisine. The use of local food in the 17 on-mountain restaurants is continuously impressive. Foodies will especially enjoy Whistler's Cornucopia Festival, which showcases culinary talents and B.C. wineries every November.

While no one would ever mistake Whistler for a thrifty resort, there are plenty of sandwich and coffee shops littered around the village. There is also a full-scale grocery store should you land a room with a kitchen.

$$$–$$$$
FRENCH
★
✕**Araxi.** Golden walls, terra-cotta tiles, antiques, and original artwork create a vibrant backdrop for the French-influenced Pacific Northwest cuisine served here, one of Whistler's finest restaurants. Local farmers grow produce exclusively for Araxi's chef, who also makes good use of cheese, game, and fish from the province. Breads and pastries are made in-house each morning. The menu changes seasonally, but dishes may include Fraser Valley rabbit and alder-smoked B.C. arctic char with saffron and oyster-mushroom sauce. The multitier seafood tower is a must-try for seafoodies who love to graze and share. Wine lovers take note: there's a 13,000-bottle inventory and three sommeliers. A heated patio is open in summer, and the lounge is a popular après-ski spot. ✉ *4222 Village Sq.* ☎ *604/932–4540* ⊕ *www.araxi.com* ⌲ *Reservations essential* ▤ *AE, DC, MC, V* ⊗ *No lunch Oct.–May.*

$$$$
PACIFIC
NORTHWEST
Fodor's Choice
★
✕**Bearfoot Bistro.** Occasionally a resort restaurant emerges with a reputation that transcends resort dining, and Bearfoot Bistro is one such place, and diners travel from Vancouver for the sole purpose of eating here. Executive chef Melissa Craig plays with local ingredients to create masterly pairings such as a rack of wild caribou with sweet corn three ways

and pepper-crusted buffalo carpaccio—you can choose either a 3-course or 5-course prix-fixe menu but there is no à la carte. The wine cellar is one of Whistler's most extensive. ⊠ *4121 Village Green* ☎ *604/932– 3433* ⊕ *www.bearfootbistro.com* ⊟ *AE, DC, MC, V* ☉ *No lunch.*

$$–$$$
CANADIAN
✕ **Christine's and Steep's.** Most world-class ski resorts offer on-mountain fine dining and Whistler-Blackcomb is no exception. Christine's, offering sit-down service and an à la carte weekend brunch in Blackcomb's Rendezvous Lodge, was once only skier accessible in the winter; the hardy can now take the Peak2Peak gondola from Whistler. At Steep's, inside Whistler's Roundhouse Lodge at the top of the Whistler Gondola, it's not uncommon to see visitors dining in saris and other decidedly nonwinter dress. The food remains very local, however, in its choice of regional cuisine and excellent B.C. wine list. If you're just eating, and not skiing, Steep's is generally easier to get to. Both Steep's and Christina's also serve during the summer months. Reservations for both Christine's and Steep's are advised. ⊠ *Blackcomb mountain, Whistler mountain* ☎ *604/905–2379 and 604/938–7437* ⊕ *www.whistler-blackcomb.com* ⊟ *AE, MC, V* ☉ *Lunch only.*

$–$$
CANADIAN
✕ **Elements Urban Tapas.** Copper accents and soft lighting accentuate the open-concept show kitchen, and a hip crowd of thirtysomethings mixed in with jet-setting families with young children occupy the comfy suede banquettes and booths. The soothing sounds of a cascading water wall can be heard in the background. The draw here is locally inspired small plates perfect for sharing. Steamed Salt Spring Island mussels with lemongrass, Kaffir lime, and coconut green curry are yummy, as is roasted duck breast with a honey-soy glaze. The Belgian chocolate mousse pyramid is the perfect way to end a day on the slopes. They're open for breakfast, too. ⊠ *Summit Lodge, 102B–4359 Main St.* ☎ *604/932–5569* ⊟ *AE, DC, MC, V.*

¢–$$
ECLECTIC
✕ **Hot Buns Bakery.** It's as if this sweet spot has been transported from a rural French town, with its stone floors, vintage skis hanging from the ceiling, and simple wooden tables and chairs. But the reason to come is not the look of the place: they serve the best *pain au chocolat,* lattes, and crepes in town. Choose a savory Tex-Mex crepe for a quick lunch or a decadent pear-and-chocolate crepe to satisfy your après-ski sweet tooth. Not a bad way to start, or end, the day. ⊠ *4232 Village Stroll* ☎ *604/932–6883* ⊟ *AE, DC, MC, V.*

¢–$$
CONTINENTAL
✕ **La Brasserie des Artistes.** "The Brass," as it's known, provides reasonably priced bistro fare, burgers, and pasta options in the heart of the Village Stroll. At breakfast there are an assortment of egg dishes to fortify you for the day ahead, or kick off the evening follies during après-ski. With one of the best patios in the Village, this is a popular spot. ⊠ *4232 Village Stroll* ☎ *604/932–3569* ⊕ *www.labrass.moonfruit. com* ⊟ *AE, DC, MC, V.*

$$–$$$
CANADIAN
✕ **The Mountain Club.** Handcrafted cocktails, inspired dishes created with the best local ingredients, a *Wine Spectator* award of excellence, and a sensual vibe make this Whistler's hottest restaurant. The menu features "earth" and "ocean" dishes such as seared sockeye salmon with roast turnip and fingerling potatoes, and Fraser Valley pork tenderloin with fig, potato, and chorizo hash. Mac-and-cheese or fish-and-chips are

simple, but no less delicious, options, and desserts are universally phenomenal. This restaurant-cum-lounge—with its warm woods, natural stone, high-back white-leather booths, and excellent down-tempo music selection—has become *the* place to see and be seen come dinnertime. An enchanting outdoor patio serves lunch in summer. ⊠ *4314 Main St.* ☎ *604/932–6009* ⊕ *www.themountainclub.ca* ⊟ *AE, DC, MC, V* ⊙ *No lunch Dec.–Feb.*

$$–$$$$
ITALIAN

✕**Quattro at Whistler.** Vancouverites who've enjoyed the Corsi family's central Italian fare at their city Quattro restaurants flock here for warming après-ski meals. The *L'Abbuffata*, a five-course Roman feast (C$60), comes on family-size platters meant for sharing. Other popular dishes include spaghetti *pescatore* (with prawns, scallops, and clams), pistachio-crusted sea bass, and shaved beef tenderloin. The seasonal three-course menu is a good deal. Dark woods, fireplaces, and an open kitchen are relaxing after a hard day on the slopes. Nine hundred wine varieties and an impressive Grappa selection fill the cellar. ⊠ *4319 Main St.* ☎ *604/905–4844* ⊕ *www.quattrorestaurants.com* ⊟ *AE, DC, MC, V* ⊙ *No lunch.*

$$$–$$$$
SEAFOOD
★

✕**Rim Rock Café.** About two miles south of the village, this restaurant is a local favorite as much for its cozy, unpretentious dining room (complete with stone fireplace) as for its great seafood. If deciding on only one item is hard, why not go for the samplers: the Rim Rock Trio combines sea bass in an almond-ginger crust, grilled prawns, and rare ahi tuna marinated in soya, sake, and mirin. If you want a booth or a coveted table near the fireplace, make a reservation. The café closes for roughly a month every fall, so call ahead. ⊠ *2117 Whistler Rd.* ☎ *604/932–5565 or 877/932–5589* ⊕ *www.rimrockwhistler.com* ⊟ *AE, DC, MC, V* ⊙ *No lunch.*

¢–$$
JAPANESE
★

✕**Sushi Village.** If you don't equate sushi with social buzz, then you haven't been to Sushi Village, one of Whistler's perennial hot spots for everything from après-ski to late-night dining. The chef's choice sashimi is a favorite, as are the dozen different house special rolls, which include the SASSs Roll (shrimp tempura, avocado, scallop, and salmon) and the mango-caterpillar roll. A score of sakes and custom sake margaritas accentuate the festive environment. ⊠ *4272 Mountain Sq.* ☎ *604/932–3330* ⊕ *www.sushivillage.com* ⊟ *AE, DC, MC, V.*

WHERE TO STAY

Price categories are based on January-to-April ski-season rates; prices will be higher during Christmas and school breaks, but lower in summer and considerably lower in the shoulder seasons. Minimum stays during all holidays are pretty much the rule. Also, Whistler Village has some serious nightlife: if peace and quiet are important to you, ask for a room away from the main pedestrian thoroughfares, book in the Upper Village, or stay in one of the residential neighborhoods outside the village. **Whistler Central Reservations** is also a good source for information on lodging. ☎ *604/932–4222, 604/664–5625 in Vancouver, 800/944–7853 in U.S. and Canada* ⊕ *www.whistler.com.*

$$$–$$$$

🛏 **Adara Hotel.** Whistler's only true boutique hotel is the Adara, sister to Vancouver's hipster Opus Hotel. With its designer furniture (think curvy white Verner Panton chairs), sheepskin throws, a vibrant color scheme

9

of reds and browns, and unexpected modish touches, like the bright-orange resin antlers that decorate the lobby's wall, the Adara provides an urban alternative to the typical large ski-lodge experience. There are four distinctive room configurations, all with spacious bathrooms with rain-shower heads and electric fireplaces, as well as sophisticated surfaces in local wood, stone, and other natural materials. Some rooms have private terraces. There's an outdoor pool in summer and a year-round hot tub. **Pros:** free Continental boxed breakfast in winter; free Wi-Fi. **Cons:** no on-site restaurant; no bathtubs, just showers. ⊠ *4122 Village Green* ☎ *604/905–4009 or 866/502–3272* ⊕ *www.adarahotel. com* ↘ *20 rooms, 21 suites* ⌂ *In-room: Safe, kitchen, Internet. In-hotel: Pool, parking (paid), some pets allowed* ⊟ *AE, D, DC, MC, V.*

$$$–$$$$ ⊡ **Delta Whistler Village Suites.** Gold-color walls, light-pine furniture, Navajo-pattern sofas, and desert-theme art create a warm Southwest look at this family-friendly hotel near the Whistler Conference Centre. The apartment-size studio and one- and two-bedroom suites have fully equipped kitchens, fireplaces, balconies—and even en suite washers and dryers. Cozy studio suites have kitchenettes. The spa offers a full range of services and exotic body massages. **Pros:** in the heart of the village with nice mountain views; gracious staff; free ski storage. **Cons:** rooms are small and those facing the street can get noisy; $20 parking fee; some common areas could use a face-lift. ⊠ *4308 Main St.* ☎ *604/905–3987, 888/299–3987, 604/966–0888 spa* ⊕ *www.deltahotels.com/ whistler* ↘ *225 suites* ⌂ *In-room: Kitchen (some), Internet. In-hotel: 2 restaurants, room service, bar, pool, gym, bicycles, children's programs (ages 4–12), laundry facilities, laundry service, parking (paid), some pets allowed, no-smoking rooms* ⊟ *AE, DC, MC, V.*

$$$–$$$$
Fodor's Choice
★
☽   ⊡ **Fairmont Château Whistler Resort.** This family-friendly fortress, just steps from the Blackcomb ski lifts, is a self-contained, ski-in, ski-out resort-within-a-resort with its own shopping arcade, golf course, and an impressive spa with exotic treatments. The lobby is filled with rustic Canadiana, handmade Mennonite rugs, overstuffed sofas, and a grand fireplace. Standard rooms are comfortably furnished and of average size, and most have mountain views. Rooms and suites on the Entrée Gold floors have fireplaces, whirlpool tubs, and their own concierge and private lounge. Ski and bike storage are convenient. The resort's Wildflower Restaurant serves fine Pacific Northwest fare against stunning mountain views. **Pros:** ski-in and ski-out option; shopping and golf on-site. **Cons:** bustling with guests and kids; not particularly intimate. ⊠ *4599 Château Blvd.* ☎ *604/938–8000 or 800/606–8244* ⊕ *www. fairmont.com* ↘ *550 rooms, 56 suites* ⌂ *In-room: Safe, Internet (some). In-hotel: 3 restaurants, room service, bar, golf course, tennis courts, pools, gym, spa, laundry facilities, laundry service, Wi-Fi, parking (paid), some pets allowed, no-smoking rooms* ⊟ *AE, D, DC, MC, V.*

$$$$
☽
Fodor's Choice
★   ⊡ **Four Seasons Resort Whistler.** This plush nine-story hotel gives alpine chic a new twist with warm earth tones and wood interiors, big leather chairs beside the fireplace in the lobby, and amazingly spacious rooms. Fifty Two 80 Bistro, the hotel's signature restaurant, is laid out around a central fire pit and has quickly become the best après-ski scene in the Upper Village. The luxurious spa has become a destination in itself

with its 15 treatment rooms and wide range of massages. Child-friendly amenities include children's programs and pint-size bathrobes. **Pros:** amazing spa and service; great restaurants; free village shuttles. **Cons:** a long walk to popular village restaurants and nightlife. ☒ *Upper Village, 4591 Blackcomb Way* ☏ *604/935–3400 or 888/935–2460* ⊕ *www. fourseasons.com* ⇆ *273 studios and suites, 3 town homes* ⚅ *In-room: Safe, DVD, Wi-Fi. In-hotel: Restaurant, room service, bar, pool, gym, spa, children's programs (ages 3–13), Wi-Fi, parking (paid), no-smoking rooms* ▭ *AE, D, DC, MC, V.*

$$$$ **Hilton Whistler Resort.** A wealth of facilities highlights this family-
☺ friendly resort complex at the base of the Whistler and Blackcomb gondolas. Attractively decorated rooms are so large that most can easily accommodate four people. Many have fireplaces, whirlpool baths, and balconies; some suites have saunas. An on-site health club and spa has a variety of soothing post-ski treatments, including acupressure and stone therapy. **Pros:** steps from the chairlift; huge rooms; free cookies served daily. **Cons:** small spa; some rooms with unremarkable street views. ☒ *4050 Whistler Way* ☏ *604/932–1982 or 800/445–8667* ⊕ *www.hiltonwhistler.com* ⇆ *287 rooms, 24 suites* ⚅ *In-room: Safe, kitchen (some), Wi-Fi. In-hotel: Restaurant, room service, bar, tennis courts, pool, gym, spa, children's programs (ages 4–12), laundry facilities, laundry service, parking (paid), some pets allowed, no-smoking rooms* ▭ *AE, DC, MC, V.*

$$–$$$$ **Nita Lake Lodge.** Timber-framed Nita Lake Lodge is the newest accom-
★ modation in the perpetually growing Whistler community; it's located away from the madding village crowd, beside Nita Lake and across Highway 99 from the Whistler Creekside Development. The overall feel is spacious yet intimate, and the rooms and suites are large, with basalt-rock fireplaces, heated floors, and capacious bathrooms with separate showers and soaking tubs. There is a 24-hour concierge, as well as a shuttle to take you around town. The lodge also has two private villas: one with five bedrooms, the other with four. **Pros:** location far from Village bustle; new property can mean good deals; serene views of Nita Lake. **Cons:** shuttle required to access slopes, services, and the village; rooms a bit dark. ☒ *2131 Lake Placid Rd.* ☏ *604/966–5700 or 888/755–6482* ⊕ *www.nitalakelodge.com* ⇆ *38 studios, 39 suites, 2 villas* ⚅ *In-room: Safe, DVD, Wi-Fi. In-hotel: Restaurants, room service, bar, gym, spa, Wi-Fi* ▭ *AE, MC, V* ⊧ *CP.*

$$$–$$$$ **Pan Pacific Whistler Village Centre.** This all-suites, full-service boutique hotel is just steps from the slopes and village activity. A full buffet breakfast and evening hors d'oeuvres are served in the Pacific Lounge, open to guests throughout the day for complimentary nonalcoholic drinks, and the outdoor patio has terrific mountain vistas. Suites come in one-to three-bedroom configurations and have fully equipped kitchens, gas fireplaces, balconies, soaker tubs, and expansive view windows. **Pros:** extraordinarily friendly staff; free breakfast buffet. **Cons:** loud ground-floor rooms; limited services. ☒ *4299 Blackcomb Way* ☏ *604/905–2999 or 888/905–9995* ⊕ *www.panpacific.com* ⇆ *82 rooms* ⚅ *In-room: Safe, kitchen, Wi-Fi. In-hotel: Room service, bar, pool, gym, laundry service, parking (paid), no-smoking rooms* ▭ *AE, DC, MC, V* ⊧ *BP.*

9

$$$–$$$$ ⊞ **Summit Lodge & Spa.** Service is gracious and attentive at this friendly boutique hotel that is also one of Whistler's best values in the luxury range of hotels. Tucked in a quiet part of the village, the spacious rooms are beautifully decorated with soft neutrals, custom-made cherrywood furnishings, original

art, and granite countertops. All units have balconies and fireplaces, and there's a shuttle to whisk guests to the nearby slopes. The full-service spa is among Whistler's most exotic, with a Javanese theme and royal heritage treatments; it claims to be North America's only authentic Indonesian-style spa. **Pros:** quiet rooms; excellent spa; free shuttle to the Village Gondola. **Cons:** small parking spots in garage; lots of pets (and their dander) so not recommended for those with allergies. ⊠ *4359 Main St.* ☎ *604/932–2778 or 888/913–8811* ⊕ *www.summitlodge.com* ➥ *75 rooms, 6 suites* ♿ *In-room: Kitchen, Internet. In-hotel: Pool, spa, laundry facilities, laundry service, parking (paid), some pets allowed, no-smoking rooms* ⊟ *MC, V* ⍓⍓ *CP.*

$$$$ ⊞ **Westin Resort & Spa.** This luxury hotel has a prime location on the edge of the village. The two-story lobby is dramatic and rooms are chic and cozy, with moss green–and–rust color schemes, gas fireplaces, extra-deep tubs, and exceptionally comfy beds. The 1,400-square-foot, split-level suites are great for families: each has a full kitchen and a loft bedroom with a whirlpool tub. The hotel's large restaurant has an open kitchen and fantastic oversize windows. The spa, with 25 treatment rooms and a mountain-view lounge, offers facials, body wraps, and holistic therapies such as herbology and acupuncture. **Pros:** complimentary Starbucks coffee; ski concierge; quiet and convenient location. **Cons:** spotty service; expensive amenities like $25 for self-park, $15 resort fee to use pool, $15 Internet. ⊠ *4090 Whistler Way* ☎ *604/905–5000 or 888/634–5577* ⊕ *www.westinwhistler.com* ➥ *204 rooms, 215 suites* ♿ *In-room: Safe, kitchen (some), Wi-Fi. In-hotel: Restaurant, room service, bar, pool, gym, spa, children's programs (ages 18 months–12 yrs), laundry facilities, laundry service, Wi-Fi, parking (paid), no-smoking rooms* ⊟ *AE, D, DC, MC, V.*

SPORTS AND THE OUTDOORS

Adventurers pour into Whistler during every season from every corner of the world. In ski season, you'll meet Australian and New Zealander skiers and guides who follow winter around the globe; in summer there are sun-baked guides who chase the warm months to lead whitewater rafting or mountain-biking excursions. These globe-trotters demonstrate how Whistler's outdoor sports culture now operates on a global, all-season scale.

The staging of sliding (bobsled, luge, skeleton) and alpine and cross-country skiing events in Whistler during the Games has yielded plenty of benefits for the adventurous, including a world-class cross-country center (and lodge) operated by the Whistler Legacies Society. The sliding center remains operational as a training facility (the ice is rumored to be

CLOSE UP

Mountain Biking

Ski resorts everywhere have recently discovered the popularity of downhill biking. Whistler-Blackcomb was not only among the first to realize the potential of converting ski runs to fat-tire trails, they also established the best downhill-biking center in the world. Located on lower Whistler Mountain, the trails are marked green through double diamond and groomed with as much care as their winter counterparts.

Riding custom bikes designed specifically for the Whistler terrain, cyclists bomb down the single-track trails, staying high on the steeply banked turns and taking air on the many tables and jumps. Expert riders might add 30-foot rock drops, leaps over streambeds, and 100-foot platform bridges to their brake-free sprints through the forest. Beginners can find plenty of comfortable dirt lanes to follow, though, and you can keep your fingers ready at the hydraulic brake should the speed become uncomfortable. After their first taste of the sport, most novice riders can't wait to sit back on the specially designed chairlift, transition onto the blue terrain, invite a few bumps, and maybe grab some air before the day is through. Downhill biking provides pure, if muddy, adrenaline-fueled bliss.

Whistler Mountain Bike Park, with experienced instructors, is a great place to learn how to downhill bike.

---

the fastest on the planet) and those who've always wanted to try out the sliding sports can. The ski mountains changed little après games, other than having some alluring signage to indicate what happened where.

Hikers and anglers, downhill and touring cyclists, free skiers and ice climbers, kayakers and golfers. there really is something for everyone here. Whistler and Blackcomb mountains are why most people are here but Garibaldi Provincial Park, adjacent to the Whistler area, is a 78,000-acre park with dense mountainous forests splashed with hospitable lakes and streams for fishing and kayaking.

9

Whistler Activity and Information Center is a good first stop for most Whistler outdoor activities: it's the place to pick up hiking, biking, and cross-country maps or find out about equipment rentals. They can even help book activities. ⊠ *4010 Whistler Way* ☎ *604/932–2394 or 604/938–2769.*

Whistler.com, the official online reservation center for Whistler, can set you up with tours, rentals, guides, and anything else you might need. ⊠ *1006 Lynham Rd.* ☎ *800/944–8537.*

Tourism Whistler has info about all aspects of Whistler. ☎ *800/944–7853, 604/664–5625 in Vancouver* ⊕ *www.whistler.com.*

BIKING AND HIKING The 28-km (45-mi) paved, car-free Valley Trail links the village to lakeside beaches and scenic picnic spots. For more challenging routes, ski lifts whisk hikers and bikers up to the alpine, where marked trails are graded by difficulty. The Peak Chair operates in summer to take hikers to the top of 7,160-foot-high Whistler. The newest addition to the high alpine-trail network is the High Note Trail, an intermediate, five-mile

Whistler is well known as a ski destination, but many of the trails are also accessible in summer for mountain biking.

route with an elevation change of 1,132 feet and fabulous coastal mountain views. Trails are clearly marked—you take the lift up and choose whichever way you want to come down, just as if you were skiing. The casual stroller can also experience the top of the mountain on the brand-new **Peak2Peak Gondola**, the largest free-span gondola expanse in the world: it crosses Fitzsimmons Valley, connecting Whistler and Blackcomb mountains in just 11 minutes. Free trail maps are available from Tourism Whistler and the Whistler Activity and Information Center.

Fanatyk Co. Ski and Cycle. This outfit rents bikes, arranges for repairs, and books bike tours. ⊠ *6–4433 Sundial Pl.* ☎ *604/938–9452.*

Whistler Gondola Base. Rent a bike, pick up a free trail map, sign up for mountain-bike lessons or a sightseeing, hiking, or walking adventure; the options are aplenty here. ⊠ *3434 Blackcomb Way* ☎ *604/905–2252.*

Fodor's Choice ★ **Whistler Mountain Bike Park.** They provide lessons, equipment, body armor, and park passes. Passes range from C$50 to C$99. ⊠ *G1 Rentals, Whistler Gondola Base* ☎ *604/904–8134* ⊕ *www.whistlerbike.com.*

BOATING Canoe and kayak rentals are available at Alta Lake at both Lakeside Park and Wayside Park. A spot that's perfect for canoeing is the River of Golden Dreams, which connects Alta Lake with Green Lake, both within a couple of miles of the village.

Canadian Outback Adventure Company. Look these adventure specialists up for guided river-rafting trips in the Whistler area. They have an easygoing trip for families. ☎ *604/921–7250 or 800/565–8735* ⊕ *www. canadianoutback.com.*

Wedge Rafting. Specializing in rafting adventures, this company features two-hour to full-day tours on the Green, Birkenhead, or Elaho-Squamish rivers. Tours depart from the village and include all equipment and experienced guides. Adventures are suitable for all levels. ☎ 604/932–7171 or 888/932–5899 ⊕ www.wedgerafting.com.

Whistler River Adventures. Contact this outfitter for river-rafting, fishing, and jet-boating trips on rivers near Whistler. ☎ 604/932–3532 or 888/932–3532 ⊕ www.whistlerriver.com.

CROSS-COUNTRY SKIING

The meandering trail around the Whistler Golf Course (⊕ www.whistlergolf.com) from the village is an ideal beginners' route. The 28 km (17 mi) of track-set trails that wind around scenic Lost Lake, Chateau Whistler Golf Course, the Nicklaus North Golf Course, and Green Lake include routes suitable for all levels; 4 km (2½ mi) of trails around Lost Lake are lighted for night skiing from 4 to 10 each evening. Trail maps and rental equipment are available in sports shops throughout the village.

Whistler Ski Hike. Operating out of the Whistler Nordic Center right in the village, Whistler Cross Country Ski & Hike and Coast Mountain Guides team up to give lessons or guided cross-country ski tours at the golf course and other locations ideal for beginners and advanced skiers. ☎ 604/932–7711 ⊕ www.whistlerski-hike.com.

Blackcomb and Whistler Mountains. When Whistler and Blackcomb Ski Resorts merged in 1997, they created a snow behemoth not seen in these parts since the last sighting of a yeti—the alpine version of the northwest's infamous Sasquatch. Whistler had already garnered #1-ski-resort status from *Ski, Skiing,* and *Powder* magazines but the addition of Blackcomb left the competition buried in the powder. The numbers are staggering: 360 inches of annual snowfall, over 8,000 skiable acres, 200 named runs, 12 alpine bowls, three glaciers, and the world's most advanced lift system. Point yourself downward on Blackcomb and you can ski or snowboard for a mile from top to bottom. And there are lots of ways to get to the top, either via the Whistler Village, Creekside, or Blackcomb Excalibur gondolas or by taking one of several chairs from the base up the mountain.

According to the locals, many of whom are world-class competitors, picking the day's mountain depends on conditions, time of day, and time of year. While most residents swear by Whistler's bowls and steeps, some prefer the long glade runs and top terrain park of Blackcomb. As of 2009, though, you can do both in the same day, thanks to the new **Peak 2 Peak Gondola,** which whisks riders along the 2.7-mile journey in just 11 minutes. ☎ 604/932–3434 or 800/766–0449 ⊕ www.whistlerblackcomb.com.

9

Mountain Adventure Centre. Get your high-performance gear rentals here—and if you want to swap equipment during the day, no problem. The center also has two alpine locations, one in the Fairmont Chateau Whistler and another at Blackcomb Day Lodge (you can return or swap equipment here, too). ✉ *Pan Pacific Lodge, 4320 Sundial Crescent* ☎ *604/905–2295.*

Ultimate Ski Adventures. This company will help you achieve your goals, whether they be to gain confidence and control on all the runs or to ski in the best terrain the mountain has to offer. ✉ *7273 Fitzsimmons Rd. S* ⊕ *www.ultimateski.com* ☎ *604/263–2390.*

WHY DO BEGINNERS LOVE WHISTLER?

For a primer on the ski facilities, drop by the resort's free Whistler Welcome Night, held at 6:30 every Sunday evening during ski season at the base of the village gondolas. First-timers at Whistler, whether beginners or experienced skiers or snowboarders, may want to try Ski or Ride Esprit. Run by the resort, these three- to four-day programs combine ski or snowboarding lessons, après-ski activities, and an insider's guide to the mountains. ⊕ *www. blackcombwhistler.com*

★ **Whistler Alpine Guides Bureau.** These expert mountain guides offer group tours, instructional clinics, and customized one-on-one trips to get you shredding untouched backcountry powder. ✉ *113–4350 Lorimer* ☎ *604/938–9242* ⊕ *www.whistlerguides.com.*

Fodor's Choice ★ **Whistler/Blackcomb Ski and Snowboard School.** The school offers lessons for skiers and snowboarders of all levels. Whistler Kids remains one of the best children's ski schools anywhere. ✉ *4545 Blackcomb Way* ☎ *604/932–3434 or 800/766–0449.*

Whistler/Blackcomb Hi Performance Rentals. They provide equipment rentals at the Whistler gondola base and at several outlets in the village. ✉ *3434 Blackcomb Way* ☎ *604/905–2252.*

FISHING Tourists first developed this region for the fishing and all five area lakes—Alta, Alpha, Lost, Green, Nita—are stocked with trout.

Whistler River Adventures. These fly-fishing specialists target five species of Pacific salmon, steelhead, trout, and char on dozens of rivers lakes in the area. They also have floatplane and heli-fishing tours, and take care of all the details, from equipment to guides, permits, and transportation. ✉ *Whistler Village Gondola Bldg., 4165 Springs La.* ☎ *604/932–3532 or 888/932–3532* ⊕ *www.whistlerriver.com.*

GOLF Few visitors associate Whistler with golf but the four championship courses vie with some of the best in the Pacific Northwest. Golf season in Whistler runs from May through October; greens fees range from C$49 to C$210. You can arrange advance tee-time bookings through **BC Golf** (⊕ *www.bcgolf.com*). The company represents most of B.C.'s golf courses and provides tee times, sometimes at substantial greens-fee discounts.

Fodor's Choice ★ **Big Sky Golf and Country Club.** This links-style par 72 course follows the Green River and faces impressive glaciers. Located just 30 minutes

One of the reasons Whistler is so popular is because it's great for experienced skiiers, and beginners, too!

north of Whistler in Pemberton, Big Sky is the local's favorite for good reason. ☎ *604/894–6106 or 800/668–7900* ⊕ *www.bigskygolf.com.*

★ **Chateau Whistler Golf Club.** Carved from the side of Blackcomb Mountain, this challenging and breathtaking par-72 course was designed by prominent golf-course architect Robert Trent Jones Jr. Make sure to carry plenty of balls, though you can reload at the turn. ✉ *4612 Blackcomb Way* ☎ *604/938–2092 or 877/938–2092.*

Nicklaus North Golf Course. Jack Nicklaus designed this challenging 18-hole, par-71 track which finishes beside lovely Green Lake. ✉ *8080 Nicklaus North Blvd.* ☎ *604/938–9898 or 800/386–9898.*

Whistler Golf Club. Often overlooked, this Arnold Palmer–designed par-72 course is surprisingly challenging, especially around "Bear Island," the traditional site of a hibernating black bear. ✉ *4010 Whistler Way* ☎ *604/932–4544 or 800/376–1777.*

HELI-SKIING AND HELI-HIKING The Coast Mountains of western Canada is one of the most glaciated regions in the world. The range is approximately 1,600 km long and 200 km wide, bordered by the Fraser River in the south and the Kelsall River in the north. Helicopter adventures consist of skiing, glacier hikes, and picnics.

Blackcomb Helicopters. Flightseeing tours over Whistler's stunning mountains and glaciers are offered year-round: there are heli-hiking, -biking, -fishing, -picnics, and even heli-weddings in summer. ☎ *604/938–1700 or 800/330–4354* ⊕ *www.blackcombhelicopters.com.*

Coast Range Heli-Skiing. This heli-skiing operator offers a shuttle service to their base in Pemberton for unique backcountry powder experiences. ☎ *604/894–1144 or 800/701–8744* ⊕ *www.coastrangeheliskiing.com.*

Fodor's Choice ★ **Whistler Heli-Skiing.** Heli-skiing tours include helicopter-accessed guided day trips with three or more glacier runs for intermediate to expert skiers and snowboarders. The cost starts at C$640 per person. Heli-hiking is available all year long and guided tours can be tailored to your group's abilities, and you can enjoy your specially prepared picnic lunch in an old-growth forest, pastoral meadow, or on a 12,000-year-old glacier. ⊠ *3–4241 Village Stroll* ☎ *604/932–4105 or 888/435–4754* ⊕ *www.whistlerheliskiing.com.*

HORSEBACK RIDING   The ultimate gentle summer activity, horseback riding in Whistler can take you through alpine meadows, old-growth forests, and along riverside beaches.

Fodor's Choice ★ **Outdoor Adventures Whistler.** Ride single-track mountain trails on horses trained specially for the mountains with this outfitter, which is just minutes from Whistler Village. ⊠ *Unit 218-4293 Mountain Sq.* ☎ *604/932–4086 or 888/297–2222* ⊕ *www.adventureswhistler.com.*

SNOWMO-BILING, SNOWSHOE-ING, AND SLEIGH RIDES   **Blackcomb Snowmobiles.** You can book guided snowmobile trips into the backcountry (from C$119 for two hours) at the outlets in the Fairmont Chateau Whistler or at the Hilton Whistler Resort. ☎ *604/932–8484* ⊕ *www.blackcombsnowmobile.com.*

★ **Outdoor Adventures Whistler.** Enjoy a snowshoe walk in the deep powder (from C$69 for 1½ hours) or mush a team on a dogsled trip (from C$140 for 2½ hours). ⊠ *Timberline Lodge, Unit 218-4293 Mountain Sq.* ☎ *604/932–4086 or 888/297–2222* ⊕ *www.adventureswhistler.com.*

★ **Meadow Park Sports Centre.** About 6 km (4 mi) north of Whistler Village, this center has a six-lane indoor pool, children's wading pool with fountains and whirlpool, ice-skating rink, hot tub, sauna, steam room, gym, aerobics studio, and two squash courts. The pool features a vortex, fountains, and even a rope swing. Day passes are C$9; family passes are C$18. ⊠ *8107 Camino Dr.* ☎ *604/935–7529.*

☾ **Whistler Blackcomb's Coca-Cola Tube Park.** Slip and slide in the snow at this family-friendly park which features 1,000 feet of lanes rated green, blue, and black diamond, a magic carpet to get back to the top, a fire pit, play area, and a snack station. There's even a minizone with minitubes for the little ones. ⊠ *Blackcomb Excalibur Gondola* ☎ *800/944–8537* ⊕ *www.whistler.com.*

ZIP-LINING AND CANOPY TOURS   **Wildplay Element Parks.** This self-contained adventure center runs skyline zip-trekking tours on a forested mountain, 10 minutes north of Whistler Village. They have tandem tours, which let you fly alongside a friend—or your child. The longest line at Cougar Mountain is 1,500 feet with a 200-foot vertical drop. Each skyline run is connected to the next by a trail, and one 150-foot suspension bridge. Wildplay has added an obstacle "tree course" of ladders, platforms, and suspension bridges. ⊠ *Unit 218-4293 Mountain Sq.* ☎ *604/932–4086 or 888/297–2222* ⊕ *www.wildplay.com.*

Fodor's Choice
★

Ziptrek Ecotours. Nestled in a valley of ancient rain forest between Whistler and Blackcomb Mountains, Ziptrek has a total of 10 zip lines offered on two tours (one for beginners and another for those with no fear of heights). They claim to have the "longest, highest and fastest zip lines in North America." With runs ranging from 200 to 2,000 feet in length, Ziptrek will give you a heart-thumping experience worth splurging on for the whole family. The less adventurous can opt for a Canopy Tour, which takes you from treetop platform to platform via suspension bridges and forest boardwalks. ✉ *4282 Mountain Sq.* ☎ *604/935–0001 or 866/935–0001* ⊕ *www.ziptrek.com.*

APRÈS-SKI, NIGHTLIFE, AND THE ARTS

Whistler has a legendary après scene, and on any given weekend, there may be more nonskiers than skiers filling the patios, clubs, and saloons. Stag and stagette parties wander the pedestrian-only village stroll, and people queue early to get inside Buffalo Bills or the GLC (Garibaldi Lift Company), where DJs and bands from Vancouver and beyond come to spin.

The night begins with après, when skiers, bikers, and hikers alike unwind on patios from the Longhorn Saloon & Grill to Citta'—think happy hour for the hyped up—and the clubs usually stay open until 2 AM except for Sundays and holidays. The minimum age is 19 and smoking is only allowed outside. When the bars close, the local constables lead a (usually) well-behaved cattle drive through the village and back to the hotels.

For entertainment listings, pick up Whistler's weekly news magazine, the *Pique.*

BARS AND PUBS

Black's Pub. You'll find Whistler's largest selection of whiskeys (more than 40 varieties) and 99 beers from around the world here. The adjoining restaurant is reasonably priced, offering mainly pizzas and pastas. ✉ *4270 Mountain Sq.* ☎ *604/932–6945.*

BrewHouse. This place brews six of its own ales and lagers in a big woodsy building with fireplaces, pool tables, seven 27-inch TVs, and a patio. Brewery tours are offered Thursday and Saturday afternoons; the attached restaurant (open to minors) is a good place for casual meals. ✉ *4355 Blackcomb Way* ☎ *604/905–2739.*

Citta'. The village-center patio is consistently touted as the best outdoor patio—it's *the* hot spot for people-watching and microbrew sipping. The place attracts a ton of late-night partiers. ✉ *Whistler Village Sq.* ☎ *604/932–4177.*

Dubh Linn Gate Pub. As its name implies, this place has an Irish theme with original decor that was actually transported all the way from the old country. The staff pours a decent pint of Guinness and serves good Irish food. Nightly live Celtic music is a highlight. Those under 19 are

9

An inukshuk—a stone landmark—stands sentry over Whistler and Blackcomb mountains.

welcome in the restaurant section. ✉ *Pan Pacific Hotel, 4320 Sundial Crescent* ☎ *604/905–4047*.

Fodor's Choice ★ **Garibaldi Lift Company.** Right at the Whistler Gondola entrance, overlooking the base of the mountain, this popular joint attracts Whistler's hipsters to its lounge, restaurant, and club. It's a cozy place to relax and watch the latest ski and snowboard videos on the flat-screen TVs during the day; it gets hopping at night with live bands or reggae and house music. ✉ *2320 London La.* ☎ *604/905–2220*.

★ **Longhorn Saloon & Grill.** The Longhorn has been at the forefront—quite literally, since it's located at the base of Blackcomb—of life in Whistler for years. The outdoor patio may be the most consistently packed terrace for early après in the village, but it's also a late-night destination. The ski saloon character suggests Steamboat Springs or Crested Butte, but the variety of local brews makes it clear you're whoopin' it up in B.C. The menu is strictly pub food. ✉ *4284 Mountain Sq., Whistler* ☎ *604/932–5999* ⊕ *www.longhornsaloon.ca*.

DANCE CLUBS **Buffalo Bill's Bar & Grill.** The DJs here play mainstream music for a younger crowd, and well-known regional bands jam once or twice a month. ✉ *1–4122 Village Green* ☎ *604/932–6613*.

Garfinkle's. One of Whistler's largest clubs hosts live rock and roll, hip-hop, funk, and jazz. It's a hangout for the young and a high point (literally) on any Whistler trip. ✉ *1–4308 Main St.* ☎ *604/932–2323*.

Maxx Fish. The who's who of DJs from around the world consider this dance club a "must play" joint. The crowd is hip and young, the music eclectic, the vibe groovy. ⊠ *Whistler Village Sq.* ☎ *604/932–1904* ⊕ *www.maxxfish.moonfruit.com.*

Moe Joes. Its hot central location makes this a perennial favorite. Theme nights from Reggae Monday to Country Thursday appeal to a diverse crowd. ⊠ *4115 Golfers Approach* ☎ *604/935–1152.*

Tommy Africa's. Guest DJs play alternative and progressive dance music. The trademark shooters (shot glasses of undiluted alcoholic concoctions) make for a lively crowd. ⊠ *4216 Gateway Dr.* ☎ *604/932–6090.*

FILM AND THEATER The Whistler Film Festival takes place early every winter, featuring Canadian and international movies. You can catch first-run movies the rest of the year.

Maurice Young Millennium Place. You can attend theatrical, dance, live music, and other performances here. The facility also has arts, child-care, and teen centers, as well as drop-in bridge, yoga, and dance classes. Ecumenical church services are held here Sunday morning. ⊠ *4335 Blackcomb Way* ☎ *604/935–8410.*

Village 8 Cinemas. This theater shows first-run movies throughout the day for C$8.50 matinee or C$12.50 after 6 PM; Cheap Tuesdays are C$8.50 all day. ⊠ *100–4295 Blackcomb Way* ☎ *604/932–5833* ⊕ *www. village8.ca.*

GALLERIES **Adele Campbell Fine Art Gallery.** This gallery has paintings and sculp-tures (many with wildlife and wilderness themes) by both established and up-and-coming B.C. artists. You'll usually be able to find some affordable pieces. ⊠ *Hilton Whistler Resort, 4050 Whistler Way* ☎ *604/ 938–0887.*

The **ArtWalk** is a weekly event that takes place throughout July and August, providing a unique opportunity to check out the ceramic, photography, jewelry, and mixed media art created by talented art-ists residing in the Sea to Sky Corridor. Hosted at numerous venues, including galleries, hotels, and retail outlets, guests can meet the artists while enjoying appetizers and live music. ☎ *604/938–9221* ⊕ *www. whistlerartscouncil.com.*

Black Tusk Gallery. Northwest Coast Native art, including limited-edition silk-screen prints, and traditional crafts such as masks, paddles, bowls, jewelry, and totem poles are the draw here. ⊠ *Hilton Whistler Resort, 108–4293 Mountain Sq.* ☎ *604/905–5540.*

Plaza Galleries. You'll see the painting efforts of Hollywood stars Tony Curtis, Anthony Quinn, and Red Skelton, as well as works by British Columbian visual artists such as Robert Bateman. ⊠ *Whistler Town Plaza, 22–4314 Main St.* ☎ *604/938–6233.*

Whistler Art Galleries. There are two locations to check out sculpture, painting, and glasswork by Canadian artists: the Hilton Whistler Resort and the Westin Resort & Spa. ⊠ *Hilton Whistler Resort, 4050 Whistler Way* ☎ *604/938–3001* ⊠ *Westin Resort & Spa, 4090 Whistler Way* ☎ *604/935–3999.*

9

SHOPPING

Whistler has almost 200 stores, including chain and designer outlets, art galleries, gift shops, and outdoor-clothing and ski shops. Most are clustered in the pedestrian-only Whistler Village Centre; more can be found a short stroll away in Village North, Upper Village, and in the shopping concourses of the major hotels.

CLOTHING **Amos and Andes.** This shop selling handmade sweaters and dresses in offbeat designs and funky colors is something of a Whistler institution. ⊠ *2–4321 Village Gate Blvd.* ☎ *604/932–7202.*

Helly Hansen. This is the place for high-quality Norwegian-made skiing, boarding, and other outdoor wear and equipment. ⊠ *Westin Resort & Spa, 115–4090 Whistler Way* ☎ *604/932–0142.*

Open Country. Casual designs for men and women by Jack Lipson, Kenneth Cole, Michael Kors, Tommy Hilfiger, and others are stocked here. ⊠ *Fairmont Chateau Whistler Resort, 4599 Chateau Blvd.* ☎ *604/938–9268.*

★ **Roots.** This Canadian-owned enterprise is known for its sweatshirts and cozy casuals, and they're something of a fixture in Whistler, especially since they outfitted both the Canadian and American Olympic teams in 2006. ⊠ *4229 Village Stroll* ☎ *604/938–0058.*

SPORTS EQUIPMENT **Can-Ski.** Their four locations have a good selection of brand-name ski gear, clothes, and accessories and they also do custom boot fitting and repairs. It's operated by Whistler-Blackcomb Resort. ⊠ *Crystal Lodge, Village Center* ☎ *604/938–7755* ⊠ *Deer Lodge, Town Plaza* ☎ *604/938–7432* ⊠ *Glacier Lodge, Upper Village* ☎ *604/938–7744* ⊠ *Creekside (winters only)* ☎ *604/905–2160.*

Fanatyk Co. Ski and Cycle. In winter you can buy skis and boots, and order custom boots, too. In summer the shop specializes in top-of-the-line mountain bikes as well as bike rentals, repairs, and tours. ⊠ *6–4433 Sundial Pl.* ☎ *604/938–9455, 604/938–9452 rentals.*

Showcase Snowboards. Voted by locals as the best snowboard shop in town, they have over 3,500 square feet of the best gear for snowboarders. ⊠ *Sundial Hotel, 4340 Sundial Crescent* ☎ *604/938–7519.*

SnowCovers Sports. Brand-name ski equipment and outerwear are sold in winter; in summer the stock is high-end bikes and cycling gear. ⊠ *126–4340 Lorimer Rd.* ☎ *604/905–4100.*

SPAS Where there's skiing, there are spas. Whistler has several terrific hotel spas as well as some independents.

Artesia Spa. Holistic and therapeutic services to gently rejuvenate the body, mind, and spirit are available here—everything from Swedish massages to infusion facials and customized treatments just for men. ⊠ *Hilton Whistler Resort, 4050 Whistler Way* ☎ *604/938–9381* ⊕ *www.hiltonworldwide.com.*

Solarice Wellness Centre & Spa. Solarice offers a mix of Eastern and Western spa treatments as well as Chinese medicine (acupuncture, Tui Na massage, and others) and naturopathic therapies. The drop-in yoga, Pilates, tai chi, and meditation classes are also a draw. ⊠ *Solarice Gate-*

A snowy night in Whistler village.

way, 202–4230 Gateway Dr. ☎ *604/935–1222* ✉ *Solarice Main St., 4–4308 Main St.* ☎ *604/966–0888* ⊕ *www.solarice.com.*

The Spa at Four Seasons Resort Whistler. Without a doubt, this is the most luxurious and decadent spa in town, featuring 14 treatment rooms, a relaxation lounge, a full-service health club, outdoor pools, whirlpools, steam rooms, and a fitness studio. ✉ *Four Seasons, 4591 Blackcomb Way* ☎ *604/966–2620.*

9

OKANAGAN WINE COUNTRY PLANNER

How Much Time Do I Need?

Three days from Vancouver is barely enough time to enjoy the Okanagan; five days to a week would be optimal.

Visitor Information

Hello BC has information about the province, including the Okanagan. The Osoyoos visitor center has information about the region. The Thompson Okanagan Tourism Association is the main tourism contact for the Okanagan. Many towns have visitor information centers, though not all are open year-round. Some, like Discover Naramata, are virtual only.

Local Tourist Information BC Visitor Centre @ Osoyoos (☎ 250/495–3366 or 888/676–9667 ⊕ www. destinationosoyoos.com). **Discover Naramata** (⊕ www. discovernaramata.com). **Hello BC** (☎ 800/435–5622 ⊕ www. hellobc.com). **Penticton Visitor Information Centre** (☎ 250/493–4055 or 800/663–5052 ⊕ www.tourismpenticton. com). **Thompson Okanagan Tourism Association** (☎ 250/860–5999 ⊕ www. totabc.com). **Tourism Kelowna** (☎ 250/861–1515 or 800/663–4345 ⊕ www. tourismkelowna.com).

When to Go

The Okanagan hosts a wine festival in May, to open the season, and in early October, to close the season; both weekends are popular, and busy, times to visit. High season is defined from wine festival to wine festival.

Winery staff and other insiders say that the best time for an Okanagan wine-tasting trip is September. Everything is open, the weather is generally fine, and the vineyards are full of grapes ready to harvest. Many wineries release new wines in the fall, so there are more tasting options.

The hot dry summer, especially July and August, is peak season here, and weekends get crowded. May and June are quieter, and most wineries are open, so either month can be a good alternative to the midsummer peak.

The Okanagan is a popular ski destination in winter, with several low-key but first-rate resorts. If your main objective is wine touring, though, many wineries close or reduce their hours from November through April.

Where to Start?

The best place to start a wine-tasting tour is at one of the two area wine info centers (Kelowna or Penticton). You can get an overview of the area's wines, get help in organizing your time, and usually taste a wine or two.

We've included a selection of wineries in this section but our list is only a small subset of the Okanagan's many producers, and new wineries open every year. Ask for current recommendations at the wine information centers or your hotel, or simply stop in when you see an appealing sign.

WHAT IT COSTS IN CANADIAN DOLLARS

	¢	$	$$	$$$	$$$$
Restaurants	under C$8	C$8–C$12	C$13–C$20	C$21–C$30	over C$30
Hotels	under C$75	C$75–C$125	C$126–C$175	C$176–C$250	over C$250

Restaurant prices are for a main course at dinner, not including 5% GST and 10% liquor tax. Hotel prices are for two in a standard double in high season, excluding 10% provincial accommodation tax, service charge, and 5% GST.

Getting Here and Around

By Air: The main airport for the Okanagan wine country is in Kelowna. There's also a small airport in Penticton.

Air Canada and WestJet both fly into Kelowna from Vancouver. From Vancouver, Air Canada also serves Penticton; flights take about one hour.

Taxis generally meet arriving flights at the Kelowna Airport.

Okanagan Shuttle provides transportation from the Kelowna Airport to local hotels for C$15 per person. They also shuttle passengers from Kelowna's airport to several of the local ski areas: Big White (C$55/C$75 one way/round-trip), Silver Star (C$60/C$80 one way/round-trip), and Apex Mountain (C$70/C$100 one way/round-trip).

By Bus: Greyhound Canada runs buses from Vancouver to Kelowna and Penticton, with connections to smaller Okanagan towns. The Kelowna Regional Transit System operates buses in the greater Kelowna area.

By Car: To get to the Okanagan by car from Vancouver, head east on Highway 1 (Trans-Canada Highway). Just east of Hope, several routes diverge. For Oliver or Osoyoos in the South Okanagan, take Highway 3 east. For the Kelowna area, the fastest route is Highway 5 (the Coquihalla toll road) north to Merritt, then follow Highway 97C (the Okanagan Connector) toward Kelowna. To reach Penticton and Naramata, you can either take the Coquihalla to 97C, then turn *south* on Highway 97, or take Highway 3 to Keremeos, where you pick up Highway 3A north, which merges into *97 north*. Allow about five hours' driving time from Vancouver to the Okanagan region.

Several major agencies, including Avis, Budget, Enterprise, Hertz, and National have offices in Kelowna.

Contacts Downtown Vancouver Bus Depot (✉ 1150 Station St. ☎ 604/683–8133). **Greyhound Canada** (☎ 800/661–8747 ⊕ www.greyhound.ca). **Kelowna Regional Transit System** (☎ 250/860–8121 ⊕ www.bctransit.com/regions/kel/). **Okanagan Shuttle** (☎ 250/766–4280 or 250/317–5631 [mobile] ⊕ www.okanaganshuttle.com). **WestJet Airlines** (☎ 888/937–8538 ⊕ www.westjet.com).

Tours

Monashee Adventure Tours has full- or half-day bike- and wine-tour combinations, and other tours around the Okanagan. Whistler Outback Adventures (WOA) also has biking tours of the Okanagan wine country.

With Okanagan Limousine you can tour the wine area in chauffeur-driven style: they offer half-day and full-day tours to wineries in Kelowna, Summerland/Peachland, Naramata, Oliver/Osoyoos, and Okanagan Falls. Okanagan Wine Country Tours offers narrated three-hour, four-hour, and full-day wine-country tours.

Wildflower Trails and Winery Tours has several options and pairs walking excursions with winery visits. Winds & Rivers Escapes runs one-day tours that combine canoeing, a winery tour, and lunch.

Contacts Monashee Adventure Tours (☎ 250/762–9253 or 888/762–9253 ⊕ www.monasheeadventuretours.com). **Okanagan Limousine** (☎ 250/717–5466 or 866/366–3133 ⊕ www.ok-limo.com). **Okanagan Wine Country Tours** (☎ 250/868–9463 or 866/689–9463 ⊕ www.okwinetours.com). **Wildflower Trails and Winery Tours** (☎ 250/979–1211 or 866/979–1211 ⊕ www.wildflowersandwine.com). **WOA** (☎ 604/935–7566 ⊕ www.whistleroutbackadventures.com). **Winds & Rivers Escapes** (☎ 250/545–4280 or 888/545–4280 ⊕ www.windsrivers.bc.ca).

9

THE OKANAGAN WINE COUNTRY

By Carolyn B.
Heller

If you think that "wine country" and "British Columbia" have as much in common as "sunshine" and "the Arctic," think again. The British Columbia region known as the Okanagan, roughly five hours east of Vancouver by car or one hour by air, is rapidly growing into a significant wine-producing area. While it may not yet live up to the promotional hype that dubs it the "Napa of the North"—Okanagan wine production is a literal drop in the bucket compared to the production in the Napa Valley—the Okanagan is a magnet for wine tourists. And it makes a perfect short getaway from Vancouver and the British Columbia coast.

The Okanagan's wineries are concentrated in three general areas: around the city of Kelowna, along the Naramata Bench outside the town of Penticton, and in the area between Oliver and Osoyoos, just north of the U.S. border. If you're planning a short trip, you might want to stick to just one of these areas. Although it's only about 125 km (75 mi) between Kelowna and Osoyoos, it takes about two hours to drive between them. The Kelowna region is more urban (and less picturesque), but it has a greater range of accommodations and other services. The Naramata and Oliver/Osoyoos areas are both prettier and more rural. With approximately 150 wineries throughout the Okanagan, there are plenty in each area to occupy several days of tasting.

The Okanagan's sandy lake beaches and hot dry climate have long made it a family-holiday magnet for Vancouverites and Albertans, and the region is still the fruit-growing capital of Canada. With the development of the wine industry, the area is shedding its "beaches and peaches" reputation, but it's still a popular spot for family holidays. While more higher-end lodgings are being built every year to cater to wine-and-food tourists, the demand for upscale and midrange rooms can exceed the supply. And even the modest roadside motels and RV camps that seem to dot every town can fill up during the summer high season. Book ahead if you're visiting on a July or August weekend.

KELOWNA

390 km (242 mi) northeast of Vancouver, 68 km (42 mi) north of Penticton.

The largest community in the Okanagan Valley, with a regional population of over 180,000, Kelowna makes a good base for exploring the region's beaches, ski hills, wineries, and golf courses. Although its edges are untidily urban, with strip malls and office parks sprawling everywhere, the town has a convenient location right on Okanagan Lake. The walkable downtown core is rapidly growing, too, with condo and office towers sprouting up, but you can still enjoy a stroll in the restful lakeside park.

Okanagan Lake splits the Kelowna region in two. On the east side of the lake is Kelowna proper, which includes the city's downtown and the winery district south of the city center that the locals call the Mission. On the west side of the lake is the community of West Kelowna, which is frequently still known by its former name, Westbank. Several wineries are on the west side, on and off Boucherie Road. The William R. Bennett Bridge connects the two sides of the lake.

A good place to start your wine country exploration is at the **Wine Museum**, in a historic packing house in downtown Kelowna. It's really more of a wineshop than an actual museum, but the staff is knowledgeable and can provide information about local wineries. They host daily wine tastings and occasional wine-related exhibits. ⊠ *1304 Ellis St.* ☎ *250/868–0441* ⊕ *www.kelownamuseum.ca* ▭ *By donation* ⊙ *Weekdays 10–6, Sat. 10–5, Sun. 11–5.*

The small **British Columbia Orchard Industry Museum**, in the same building as the Wine Museum, has displays about the area's fruit industry. ⊠ *1304 Ellis St.* ☎ *250/763–0433* ▭ *By donation* ⊙ *Weekdays 10–5, Sat. 10–4.*

The **Kelowna Art Gallery** is an elegant public museum with a variety of local and international exhibits. ⊠ *1315 Water St.* ☎ *250/762–2226* ▭ *C$5* ⊙ *Tues.–Sat. 10–5, until 9 on Thurs., Sun. 1–4.*

Much of the Okanagan valley is still covered with apple orchards, and one of the largest and oldest (dating from 1904) is the **Kelowna Land & Orchard Company**, which you can tour on foot or in a tractor-drawn covered wagon. The farm animals are a hit with kids, but grown-ups might prefer samples from the Raven Ridge Cidery, which turns Fuji,

9

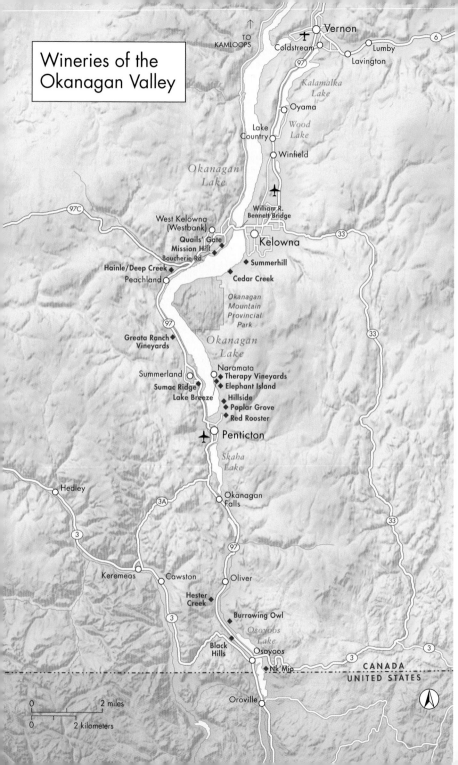

Braeburn, and Granny Smith apples into still wine, sparkling cider, and iced ciders. The lake-view **Ridge Restaurant** ($–$$) serves lunch daily from mid-April through October. ⊠ *3004 Dunster Rd., 8 km (5 mi) east of Kelowna,* ☎ *250/763–1091, 250/712–9404 restaurant reservations* ⊕ *www.k-l-o.com* ⊡ *Site free, tours C$7.50* ⊙ *Mid-Apr.–Oct., daily 9–4:30; tours mid-Apr.–Oct., call for times.*

WINERIES   Almost all of the wineries in and around Kelowna offer tastings and tours throughout the summer and during the Okanagan Wine Festivals held in May and October; several have restaurants and most also have wineshops open year-round. Many wineries charge a nominal fee (C$2–C$5) for tastings.

■ **TIP**➔ As you plan your tour route, note that Cedar Creek and Summerhill are on the east side of the lake, while Mission Hill and Quails' Gate are on the west.

Cedar Creek Estate Winery, south of Kelowna, has a scenic location overlooking the lake. Recent award-winning wines include several of their 2005 Platinum Reserve reds. Tours of the winery are given daily May to October; the wineshop is open for tastings year-round. Offering wine-friendly salads, sandwiches, seafood, and other light contemporary fare, the outdoor **Vineyard Terrace Restaurant** ($$) serves lunch mid-June through mid-September, weather permitting. Cedar Creek has a sister winery, **Greata Ranch Vineyards** (⊠ *697 Hwy. 97S, Peachland* ☎ *250/767–2768* ⊙ *Apr. –Oct., daily 10–6),* 9 km south of Peachland. ⊠ *5445 Lakeshore Rd.* ☎ *250/764–8866 or 800/730–9463* ⊕ *www. cedarcreek.bc.ca* ⊡ *Tours C$5, tastings C$2–C$5* ⊙ *Tours May–Oct., daily 11, 1, and 3. Wineshop May–Oct., daily 10–6; Nov.–Apr., daily 11–5.*

Atop a hill overlooking Okanagan Lake, **Mission Hill Family Estate** was built to look, as the owner describes it, like "a combination monastery, Tuscan hill village, and French winery," complete with a vaulted cellar blasted from volcanic rock and a 12-story bell tower. Mission Hill produces a wide variety of wines, and several different winery tours are offered, from a basic tour with a tasting of three wines, to a more in-depth visit that includes wine-and-food pairings. Wine aficionados might consider the "Sommelier Selected Tasting," which offers samples of higher-end wines, guided by the resident sommelier. An outdoor amphitheater hosts music and theater events on some summer evenings, and **The Terrace Restaurant** (⇨ *Where to Eat, below*) is one of the Kelowna area's best dining options. ⊠ *1730 Mission Hill Rd., West Kelowna* ☎ *250/768–6448 or 800/957–9911* ⊕ *www.missionhillwinery. com* ⊡ *Tours C$7–C$45* ⊙ *July–early Sept., daily 9:30–7; Apr.–June and early Sept.–early Oct., daily 10–6; early Oct.–Nov., daily 10–5; Dec.–Mar., daily 10–4; call or check the Web site for tour times.*

Quails' Gate Estate Winery, set on 125 acres above the western edge of Okanagan Lake, gives tours several times daily from May through mid-October. The winery produces more than a dozen different varieties, although they're best known for their Chardonnay and Pinot Noir. Complimentary tastings are offered in the spacious wineshop, and the **Old Vines Restaurant** (⇨ *Where to Eat, below*) is open year-round.

9

MORE OKANAGAN TIPS

OKANAGAN WINERIES: LARGE OR SMALL?

Is it better to visit large wineries or small ones? It depends. Starting your trip at a larger winery can be a useful orientation. The big ones generally have organized tours, where you can learn about the types of wine they make and the wine-making process, and you can pick up general information about the region as well. They usually have restaurants, too, where you can refuel.

On the other hand, at the smaller producers you may get to talk with the owners or winemakers themselves and get a more personal feel for their wines and the wine-making business. Our recommendation is to include a mix of larger and smaller wineries in your itinerary.

OKANAGAN: NORTH OR SOUTH?

The Okanagan is a large region, with many winding, stop-and-go roads. If your time is limited, consider concentrating on one area:

■ Go to Osoyoos/Oliver if you prefer smaller wineries, a more rural place, and a dry, desertlike climate.

■ Visit Penticton/Naramata also for smaller wineries and if you prefer cycling or other outdoor adventures; there are several biking and hiking options here.

■ Head for Kelowna if you're arriving by plane (it has the region's only significant airport), if you prefer a more developed urban setting, or if you want to check out the largest wineries. Kelowna isn't appealing, though, so if you're envisioning idyllic wine country, go farther south.

■ What to Do Besides Winery Tours?

Before developing its reputation as a wine-and-food destination, the Okanagan was a family holiday spot, best known for its "beaches and peaches"—the lakes with their sandy shores, boating or waterskiing opportunities, and waterfront lodges and campgrounds, as well as the countless farm stands offering fresh produce. The beaches and peaches are still there, and the Okanagan still welcomes families. With its mild dry climate, the region is also popular with golfers, and there are trails for biking and hiking.

The restaurant scene in the Okanagan is evolving too, and a growing number of high-end eateries emphasize food-and-wine pairings. Some of the best are at the wineries, especially the Sonora Room at Burrowing Owl in Oliver and the Terrace at Mission Hill in the Kelowna area. Surprisingly, outside of Kelowna, it can be hard to find good-quality cheap eats: your best bet, particularly in the summer and fall, is to stop at one of the many roadside farm stands to pick up fruits, veggies, and picnic fare. Some wineries have "picnic licenses," which means that they're allowed to sell you a glass (or a bottle) of wine that you can enjoy on their grounds, paired with your own picnic supplies or with picnic fare that the winery sells.

3303 Boucherie Rd. ☎250/769–4451 or 800/420–9463 ⊕www. quailsgate.com 🎫Tours C$5 ⊙ Tours May–mid-Oct.; call for schedule. Wineshop May and June, daily 10–7; July–early Sept., daily 9:30–7; early Sept.–Apr., daily 10–6.

Summerhill Estate Winery, south of Kelowna on the east side of the lake, is an organic producer best known for its sparkling and ice wines. What tends to startle visitors, though, is the four-story-high replica of the Great Pyramid of Cheops; it's used to age and store the wine. You can tour the winery and visit the wineshop, as well as a preserved settler's cabin, and a re-created First Nations earth house. The **Summerhill Sunset Bistro** ($$$–$$$$), with a veranda overlooking Okanagan Lake, serves lunch and dinner daily (closed January through early February). *4870 Chute Lake Rd. ☎250/764–8000 or 800/667–3538 ⊕www. summerhill.bc.ca 🎫Tours C$5, tastings C$5 ⊙ Tours May–mid-Oct., daily noon, 2, and 4; mid-Oct.–Apr., daily noon and 2. Wineshop May–mid-Oct., daily 9–7; mid-Oct.–Apr., daily 11–5.*

WHERE TO EAT

$$$–$$$$

FRENCH

✕**Bouchons Bistro.** Lots of windows and crisp white-linen tablecloths make this restaurant as bright as a French café, and the menu offers an array of French classics. Signature dishes include a mouthwatering bouillabaisse containing everything from fresh scallops to shrimp, salmon, halibut, and mussels; and a hearty cassoulet that includes duck confit, smoked pork belly, and Toulouse sausage over white beans. For dessert, you might opt for a cheese plate or go sweet with pears poached in local Syrah or a warm chocolate cake with strawberry coulis. The bistro is justifiably proud of its two certified sommeliers and its wine list of roughly 170 bottles, primarily Okanagan and French labels. *105–1180 Sunset Dr. ☎250/763–6595 ⊕ www.bouchonsbistro.com* ▭AE, MC, V ⊙ Closed Jan. No lunch.

$$$–$$$$

MODERN CANADIAN

✕**Old Vines Restaurant.** This contemporary restaurant at the Quails' Gate Winery is open year-round, making it a good choice for off-season visits. When the weather is fine, you can dine on the patio overlooking the lake. You might start with a salad of local tomatoes, goat feta, and basil, or beef carpaccio served on a bed of arugula. Among the mains, roast lamb sirloin might be paired with lentils, and seafood is another good option, from Pacific sablefish to scallops to bouillabaisse; the staff can suggest wine pairings. *3303 Boucherie Rd. ☎250/769–2500 or 800/420–9463 Ext. 252 ⊕ www.quailsgate.com* ▭AE, MC, V.

$$–$$$

MODERN CANADIAN

✕**RauDZ.** Chef-owner Rod Butters, one of B.C.'s better-known chefs who previously operated the high-end Fresco Restaurant at this downtown location, has revamped his contemporary eatery to deliver an equally creative but more casual dining experience. The kitchen still emphasizes seasonal, locally sourced fare, but it's not afraid to offer chili dogs (albeit made with merguez sausages) or cheeseburgers (topped with artisanal cheddar or blue) alongside more innovative dishes, from spaghetti with venison meatballs to jumbo scallops paired with a root vegetable torte and celeriac fondue. The interior is simple, with an open kitchen, a 21-foot communal table, and exposed brick and beams revealing the historic building's architectural roots. P.S. The name is

9

pronounced "Rod's." ✉ *1560 Water St.* ☎ *250/868–8805* ⊕ *www.raudz.com* ⌕ *Reservations not accepted* ▤ *AE, MC, V* ☾ *No lunch.*

\$\$\$
MODERN
CANADIAN
★

✕ **The Terrace at Mission Hill.** One of the most romantic of the winery dining rooms, this outdoor restaurant at the Mission Hill Family Estate has panoramic views across the vines and the lake. It's tough to compete with such a classic wine-country locale, but the creative kitchen here is up to the task. You might start with a simple salad of perfectly ripe tomatoes and locally made feta cheese, or a tart of duck prosciutto, leeks, and potatoes, before moving on to pan-seared sablefish paired with a pea purée, or braised venison with figs. Every menu item is matched with an appropriate wine. Linger over a tasting plate of cheeses or the decadent "Progression of Valrhona Chocolate," an assortment of chocolate creations. Because the restaurant is outdoors, service stops in inclement weather. ✉ *1730 Mission Hill Rd., West Kelowna* ☎ *250/768–6467* ⊕ *www.missionhillwinery.com* ▤ *AE, MC, V* ☾ *Closed early Oct.–Apr. No dinner.*

\$\$\$
MODERN
CANADIAN
★

✕ **Waterfront Restaurant & Wine Bar.** The kind of laid-back place every neighborhood should have, this bistro and wine bar concentrates on small—and larger—plates paired with local wines (which are also sold in the adjacent Metro Liquor shop). They make a first-rate, garlicky Caesar salad, and locals rave about the masala-spiced calamari. If you're in the mood for something heartier, you might try the duck breast with ricotta gnocchi or the roast halibut in a white miso broth. The helpful staff know their wines, so you can do well by heeding their suggestions. ✉ *104–1180 Sunset Dr.* ☎ *250/979–1222* ⊕ *www.waterfrontrestaurant.ca* ▤ *MC, V* ☾ *No lunch.*

WHERE TO STAY

\$–\$\$

🛏 **A View of the Lake B&B.** Attention, foodies! Owner Steve Marston and his wife Chrissy run this bed-and-breakfast in their contemporary home. He's a former restaurant chef who whips up elaborate breakfasts and offers periodic cooking demonstrations and dinners in his lavish Food Network–style kitchen. Perched high on a hill, the house has expansive views of the lake and the entire valley, particularly from the huge deck. Inside, you'll find soaring ceilings and bright yellow walls in the living room, and clean modern furnishings in the guest rooms. **Pros:** lake views and the to-die-for kitchen (take a cooking class if you can). **Cons:** guest room furnishings are a bit minimalist. ✉ *1877 Horizon Dr., West Kelowna* ☎ *250/769–7854* ⊕ *www.aviewofthelake.com* ⇦ *3 rooms* ⌕ *In-room: No TV, Wi-Fi. In-hotel: No kids under 12, no-smoking rooms* ▤ *MC, V* ⧖ *BP.*

\$–\$\$

🛏 **Apple Blossom B&B.** Set on the western slopes above Okanagan Lake, this cheery B&B offers terrific views and genuine hospitality. A separate guest entrance opens to a comfy communal lounge with a large-screen TV and DVD player, lots of local information, the Internet, and a small kitchenette. The bedrooms are simple but cozy, and true to its name, an apple theme permeates everything, especially at breakfast where apple motifs adorn linens and dishes. If you're home by midevening, you'll also be offered a delicious dessert. **Pros:** the warm welcome from owners Jeanette and John Martens; moderate prices. **Cons:** if you need high style, look elsewhere. ✉ *3582 Apple Way Blvd.,*

West Kelowna ☎ 250/768–1163 or 888/718–5064 ⊕ www.applebnb. com ↪ 3 rooms ⚠ In-room: Wi-Fi. In-hotel: Internet, no kids under 5 ⊟ MC, V ⍾◯ BP.

$$$$ ⊡ **The Cove Lakeside Resort.** At this all-suites resort hotel on the western shore of Okanagan Lake, the guest suites, done in smart beiges and browns, have all the comforts of home and then some: fully equipped modern kitchens complete with special fridges to chill your wine, 42-inch plasma TVs, and fireplaces. Kids can amuse themselves at the pools, in the game room, or watching a movie in the media center, while active adults gravitate to the small fitness room or take a yoga class. The chic, Southwestern-style **Bonfire Restaurant & Bar** ($$–$$$), which is run separately from the hotel, is a striking setting for a drink. **Pros:** lakeside location; in-suite wine coolers; the washer-dryers. **Cons:** the restaurant gets mixed reviews. ⊠ *4205 Gellatly Rd., West Kelowna ☎ 250/707–1800 or 877/762–2683 ⊕ www.covelakeside.com ↪ 150 suites ⚠ In-room: Kitchen, DVD, Wi-Fi. In-hotel: Restaurant, room service, bar, tennis court, pools, gym, spa, beachfront, water sports, children's programs (ages 5 and up), laundry facilities, Wi-Fi, no-smoking rooms ⊟ AE, MC, V.*

$$$$ ⊡ **Delta Grand Okanagan Resort.** On the shore of Okanagan Lake, this resort is a five-minute stroll from downtown Kelowna, though you may never have to leave the grounds because of all the amenities—there's even a casino on-site. Most standard rooms and suites are spacious, with balconies, sitting areas, and appealing modern furnishings. About half the rooms have views over the lake and the surrounding hills. The two-bedroom waterfront condo suites are a good option for families: suites have two full baths, full kitchens, washer-dryers, and gas fireplaces. The villas in the adjacent Royal Private Residence Club are another option; they have one to three bedrooms, sleeping two to eight people. **Pros:** a full menu of resort activities, from spa treatments to slot machines. **Cons:** can feel like a big convention hotel; not the hippest choice in town. ⊠ *1310 Water St. ☎ 250/763–4500 or 800/465–4651 ⊕ www. deltahotels.com ↪ 260 rooms, 60 condominiums, 70 villas ⚠ In-room: Kitchen (some), Wi-Fi. In-hotel: 3 restaurants, room service, bar, pools, gym, spa, bicycles, laundry service, parking (paid), some pets allowed, no-smoking rooms ⊟ AE, D, DC, MC, V.*

$$$–$$$$ ⊡ **Hotel El Dorado.** Combining a 1926 building with a modern addition, this boutiquey, adult-oriented, lakeside hotel a short drive south of downtown Kelowna is one of the area's more stylish options. In the older "heritage" wing, the rooms are all different, but done with 1930s-style furniture, vintage radios, and claw-foot tubs. Rooms in the new wing, many of which are quite large, feel more like an upscale summer cottage, with cork floors, fridges, and plush furnishings. The traditional **Lakeside Dining Room** ($$$–$$$$) serves steaks and seafood. **Pros:** eclectic style; lake views. **Cons:** busy on-site liquor store—a benefit to some, a nuisance for others. ⊠ *500 Cook Rd. ☎ 250/763–7500 or 866/608–7500 ⊕ www.eldoradokelowna.com ↪ 49 rooms, 6 suites ⚠ In-room: Refrigerator (some), DVD, Wi-Fi. In-hotel: 2 restaurants, bar, pool, gym, spa, beachfront ⊟ AE, MC, V.*

9

$$$$ 🏨 **Manteo Resort Waterfront Hotel & Villas.** This striking Tuscan-looking resort painted in vivid yellows and reds sits on a sandy swimming beach on Okanagan Lake. All the water sports are here, from windsurfing to parasailing to waterskiing. Accommodation choices include rooms and suites—all with balconies—in the main building and two- and three-bedroom villas with full kitchens. The villas are especially handsome, with gas fireplaces, terra-cotta tiles, high ceilings, and patios. The **Wild Apple Grill** ($$–$$$) serves Pacific Northwest cuisine inside and on its big lakeside patio. **Pros:** lots of activities for kids and teens. **Cons:** rooms look rather generic. ⊠ *3762 Lakeshore Rd.* ☎ *250/860–1031 or 800/445–5255* ⊕ *www.manteo.com* ⟿ *48 rooms, 30 suites, 24 villas* ⚹ *In-room: Kitchen (some), refrigerator (some), DVD (some), Wi-Fi. In-hotel: Restaurant, room service, bar, tennis court, pools, gym, spa, bicycles, children's programs (ages 3–12), laundry service, no-smoking rooms* ▭ *AE, DC, MC, V.*

$$–$$$$ 🏨 **Predator Ridge Golf Resort.** Set right on an 18-hole golf course (with a second course slated to open in 2010) that's part of a vacation-home community, this full-service resort offers a range of accommodations, from studio, one-bedroom, and two-bedroom units in the modern Craftsman-style lodge, to two- and three-bedroom townhouse-style cottages. All units have full kitchens (useful, since the resort is not right in town), though on-site dining options include the steak-focused **Range Restaurant** ($$$–$$$$), the casual Clubhouse Lounge, and a small café. Greens fees for 18 holes are C$140 (cart rentals included), but lodging and golf packages are available (note that the golf course is closed early Oct.–Apr., though the hotel stays open). Individual and small-group golf lessons are offered, as are a variety of golf camps. The resort is in the hills 40 km (25 mi) north of Kelowna and 15 km (9 mi) south of Vernon, off Highway 97. **Pros:** you can stumble out of bed onto the links. **Cons:** location is rather remote, especially for wine touring. ⊠ *301 Village Centre Pl., Vernon* ☎ *250/542–3436 or 888/578–6688* ⊕ *www.predatorridge.com* ⟿ *75 suites, 51 cottages* ⚹ *In-room: Kitchen, DVD, Wi-Fi (some). In-hotel: 3 restaurants, bar, golf course, tennis court, pools, gym, spa, children's programs (ages 5–12), Wi-Fi* ▭ *AE, MC, V.*

SPORTS AND THE OUTDOORS

BIKING AND HIKING   Bikers and hikers can follow the **Kettle Valley Rail Trail**, a 455-km (283-mi) multiuse trail that begins west of the Okanagan Valley near the town of Brodie (along Highway 5) and meanders east to the town of Midway (on Highway 3). A popular day trip for cyclists is to follow the trail between Penticton or Naramata and the Kelowna area. The trail doesn't go into central Kelowna but you can pick it up south of the city. You can get up-to-date maps and information from the visitor center in Kelowna. The "Click, Hike & Bike" interactive map on the Regional District Okanagan-Similkameen Web site (⊕ *www.rdos.bc.ca*) is also a useful planning tool.

GOLF   With four championship golf courses close to town, Kelowna is a major golf destination.

Gallagher's Canyon Golf and Country Club, about 15 km (9 mi) southeast of downtown Kelowna, has an 18-hole, par-72 championship course and a 9-hole, par-32 course; greens fees for the 18-hole course are C$118 in high season. ⌧ *4320 Gallagher's Dr. W* ☎ *250/861–4240 or 800/446–5322* ⊕ *www.golfbc.com.*

Surrounded by orchards (golfers can pick fruit as they play), **Harvest Golf Club** is an 18-hole championship par-72 course. Greens fees in high season are C$115. The Harvest Grille ($$–$$$; ⊙ *Closed mid-Nov.–mid-Mar.*) serves breakfast, sandwiches, salads, and other casual fare by day, and more substantial meals in the evening. ⌧ *2725 KLO Rd.* ☎ *250/862–3103 or 800/257–8577* ⊕ *www.harvestgolf.com.*

The **Okanagan Golf Club** has two 18-hole, par-72 championship courses with Okanagan Valley views. The Quail Course is a challenging hillside course with tight tree-lined fairways; the newer Bear Course, designed by the Jack Nicklaus Group, is more forgiving. High-season greens fees are C$115 for either course. ⌧ *3200 Via Centrale* ☎ *250/765–5955 or 800/446–5322* ⊕ *www.golfbc.com.*

SHOPPING

Carmelis Goat Cheese. If your only experience with chèvre is the super-market cheese logs, you may be surprised by the variety—and the rich flavors—of the goats'-milk cheeses that this family-owned artisanal cheese company produces. You can sample many of the cheeses in the shop, which is 12 km (8 mi) south of downtown Kelowna (and you'll likely see Carmelis cheeses on many area menus). To arrange a tour of the cheese-production facilities and the goat barns, phone a week in advance. ⌧ *170 Timberline Rd.* ☎ *250/870–3117* ⊕ *www.carmelisgoatcheese.com* ⌧ *Tours C$5, tastings free* ⊙ *Mar.–Apr., daily 11–5; May–mid-Oct., daily 10–6; mid-Oct.–Dec., Mon.–Sat. 11–4.*

Okanagan Grocery Artisan Breads. A good place to start if you're assembling a picnic, this first-rate bakery sells a variety of hearty loaves. They also offer a selection of local cheeses and other gourmet items. It's in the Guisachan Village shopping complex, which also houses a produce market, seafood and meat shops, and a chocolate maker. ⌧ *2355 Gordon Dr.* ☎ *250/862–2811* ⊕ *www.okanagangrocery.com* ⊙ *Tues.–Sat. 9:30–5:30.*

9

EN ROUTE **The Sunmore Ginseng Spa.** If you're passing through the town of Kamloops, 200 km (125 mi) northwest of Kelowna, plan to stop off at this serene spa that offers a range of traditional and ginseng-based therapies, including ginseng soaks, scrubs, facials, and massage. Run by Sunmore Healthtech Ltd. as an offshoot of its successful ginseng-processing factory, the spa also has a teahouse that serves Asian-inspired ginseng-flavored cuisine and offers guests a traditional Chinese tea ceremony. Each treatment room in the elegant spa takes its theme from a different Chinese element: earth, water, fire, wood, and gold. Be sure to visit the ginseng information center and showroom, too. ⌧ *925 McGill Pl., Kamloops* ☎ *250/372–2814 spa, 250/374–3017 showroom* ⊕ *www.sunmoreginseng.com.*

SUMMERLAND AND PEACHLAND

Summerland is 52 km (31 mi) south of Kelowna, Peachland is 25 km (15 mi) southwest of Kelowna.

Between Kelowna and Penticton, Highway 97 winds along the west side of Okanagan Lake, past vineyards, orchards, fruit stands, beaches, picnic sites, and some of the region's prettiest lake and hill scenery.

One way to tour the area is aboard the historic **Kettle Valley Steam Railway,** which has 90-minute trips along 16 km (10 mi) of the 1915 rail line, pulled by a restored 1912 steam locomotive. The train runs twice daily Saturday through Monday in May, June, September, and October and Thursday through Monday in July and August. Several times a year, they also host a "Great Train Robbery" reenactment, combined with a barbecue dinner and musical entertainment. ⊠ *18404 Bathville Rd., 7 km (4 mi) west of Hwy. 97, Summerland* ☎ *250/494–8422* ⊕ *www. kettlevalleyrail.org* 🎫 *C$21; Great Train Robbery and barbecue C$50* ⊙ *Mid-May–early Oct.*

WINERIES **Hainle Vineyards Estate Winery,** British Columbia's first organic winery and the first to make ice wines, is a small producer open for tastings (though not tours). The Trepanier Manor Hotel, a luxury boutique property, is under construction adjacent to the winery, slated to open in 2011. ⊠ *5355 Trepanier Bench Rd., Peachland* ☎ *250/767–2525 or 800/767–3109* ⊕ *www.hainle.com* ⊙ *Mid-Apr.–Oct., daily 11–5; Nov.– mid-Apr., by appointment only.*

Sumac Ridge Estate Winery offers tours combined with tastings, a "founder's tasting" of their premium wines, and a "founder's tasting with food" including wine-and-food pairings. The **Cellar Door Bistro** (⇨ *Where to Eat and Stay, below*) is open for lunch and dinner. ⊠ *17403 Hwy. 97 N, Summerland* ☎ *250/494–0451* ⊕ *www.sumacridge.com* 🎫 *Tours C$7, founder's tastings C$15–C$30* ⊙ *Tours May–late June, daily at 11, 2, and 4; late June–early Oct., 11, 1, and 3. Wineshop late June– early Sept., daily 9:30–9 (tastings until 6); early Sept.–late June, daily 10–8 (tastings until 5).*

WHERE TO EAT AND STAY

¢ ✕ **Bliss Bakery.** Across the street from Okanagan Lake, along Peach-

CAFÉ land's tiny commercial strip, this bakery-café is the best place in the area for muffins, pastries, and coffee. The hearty breads are excellent, too, and there's a small selection of sandwiches on offer. Popular items often sell out, so come early in the day. ⊠ *4200 Beach Ave., Peachland* ☎ *250/767–2711* ⊕ *www.blissbakery.ca* ⚐ *Reservations not accepted* ⊟ *MC, V* ⊙ *No dinner.*

$$–$$$ ✕ **Cellar Door Bistro.** Simple fresh fare takes the stage at this bistro in

MODERN the Sumac Ridge Estate Winery. Salads are made with local greens, a

CANADIAN cheese plate features artisan products, and a simple charcuterie assortment is designed to share. If you want a more substantial meal, you might opt for grilled salmon with a vegetable hash or Mediterranean-flavored lamb shank served with a warm lentil-and-olive salad. And—you guessed it—it's all paired with Sumac Ridge wines. ⊠ *17403 Hwy.*

97 N, Summerland ☎ 250/494–0451 ⊕ www.sumacridge.com ▭ AE, MC, V ✆ Closed mid-Dec.–mid-Jan.

$$$–$$$$ ⊞ **Summerland Waterfront Resort.** Designed for families who like the feel of a summer cottage but want the amenities of a resort, the rooms at this modern lakeside hotel are bright and beachy, done in sunny yellows and ocean blues. All have fireplaces and kitchen facilities, and the majority have lake views. There's plenty to keep the kids busy, with a pool, boat rentals, and a small beach; additional offerings for the adults include wine-touring and cooking-school packages. **Pros:** prime location right on the lake; family-friendly. **Cons:** not many interesting dining options nearby. ⊠ 13011 Lakeshore Dr. S, Summerland ☎ 250/494–8180 or 877/494–8111 ⊕ www.summerlandresorthotel.com ⤳ 115 suites ⏸ In-room: Kitchen, DVD, Internet. In-hotel: Restaurant, pool, gym, spa, beachfront, water sports, laundry facilities ▭ AE, MC, V.

PENTICTON AND NARAMATA

16 km (10 mi) south of Summerland, 395 km (245 mi) east of Vancouver.

Penticton, with its long sandy beach backed by motels and cruising pickup trucks, is a nostalgia-inducing family-vacation spot. Drive through the city center to the east side of Okanagan Lake, though, and you'll be in the heart of the burgeoning Naramata wine country. The route along the Naramata Benchlands is peppered with one winery after another, so the seemingly short drive could take all afternoon.

The knowledgeable staff at the **British Columbia Wine Information Centre** will tell you what's new at area wineries and help you plan a self-drive winery tour. The center also stocks more than 500 local wines and offers complimentary tastings daily. They'll pack wine for travel and can arrange shipping within Canada. The Visitor Information Centre (⇨ *the Okanagan Planner, above*), in the same building, has information about places to stay and eat. ⊠ 553 Railway St., Penticton ☎ 250/490–2006 ⊕ www.bcwineinfo.net ✆ July–Aug., daily 9–7; Sept.–Jun., Mon.–Sat. 9–6, Sun. 10–5.

WINERIES May through October is high season for the Naramata wineries. Some close or scale back their hours between November and April.

Elephant Island Orchard Wines creates some delightful table and dessert wines from fruits such as pear, cherry, and black currant. Many of the recipes are generations old. Tastings are complimentary. ⊠ 2730 Aikens Loop, Naramata ☎ 250/496–5522 ⊕ www.elephantislandwine.com ✆ May–mid-Oct., daily 10:30–5:30; Mid-Oct.–Apr., by appointment.

It's hard to miss the 72-foot tower at **Hillside Estate Winery** as you drive along the road between Penticton and Naramata. Their first commercial release was in 1989, and their Old Vines Gamay Noir, Cabernet Franc, Riesling, and Gewürztraminer are recent award winners. They also produce an unusual white wine called Muscat Ottonel. The **Barrel Room Bistro** ($$–$$$) (⇨ *Where to Eat, below*) feeds visitors between April and mid-October. ⊠ 1350 Naramata Rd., Penticton ☎ 250/493–6274 or 888/923–9463 ⊕ www.hillsideestate.com ✆ Apr–Oct., daily 10–6; Nov.–Mar., by appointment.

9

DID YOU KNOW?

Lake Breeze Vineyards, overlooking Okanagan Lake, is an enticing spot to stop for a wine tasting, or for lunch at the Patio restaurant.

Set on the Naramata Benchlands above Okanagan Lake, **Lake Breeze Vineyards** is one of the region's most attractively located small wineries and their white wines, particularly their Gewürztraminer, Pinot Gris, and Pinot Blanc, are well regarded. Tastings are available but not tours. The outdoor **Patio Restaurant** ($$–$$$) (⇨ *Where to Eat, below*) is open for lunch (weather permitting) between May and the second week of October. ✉ *930 Sammet Rd., Naramata* ☎ *250/496–5659* ⊕ *www. lakebreeze.ca* ⬚ *Tastings C$2* ⊗ *Apr., Fri.–Sun. 12–4; May–mid-Oct., daily 11–5.*

Small producer **Poplar Grove** makes respected Merlot, Chardonnay, and Pinot Gris, but the company is perhaps even better known for its first-rate cheeses. Stop by the cheese shop for the soft and pungent double-cream Camembert or the intense Tiger Blue. A winery is under construction, expected to open in 2010. ✉ *1060 Poplar Grove Rd., Naramata* ☎ *250/493–9463 winery, 250/492–4575 cheese shop* ⊕ *www.poplargrove.ca* ⊗ *Call for winery and cheese-shop hours.*

Red Rooster Winery has a spacious tasting room that showcases wine alongside the work of local artists. For those who fantasize about owning a vineyard, Red Rooster has an Adopt A Row program: you "adopt" a row of 50 vines, with the guarantee of 12 bottles of wine. ✉ *891 Naramata Rd., Naramata* ☎ *250/492–2424* ⊕ *www.redroosterwinery. com* ⊗ *Apr.–Oct., daily 10–6; Nov.–Mar., daily 11–5.*

Though the names of the wines at **Therapy Vineyards**—Super Ego, Pink Freud, Freudian Sip—may have you running for the analyst's couch, this small winery does make a number of well-regarded varieties. And they're great gifts for your psychiatrist friends. ✉ *940 Debeck Rd., Naramata* ☎ *250/496–5257* ⊕ *www.therapyvineyards.com* ⊗ *May–Oct., weekdays 10–5, weekends 10–6.*

WHERE TO EAT

$$–$$$ ✕ **Barrel Room Bistro at Hillside Estate Winery.** The straightforward lunch
MODERN menu—salads, sandwiches, pizzas, and pastas—brings in the wine tour-
CANADIAN ists, who sip and chew on one of the two patios or in the rustic-style dining room. In the evening, more substantial fare includes grilled steak with a Tiger Blue cheese sauce, duck with cherry chutney, and citrus- and honey-glazed salmon. The restaurant can get busy with tour groups. ✉ *1350 Naramata Rd., Penticton* ☎ *250/493–6274 or 888/923–9463* ⊕ *www.hillsideestate.com* ⊟ *AE, MC, V* ⊗ *Closed mid-Oct.–early Apr. No dinner Apr. No dinner Mon.–Thurs. May and June.*

¢–$ ✕ **The Bench Artisan Food Market.** In the morning, you can pop into this
CAFÉS foodie-friendly market and café for coffee and pastries or a bowl of homemade granola. Then at midday, there are soups, salads, sand- wiches, and daily specials. They'll make picnic platters to go, or you can assemble your own from the locally made cheeses, fresh-baked breads, and signature molten-chocolate brownies. ✉ *368 Vancouver Ave., Penticton* ☎ *250/492–2222* ⊕ *www.thebenchmarket.com* ⊟ *MC, V* ⊗ *No dinner.*

$$–$$$ ✕ **The Patio at Lake Breeze.** A seat at this tiny outdoor restaurant at Lake
MODERN Breeze Vineyards is one of the hottest tickets in town, so plan on an
CANADIAN early lunch if you hope to nab a table. Among the intriguing, wine-

friendly dishes, you might find a warm seafood salad with chipotle cream sauce; roasted chicken breast with grilled pears, blackberries, and blue cheese served on a bed of greens; or a beef-tenderloin sandwich with truffle butter, Parmesan cheese, and arugula. Because the tables are all outdoors, the restaurant closes in inclement weather. Reservations are accepted only for groups of six or more. ⊠ *930 Sammet Rd., Naramata* ☎ *250/496–5619* ⊕ *www.lakebreeze.ca* ⊟ *AE, MC, V* ⊙ *No dinner. Closed mid-Oct.–Apr.*

WHERE TO STAY

$$$$ ⊞ **Apple D'Or.** If "log house" brings to mind Abe Lincoln's bare-bones childhood cabin, think again. This massive house built of logs is a deluxe B&B that overlooks Okanagan Lake and has amenities Honest Abe never dreamed of, from the solid, well-insulated walls to the in-room music systems, flat-screen TVs, and fireplaces. Each of the three rooms on the lower level is furnished differently, but all have a mix of antiques and traditional pieces and open to a private patio and the lovely gardens. You can borrow a DVD from the 250-disk library, take a dip in the pool, or steam in the sauna. **Pros:** convenient location in the heart of the Naramata wine district. **Cons:** who'll sleep in the bunk beds (in the second bedroom of one suite) if kids aren't allowed? ⊠ *2587 Naramata Rd., Naramata* ☎ *250/496–4045* ⊕ *www.appledor. ca* ⇆ *3 suites* ⚐ *In-room: Kitchen, DVD, Wi-Fi. In-hotel: Pool, laundry service, no kids under 12, no-smoking rooms* ⊟ *AE, MC, V* ⊙ *Closed Nov.–Mar.* ⏚ *CP.*

$$–$$$ ⊞ **God's Mountain Estate.** This quirky Mediterranean-style villa sits on 115 acres of sunny hilltop overlooking Skaha Lake, 4 km (2½ mi) south of Penticton, and a stay at this rambling property is a bit like a visit with a gracious, if eccentric, aunt. The three spacious common rooms are filled with an eclectic mix of antiques, plush cushions, and theatrical props, and you are free to use the large common kitchen. Among the guest rooms, the Roofless Room is the most fun: the four-poster bed is sheltered under a canopy, but the rest of the room, including a fireplace and private hot tub, is open to the stars. Although the other rooms vary, several have expansive lake views. On most Sunday evenings in July and August, the inn hosts an elaborate four-course dinner that's open to guests and to the public (C$95 per person, including wine); on summer Wednesdays, it's dinner with a local winemaker (C$105). **Pros:** a roofless room—how romantic is that? And owner Sarah Allen has a wealth of local knowledge, particularly about area restaurants and shops. **Cons:** if you're more comfortable in the Four Seasons, the funky style here may not be for you. ⊠ *4898 Lakeside Rd., Penticton* ☎ *250/490–4800* ⊕ *www.godsmountain.com* ⇆ *10 rooms, 4 suites* ⚐ *In-room: No a/c (some), no phone, refrigerator (some), no TV. In-hotel: Pool, Wi-Fi, no kids under 12, no-smoking rooms* ⊟ *MC, V* ⏚ *BP.*

$$$–$$$$ ⊞ **Naramata Heritage Inn.** Built as a hotel in 1908, this historic structure did time as a girls' school before the current owners converted it, in 2001, back to an inn. Many of the Mission-style furnishings, wood floors, and claw-foot tubs are original, but plenty of the amenities— heated bathroom floors, fluffy duvets, central air-conditioning—are au courant. The **Cobblestone Wine Bar** ($$–$$$) has a large selection of

Okanagan wines, which are paired with contemporary cuisine, including grilled salmon, morel-studded pasta, and top-your-own focaccia; there's a sunny patio for summer lunches. **Pros:** to sample a wide range of wines, you need only go downstairs. **Cons:** many of the rooms are a bit cramped. ⊠ *3625 1st St., Naramata* ☎ *250/496–6808 or 866/617–1188* ⊕ *www.naramatainn.com* ⊅ *11 rooms, 1 suite* ⚒ *In-room: No TV (some). In-hotel: Restaurant, bar, spa, bicycles, no-smoking rooms* ⊟ *AE, MC, V* ⊗ *Closed Nov.–Jan.* ⏸*CP.*

$$$ 🛏 **Therapy Vineyards Guesthouse.** Independent travelers who want to get away from it all might consider a room at this cozy winery guesthouse. There's no restaurant, guest lounge, or other resort amenities, but there are two well-designed (if smallish) rooms furnished with king beds and Mission-style pieces. A breakfast basket is delivered to your door each morning and you can bring your own wine to enjoy on your private terrace. **Pros:** the terraces overlooking the lake. **Cons:** no common space for guests. ⊠ *940 Debeck Rd., Naramata* ☎ *250/496–5217 Ext. 6* ⊕ *www.therapyvineyards.com* ⊅ *2 rooms* ⚒ *In-room: Refrigerator, DVD, Internet* ⊟ *MC, V* ⊗ *Closed Nov.–Apr.* ⏸*CP.*

SPORTS AND THE OUTDOORS

BIKING AND HIKING A section of the **Kettle Valley Rail Trail** between Penticton and Kelowna runs through the Naramata area. You can easily detour off the trail for winery visits.

SHOPPING

Penticton Farmers' Market. To pick up fresh fruits and vegetables, baked goods, and crafts—or the local gossip—head for this seasonal Saturday market. ⊠ *100 block of Main St., Penticton* ☎ *250/770–3276* ⊕ *www. pentictonfarmersmarket.org* ⊗ *May–Oct., Sat. 8:30* AM*–noon.*

OLIVER AND OSOYOOS

58 km (36 mi) south of Penticton, 400 km (250 mi) east of Vancouver.

South of Penticton between the southern tip of Lake Okanagan and the U.S. border, Highway 97 runs along a chain of lakes: Skaha, Vaseaux, and Osoyoos, and through Canada's only desert. With a hot dry climate, the sandy lakeshores can be crowded with families in summer, and it's also a popular winter destination for snowbirds from the Canadian prairies. The climate makes this a prime wine-producing area and the roads on both sides of Osoyoos Lake between the towns of Oliver and Osoyoos are lined with wineries.

Oliver bills itself as "the Wine Capital of Canada" and despite the ever-growing number of wineries in the area, this sleepy town of about 4,700 is still growing into its "Wine Capital" ambitions. The community has plans to construct a "wine village" that will include an upscale inn and spa, although the village has remained in the planning stage for the past several years.

The southernmost town in the Okanagan region, Osoyoos, has a significant First Nations population among its roughly 5,000 residents. The Osoyoos Indian Band operates North America's first aboriginal-owned winery and also runs an informative cultural center that's well worth a visit.

If you're approaching the Oliver/Osoyoos area from the west along Highway 3, keep your eye out for **Spotted Lake**. Containing one of the world's highest concentrations of minerals, this 15.2-hectare (38-acre) lake dries up as the summer progresses, leaving mineral deposits in a distinctive "spotted" pattern. The Osoyoos Indian Band, which lives in the area, considers the lake sacred, believing its minerals have healing properties. The lake is on private property, but it's visible from the highway; it's east of Cawston and about 8 km (5 mi) west of Osoyoos.

Desert Centre. The northern tip of the Great Basin Desert is home to flora and fauna found nowhere else in the country. You can learn more about the unique local ecology at this interpretive center, where you can take a one-hour guided tour along a boardwalk desert trail. ⊠ *146th St., off Hwy. 97, 4 km (3 mi) north of Osoyoos* ☎ *250/495–2470 or 877/899–0897* ⊕ *www.desert.org* ☜ *C$7, including tour* ☉ *Late Apr.– mid-May and mid-Sept.–mid-Oct., daily 10–2; mid-May–mid-Sept., daily 9:30–4:30; guided tours mid-May–mid-Sept. at 10, noon, and 2.*

☖ **Nk'Mip Desert Cultural Centre.** Run by the Osoyoos Indian Band, this ★ well-designed museum—the name is pronounced "in-ka-meep"—has exhibits about the area's aboriginal community, the region's natural setting, and the creatures which make their home in this desert environment. Don't miss "Sssnakes Alive!," a presentation featuring live rattlesnakes native to the area. You can also walk to a reconstructed village that includes two pit houses, a teepee, and a sweat lodge (bring water, since there's little shade along the desert trails). In July and August, the center opens one evening a week for the "Wild Wednesdays" program, which includes entertainment and other special events. The center's exterior is a striking, environmentally friendly earth wall built of a mix of soil, water, a small amount of cement, and pigment. ⊠ *1000 Rancher Creek Rd., Osoyoos* ☎ *250/495–7901* ⊕ *www.nkmipdesert. com* ☜ *C$12; "Wild Wednesdays" full-day C$18, evening only C$11* ☉ *Early Mar.–early May, Tues.–Sat. 9:30–4:30; early May–June and Sept.–Oct., daily 9:30–4:30; Jul.–Aug., Thurs.–Tues. 9:30–4:30, Wed. 9:30–4:30 and 5–9.*

9

Wineries line the roads between Osoyoos and Oliver, and continuing north toward the town of Okanagan Falls. Many of these are fairly small operations, but some notable larger producers are here, too. Many wineries close or reduce their operations between November and April, so call first if you're traveling off-season.

Something of a cult find among Okanagan aficionados, **Black Hills Estate Winery,** on the Black Sage Bench between Osoyoos and Oliver, frequently sells out of its much-admired wines (and when the wine is gone, the tasting room closes). But it's worth calling to check on the status of their Nota Bene (a blend of Cabernet Sauvignon, Merlot, and Cabernet Franc), Chardonnay, Alibi (Sauvignon Blanc with a bit of Sémillon), or whatever the winemaker dreams up next. ⊠ *30880 Black Sage Rd., Oliver* ☎ *250/498–0666* ⊕ *www.blackhillswinery.com* ☉ *Sat., by appointment only.*

CLOSE UP

A Crash Course in Okanagan Wines

GETTING ORIENTED

A great source of information about Okanagan wines is the British Columbia Wine Institute. Their Web site, ⊕ www.winebc.com, includes a helpful guide to B.C. wines, as well as detailed itinerary suggestions for Okanagan wine touring. It also includes a calendar of wine-related dinners, tastings, and other events around the province.

A DROP OF HISTORY

Most wine experts agree that back in the dark ages (aka the 1970s), the wine produced in British Columbia was, to put it charitably, plonk. Okanagan Riesling and sparkling Labrusca were the best sellers. Beginning in the late '70s, however, growers began replacing their vines with high-quality Vinifera varieties to start producing more sophisticated wines. In 1984, B.C. had 13 wineries. By 2009, there were more than 150.

WHAT TO DRINK

In British Columbia overall, the top white varietals are Chardonnay, Pinot Gris, Gewürztraminer, Pinot Blanc, and Sauvignon Blanc. The top reds are Merlot, Pinot Noir, Cabernet Sauvignon, Syrah, and Cabernet Franc. Many Okanagan wineries also produce ice wine, a late-harvest dessert wine made from grapes that have frozen on the vine.

As you tour the Okanagan, ask the wineries about their specialties. The B.C. Wine Institute also posts regularly updated lists of award-winning wines on their Web site (⊕ www.winebc. com).

WHAT IS VQA?

British Columbia wines that carry a "VQA" (Vintners Quality Alliance) label must meet certain production and quality standards. A professional tasting panel approves each VQA wine. Participation in the VQA program is voluntary, and there are plenty of fine B.C. wines that have opted not to take part.

TO SPIT OR NOT TO SPIT?

On a day-long wine-tasting excursion, you can taste a good deal of wine. To avoid getting fatigued, or overly inebriated, do as the pros do: sip, swirl, and spit. Most wineries have a bucket on the tasting bar for that purpose, so don't be shy. You'll enjoy your tour more in the long run. And if the sample in your glass is more than you can drink, simply pour it into the bucket.

TRANSPORTING WINE

If you're buying wine at the wineries, be sure you have some way to keep it cool, particularly in summer when it gets hot and wine can spoil quickly. If you must transport wine in your car, put it in a cooler or keep it on ice.

Most wineries will ship wines for you but *only within Canada;* they cannot send wine over the border. If you're traveling back to the United States, your best bet may be to have your wine packed for travel and transport it yourself. Check at one of the wine information centers for more details.

UH-OH: SOLD OUT?

It's not uncommon for smaller Okanagan wineries to sell out of their wine in a given year. And when there's limited wine left, they generally close or reduce the hours in their tasting rooms. If you have your heart set on visiting a particular winery, check their Web site or phone in advance to be sure they have wine available.

From the viewing tower and patio at **Burrowing Owl Estate Winery,** you get sweeping views of the vineyards and Osoyoos Lake. Among their award-winning wines are their 2008 Pinot Gris, 2007 Chardonnay, and 2007 Cabernet Franc. Winery tours are offered on weekends from May through October, and tastings are available year-round. At the 25-foot tasting bar, donations (C$2) for tastings are put toward the Burrowing Owl Recovery Society. Save time for a meal at the terrific **Sonora Room Restaurant** (⇨ *Where to Eat, below*). ⊠ *100 Burrowing Owl Pl., off Black Sage Rd., Oliver* ☎ *250/498–0620 or 877/498–0620* ⊕ *www. bovwine.ca* 🎫 *Tours C$5.* ⊙ *Tours May–Oct., weekends 11 AM and 2 PM. Wineshop May–mid-Oct., daily 10–5; call for off-season hrs.*

Hester Creek Estate Winery, set high on a bluff between Osoyoos and Oliver, offers complimentary tastings daily. They also have a picnic area where you can enjoy a snack and a glass of wine. Their Pinot Blanc, Pinot Gris, Merlot, and Cabernet Franc are well regarded. ⊠ *13163 326th Ave., Oliver* ☎ *250/498–4435* ⊕ *www.hestercreek.com* ⊙ *May–mid-Oct., daily 10–5:30; mid-Oct.–Apr., daily 10–4.*

Just east of downtown Osoyoos lies **The Nk'Mip Cellars,** North America's first aboriginal-owned and -operated winery. On a ridge overlooking Osoyoos Lake, this stunningly designed winery is surrounded by both desert and vineyards. The winery released its first wine in 2002 and now produces 18,000 cases annually, including their premium label, Qwam Qwmt; it's pronounced "kw-em kw-empt" and means "achieving excellence." In addition to wine, the tasting room sells aboriginal art and gift items. The **Patio Restaurant** (⇨ *Where to Eat, below*) serves contemporary fare. ⊠ *1400 Rancher Creek Rd., Osoyoos* ☎ *250/495–2985* ⊕ *www.nkmipcellars.com* 🎫 *Tours C$5. Reserve tastings C$35–C$55* ⊙ *Tours May–Oct., daily 11, 1, and 3. Wineshop Apr.–May and Sept.–Oct. 9–5; June–Aug. 9–6; Nov.–Mar. 10–4.*

WHERE TO EAT

¢–$
CAFÉ
✕ **Cantaloupe Annie's Delicatessen & Tea Room.** Named for the 1930s steam engine that hauled cantaloupes to market (when Oliver was known not as a wine center but as "home of the cantaloupe"), this cute little spot has dine-in and take-out options. You can assemble a picnic of sandwiches and salads, or sit down for *spanakopita,* cabbage rolls, or a British-style meat pie. The cinnamon-scented iced tea is especially refreshing, and you can take time out from wine tasting with a slice of apple strudel, a cream scone, or some fig-ginger cake. It's also one of the few spots in the area with free Wi-Fi. ⊠ *34845 Main St. (Hwy. 97), Oliver* ☎ *250/498–2955* ⊕ *www.cantaloupeannies.com* ⊟ MC, V ⊙ *No dinner. Closed Sun. Oct.–Apr.*

$–$$
MODERN
CANADIAN
✕ **The Patio at Nk'Mip Cellars.** Set on a lovely terrace overlooking the Nk'Mip vines, this winery restaurant is a relaxing spot to rest away from the desert heat. The menu includes salads, a cheese plate, and other light meals; dishes sometimes feature aboriginal influences, such as wild salmon or bison steak. Like many winery dining rooms, this one is outdoors and closes when the weather turns. Although it's primarily a place for lunch, they serve dinner on Friday and Saturday evenings in July and August. ⊠ *1400 Rancher Creek Rd., Osoyoos* ☎ *250/495–2985*

9

⊕ *www.nkmipcellars.com* ▭ *AE, MC, V* ⊙ *Closed Oct.–Apr. No dinner May–June or Sept; no dinner Sun.–Thurs. July–Aug.*

$$$–$$$$

MODERN

CANADIAN

Fodor's Choice

★

✕ **Sonora Room Restaurant at Burrowing Owl.** Start with a picture-perfect backdrop overlooking the vineyards, add a contemporary market-driven menu matched with Burrowing Owl wines and expert service, and the result is one of the Okanagan's finest dining experiences. With its high, beamed ceilings and wood floors, the interior is winery-rustic, but the best seats are on the terrace looking out across the fields. Ask for the daily special, or try wild salmon served with shrimp risotto; duck breast paired with a roasted apple fritter and grilled vegetables; or a sophisticated vegetarian plate that might include chickpea-crusted tofu, a salad of quinoa and Brussels sprouts, and roasted cauliflower purée. The restaurant is open for lunch and dinner daily from May through mid-October but keeps more limited hours off-season; call before visiting. ✉ *100 Burrowing Owl Pl., Oliver* ☎ *250/498–0620 or 877/498–0620* ⊕ *www.bovwine.ca* ▭ *AE, MC, V.*

WHERE TO STAY

$$$$

🖬 **The Guesthouse at Burrowing Owl.** You could be forgiven for thinking you're in Tuscany while sitting on your balcony sipping a glass of Chardonnay, overlooking the vineyards, at this romantic inn. The tiled floors, creamy-beige linens, and stucco exterior say "Mediterranean," but the flat-screen TVs, fireplaces, and commodious bath and dressing areas all say "luxe." In mild weather, breakfast is served beside the saltwater pool (there's an indoor dining room, too). The excellent **Sonora Room Restaurant** (⇨ *Where to Eat, above*) is adjacent to the Guesthouse. There's no spa facility, but you can book in-room services. **Pros:** the views over the vineyards; the wines. **Cons:** if you're looking for resort-style amenities (golf, tennis), you'll have to look elsewhere. ✉ *100 Burrowing Owl Pl., Oliver* ☎ *250/498–0620 or 877/498–0620* ⊕ *www. bovwine.ca* ⤶ *10 rooms, 1 suite* ⚿ *In-room: Refrigerator, Wi-Fi. In-hotel: Restaurant, pool, laundry facilities* ▭ *AE, MC, V* ⊙ *Closed mid-Dec.–mid-Feb.* ⑩ *BP.*

$$$$

🖬 **Spirit Ridge Vineyard Resort & Spa.** Owned and operated jointly by the Osoyoos Indian Band and Bellstar Hotels & Resorts, this Southwestern-inspired resort on a vine-covered hillside east of downtown Osoyoos is designed for upscale families; all the units, from the one-, two-, and three-bedroom suites in the lodges to the one- and two-bedroom "villas" in adjacent townhouses, have kitchens and sleep at least four. Although the hotel is not on the lake, you can rent kayaks, canoes, and motorboats down the hill in the affiliated lakefront campground. The stylish **Passa Tempo Restaurant** ($$$–$$$$), open for three meals a day as well as afternoon tapas, serves contemporary fare with an emphasis on regional ingredients; nab a seat on the patio above the pool and vineyard if you can. For coffee or a quick bite, you can stop into the Market Deli ($). **Pros:** there's plenty to do, particularly with the Nk'Mip Desert Cultural Centre, Nk'Mip Cellars Winery, and Sonora Dunes Golf Course all next door. **Cons:** access to the lake through the campground is a little awkward. ✉ *1200 Rancher Creek Rd., Osoyoos* ☎ *250/495–5445 or 877/313–9463* ⊕ *www.spiritridge.ca* ⤶ *226 suites* ⚿ *In-room: Kitchen, DVD, Internet. In-hotel: 2 restaurants, bar, golf*

*course, pools, gym, spa, water sports, bicycles, laundry facilities, Wi-Fi,
some pets allowed, no-smoking rooms* ⊟ *AE, MC, V.*

$$$$ ⊞ **Veranda Beach Lakeside Cottages.** Infused with a homey "Leave it to
Beaver" vibe, this colony of brightly painted, two- to four-bedroom
cottages mixes modern comforts with vintage details like large screened
porches, 1950s-style appliances, and white picket fences. Though the
cottages are individually owned, the decor is generally upscale beachy,
with oversize chairs, large dining tables, and plenty of room for friends
and family. Set on the eastern shore of Osoyoos Lake, Veranda Beach
is in the slow-paced town of Oroville, Washington (population 1,670),
about a 20-minute drive from Osoyoos. The border crossing from Canada generally takes less than 15 minutes, but don't forget your passport.
From mid-June through mid-September, a three-night minimum stay
is usually required, but two-night rentals are available at other times.
The development will eventually include an inn, equestrian center, and
tennis courts. **Pros:** an idyllic lakefront backdrop; plenty of room for
the family. **Cons:** crossing the border; ongoing construction can be a bit
disruptive. ⊠ *229 E. Lake Rd., Oroville, WA* ⬠ *Box 3000, Oroville,
WA 98844* ☎ *509/476–4000 or 888/476–4001* ⊕ *www.verandabeach.
com* ⊅ *110 cottages* ⚬ *In-room: Kitchen, DVD, Wi-Fi. In-hotel: Restaurant, pool, gym, beachfront, water sports, laundry facilities, some
pets allowed* ⊟ *MC, V.*

$$$$ ⊞ **The Villa at Hester Creek.** All the rooms in this Mediterranean-style
B&B on the grounds of the Hester Creek winery overlook rows of
grapevines, and you can enjoy the views from your private patio. It's
not a villa in the sense of a grand home in Tuscany—it's more a block
of well-appointed rooms—but all the accommodations have king-size
beds, fireplaces, tile floors, and sizeable bathrooms. With a separate
bedroom and sitting area, La Serena is considered the "executive suite,"
though like all the rooms, it's more romantic than businesslike. **Pros:**
serene environment; spacious rooms. **Cons:** no restaurant or common
space for guests. ⊠ *13163 326th Ave., Oliver* ☎ *250/498–4435 or
866/498–4435* ⊕ *www.hestercreek.com* ⊅ *5 rooms, 1 suite* ⚬ *In-room:
Kitchen, Wi-Fi. In-hotel: No kids under 12, no-smoking rooms* ⊟ *MC,
V* ☉ *Closed Nov.–mid-Feb.* ⋈ *CP.*

SPORTS AND THE OUTDOORS

BIKING AND If you want to travel from winery to winery under your own power,
HIKING follow the **International Bicycling and Hiking Trail.** This relatively flat trail
begins at the north end of Osoyoos Lake and runs north along the Okanagan River for 18.4 km (11 mi), parallel to Highway 97 and Black
Sage Road. The trail ends at the McAlpine Bridge, between Oliver and
Okanagan Falls. None of the wineries is directly on the trail, but they're
within easy access. To get to the trail parking lot from Osoyoos, follow
Highway 97 north for 8 km (5 mi), then head east of Road 22. Trail
information is available online from Destination Osoyoos, ⊕ *www.
destinationosoyoos.com.*

9

TOFINO, UCLUELET, AND THE PACIFIC RIM PLANNER

How Much Time?

Three full days are about the minimum, once you've made the five-hour trek from Vancouver.

Off the Beaten Path

Tour operators, water taxis, and floatplanes will take you into the rain forest on trips to Meares Island and other parts of Clayoquot Sound. With Tla-ook Cultural Adventures, you can travel to a former aboriginal summer village with archaeological middens, on Echachist Island. The hot springs in Maquinna Marine Provincial Park (accessible only by boat) are popular, too, and kayakers may want to venture into the Broken Group Islands, part of Pacific Rim National Park Reserve.

Visitor Information

The Pacific Rim Visitors Centre sells permits and provides information on Pacific Rim National Park Reserve and the Tofino-Ucluelet area.

Contacts Pacific Rim Visitors Center (☎ 250/726-4212 ⊕ www.pacificrimvisitor.ca).

Kayak Trips

Several companies conduct multiday sea-kayaking trips to the coastal areas of Vancouver Island with overnights in campgrounds or lodges. Some excursions are suitable for beginners, and many trips provide an excellent chance to view orcas and other sea mammals. Gabriola Sea Kayaking, Majestic Ocean Kayaking, and Island Adventure Tours are good options.

Contacts Gabriola Sea Kayaking (☎ 250/247-0189 ⊕ www.kayaktoursbc.com). **Island Adventure Tours** (☎ 250/812-7103 or 866/812-7103 ⊕ www.islandadventuretours.com). **Majestic Ocean Kayaking** (☎ 250/726-2868 or 800/889-7644 ⊕ www.oceankayaking.com).

Local Food and Lodging

Vancouver Islanders are often credited with starting the recent "locavore" movement. Wild salmon, locally made artisanal cheeses, Pacific oysters, forest-foraged mushrooms, organic vegetables, local microbrews, and even wines and spirits from the island's family-run wineries and distilleries can all be sampled here. Restaurants are generally casual and few are "late night."

Prices for lodging and dining are relatively high for such a remote destination. Rates vary widely through the seasons, winter being the lowest: luxury lodge stays during the winter storm-watching season can cost as little as a third of regular rates.

WHAT IT COSTS IN CANADIAN DOLLARS

	¢	$	$$	$$$	$$$$
Restaurants	under C$8	C$8–C$12	C$13–C$20	C$21–C$30	over C$30
Hotels	under C$75	C$75–C$125	C$126–C$175	C$176–C$250	over C$250

Restaurant prices are for a main course at dinner, not including 5% GST and 10% liquor tax. Hotel prices are for two in a standard double in high season, excluding 10% provincial accommodation tax, service charge, and 5% GST.

By Air

The major airports on Vancouver Island are Victoria International Airport (YYJ), Nanaimo Airport (YCD), and Comox Valley Airport (YQQ). Only Orca flies regular scheduled flights into the tiny Tofino-Ucluelet Airport (YAZ) from Vancouver, Victoria, and Qualicum Beach.

A Tofino shuttle service delivers passengers to major resorts. Pacific Coastal Airlines runs charters to Tofino from Vancouver's South Terminal in summer. Seattle-based Kenmore flies from Washington State to several B.C. communities. Northwest Seaplanes runs charter flights from Renton, near Seattle, to Tofino and Ucluelet. Baxter Aviation runs seaplane charters from Vancouver, Victoria, Nanaimo, and other B.C. destinations.

Contacts Baxter Aviation (☎ 800/347–2222 ⊕ www. westcoastair.com). **Kenmore Air Harbor** (☎ 425/486–1257 or 866/435–9524 ⊕ www.kenmoreair.com). **Orca Air** (☎ 888/359–6722 ⊕ www.flyorcaair.com). **Pacific Coastal Airlines** (☎ 604/273–8666 or 800/663–2872 ⊕ www. pacific-coastal.com). **Northwest Seaplanes** (☎ 425/277–1590 or 800/690–0086 ⊕ www.nwseaplanes.com).

By Boat and Ferry

BC Ferries has frequent, year-round passenger and vehicle service to Vancouver Island: it's a 1½-hour crossing from Horseshoe Bay (a 30-minute drive north of Vancouver) to Departure Bay, 3 km (2 mi) north of Nanaimo. From here it's a two- to three-hour drive, via Port Alberni, to Ucluelet, and on to Tofino. There's also a two-hour crossing from Tsawwassen (about a 40-minute drive south of Vancouver) to Duke Point, 15 km (9 mi) south of Nanaimo; or a 1½-hour crossing from Tsawwassen to Swartz Bay (a 30-minute drive north of Victoria).

Lady Rose Marine Services takes passengers on heritage packet freighters from Port Alberni to Vancouver Island's west coast. The M. V. *Lady Rose* makes a popular 4½-hour trip to Bamfield, on the edge of Barkeley Sound opposite Ucluelet, on Tuesday, Thursday, and Saturday year-round. The M. V. *Francis Barkley* sails from Port Alberni to the Broken Group Islands and Ucluelet on Monday, Wednesday, and Friday between early June and late September.

Contacts BC Ferries (☎ 250/386–3431, 888/223–3779 in B.C. ⊕ www.bcferries.com). **Lady Rose Marine Services** (☎ 250/723–8313, 800/663–7192 reservations ⊕ www. ladyrosemarine.com).

By Car

Tofino is 314 km (195 mi) from Victoria, about a four-hour drive. If you're coming from Vancouver by ferry (to Victoria or Nanaimo), you will pass through Nanaimo and Port Alberni to access Highway 4. The Trans-Canada Highway (Highway 1) runs from Victoria to Nanaimo. The Island Highway (Highway 19) connects Nanaimo to Parksville. Highway 4 crosses the island from Parksville to Port Alberni, Ucluelet, Tofino, and Pacific Rim National Park Reserve. It's 203 km (126 mi) between Nanaimo and Tofino on a well-maintained, if twisting and mountainous, secondary highway.

Budget Car and Truck Rental and Tofino Car Rental rent vehicles at Tofino-Ucluelet Airport.

Contacts Budget Car (☎ 250/725–2060 ⊕ www. bcbudget.com). **Tofino Rental Car** (⊕ www.kayak.com).

Taxi Travel

Tofino West Coast Taxi provides service to Tofino, including airport pickup. Book in advance for night or off-hours service. The Tofino Water Taxi is a boat shuttle to Meares Island, Hot Springs Cove, and other remote offshore (including camping) sites.

Contacts Tofino West Coast Taxi (☎ 250/725–3333). **Tofino Water Taxi** (☎ 250/726–5485 or 877/726–5485 ⊕ www. tofinowatertaxi.com).

9

TOFINO, UCLUELET, AND
THE PACIFIC RIM

Updated by
Crai S. Bower

Tofino may be the birthplace of North American storm watching, but the winter's roiling waves serve as just one of many lures to the Pacific Northwest's wildest coastline. Exquisite tide pooling, surfing, and the potential to see some of the continent's largest sea mammals lure thousands of visitors to Pacific Rim National Park Reserve, sleepy Ucluelet, and Tofino, Canada's premier surfer village.

No one "happens" upon Tofino, where Highway 4 ends at the mouth of Clayoquot Sound—though today's visitors can cap their days with luxuries like glasses of exceptional B.C. wines and spa treatments. Area attractions include old-growth forests, pristine beaches, and the chance to see whales, bears, eagles, river otters, and other wildlife in a natural setting. Campers, hikers, kayakers, and sport fishermen are drawn to the region, but so are visitors simply in search of an unspeakably gorgeous location. It can be enjoyed in the comfort of a youthful hostel, a cozy B&B, a modestly priced motel, or a luxury lodge. The harbor towns of Ucluelet and Tofino are chock-a-block with character, funky shops, services, and eateries—and, in Tofino, fine-dining restaurants. Indeed, the burgeoning culinary culture on Vancouver Island definitely extends to the Pacific Rim region. Permanent residents include this coast's ancestral aboriginal people, cold-water surfers and adventure-sports types, artists and craftspeople, fishers and loggers, environmentalists—and ordinary people who've sought the laid-back life.

Tofino, the more northerly village on Clayoquot Sound, is geared to tourism. Most tour operators are based here, and most accommodations are in the immediate area. It's the proverbial end of the road—and marvelous on that basis alone. Ucluelet, a resource industry town, has embraced tourism more recently and is growing. Pacific Rim National Park Reserve stretches between the two communities.

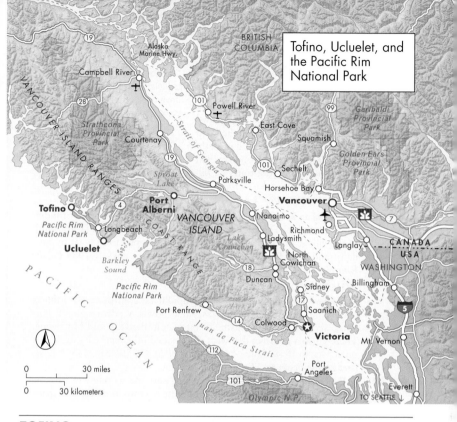

Map caption box: Tofino, Ucluelet, and the Pacific Rim National Park

TOFINO

42 km (26 mi) northwest of Ucluelet, 337 km (209 mi) northwest of Victoria.

Tofino combines the rugged Canadian frontier (the road ends here, literally) with the mellow vibe of a California surf town—think Mendocino in a toque. Cafés line the streets; foodies line up at Sobo; and a hike, bike, or paddle is right outside your door. Old-growth forest meets the relentless surf of the Pacific and explorers from age two to 102 dig into sand, tide pools, and surf. Talk to the locals and you'll be sure to hear some interesting "How I came to live in Tofino" anecdotes.

Tofino's 1,400 or so permanent residents host about a million visitors every year, but they've made what could have been a tourist trap into a funky little town with several art galleries, good restaurants, and plenty of opportunity to get out to the surrounding wilds. Reservations are recommended any time of year. While many outdoor activities are confined to spring through fall, surfing continues year-round, despite the chilly water. November through February is devoted to storm watching (best enjoyed from a cozy waterfront lodge).

For side trips, boats and floatplanes provide access to the surrounding roadless wilderness. The most popular day trip is to **Hot Springs**

Cove, where you can soak in natural rock pools. On **Meares Island,** an easy 20-minute boardwalk trail leads to trees up to 1,600 years old. The remote sand beaches of Vargas Island are popular in warm weather. On **Flores Island,** a challenging five-hour hike called Walk on the Wild Side leads through the old growth. These destinations can be reached on various adventure tours (⇨ *below*), or by water taxi (⇨ *the Planner for contact info*).

At the **Tofino Botanical Gardens,** trails wind through displays of indigenous plant life. The 12-acre waterfront site, about 2 km (1 mi) south of the village on the Pacific Rim Highway, is open from 9 AM to dusk daily, and the C$10 admission is good for three days. ⊠ *1084 Pacific Rim Hwy.* ☎ *250/725–1220* ⊕ *www.tbgf.com.*

WHERE TO EAT

¢–$
ECLECTIC

✕ **Breakers Wholefood Eatery.** This popular takeout place on Tofino's main drag serves delicious pizzas, salad bowls, sandwich wraps, burritos, and all-day breakfasts, all on an ultrahealthy and hip theme. There's also a gourmet deli with cheeses and other specialty items. It's open 7 AM to 10 PM daily. ⊠ *430 Campbell St.* ☎ *250/725–2558* ⊕ *www.breakersdeli.com* ▭ *AE, MC, V.*

$$$–$$$$
CANADIAN
★

✕ **The Pointe.** With views of the crashing surf and its renowned Pacific Northwest cuisine, the dining at the Pointe is a top-notch Tofino experience. Local bounty from the water—including oysters, shrimp, salmon, and a variety of other fish—and land (whatever's in season, such as wild mushrooms, and fresh herbs) are the ingredients in innovative but not too outlandish dishes, which are well paired with options from the award-winning wine list. Service is formal but friendly. ⊠ *The Wickaninnish Inn, Osprey La., at Chesterman Beach* ☎ *250/725–3100* ⊕ *www.wickinn.com* ▭ *AE, DC, MC, V.*

$$–$$$
ECLECTIC
★

✕ **RainCoast Café.** This small and casual-yet-chic village-center restaurant has a stellar reputation for its Asian take on local seafood and vegetarian options. Sustainably harvested or organic entrées include pan-seared halibut from the coastal waters and duck from B.C.'s Fraser Valley Lower Mainland. ⊠ *101–120 4th St.* ☎ *250/725–2215* ⊕ *www.raincoastcafe.com* ▭ *AE, MC, V* ☿ *No lunch.*

$$–$$$
SEAFOOD
Fodor's Choice
★

✕ **The Schooner on Second.** An institution in downtown Tofino, the main-floor dining room is comfortable and casually upscale. The seafood dishes change frequently, but try, if it's available, the halibut Bawden Bay: halibut fillet stuffed with Brie, crab, pine nuts, and shrimp in an apple-peppercorn brandy sauce. The Schooner is also popular for its hearty breakfasts and lunchtime sandwiches, burgers, and pastas, and the summer patio is a plus. The evening-only Schooner Upstairs is both a fine-dining restaurant and a lounge with exceptional views to Meares Island. Small plates are served in the lounge, a popular gathering place for hip locals. ⊠ *331 Campbell St.* ☎ *250/725–3444* ▭ *AE, MC, V.*

Pacific Rim Storm Watching

No one's really sure when the concept of "bad weather" morphed into "good weather," but on the tourism-friendly Pacific Rim, nasty storms are usually considered quite fine indeed.

November through March is formally storm-watching season around here, and thousands of people travel from around the world to witness the spectacularly violent weather. Veteran storm watchers are known to keep an eye on the weather channels and pack their bags quickly for Tofino or Ucluelet when storm predictions are particularly, well, grim.

Throughout the winter, but particularly during the "peak season" of December through February, as many as 15 "good storms," major blasts of Sturm und Drang, arrive per month. Winds from the ocean exceed 50 kph (30 mph) and teeming rain—even sleet or snow—arrives horizontally. Massive waves thunder onto the beaches and crash over the rocky headlands and islets, sending spray soaring. Towering evergreen trees crackle and lean; logs are tossed helter-skelter, high onto kelp-strewn beaches. Unusual storm clouds, mists, and rainbows add to the beauty. And as if the sights weren't enough, expect to hear the eerie sounds of a screaming wind, pounding surf—even the rattling of double-paned windows.

The hotels and B&Bs love the storm season because it fills rooms in what could otherwise be a bleak time of year. And it must be admitted that most storm watching takes place in considerable comfort—particularly at the luxury hotels along Cox Bay, Chesterman Beach, and MacKenzie Beach. These and other waterfront properties in the Tofino-Ucluelet region have shrewdly developed "storm-watching packages," in which treats abound (and rates tumble). Champagne on arrival, fashionable wet-weather gear, complimentary nature walks, and gourmet dinners are among the offerings. Perhaps most importantly, expect a cozy room, often with a fireplace and a soaker tub with an ocean outlook, in which you relax in security, while the outer world rages on.

Storms are known to generate communal excitement—and wonder. One Cox Bay lodge reports that staff, too, rush to the windows when things get wild. And patrons particularly enjoy watching surfers who continue to ride the waves when it snows; those crazy locals.

Serious thrill seekers take to the beaches and lookouts to experience storms firsthand. That said, conditions can be decidedly unfriendly, and visitors should remember that this is a coastline famed for its shipwrecks. Storm watchers planning on walking the Wild Coast Trail, for example, should do so with an experienced naturalist or guide. Other notable storm-watching spots include Wickaninnish Beach, with the largest swells and greatest concentration of logs and driftwood; Second Bay, where powerful swells funnel through the rocks and islets; Long Beach, famed for its rolling swells, wave-washed islands, and panoramic views; Cox Bay, said to receive the largest and most powerful waves; and Chesterman Beach, beloved for its varied conditions and outlooks.

9

CLOSE UP

Pacific Rim Festivals

MAR.: The Pacific Rim Whale Festival marks the spring migration of as many as 22,000 Pacific gray whales between Mexico and the Arctic, with craft, cultural, and food events for the whole family, from sand-sculpture building to sea creature-cookie decorating and more. (⊕ www.pacificrimwhalefestival.org)

APRIL–MAY: The Tofino Shorebird Festival celebrates the thousands of shorebirds that migrate north from Central and South America to tundra breeding grounds in Alaska. The date changes annually so check with Tourism Tofino. (⊕ www.tourismtofino.com)

JUNE: Area lodges and food and wine producers sponsor the three-day Tofino Food and Wine Festival. (⊕ www.tofinofoodandwinefestival.com)

JULY: The Pacific Rim Summer Festival is a festival of music, dance, and the arts during the first two weeks of July. (⊕ www.pacificrimarts.ca)

NOV.: The humble bivalve is celebrated during the Clayoquot Oyster Festival, with three days of outings and culinary events. (⊕ www.oystergala.com)

$$–$$$ ✕ **Shelter Restaurant.** The centrally located Shelter has a lounge and patio
SEAFOOD for casual dining and an upstairs dining room; it's popular with locals and visitors. Fare ranges from char-grilled beef burgers and a seared-chicken rice bowl to Pacific halibut and Dungeness crab. Small plates on a coastal theme, such as steamed B.C. mussels and rain-forest greens, are also a draw. ⊠ *601 Campbell St.* ☎ *250/725–3353* ▭ *AE, DC, MC, V* ⊘ *No lunch.*

$$–$$$ ✕ **Sobo.** The name, short for "sophisticated bohemian," sums up the
CANADIAN style here: a classically trained chef serving casual fare influenced by
Fodor's Choice international street food. Tapas might be halibut cheeks, sushi rice
★ pockets, or forest-mushroom risotto bullets. Mains range from cedar-plank wild salmon to mushroom enchiladas. There's talk that they'll close Monday or Tuesday in winter, so call first. There's a deli counter, too. ⊠ *311 Neil St.* ☎ *250/725–2341* ▭ *AE, MC, V* ⊘ *No dinner Oct.–May.*

$$$–$$$$ ✕ **The Wickaninnish Restaurant.** Not to be confused with the restaurant
SEAFOOD at the nearby Wickaninnish Inn, this spectacular wood-beam room
★ is right on Long Beach, in Pacific Rim National Park Reserve. Commercial signage is, by park regulation, constrained: all you'll see is the word "restaurant," alongside "Wickaninnish Interpretive Centre," on a green park sign on the Pacific Rim Highway, about 11 km (7 mi) north of Ucluelet; turn onto Wick Road and drive to the ocean. While the locally caught salmon and crab are extremely good (meat and vegetarian options are available, too)—the room itself is reason enough to make the trip. The wine list includes a selection of B.C. ice wines. Dress is casual. ⊠ *Wick Rd., Long Beach, Pacific Rim National Park Reserve* ☎ *250/726–7706* ▭ *AE, DC, MC, V* ⊘ *Closed Oct.–Feb.*

WHERE TO STAY

$$$$
Fodor's Choice
★

🏨 **Clayoquot Wilderness Resort: Outpost at Bedwell River.** Glampers (glamorous campers) arrive via floatplane or boat from all over the globe to experience one of the top wilderness resorts on the planet for three- or seven-day packages. Typical days may include a wild-salmon Eggs Benedict breakfast, ocean fishing, horseback riding through the rain forest, a little skeet shooting, or perhaps river rafting or sea kayaking, followed by a five-star dinner. Guests then return along torch-lit boardwalks to discover the antique furniture in their platform tents illuminated with candles and kerosene lanterns. But perhaps the most luxurious experience of all is spent sipping local wines in the outdoor living room before the huge river-stone fireplace. Prices are all-inclusive except for spa treatments. **Pros:** escapism at its best, with no phone or other distractions; excellent food. **Cons:** it's pricey; travel time getting here. ⊠ *Bedwell River* ☎ *250/726–8235 or 888/333–5405* ⊕ *www.wildretreat.com* ➷ *20 tents* ⚷ *In-room: No a/c, no phone, no TV. In-hotel: Restaurant, room service, bar, gym, spa, bicycles, Wi-Fi, no-smoking rooms* ⊟ *AE, MC, V* ⊘ *Closed Nov.–Apr.* ⧖ *FAP.*

$–$$$

🏨 **Inn at Tough City.** Vintage furnishings and First Nations art make this harborside inn funky, if a bit cluttered. The name is derived from Tofino's old nickname, when life here was pretty rough: it certainly isn't anymore. Guest rooms have bold colors, stained-glass windows, hardwood floors, antiques, and decks or balconies. Several have views over Tofino Harbour and Clayoquot Sound, and fireplaces. The hotel's water-view restaurant, Tough City Sushi ($$–$$$), uses fresh local seafood. **Pros:** prime Tofino location. **Cons:** the lobby is small and cluttered; front-desk staffing can be iffy. ⊠ *350 Main St., Box 8* ☎ *250/725–2021 or 877/725–2021* ⊕ *www.toughcity.com* ➷ *8 rooms* ⚷ *In-room: No a/c. In-hotel: Restaurant, bar, no-smoking rooms* ⊟ *AE, MC, V.*

$$$–$$$$
★

🏨 **Long Beach Lodge Resort.** Dramatic First Nations art, a tall granite fireplace, and expansive views of the crashing surf define the striking great room at this luxury lodge, which overlooks Cox Bay. Throughout the lodge and cabins are handcrafted furniture, exposed fir beams, and such artful details as handwoven kelp amenities baskets. Accommodations include comfortable lodge rooms and two-bedroom cottages. The chef uses local organic ingredients whenever possible for the lunch and dinner menus ($$–$$$), the shared plates served in the great room, and even for picnic lunches. As at other area lodges, winter storms are a major draw: rainwear is provided. Year-round, the lodge organizes adventure outings with preferred tour operators. **Pros:** the exceptional forested beachfront location; the restaurant; the pleasant lounge and rooms. **Cons:** the time-share complex is uncomfortably close; no spa or pool. ⊠ *1441 Pacific Rim Hwy., Box 897* ☎ *250/725–2442 or 877/844–7873* ⊕ *www.longbeachlodgeresort.com* ➷ *41 rooms, 20 cottages* ⚷ *In-room: No a/c, kitchen (some), DVD, Wi-Fi. In-hotel: Restaurant, bar, gym, some pets allowed, no-smoking rooms* ⊟ *AE, MC, V* ⧖ *CP.*

$$–$$$
★

🏨 **Middle Beach Lodge.** This longtime favorite, set on a bluff over a mile of private beach, has several options: adults-only phone- and TV-free rooms in the Lodge at the Beach; ocean-view rooms and suites, most with kitchenettes, at the Headlands; and self-contained cabins, some

9

with hot tubs, suitable for families. The style throughout defines West Coast rustic elegance, with recycled timbers, woodsy colors, and a smattering of antiques. Each lodge has an expansive common room with a floor-to-ceiling stone fireplace and far-reaching ocean views. **Pros:** it's truly secluded, with an (almost) exclusive beach; ideal for adults seeking peace and privacy, and families seeking spacious cabins at reasonable prices; there's a good dining room, too. **Cons:** a lack of amenities like room service and in-room Wi-Fi. ⊠ *400 MacKenzie Beach Rd., Box 100* ☎ *250/725–2900* ⊕ *www.middlebeach.com* ⇗ *35 rooms, 10 suites, 19 cabins* ⟑ *In-room: No a/c, no phone (some), kitchen (some), DVD (some), no TV (some), Internet (some). In-hotel: Restaurant, bar, gym, laundry facilities, Wi-Fi, some pets allowed, no-smoking rooms* ▤ *AE, MC, V* ⊗ *Restaurant closed Nov.–Mar. Sun.–Thurs. No lunch* ⦿| *CP.*

$$$–$$$$
☺
★
🔲 **Pacific Sands Beach Resort.** On 45 marvelous acres along Cox Bay, this resort with beach villas, a lodge, and waterfront suites and studios, is popular with couples, families, and groups. Cox Bay draws surfers, and the beach and adjacent forest are a walker's and nature-lover's paradise. In winter this is prime storm-watching territory. There's no on-site dining but the Long Beach Lodge restaurant is a five-minute walk down the beach. Beachfront villas have full kitchens, fireplaces, and private decks. Rain gear, and bookings for regional adventure outings, are available year-round. **Pros:** gorgeously situated on prime Cox Bay beachfront. **Cons:** no restaurant; no elevators. ⊠ *1421 Pacific Rim Hwy.* ☎ *250/725–3322 or 800/565–2322* ⊕ *www.pacificsands.com* ⇗ *22 villas, 57 suites* ⟑ *In-room: No a/c, no phone (some), kitchen, DVD, Internet (some). In-hotel: Beachfront, water sports, bicycles, children's programs (ages 7 and up), laundry facilities, Internet terminal, parking (free), some pets allowed, no-smoking rooms* ▤ *AE, DC, MC, V.*

$–$$$
🔲 **Red Crow on the Oceanfront B&B.** Serene is the word used by co-owner Stephen Ashton to describe this retreat made up of two ground-level waterfront rooms and a self-catering forest cottage at the end of a leafy lane, on Grice Bay, a few kilometers south of Tofino. You can't see the town from here, so the night sky is a star-filled canopy. The spacious king and queen guest rooms are elegantly appointed; the cottage rustic and cozy. The B&B is also close to Chesterman and MacKenzie beaches, on the opposite side of the Pacific Rim Highway, and just a five-minute walk to the Tofino Botanical Gardens. **Pros:** the discrete location just south of Tofino (note that the sign—a simple crow—is a bit hard to spot). **Cons:** no TV. ⊠ *1084 Pacific Rim Hwy.* ☎ *250/725–2275* ⊕ *www. tofinoredcrow.com* ⇗ *2 rooms, 1 cottage* ⟑ *In-room: No a/c, no phone, refrigerator, no TV, Wi-Fi. In-hotel: Water sports, bicycles, laundry service, parking (free), no-smoking rooms* ▤ *MC, V.*

¢–$$
Fodor's Choice
★
🔲 **Whalers on the Point Guesthouse.** With its harbor-view picture windows and big stone fireplace, this modern seaside hostel looks more like an upscale lodge than a backpackers' haven. It also has pretty much everything a budget traveler could want: a game room and TV lounge, a shared kitchen and living room, even surfboard storage. Accommodation is available in private rooms with shared bathrooms, family rooms (for four) with private bathrooms, and four- and six-bed dorm rooms with shared bathrooms. Advance reservations are highly recommended.

Pros: unbeatable location in Tofino; ideal for youthful, budget-minded travelers. **Cons:** no restaurant. ⊠ *81 West St., Box 296* ☎ *250/725–3443* ⊕ *www.tofinohostel.com* ⬎ *7 rooms, 11 dorm rooms.* ⟁ *In-room: No a/c, no phone, no TV. In-hotel: Kitchen, laundry facilities, Internet terminal, Wi-Fi, no-smoking rooms* ▭ *MC, V.*

$$$$
Fodor's Choice
★

⊡ **The Wickaninnish Inn.** On a rocky promontory above Chesterman Beach, with open ocean on three sides and old-growth forest as a backdrop, this cedar-sided inn has exceptional First Nations and coastal art. Every room in this Relais & Châteaux property has an ocean or beach view, balcony, soaker tub, and fireplace; the Ancient Cedars Spa gives hot-stone massages and couples massages in mind-blowing oceanfront treatment rooms; yoga classes are held daily. The Pointe Restaurant ($$$$) offers Tofino's finest dining. **Pros:** the inn is spectacularly sited on a headland at the end of a superb crescent beach. **Cons:** it's pricey; no pool. ⊠ *Osprey La., at Chesterman Beach* ☎ *250/725–3100 or 800/333–4604* ⊕ *www.wickinn.com* ⬎ *64 rooms, 11 suites* ⟁ *In-room: Safe, kitchen (some), DVD, Internet. In-hotel: Restaurant, room service, bar, gym, spa, beachfront, laundry service, Wi-Fi, some pets allowed, no-smoking rooms* ▭ *AE, DC, MC, V.*

SPORTS AND THE OUTDOORS

FISHING **Chinook Charters** leads fishing charters in the area. ⊠ *331 Main St.* ☎ *250/725–3431.*

Weigh West Marine Resort Adventure Centre operates a marina and conducts fishing charters, including saltwater fly-fishing. They can arrange accommodation, meals, and guides for kayaking, whale-watching, hot-springs tours, and surf trips. ☎ *250/725–3277 or 800/665–8922* ⊕ *www.weighwest.com.*

FLIGHTSEEING **Tofino Air** runs 20-minute flightseeing tours over outlying forests and beaches, flights to Hot Springs Cove, trips to the lakes and glaciers of Strathcona Provincial Park, and flights to Cougar Annie's Garden—a century-old wilderness homestead, once the home of the eponymous legendary local character. ☎ *250/725–4454 or 866/486–3247* ⊕ *www.tofinoair.ca.*

KAYAKING **Remote Passages** has relaxed guided paddles in sheltered waters; no expe-
★ rience is necessary. ⊠ *71 Wharf St.* ☎ *250/725–3330 or 800/666–9833* ⊕ *www.remotepassages.com.*

Tofino Sea-Kayaking Company rents kayaks, runs a kayaking school, and provides day and multiday wilderness kayaking trips. No experience is necessary. ⊠ *320 Main St.* ☎ *250/725–4222 or 800/863–4664* ⊕ *www. tofino-kayaking.com.*

SURFING The coast from Tofino south to Ucluelet is, despite perpetually chilly waters, an increasingly popular surf destination—year-round.

You can rent boards and other gear at **Live to Surf.** Jean-Paul Froment runs the business (founded in 1984 by his parents) with his sister Pascale, from the funky Outside Break commercial hub south of Tofino, which is conveniently close to the major surfing spots of Long Beach, Cox Bay, Chesterman Beach, and MacKenzie Beach. The shop sells boards, wet suits, and accessories, as well as providing rentals and lessons. ⊠ *1184 Pacific Rim Hwy.* ☎ *250/725–4464* ⊕ *www.livetosurf.com.*

9

CLOSE UP

Pacific Rim Surfing

The waters might be chilly but Tofino has skimmed its way onto the international surfing map for several reasons. The curvaceous hard-sand beaches framed by rocky headlands are smack on the open Pacific and long swells and sizeable waves are guaranteed year-round; the area is also a rain forest, providing a genuine wilderness experience; and the Tofino region, literally at the end of the road, nurtures a laid-back, even mildly anarchic lifestyle. No surprise then that a distinctive "free style" of surfing has taken root here. Many local surfers eschew competitions in favor of doing their own (surfing) thing.

Unlike warm-weather destinations, full-length wet suits are worn winter and summer alike here, and warm-climate surfers travel to Tofino to test themselves in what's considered a more challenging environment. What they find, along 20 miles of rugged shoreline between Ucluelet and Tofino, are at least four spectacular surfing beaches.

The most famous, Long Beach, together with Wickaninnish Beach, is within the Pacific Rim National Park Reserve. The next beach northward is Cox Bay, arguably the most popular—and most challenging—of the surfing beaches located outside the park. This is where the most skilled surfers launch their boards and where competitions, when they're held, take place. That said, there's space for everyone on this long and lovely stretch of forgiving sand, even for beginners. Several lodges, suitable for families, are located on Cox Bay. Chesterman Beach, the next major beach as you travel towards Tofino, is similarly picturesque and is considered the best beach for those starting out

in the sport. Finally, MacKenzie Beach is conveniently close to the town of Tofino.

Take note that the waves and rip currents here present real danger, and first-time surfers are advised to take lessons. Parks Canada employs surf guards at Long Beach in the summer. Wave-hazard signs are posted along the highway and updated daily.

The Pacific Rim Highway, running the length of the Tofino peninsula, includes a separate bike path, and almost any day of the year you'll see surfers, a long board under one arm, cycling their way to their preferred destination. Shorter surfing "skate boards" and "skim boards" are also used here. And as in every sport, surfing has its fashionistas and accessories freaks. Numerous regional surfing shops sell all kinds of add-ons, from trendy outer gear to special surf watches—even "fins" and "traction pads."

While only the most dramatic storms—and they happen here in winter—keep surfers away (and local surfers are out there when it snows), the best surfing is said to take place in spring and fall, when the waves are strong and consistent and the weather more or less cooperates. Lessons and equipment rentals are available year-round (see the individual listings in this section).

For surfing lessons at all levels, contact the **Pacific Surf School.** ✉ *430 Campbell St.* ☎ *250/725–2155 or 888/777–9961* ⊕ *www.pacificsurf-school.com.*

Storm, the Tofino Surf Shop is a hip surf shop in downtown Tofino. ✉ *444 Campbell St.* ☎ *250/725–3344* ⊕ *www.stormcanada.ca.*

Surf Sister has women-only and coed surfing lessons. ✉ *1180 Pacific Rim Hwy.* ☎ *250/725–4456 or 877/724–7873* ⊕ *www.surfsister.com.*

WHALE-
WATCHING
AND MARINE
EXCURSIONS

In March and April, an estimated 20,000 gray whales migrate along the coast here; resident grays can be seen anytime between March and October. In addition, humpback whales, sea otters, sea lions, orca, black bears, and other wildlife are increasingly seen in the area. Most whale-watching operators lead excursions along the coast and to the region's outlying islands, including Meares Island, Flores Island, and Hot Springs Cove. Services range from no-frills water-taxi drop-off to tours with experienced guides; prices vary accordingly.

Jamie's Whaling Station & Adventure Centre is one of the most established whale-watching operators on the coast. It has both Zodiacs (motorized inflatable boats) and more comfortable covered 65-foot tour boats. You can book a whole range of adventures here, including kayaking, bear watching, and trips to Meares Island or Hot Springs Cove in Maquinna Marine Provincial Park in Clayoquot Sound. Jamie's operates from February 15 to October 31. ✉ *606 Campbell St.* ☎ *250/725–3919 or 800/667–9913* ⊕ *www.jamies.com.*

★ **Remote Passages Marine Excursions,** a well-established operator, runs whale-watching, bear-watching, and other wildlife-viewing trips with an ecological and educational focus using Zodiacs and covered boats. ✉ *71 Wharf St.* ☎ *250/725–3330 or 800/666–9833* ⊕ *www.remotepas-sages.com.*

★ With **Tla-ook Cultural Adventures** you can paddle a traditional Nuu-chah-nulth dugout canoe with a First Nations guide. Trips go to traditional native territory on Meares Island and to Echachist Island, an early Nuu-chah-nulth summering territory. The latter is an all-day trip featuring a seafood feast in an old summer village dotted with historic middens. ☎ *250/725–2656 or 877/942–2663* ⊕ *www.tlaook.com.*

The **Whale Centre** has a maritime museum with a 40-foot whale skeleton you can study while waiting for your boat. The company runs whale-watching, hot springs, and bear- and bird-watching tours, year-round. ✉ *411 Campbell St.* ☎ *250/725–2132 or 888/474–2288* ⊕ *www. tofinowhalecentre.com.*

SHOPPING

In a traditional longhouse, the magnificent **Eagle Aerie Gallery** houses a collection of prints, paintings, and carvings by the renowned B.C. artist Roy Henry Vickers. ✉ *350 Campbell St.* ☎ *250/725–3235.*

House of Himwitsa sells First Nations crafts, jewelry, and clothing. The complex also has a seafood restaurant and lodge rooms. ✉ *300 Main St.* ☎ *250/725–2017 or 800/899–1947.*

Photographs, paintings, carvings, pottery, and jewelry by local artists are available at **Reflecting Spirit Gallery.** ⊠ *411 Campbell St.* ☎ *250/725–2472* ⊕ *www.reflectingspirit.ca.*

Shorewind Gallery is a lovely store specializing in nonnative West Coast fine art, including paintings, sculpture, and other handcrafted objects and jewelry. ⊠ *120 Fourth St.* ☎ *250/725–1222.*

Wildside Booksellers has an extensive selection of books and kites and houses an espresso bar. ⊠ *320 Main St.* ☎ *250/725–4222.*

SPAS

Sacred Stone Spa. A small spa above the harbor in downtown Tofino, Sacred Stone does several types of massages. ⊠ *421 Main St.* ☎ *250/725–3341* ⊕ *www.sacredstone.ca.*

UCLUELET

295 km (183 mi) northwest of Victoria.

Ucluelet, which in the Nuu-chah-nulth First Nations language means "people with a safe landing place," along with the towns of Bamfield and Tofino, serves the Pacific Rim National Park Reserve. A longtime resource industry town, Ucluelet is less visited than Tofino and has a more relaxed pace. Despite a growing number of crafts shops and B&Bs, it's still more of a fishing village than an ecotourism retreat. The Black Rock Resort, though, competes with Tofino's upscale dining-and-lodging market.

As in Tofino, whale-watching is an important draw, though visitors also come in the off-season to watch the dramatic winter storms. It's also a regional base for sportfishing and kayaking to the Broken Group Islands, in the Pacific Rim National Park Reserve. Various charter companies also take boats to greet the 20,000 gray whales that pass close to Ucluelet on their migration to the Bering Sea every March and April.

Ucluelet is the starting point for the **Wild Pacific Trail** (⊕ *www.wildpacifictrail.com*), a hiking path that winds along the coast and through the rain forest; it's a work in progress that will eventually link Ucluelet to the Pacific Rim National Park Reserve. A 2.7-km (1.7-mi) loop starts at **He-Tin-Kis Park** off Peninsula Road and can also be reached from the **Amphitrite Point Lighthouse** at the end of Coast Guard Road. Another 4-km (2½-mi) stretch starts at **Big Beach** at the end of Matterson Road and continues to the bike path just outside Ucluelet.

WHERE TO EAT AND STAY

$–$$
CONTEMPORARY

✕ **Matterson House.** In a tiny 1931 cottage with seven tables and an outdoor deck, husband-and-wife team Sandy and Jennifer Clark serve generous portions of seafood, burgers, pasta, and filling standards such as prime rib and veal cutlets. It's simple food, prepared well with fresh local ingredients; everything, including soups, desserts, and the wonderful bread, is homemade. The wine list has local wines worth trying. ⊠ *1682 Peninsula Rd.* ☎ *250/726–2200* ▭ MC, V.

$$$–$$$$

⊞ **A Snug Harbour Inn.** Set on a cliff above the Pacific, this beachfront couples-oriented B&B has some of the most dramatic views anywhere. The rooms, all with fireplaces, private balconies or decks, and whirlpool baths, are decorated in a highly individual style. The Lighthouse room winds up three levels for great views, the Valhalla has a nautical theme, and the Atlantis room is the largest, with dramatic First Nations art and a Jacuzzi tub for two. Eagles nest nearby, and a staircase leads down to a rocky beach. Two rooms in a separate cottage, one of which is wheelchair accessible, have forest views. **Pros:** friendly vibe. **Cons:** somewhat remote Ucluelet location; no on-site dining; no children allowed, so definitely not for families. ⊠ *460 Marine Dr., Box 318* ☎ *250/726–2686 or 888/936–5222* ⊕ *www.awesomeview.com* ⤴ *6 rooms* ♿ *In-room: No a/c, refrigerator (some), DVD, Wi-Fi. In-hotel: Bicycles, some pets allowed, no kids under 16, no-smoking rooms* ▤ *MC, V* ⦿*BP.*

$$$$ ▢ **Black Rock Oceanfront Resort.** On a rocky ledge at the edge of a shal-
★ low inlet, the Black Rock Resort is the first upscale, full-service resort to appear in the Ucluelet area. The views over the Pacific Ocean from the windows and balconies are dramatic. The hotel's modern interior combines glass, rock, steel, and wood to create an airy yet comfortable-and-welcoming aura, and each of the rooms has a gas fireplace. There are several in-house dining options: the Float Lounge serves cocktails, small plates, and views of the water and shoreline; Fetch Restaurant sits on a promontory above the sea; the Wine Cellar, which can be rented for private events or dinners, has floor-to-ceiling windows from which you can see surging waves. The property also has two "hot pools"—smaller than a swimming pool but larger than a Jacuzzi. Drift Spa completes the pampering. **Pros:** gorgeous backdrop; überchic aesthetic. **Cons:** limited beach access; austere design is not for everyone. ⊠ *596 Marine Drive* ☎ *250/726–4800 or 877/762–5011* ⊕ *www.blackrockresort.com* ⤴ *71 rooms, 62 suites* ♿ *In-room: Kitchen, Wi-Fi. In-hotel: Restaurant, bar, gym, spa* ▤ *AE, DC, MC, V* ⦿*CP.*

$–$$$ ▢ **Canadian Princess Resort.** You can book a cabin on this 1932 steam-powered survey ship moored at Ucluelet's marina. Though hardly opulent, the staterooms are comfortable, with one to four berths and shared bathrooms. The captain's cabin is a full suite with a private bath. The resort's shoreside rooms are bigger, if less atmospheric, with private entrances, contemporary furnishings, and patios or balconies; a few have fireplaces, and some are large enough to sleep six. Most people come here to fish or whale-watch—the resort is home to the area's largest charter company, Oak Bay Marine Group. **Pros:** ideal downtown Ucluelet location; laid-back character. **Cons:** shared bathrooms; large fishing cruisers sometimes fire up their engines at an early hour. ⊠ *1943 Peninsula Rd., Box 939* ☎ *250/726–7771 or 800/663–7090* ⊕ *www. canadianprincess.com* ⤴ *46 shoreside rooms, 27 shipboard cabins without bath, 1 suite* ♿ *In-room: No a/c, no phone, no TV (some). In-hotel: Restaurant, bar, parking (free), some pets allowed, no-smoking rooms* ▤ *AE, DC, MC, V* ⊗ *Closed mid-Sept.–mid-Mar.*

$$ ▢ **Majestic Ocean B&B.** Longtime kayaking-business operator Tracy Eeftink and her husband Ted have three fetching ground-level rooms opening onto Ucluelet Harbour. All have private entrances from a patio seating area and all feature handcrafted cedar furniture and local artwork. A sitting room has a fireplace, breakfast area, TV, and computer. **Pros:** it's on Ucluelet Harbour, adjacent to its own ocean-kayaking

outfit (Majestic Ocean). **Cons:** a long walk into town; no nearby restaurant. ⊠ *1183 Helen Rd.* ☎ *250/726–2828 or 800/889–7644* ⊕ *www. majesticoceanbb.ca* ↝ *3 rooms* ⚭ *In-room: No a/c, no phone, no TV. In-hotel: Laundry facilities, Internet terminal, Wi-Fi, parking (free), some pets allowed, no-smoking rooms* ☰ *AE, MC, V.*

SPORTS AND THE OUTDOORS

ECOTOURS **Long Beach Nature Tours.** A great way to learn about the area's natural history and ecosystems is on a guided walk or hike with this ecotour group. Led by Bill McIntyre, former chief naturalist at Pacific Rim National Park Reserve, and his team of naturalist–biologists, half- and full-day outings range from easy to challenging and include hikes through old-growth forest, beach, and headlands, and storm watching during fall and winter. Following safe routes and cliff-top trails, you can experience the fury of winter storms and relive the experience of shipwrecked mariners along this shoreline dubbed "the Graveyard of the Pacific." ☎ *250/656–1236* ⊕ *www.oceansedge.bc.ca.*

★ The **Canadian Princess Resort** is part of the prominent Oak Bay Marine Group and has 10 comfortable fishing and whale-watching cruisers with heated cabins and bathrooms. Fishing trips go out several times a day in pursuit of salmon, halibut, and various bottom fish. The charteres are relatively inexpensive. ⊠ *1943 Peninsula Rd.* ☎ *250/726–7771 or 800/663–7090* ⊕ *www.canadianprincess.com.*

Island West Fishing Resort specializes in fishing charters and also has floatplane sightseeing tours in the Ucluelet area. ⊠ *Foot of Bay St.* ☎ *250/726–7515* ⊕ *www.islandwestresort.com.*

KAYAKING Experienced guides with **Majestic Ocean Kayaking** can take you out to explore the clear waters surrounding the Broken Group Islands and Barkley Sound, as well as Clayoquot Sound and Deer Group Islands. Trips range from three hours to six days. A whale-watching trip for experienced paddlers goes to outside waters. ⊠ *1167 Helen Rd.* ☎ *250/726–2868 or 800/889–7644* ⊕ *www.oceankayaking.com.*

SURFING Ucluelet, like Tofino, is a popular year-round surf destination, though the water is chilly so bring your full dry suit any time of year. **Inner Rhythm Surf Camp** has lessons, rentals, surf camps, and surf tours to remote beaches. ⊠ *1685 Peninsula Rd.* ☎ *250/726–3456 or 877/393–7873* ⊕ *www.innerrhythm.net.*

WHALE-
WATCHING **Jamie's Whaling Station** has guaranteed sightings: if you don't see a whale on your first trip, you can take another at no charge. You can book a range of adventures, including kayaking and hot-springs tours. They're open March 15 through October 31. ⊠ *168 Fraser La., on waterfront promenade* ☎ *250/726–7444 or 877/726–7444* ⊕ *www.jamies.com.*

Subtidal Adventures specializes in whale-watching and nature tours to the Broken Group Islands; you can choose a Zodiac or a 36-foot former coast-guard rescue boat. ⊠ *1950 Peninsula Rd.* ☎ *250/726–7336 or 877/444–1134* ⊕ *www.subtidaladventures.com.*

9

PACIFIC RIM NATIONAL PARK RESERVE

Fodor's Choice *105 km (63 mi) west of Port Alberni, 9 km (5 mi) south of Tofino.*

★ This national park has some of Canada's most stunning coastal and rain-forest scenery, abundant wildlife, and a unique marine environment. It comprises three separate units—Long Beach, the Broken Group Islands, and the West Coast Trail—for a combined area of 123,431 acres, and stretches 130 km (81 mi) along Vancouver Island's west coast. The **Pacific Rim Visitor Centre** (⊠ *Tofino-Ucluelet junction on Hwy. 4* ☎ *250/726–4212* ⊕ *www.pacificrimvisitor.ca*) is open daily mid-March through August, from 9 AM to 7 PM, and until mid-October, 9 AM to 5 PM. General adult fee for entry to the park is C$7.80 in 2010. Park users must display a permit, available from the visitor center and valid for 24 hours, in their vehicle.

☾ The **Long Beach** unit gets its name from a 16-km (10-mi) strip of hard-packed sand strewn with driftwood, shells, and the occasional Japanese, glass fishing float. Long Beach is the most accessible part of the park and can get busy in summer. People come in the off-season to watch winter storms and to see migrating whales in early spring.

A first stop for many Pacific Rim National Park visitors, the **Wickaninnish Interpretive Centre** (⊠ *Hwy. 4* ☎ *250/726–7721*) is on the ocean's edge about 16 km (10 mi) north of Ucluelet. It's a great place to learn about the wilderness; theater programs and exhibits provide information about the park's marine ecology and rain-forest environment. It's open daily mid-March to mid-October 10 to 6. The fabulous, high-end Wickaninnish Restaurant is next door. The 100-plus islands of the **Broken Group Islands** archipelago can be reached only by boat. The islands and their clear waters are alive with sea lions, seals, and whales, and the inner waters are good for kayaking. Guided kayak and charter-boat tours are available from Ucluelet, Bamfield, and Port Alberni.

The third element of the park, the **West Coast Trail**, runs along the coast from Bamfield to Port Renfrew. It's an extremely rugged 75-km (47-mi) trail for experienced hikers; it can be traveled only on foot, takes an average of six days to complete, and is open from May 1 to September 30. A quota system helps the park manage the number of hikers on the trail, and reservations are recommended between mid-June and mid-September, though some spaces are available on a first-come, first-served basis at each end of the trail during this time. A number of fees apply: C$24.75 for a reservation, C$128.75 for a hiker's permit, and C$30 for two ferry crossings. ☎ *800/435–5622, 604/435–5622 in Greater Vancouver, 250/387–1642 international* ⊕ *www.pacificrimvisitor.ca.*

SPORTS AND THE OUTDOORS

Ecosummer Expeditions has guided hiking trips along the West Coast Trail in Pacific Rim National Park. (☎ *250/674–0102 or 800/465–8884* ⊕ *www.ecosummer.com*).

Travel Smart

GETTING HERE AND AROUND

Most visitors to British Columbia arrive by car via the I–5 interstate highway (called Highway 99 in Canada) or fly into the province's main airport in Vancouver. For visitors who plan to rent a car, well-maintained roads and highways make it easy to drive to destinations such as Victoria, Ucluelet and Tofino on Vancouver Island, Whistler (two hours outside Vancouver), or the Okanagan. Public transportation in Vancouver is accessible and well run.

■ AIR TRAVEL

Flying time to Vancouver is 5½ hours from New York, 6½ hours from Montréal, 4 hours from Chicago, and 2½ hours from Los Angeles.

Security measures at Canadian airports are similar to those in the United States. Be sure you're not carrying anything that could be construed as a weapon: a letter opener, Swiss Army knife, or a toy weapon, for example.

Passengers departing from Vancouver must pay an airport-improvement fee before they can board their plane; however, this fee is now included directly in the cost of tickets, simplifying the process. The fee is C$5 for flights within British Columbia and the Yukon, C$15 for all other flights.

Airlines and Airports Airline and Airport Links.com (⊕ www.airlineandairportlinks.com) has links to many of the world's airlines and airports.

Airline Security Issues Transportation Security Administration (⊕ www.tsa.gov) has answers for almost every question that might come up.

AIRPORTS

The major airport is Vancouver International Airport (YVR), in the suburb of Richmond about 16 km (10 mi) south of downtown Vancouver.

Vancouver International Airport is Canada's second-busiest airport, but it's easy to get around this spacious facility, and lineups and congestion are rare. Extensive duty-free shopping, dining, spa, children's play areas, and other services are available, plus free Wi-Fi. Regular courtesy shuttles run between the Main and South Terminals.

Vancouver Island is served by Victoria International Airport. Otherwise, there are domestic airports in or near many towns on the island, including Campbell River, Comox, and Nanaimo. Smaller communities without airports are served by floatplanes.

GROUND TRANSPORTATION

There are many options for getting downtown from Vancouver International Airport, a drive of about 20 to 45 minutes, depending on traffic. If you're driving, go over the Arthur Laing Bridge and north on Granville Street (also signposted as Highway 99). Signs direct you to Vancouver City center.

The fastest and cheapest way to travel downtown or to points en route is via the Canada Line, the newest addition to Vancouver's rapid-transit system, which runs downtown from the Vancouver International Airport in 25 minutes. The station is inside the airport, on level four, between the domestic and international terminals. The trains, which are fully wheelchair accessible and allow plenty of room for luggage, leave every six minutes from the airport and every three minutes from downtown Vancouver. Fares are C$3.75 each way.

Taxi stands are in front of the terminal building on domestic- and international-arrivals levels. The taxi fare to downtown is about C$35. Area cab companies include Black Top and Yellow.

Limousine service from LimoJet Gold costs about C$70 to C$80 one way; they also offer service from the airport to Whistler for C$300 each way.

Taxis and Shuttles Black Top Cabs (☏ 604/681–2181). **LimoJet Gold** (☏ 604/273–1331 or 800/278–8742 ⊕ www. limojetgold.com). **TransLink** (☏ 604/953–3333 ⊕ www.translink.ca). **Yellow Cab** (☏ 604/681–1111).

FLIGHTS

Of the U.S. airlines, American, Continental, Delta, Northwest, and United fly to Vancouver. Among smaller carriers, Horizon Air (an affiliate of Alaska Airlines) flies to Vancouver and Victoria from many western U.S. cities. From the United Kingdom, Air Canada and British Airways fly to Vancouver. Canadian charter line Air Transat flies to Vancouver, usually at lower rates than the other airlines offer.

Within Canada, regularly scheduled flights to every major city and to most smaller cities are available on Air Canada. WestJet, a regional carrier, serves most Canadian cities.

Airline Contacts Air Canada (☏ 888/247–2262 ⊕ www.aircanada.ca). **Alaska Airlines** (☏ 800/252–7522 ⊕ www.alaskaair.com). **American Airlines** (☏ 800/433–7300 ⊕ www. aa.com). **Continental Airlines** (☏ 800/523–3273 for U.S. and Mexico reservations, 800/231–0856 for international reservations ⊕ www.continental.com). **Delta Airlines** (☏ 800/221–1212 ⊕ www.delta.com). **Northwest Airlines** (☏ 800/225–2525 ⊕ www.nwa. com). **United Airlines** (☏ 800/864–8331 for U.S. reservations, 800/538–2929 for international reservations ⊕ www.united.com). **US Airways** (☏ 800/428–4322 for U.S. and Canada reservations, 800/622–1015 for international reservations ⊕ www.usairways.com). **WestJet Airlines** (☏ 800/538–5696 ⊕ www. westjet.com).

▌ BIKE TRAVEL

Despite British Columbia's demanding landscape, bicycle travel is extremely popular. One of the most spectacular

routes follows the abandoned 600-km-long (370-mi-long) Kettle Valley Railway through the mountains of the B.C. interior; Tourism Kelowna has details. Gentler options include the 100-km (62-mi) Galloping Goose Regional Trail near Victoria and the rolling hills of the Gulf Islands. Cycle Vancouver Island has information about bike touring on Vancouver Island and the Gulf Islands. Mountain biking enthusiasts gravitate toward the trails on Vancouver's North Shore Mountains and up at Whistler.

Bike Maps Cycle Vancouver Island (⊕ www. cyclevancouverisland.ca). **Galloping Goose Regional Trail** (☏ 250/478–3344 ⊕ www.crd. bc.ca/parks). **Tourism Kelowna** (☏ 250/861–1515 or 800/663–4345 ⊕ tourismkelowna. com). **TransLink, the Greater Vancouver Transit Authority** (☏ 604/953–3333 ⊕ www. translink.ca/en/Cycling/Cycling-Routes.aspx).

BIKES IN FLIGHT

Most airlines accommodate bikes as luggage, provided they are dismantled and boxed; check with individual airlines about packing requirements. Some airlines sell bike boxes, which are often free at bike shops, for about $20 (bike bags can be considerably more expensive). International travelers often can substitute a bike for a piece of checked luggage at no charge; otherwise, the cost is about $100. Most U.S. and Canadian airlines charge $50–$100 each way, though fees are increasing steadily. Many also ask that the bike be preregistered when you book your ticket.

▌ BOAT AND FERRY TRAVEL

Ferries play a central role in British Columbia's transportation network. In some areas, ferries provide the only access (besides floatplanes) into and out of communities. For visitors, ferries are one of the best ways to get a sense of the region and its ties to the sea. BC Ferries operates one of the largest ferry fleets in the world, serving about 40 ports of call on B.C.'s west coast. The ferries carry all vehicles as well as bicycles and foot passengers.

Reservations are optional between Vancouver and Vancouver Island and on most sailings between Vancouver and the Southern Gulf Islands. Most other services do not accept reservations and load vehicles on a first-come, first-served basis.

BC Ferries operates two major ferry terminals outside Vancouver. From Tsawwassen to the south (an hour's drive from downtown), ferries sail to Swartz Bay near Victoria, to Nanaimo on Vancouver Island, and to the Gulf Islands (the small islands between the mainland and Vancouver Island). From Horseshoe Bay (45 minutes north of downtown), ferries sail to the Sunshine Coast and to Nanaimo on Vancouver Island. Vehicle reservations on Vancouver to Victoria and Nanaimo and Vancouver to the Sunshine Coast routes are optional and cost C$15 to C$17.50 in addition to the fare. There's no extra charge for reservations on Gulf Island routes.

There are several options for getting to Vancouver Island from Washington State: Black Ball Transport operates the *MV Coho*, a car ferry, daily year-round between Port Angeles, Washington, and Victoria's Inner Harbour. The car and passenger fare is US$50; bikes are carried for US$5.25. The *Victoria Clipper* runs daily, year-round passenger-only service between downtown Seattle and downtown Victoria. Sailings take about 3 hours, and the one-way fare from mid-May to late September is US$87; bicycles are carried for an extra US$10, bike reservations are recommended. Between late June and early September, the Victoria Express provides daily passenger-only service between Port Angeles, Washington, and downtown Victoria. From late May to late June, and early to mid-September, the service runs Friday to Monday only. Sailings cost US$12.50 (US$5.50 for bikes or kayaks) and take an hour. Washington State Ferries runs a car ferry daily from April through December from Anacortes,

Washington, to Sidney (some runs make stops at different San Juan Islands), about 30 km (18 mi) north of Victoria. Bikes are welcome and the sailing takes about three hours. One-way high-season fares are US$53.70 for a vehicle and driver.

Between late June and late September, Victoria San Juan Cruises offer narrated foot-passenger day trips from Bellingham, Washington, to Victoria with a salmon barbecue dinner on the return trip; Victoria city tours, the Butchart Gardens trips, tea at the Empress, and overnight packages are also available. One-way high-season fare is US$59; a return trip with dinner is US$99.

Boat and Ferry Information BC Ferries (☎ 250/386–3431, 888/223–3779 in B.C., Alberta, and Washington State ⊕ www. bcferries.com). **Black Ball Transport** (☎ 250/386–2202 or 360/457–4491 ⊕ www. ferrytovictoria.com). **Victoria Clipper** (☎ 206/ 448–5000, 250/382–8100, or 800/888–2535 ⊕ www.clippervacations.com/). **Victoria Express** (☎ 360/452–8088 or 250/361–9144 ⊕ www.victoriaexpress.com). **Victoria San Juan Cruises** (☎ 360/738–8099 or 800/443–4552 ⊕ www.whales.com). **Washington State Ferries** (☎ 206/464–6400 or 888/808–7977 ⊕ www.wsdot.wa.gov/ferries).

▌BUS TRAVEL

Greyhound serves most towns in the province and provides frequent service on popular runs. IslandLink Bus operates bus service to most towns on Vancouver Island and connects with BC Ferries at Departure Bay in Nanaimo. The same company operates AirportLink, Valley-Link, and WhistlerLink buses, which serve the Vancouver International Airport, the Fraser Valley, and Whistler respectively. Pacific Coach Lines operates frequent service between Victoria and Vancouver (both downtown and the airport) on BC Ferries. The Tofino Bus provides daily service from Vancouver, Vancouver Airport, Victoria, Nanaimo, and points en route to Port Alberni, Tofino, and Ucluelet. From

May to September, the West Coast Trail Express shuttles hikers from Victoria and Nanaimo to the trailheads of the West Coast and Juan de Fuca trails. All bus companies ban smoking, and most long-distance buses have washrooms on board. Some long-haul buses even play videos. Greyhound's North America Discovery Pass provides unlimited bus travel for 7, 15, 30, or 60 days anywhere in Canada or the United States served by Greyhound. The passes can be purchased at U.S. bus stations (if your travel starts in the United States); Canadian and overseas residents must buy them online two weeks in advance. These passes are an excellent value for travelers who want to wander the highways and byways of the country, packing many miles into a relatively short period of time. For occasional, short day trips, however, they're hardly worth it.

Bus terminals in major cities and even in many smaller ones are usually efficient operations with service all week and plenty of agents on hand to handle ticket sales. In villages and some smaller towns, the bus station is simply a counter in a local convenience store, gas station, or snack bar. Getting information on schedules beyond the local ones is sometimes difficult in these places.

In major bus terminals, most bus lines accept at least some of the major credit cards. Some smaller lines require cash or take only Visa or MasterCard. To buy a ticket in really small centers, it's best to use cash. You should plan on picking up your tickets at least 45 minutes before the bus's scheduled departure time.

Contacts Greyhound Lines ☏ 800/661–8747 in Canada, 800/231–2222 in U.S., 214/849–8100 outside the U.S. and Canada ⊕ www.greyhound.ca or www.discoverypass.com. **IslandLinkBus** (⊕ www.islandlinkbus.com). **Pacific Coach Lines** (☏ 604/662–8074 or 800/661–1725 ⊕ www.pacificcoach.com). **Tofino Bus** (☏ 250/725–2871 or 866/986–3466 ⊕ www.tofinobus.com). **West Coast Trail Express** (☏ 250/477–8700 or 888/999–2288 ⊕ www.trailbus.com).

▌ CAR TRAVEL

Canada's highway system is excellent. It includes the Trans-Canada Highway, or Highway 1, the longest highway in the world—running about 8,000 km (5,000 mi) from Victoria, British Columbia, to St. John's, Newfoundland, using ferries to bridge coastal waters at each end. The second-longest Canadian highway, the Yellowhead Highway (Highway 16), follows a route from the Pacific Coast and over the Rockies to the prairies. North of the population centers, roads become fewer and less developed.

Within British Columbia itself, the Trans-Canada Highway (Highway 1), Highway 3, and the Coquihalla Highway (Highway 5) offer easy access to the Okanagan. Speed limits range between 30 mph (50 kph) in cities to a maximum of 60 mph (100 kph) on highways. The Sea-to-Sky Highway between Vancouver and Whistler is full of twists and turns, and although it was upgraded and widened prior to the 2010 Winter Olympics, drivers should still exercise caution. Landslides occasionally occur along this highway, also noted for its spectacular scenery along Howe Sound.

FROM THE UNITED STATES

Drivers must carry owner registration and proof-of-insurance coverage, which is compulsory in Canada. The Canadian Non-Resident Inter-Provincial Motor Vehicle Liability Insurance Card, available from any U.S. insurance company, is accepted as evidence of financial responsibility in Canada. If you're driving a car that is not registered in your name, carry a letter from the owner that authorizes your use of the vehicle.

The main entry point into British Columbia from the United States by car is on Interstate 5 at Blaine, Washington, 48 km (30 mi) south of Vancouver. Three highways enter British Columbia from the east: Highway 1, or the Trans-Canada Highway; Highway 3, or the Crowsnest Highway, which crosses southern British

Columbia; and Highway 16, the Yellow-head Highway, which runs through northern British Columbia from the Rocky Mountains to Prince Rupert. From Alaska and the Yukon, take the Alaska Highway (from Fairbanks) or the Klondike Highway (from Skagway or Dawson City).

Border-crossing procedures are usually quick and simple (⇨ *Passports and Visas*). Most British Columbia land-border crossings are open 24 hours; exceptions are the crossing at Aldergrove and smaller border posts in eastern British Columbia, which are typically open 8 AM to midnight. The Interstate 5 border crossing at Blaine, Washington (also known as the Douglas, or Peace Arch, border crossing), is one of the busiest border crossings between the United States and Canada. Weekend and holiday traffic tends to be heaviest; listen to local radio traffic reports for information about wait times. The Canada Border Services Agency posts estimated wait times on its Web site.

Insurance Information Canada Border Services Agency (⊕ *www.cbsa-asfc.gc.ca*). **Insurance Corporation of British Columbia** (☎ *604/661–2800 or 800/663–1466* ⊕ *www. icbc.com*).

GASOLINE

Gasoline prices vary significantly from neighborhood to neighborhood in British Columbia. Expect to pay at least C$1 per liter (1 gallon = 3.78 liters), with prices slightly higher in Vancouver. In B.C., the price includes 10 cents in federal excise tax, a 5% goods and services tax, 14.5 cents in provincial taxes (including a gradually increasing carbon emissions tax), and in the Greater Vancouver region, 15 cents per liter of local transit tax.

Most gas stations are self-serve and most are automated, so you can pay at the pump using a credit card; major credit cards are widely accepted. A local law requires customers to pay for the gas before it's dispensed, so if you want to pay cash you'll have to estimate how much you'll need. It's not customary to tip attendants.

PARKING

More than 300 parking lots (above- and belowground) are available in Vancouver. Underground parking prices downtown typically run between C$3 to C$5 per hour, depending on location. Parking meters are in effect 9 AM to 8 PM daily. On-street parking can be hard to find downtown, especially during workdays and on weekends. Read signs carefully to avoid being towed or fined. Fines can run between C$30 and C$75, depending on location.

ROAD CONDITIONS

Snow tires are recommended when traveling the Sea-to-Sky Highway between Vancouver and Whistler or driving on the Coquihalla or Trans-Canada highways during the winter. Keep in mind that speed limits are expressed in kilometers, not miles, in Canada.

ROADSIDE EMERGENCIES

In case of emergency anywhere in B.C., call 911; if you are not connected immediately, dial "0" and ask for the operator. The British Columbia Automobile Association (BCAA) provides 24-hour roadside assistance to AAA and CAA members.

Emergency Services BCAA (☎ *604/268–5555, 800/663–1956 nonemergencies, 604/293–2222 or 800/222–4357 emergencies* ⊕ *www.bcaa.com*).

RULES OF THE ROAD

In Canada your own driver's license is acceptable. By law, you're required to wear seat belts and to use infant seats. In B.C., babies under the age of one and under 20 pounds must travel in a rear-facing infant seat and not in a front seat with an active air bag; children over one year old and between 20 and 40 pounds need to be secured in child seats, while kids up to age nine or four-foot-nine inches tall (whichever comes first) must use booster seats. These rules don't apply in bus or taxi travel. Motorcycle and bicycle helmets are mandatory. Right turns are permitted on red signals. Speed limits, given in kilometers, are usually within the 50–100 kph

(30–60 mph) range outside the cities. The BC Automobile Association (BCAA) has details about regulations in B.C.

WINTER DRIVING

In coastal areas, the mild damp climate contributes to roadways that are frequently wet. Winter snowfalls are not common (generally only once or twice a year), but when snow does fall, traffic grinds to a halt and the roadways become treacherous and stay that way until the snow melts.

Tire chains, studs, or snow tires are essential equipment for winter travel in the north and in mountain areas such as Whistler. If you're planning to drive into high elevations, be sure to check the weather forecast beforehand. Even the main-highway mountain passes can be forced to close because of snow conditions. The Ministry of Transportation Web site has up-to-date road reports.

Road Reports BC Ministry of Transportation (⊕ www.drivebc.ca). **BCAA** (☎ 604/268–5555, 800/663–1956 ⊕ www.bcaa.com).

CAR RENTAL

When you reserve a car, ask about cancellation penalties, taxes, drop-off charges (if you're planning to pick up the car in one city and leave it in another), and surcharges (for being under or over a certain age, for additional drivers, or for driving across state or country borders or beyond a specific distance from your point of rental). All these things can add substantially to your costs. Request car seats and extras such as GPS when you book.

Rates are sometimes—but not always—better if you book in advance or reserve through a rental agency's Web site. There are other reasons to book ahead, though: for popular destinations, during busy times of the year, or to ensure that you get certain types of cars (vans, SUVs, exotic sports cars).

■**TIP→** Make sure that a confirmed reservation guarantees you a car. Agencies sometimes overbook, particularly for busy weekends and holiday periods.

Renting a car is a good option if you're getting out of the cities. If you plan to spend most or all your time in downtown Vancouver, you won't need a car: parking can be difficult to secure and most attractions are within walking distance or a short cab or bus ride away. Downtown Victoria is even more compact. Rates in Vancouver begin at about C$40 a day or C$230 a week, usually including unlimited mileage. Car rentals in B.C. also incur a 5% Goods-and-Services Tax and a 7% sales tax (on July 1, 2010, these two taxes will be replaced with a 12% Harmonized Sales Tax), as well as a C$1.50-per-day road tax, and a vehicle-licensing fee of C$0.84 per day. An additional 17% Concession Recovery Fee (also known as a premium location fee), an extra fee charged by the airport authority for retail space in the terminal, is levied at airport locations. Some companies located near Vancouver International Airport offer free customer pick-up and drop-off at the airport, enabling you to avoid the latter fee. Some companies also tack on other fees, such as an Energy Recovery Fee, or a Vehicle Maintenance Fee, of about C$1 per day. If you prefer a manual-transmission car, check whether the rental agency of your choice offers stick shifts; some companies don't in Canada.

Car-rental rates vary by supply and demand, so it pays to shop around and to reserve well in advance. Vancouver's airport and downtown locations usually have the best selection. When comparing costs, take into account any mileage charges: an arrangement with unlimited mileage is usually the best deal if you plan to tour the province.

Additional drivers are charged about C$10 per day. Child seats and booster seats, which are required for children up to age 9, also cost about C$10 per day, so if you need one for more than a few days, it's worth bringing your own or buying one locally.

∎ CAR RENTAL RESOURCES

Local Agencies Lo-Cost Rent A Car
(☎ 888/556-2678 ⊕ www.locost.com).

Major Agencies Alamo (☎ 800/522-9696
⊕ www.alamo.com). **Avis** (☎ 800/331-1084
⊕ www.avis.com). **Budget** (☎ 800/472-3325
⊕ www.budget.com). **Hertz** (☎ 800/654-3001
⊕ www.hertz.com). **National Car Rental**
(☎ 800/227-7368 ⊕ www.nationalcar.com).

∎ CRUISE TRAVEL

Vancouver is, with Seattle, a major embarkation point for Alaska cruises, and virtually all Alaska-bound cruise ships call there; some also call at Victoria and Prince Rupert. After leaving Vancouver, however, most luxury liners make straight for Alaska, leaving the fjords and islands of B.C. to smaller vessels and expedition ships. Some operators lead sailing trips around B.C.'s islands; independent travelers can explore the coast on BC Ferries or on one of the coastal freighters serving remote outposts.

The small, expedition-style ships operated by American Safari Cruises and Cruise West explore the British Columbia coast on their way to Alaska; some offer cruises exclusively in B.C. Bluewater Adventures has 8- to 10-day sailing cruises of the B.C. coastline, including the Queen Charlotte Islands.

Cruise Lines American Safari Cruises
(☎ 206/284-0300 or 888/862-8881 ⊕ www.
amsafari.com). **Bluewater Adventures**
(☎ 604/980-3800 or 888/877-1770 ⊕ www.
bluewateradventures.ca). **Cruise West**
(☎ 206/441-8687 or 888/851-8133 ⊕ www.
cruisewest.com).

∎ TRAIN TRAVEL

Amtrak has service from Seattle to Vancouver, providing connections between Amtrak's U.S.-wide network and VIA Rail's Canadian routes. VIA Rail Canada provides transcontinental rail service. In B.C. VIA Rail has three routes: Victoria to Courtenay on Vancouver Island, Vancouver to Jasper, and Jasper to Prince Rupert with an overnight stop in Prince George. Rocky Mountaineer Vacations operates a variety of spectacular all-daylight rail trips between the Canadian Rockies and the west coast as well as the Whistler Mountaineer between North Vancouver and Whistler. All trains are no-smoking.

If you're planning to travel much by train, look into the Canrail pass. It allows 12 days of coach-class travel within a 30-day period; sleeping cars are available, but they sell out early and must be reserved at least a month in advance during the high season (June through mid-October), when the pass is C$923. Low-season rates (October 16 through May) are C$576. For more information and reservations, contact VIA Rail, or a travel agent in the United States or Canada.

All the train services accept major credit cards, traveler's checks, and cash. VIA Rail will accept U.S. and Canadian currency.

Reservations are essential on the Rocky Mountaineer and highly recommended on Amtrak and VIA routes. There's no extra charge for reservations on any of the train services listed.

Information Amtrak (☎ 800/872-7245
⊕ www.amtrak.com). **Rocky Mountaineer Vacations** (☎ 800/665-7245 ⊕ www.
rockymountaineer.com). **VIA Rail Canada**
(☎ 888/842-7245 ⊕ www.viarail.ca).

ESSENTIALS

▮ ACCOMMODATIONS

In Vancouver and Victoria you have a choice of luxury hotels; moderately priced modern properties; bed-and-breakfasts, both simple and luxurious; and smaller older hotels with perhaps fewer conveniences but more charm. Options in smaller towns and in the country include large, full-service resorts; remote wilderness lodges; small, privately owned hotels; roadside motels; and B&Bs. Even here you need to make reservations at least on the day on which you plan to pull into town.

Canada doesn't have a national-government rating system, but in British Columbia, a blue Approved Accommodation decal on the window or door of a hotel or motel indicates that it has met provincial hotel-association standards for courtesy, comfort, and cleanliness.

Expect accommodations to cost more in summer than in the off-season (except for places such as ski resorts, where winter and spring break are high season). If you're planning to visit in high season, book well in advance. As a rule, hotels in downtown Vancouver are substantially pricier than those located 10 or 15 minutes away outside the downtown core. Also be aware of any special events or festivals that may coincide with your visit and fill every room for miles around. Note also that many out-of-the-way lodgings are closed during the winter.

The lodgings we list are the cream of the crop in each price category. We always list the facilities that are available, but we don't specify whether they cost extra; when pricing accommodations, always ask what's included and what costs extra. Properties are assigned price categories based on the range between their least and most expensive standard double rooms at high season (excluding holidays). Price charts are at the start of each relevant chapter.

Most hotels and lodgings require you to give your credit-card details before they will confirm your reservation. If you don't feel comfortable e-mailing this information, ask if you can fax it (some places even prefer faxes). However you book, get confirmation in writing and have a copy of it handy when you check in.

Be sure you understand the hotel's cancellation policy. Some places allow you to cancel without any kind of penalty—even if you prepaid to secure a discounted rate—if you cancel at least 24 hours in advance. Others require you to cancel a week in advance or penalize you the cost of one night. Small inns and B&Bs are most likely to require you to cancel far in advance. Most hotels allow children under a certain age to stay in their parents' room at no extra charge, but others charge for them as extra adults; find out the cutoff age for discounts.

▮TIP➔ Assume that hotels operate on the European Plan (EP, no meals) unless we specify that they use the Breakfast Plan (BP, with full breakfast), Continental Plan (CP, Continental breakfast), Full American Plan (FAP, all meals), Modified American Plan (MAP, breakfast and dinner) or are all-inclusive (AI, all meals and most activities).

APARTMENT AND HOUSE RENTALS

Rental houses, apartments, and cottages are popular in British Columbia, particularly on the coast and the islands, and in Whistler. Whistler condos are usually time-share or consortium arrangements and can be booked directly through Tourism Whistler. Vacation rentals elsewhere are usually privately owned and range from simple summer cottages to luxurious waterfront homes. Rates range from C$800 per week to several thousand; popular places book up as much as a year in advance.

Local Agents Chalet Select (☎ 613/830–1124 or 800/741–1617 ⊕ www.chaletselect.com). **Sojourn Vacation Properties** (☎ 250/479–8600 or 888/479–8600 ⊕ www.bcacc.com). **Tourism Whistler** (☎ 604/664–5625 or 800/944–7853 ⊕ www.tourismwhistler.com).

BED-AND-BREAKFASTS

B&Bs are in both the country and the cities. In Vancouver, many of the top B&Bs are scattered throughout the West End, between Stanley Park and downtown. In Victoria, try the historic neighborhoods of Oak Bay and Rockland, or James Baynear, the Inner Harbour, and downtown. For assistance in booking these and other B&B lodgings, contact Tourism British Columbia. Be sure to check out the B&B's Web site, which may have useful information, although you should also find out how up-to-date it is. Room quality varies from house to house as well, so you should ask to see a room before making a choice.

Reservation Services (U.S.-based) Bed and Breakfast.com (☎ 512/322–2710 or 800/462–2632 ⊕ www.bedandbreakfast.com). **Bed & Breakfast Inns Online** (☎ 310/280–4363 or 800/215–7365 ⊕ www.bbonline.com). **BnB Finder.com** (☎ 212/837–7865 or 888/547–8226 ⊕ www.bnbfinder.com).

Reservation Services (Canada-based) Hello BC (Tourism B.C.) (☎ 800/435–5622 ⊕ www.hellobc.com). **Victoria Bed and Breakfast Guide** (⊕ www.bestinnsofvictoria.com).

▌ COMMUNICATIONS

INTERNET

As in most North American cities, Internet cafés and Wi-Fi service can be found throughout Vancouver and Victoria. Most hotels and B&Bs also have Internet connections; many of the larger properties have Wi-Fi, sometimes free. It's harder to find Internet cafés in smaller towns in the Okanagan, Tofino, and Ucluelet, but many lodgings have some kind of connection that you can use. Vancouver Wi-Fi Mug is a directory of more than 100 free wireless cafés around the city. Internet and Wi-Fi access are available free at all 22 branches of the Vancouver Public Library. Internet cafés throughout the city charge about C$3 per half hour.

Contacts Cybercafes (⊕ www.cybercafes.com) lists over 4,000 Internet cafés worldwide. **Vancouver WiFi Mug** (⊕ www.vancouver.wifimug.org). **Vancouver Public Library Central Branch** (✉ 350 W. Georgia St., Downtown ☎ 604/331–3600 ⊕ www.vpl.vancouver.bc.ca).

PHONES

The good news is that you can now make a direct-dial telephone call from virtually any point on earth. The bad news? You can't always do so cheaply. Calling from a hotel is almost always the most expensive option; hotels usually add huge surcharges to all calls, particularly international ones. In some countries you can phone from call centers or even the post office. Calling cards usually keep costs to a minimum, but only if you purchase them locally. And then there are mobile phones (⇨ *below*), which are sometimes more prevalent—particularly in the developing world—than landlines; as expensive as mobile phone calls can be, they are still usually a much cheaper option than calling from your hotel.

CALLING WITHIN CANADA

Vancouver uses 10-digit calling for local calls (i.e. 604/555–1212). The city's area codes are 604 and 778. Whistler and the Sunshine Coast also use a 604 area code, and for the rest of British Columbia, including Victoria and Vancouver Island, it's 250. Pay phones are easy to find, and new ones accept credit cards and prepaid calling cards. Dial 411 for directory assistance, 0 to reach an operator, and 911 for emergencies. All long-distance calls, including calls to the United States, must be prefixed with a 1.

CALLING OUTSIDE CANADA

The country code for the United States is 1.

MOBILE PHONES

If you have a multiband phone (some countries use different frequencies than what's used in the United States) and your service provider uses the world-standard GSM network (as do T-Mobile, Cingular, and Verizon), you can probably use your phone abroad. Roaming fees can be steep, however: 99¢ a minute is considered reasonable. And overseas you normally pay the toll charges for incoming calls. It's almost always cheaper to send a text message than to make a call, since text messages have a really low set fee (often less than 5¢).

If you just want to make local calls, consider buying a new SIM card (note that your provider may have to unlock your phone for you to use a different SIM card) and a prepaid service plan in the destination. You'll then have a local number and can make local calls at local rates. If your trip is extensive, you could also simply buy a cell phone in your destination, as the initial cost will be offset over time.

■TIP➜ If you travel internationally frequently, save one of your old mobile phones or buy a cheap one on the Internet; ask your cell phone company to unlock it for you, and take it with you as a travel phone, buying a new SIM card with pay-as-you-go service in each destination.

To avoid roaming charges, you can rent a cell phone in Vancouver. Cita Communications, at the Visitor Information Centre at the Vancouver International Airport international- and domestic-arrival terminals, offers cell phone rentals for C$4.99 a day, with local calls costing C$0.49 a minute, and SIM cards for $1 a day with calls costing C$0.35 a minute. Alternatively, cell-phone stores abound throughout downtown Vancouver.

Contacts Cellular Abroad (☎ 800/287–5072 ⊕ www.cellularabroad.com) rents and sells GMS phones and sells SIM cards that work in many countries. **Cita Communications** (☎ 604/671–4655 or 888/593–2482 ⊕ www.cita.info). **Mobal** (☎ 888/888–9162 ⊕ www.mobalrental. com) rents mobiles and sells GSM phones (starting at $49; $99 for a phone that works in North America) that will operate in 150 countries. Per-call rates vary, but are typically more than $1 per minute. **Planet Fone** (☎ 888/988–4777 ⊕ www.planetfone.com) rents cell phones, but the per-minute rates are expensive.

▐ CUSTOMS AND DUTIES

You're always allowed to bring goods of a certain value back home without having to pay any duty or import tax. But there's a limit on the amount of tobacco and liquor you can bring back duty-free, and some countries have separate limits for perfumes; for exact figures, check with your customs department. The values of so-called "duty-free" goods are included in these amounts. When you shop abroad, save all your receipts, as customs inspectors may ask to see them as well as the items you purchased. If the total value of your goods is more than the duty-free limit, you'll have to pay a tax (most often a flat percentage) on the value of everything beyond that limit.

Visitors may bring certain goods into Canada for their own use as "personal baggage." Clothing, camping and sports equipment, cameras, tape recorders, and even personal computers are considered to be personal baggage. Vehicles, vessels, and aircraft may also be imported. Provided these goods are declared upon arrival and taken back out of Canada when you leave, they will not be subject to any duties or taxes. A (refundable) deposit is sometimes required. A visitor's goods cannot be used by a resident of Canada, or on behalf of a business based in Canada.

Visitors may bring in the following items duty-free: 200 cigarettes, 50 cigars, and 7 ounces of tobacco; 1 bottle (1.14 liters or 40 imperial ounces) of liquor or 1.5 liters of wine, or 24 355-milliliter (12-ounce) bottles or cans of beer for personal consumption. Any alcohol and tobacco products in excess of these amounts are subject to duty, provincial fees, and taxes. You can also bring in gifts up to a total value of C$60 per gift as long as the gifts do not include alcohol or tobacco.

Information in Canada Canada Border Services Agency (☎ 204/983–3500, 800/461–9999 in Canada ⊕ www.cbsa.gc.ca). **Canadian Firearms Centre** (☎ 800/731–4000 ⊕ www.cfc-cafc.gc.ca).

U.S. Information U.S. Customs and Border Protection (⊕ www.cbp.gov).

∎ EATING OUT

The restaurants we list are the cream of the crop in each price category.

In Vancouver, where several thousand eateries represent almost every cuisine on the planet, deciding what to eat is as important as deciding what to see and do. Vancouverites are a health-conscious lot, so light, organic, and vegetarian meals are easy to find, and every restaurant and even most of the pubs in the province ban smoking indoors and out. Good coffee is everywhere—downtown you'll never have to walk more than half a block for a cup of high-test cappuccino. You won't find much street food in town (only hot dog vendors are permitted on city streets), but you can grab takeout and picnic at any city beach or park.

In Victoria and on Vancouver Island, many chefs work with local organic farmers to create a distinctive regional cuisine; Whistler has some of the most highly regarded, and priciest, restaurants in the province. Elsewhere, excellent food is available even in the most out-of-the-way places, as chefs passionate about their ingredients locate close to the source and let their diners come to them. Neighborhood pubs, both in and outside cities, are your best bet for a casual meal. Many have a separate restaurant section where you can take kids.

Although the Canadian dollar is no longer the steal it once was, dining in British Columbia is still one of North America's great bargains. To be sure, high-end entrées, especially where seafood is involved, can top C$35, but C$20 to C$25 is more the norm. Bargains abound: the densest cluster of cheap eats in Vancouver is along Denman Street in the West End. Another budget option is to check out the lunch specials at any of the small Asian restaurants lining Vancouver's streets and shopping malls. They serve healthy hot meals for about the same cost as a take-out burger and fries. But even though food is a deal in B.C., alcohol is pricey. A bottle of wine can easily double your bill.

MEALS AND MEALTIMES

Despite dwindling stocks, wild Pacific salmon—fresh, smoked, dried, candied, barbecued, or grilled on an alder wood plank in the First Nations fashion—remains British Columbia's signature dish. Other local delicacies served at B.C.'s upmarket restaurants include Fanny Bay or Long Beach oysters and Salt Spring Island lamb. Another homegrown treat is the Nanaimo Bar. Once a Christmas bake-sale standard, this chocolate-and-icing concoction has made its way to trendy city cafés.

Most upscale restaurants in Vancouver, Victoria, and Whistler observe standard North American mealtimes (5:30 to 9 or so for dinner, roughly noon to 2 if open for lunch); though some offer a lighter tapas-style menu (or, in Victoria, afternoon tea) in the afternoon. Casual places and pubs typically serve food all afternoon and into the evening. Restaurants that do stay open late (meaning midnight or 1 AM) usually morph into bars after about 9 PM, but the kitchen stays open. In Vancouver, the West End and Kitsilano have the most late-night choices; pubs are your best bet if you're eating late in Victoria.

Unless otherwise noted, the restaurants listed in this guide are open daily for lunch and dinner.

PAYING

Credit cards are widely accepted, but a few smaller restaurants accept only cash. Discover Cards are little known in Canada, and many restaurants outside of Vancouver do not accept American Express. Our restaurant reviews indicate what credit cards are accepted (or not) at each establishment.

For guidelines on tipping *see* Tipping *below.*

RESERVATIONS AND DRESS

Regardless of where you are, it's a good idea to make a reservation if you can. In some places, it's expected. We only mention them specifically when reservations are essential (there's no other way you'll ever get a table) or when they are not accepted. For popular restaurants, book as far ahead as you can (often 30 days), and reconfirm as soon as you arrive. (Large parties should always call ahead to check the reservations policy.) We mention dress only when men are required to wear a jacket or a jacket and tie. In British Columbia, smart casual dress is acceptable everywhere.

At the hottest restaurants in Vancouver, Victoria, and Whistler, you need to make reservations at least a few days in advance, especially if you want to dine between 7 and 9, or on a Friday or Saturday night. On weeknights or outside of the peak tourist season, you can usually secure a table by calling the same day. Just showing up can work, too, though there's no guarantee you'll get a table.

If you want to dine, but not sleep, at one of B.C.'s better-known country inns, such as the Sooke Harbour House, the Aerie, or the Wickaninnish Inn, make your reservation as far ahead as possible. Guests staying at these inns are given first choice for dining reservations, which means spaces for nonguests are limited. Remember also to call the restaurant should you need to cancel your reservation—it's only courteous.

WINES, BEER, AND SPIRITS

Though little known and virtually unobtainable outside the province, British Columbia wines have beaten many more established regions in international competitions. A tasting tour of B.C.'s Okanagan wine region is a scenic way to experience some of these vintages. British Columbians are also choosy about their beer, brewing and drinking (per capita) more microbrewed ales and lagers than anyone else in the country. The liquor stores sell a daunting selection of oddly named brews, but many cottage breweries produce only enough for their local pubs, so it's always worth asking what's on draft.

■ ELECTRICITY

Canada uses the same voltage as the United States, so all of your electronics should make the transition without any fuss at all. No need for adapters.

■ EMERGENCIES

Foreign Embassies U.S. Consulate General (✉ *1095 W. Pender St., Vancouver* ☎ *604/685–4311* ⊕ *www.vancouver.usconsulate.gov/ content/index.asp*).

■ HEALTH

OVER-THE-COUNTER REMEDIES

Virtually all major brand-name American medications are available at pharmacies as well as chain stores like Shoppers Drug Mart and London Drugs.

■ HOURS OF OPERATION

Most banks in British Columbia are open Monday–Thursday 10–3:30 and Friday 10–5 or 6. Some banks, especially in

Vancouver, are open longer hours and also on Saturday morning. All banks are closed on national holidays. Most banks (and some gas stations and convenience stores) have automatic teller machines (ATMs) that are accessible around the clock. Hours at museums vary, but most open at 10 or 11 and close in the evening. Many museums are closed on Monday; some make up for it by staying open late on Wednesday or Thursday, often waiving admission.

Stores in B.C. are usually open Monday–Saturday 9–6. Shops in the major cities and in areas frequented by tourists are usually open Sunday as well. Stores often stay open Thursday and Friday evenings, most shopping malls are open until 9 PM. Many supermarkets are open 7:30 AM–9 PM, and some food and convenience stores in Vancouver are open 24 hours.

HOLIDAYS

Canadian national holidays for 2010 are as follows: New Year's Day, Good Friday (April 2), Easter Monday (April 5), Victoria Day (May 24), Canada Day (July 1), Labor Day (September 6), Thanksgiving (October 11), Remembrance Day (November 11), Christmas, and Boxing Day (December 26). British Columbia Day (August 2) is a provincial holiday.

▌ MAIL

In British Columbia you can buy stamps at the post office or from many retail outlets and some newsstands. If you're sending mail to or within Canada, be sure to include the postal code (six digits and letters). Note that the suite number often appears before the street number in an address, followed by a hyphen. The postal abbreviation for British Columbia is BC.

Within Canada, postcards and letters cost C$0.54 for up to 30 grams, C$0.98 for between 31 and 50 grams, and C$1.18 for between 51 and 100 grams. Letters and postcards to the United States cost C$0.98 for up to 30 grams, C$1.18 for

between 31 and 50 grams, and C$1.96 for up to 100 grams.

International mail and postcards are C$1.65 for up to 30 grams, C$2.36 for between 31 and 50 grams, and C$3.90 for between 51 and 100 grams. All postage rates also incur a 5% Goods-and-Services Tax (GST).

Post Office Canada Post (✉ *Bentall Centre, 595 Burrard St., Downtown* ☎ *604/482–4296 or 800/267–1177* ⊕ *www.canadapost.ca*).

SHIPPING PACKAGES

Small packages can be sent via the Small Packets service offered by Canada Post. Up to 250 grams to the United States is C$6.70 by air and C$5.25 surface; 250–500 grams is C$8.90 by air and C$7.50 surface; 500 grams to 1 kilo is C$13.80 by air and C$11.15 surface. Internationally, up to 250 grams starts at C$8.01 by air and C$5.86 surface; 250–500 grams is C$16.02 by air and C$8.22 surface; 500 grams to 1 kilo is C$30.93 by air and C$13.60 surface.

Express Services DHL (☎ *800/225–5345* ⊕ *www.dhl.ca/ca*). FedEx (☎ *800/463–3339* ⊕ *www. fedex.ca*). ICS Courier (business-to-business ⊕ *www.ics-canada.net*). Purolator (☎ *888/744–7123* ⊕ *www.purolator.com*). UPS (☎ *800/742–5877* ⊕ *www.ups.ca*).

▌ MONEY

Throughout this book, unless otherwise stated, all prices, including dining and lodging, are given in Canadian dollars.

ITEM	AVERAGE COST
Cup of Coffee	C$3
Glass of Wine	C$5
Glass of Beer	C$4
Sandwich	C$5
One-Mile Taxi Ride in Capital City	C$7
Museum Admission	C$10

Prices throughout this guide are given for adults. Substantially reduced fees are almost always available for children, students, and senior citizens.

■ TIP→ Banks never have every foreign currency on hand, and it may take as long as a week to order. If you're planning to exchange funds before leaving home, don't wait until the last minute.

ATMS AND BANKS
Your own bank will probably charge a fee for using ATMs abroad; the foreign bank you use may also charge a fee. Nevertheless, you'll usually get a better rate of exchange at an ATM than you will at a currency-exchange office or even when changing money in a bank. And extracting funds as you need them is a safer option than carrying around a large amount of cash.

■ TIP→ PIN numbers with more than four digits are not recognized at ATMs in many countries. If yours has five or more, remember to change it before you leave. ATMs are available in most bank and credit-union branches across British Columbia, as well as in many convenience stores, malls, and gas stations. Major banks include RBC Royal Bank, BMO Bank of Montreal, TD Bank Financial Group, Scotiabank, and the Canadian Imperial Bank of Commerce.

CREDIT CARDS
Throughout this guide, the following abbreviations are used: **AE**, American Express; **D**, Discover; **DC**, Diners Club; **MC**, MasterCard; and **V**, Visa.

It's a good idea to inform your credit-card company before you travel, especially if you're going abroad and don't travel internationally very often. Otherwise, the credit-card company might put a hold on your card owing to unusual activity—not a good thing halfway through your trip. Record all your credit-card numbers—as well as the phone numbers to call if your cards are lost or stolen—in a safe place, so you're prepared should something go wrong. Both MasterCard and Visa have general numbers you can call (collect if you're abroad) if your card is lost, but you're better off calling the number of your issuing bank, since MasterCard and Visa usually just transfer you to your bank; your bank's number is usually printed on your card.

If you plan to use your credit card for cash advances, you'll need to apply for a PIN at least two weeks before your trip. Although it's usually cheaper (and safer) to use a credit card abroad for large purchases (so you can cancel payments or be reimbursed if there's a problem), note that some credit-card companies *and* the banks that issue them add substantial percentages to all foreign transactions, whether they're in a foreign currency or not. Check on these fees before leaving home, so there won't be any surprises when you get the bill.

■ TIP→ Before you charge something, ask the merchant whether or not he or she plans to do a dynamic currency conversion (DCC). In such a transaction the credit-card *processor* (shop, restaurant, or hotel, not Visa or MasterCard) converts the currency and charges you in U.S. dollars. In most cases you'll pay the merchant a 3% fee for this service in addition to any credit-card company and issuing-bank foreign-transaction surcharges.

Dynamic-currency-conversion programs are becoming increasingly widespread. Merchants who participate in them are supposed to ask whether you want to be charged in U.S. dollars or the local currency, but they don't always do so. And even if they do give you a choice, they may well avoid mentioning the additional surcharges. The good news is that you *do* have a choice. And if this practice really gets your goat, you can avoid it entirely thanks to American Express; with its cards, DCC simply isn't an option.

Reporting Lost Cards American Express (☎ 800/528–4800 in the U.S., 336/393–1111 collect from abroad ⊕ www.americanexpress. com). **Diners Club** (☎ 800/234–6377 in the U.S., 303/799–1504 collect from abroad ⊕ www.dinersclub.com). **MasterCard** (☎ 800/627–8372 in the U.S., 636/722–7111 collect from abroad ⊕ www.mastercard. com). **Visa** (☎ 800/847–2911 in the U.S. and Canada, 410/581–9994 collect from abroad ⊕ www.visa.com).

CURRENCY AND EXCHANGE

U.S. dollars are accepted in much of Canada (especially in communities near the border) but you won't get the exchange rate offered at banks. Major U.S. credit cards are accepted in most areas.

The units of currency in Canada are the Canadian dollar (C$) and the cent, in almost the same denominations as U.S. currency ($5, $10, $20, 1¢, 5¢, 10¢, 25¢, etc.). The C$1 and C$2 bill have been replaced by C$1 and C$2 coins—known as a "loonie," because of the loon that appears on the coin, and a "toonie," respectively.

ATMs are ubiquitous in Vancouver and Victoria and credit cards are accepted virtually everywhere.

In Vancouver and the rest of British Columbia, attire tends to be casual but neat. T-shirts, polo shirts, and slacks are fine at tourist attractions and all but the most upscale restaurants. Waterproof, breathable fabrics are recommended for those planning outdoor excursions. Weather in British Columbia is changeable and varied; you can expect cool evenings and some chance of rain even in summer, so don't forget your umbrella. If you plan on camping or hiking in the deep woods in summer, particularly in northern British

Columbia, definitely take insect repellent. In wilderness areas it's also a good idea to carry bear spray and/or wear bells to warn bears of your presence. Both are available in camping and hardware stores in B.C.

SHIPPING LUGGAGE AHEAD

Imagine globe-trotting with only a carry-on in tow. Shipping your luggage in advance via an air-freight service is a great way to cut down on backaches, hassles, and stress—especially if your packing list includes strollers, car seats, etc. There are some things to be aware of, though.

First, research carry-on restrictions; if you absolutely need something that isn't practical to ship and isn't allowed in carry-ons, this strategy isn't for you. Second, plan to send your bags several days in advance to U.S. destinations and as much as two weeks in advance to some international destinations. Third, plan to spend some money: it will cost least $100 to send a small piece of luggage, a golf bag, or a pair of skis to a domestic destination, much more to places overseas.

Some people use Federal Express to ship their bags, but this can cost even more than air-freight services. All these services insure your bag (for most, the limit is $1,000, but you should verify that amount); you can, however, purchase additional insurance for about $1 per $100 of value.

Contacts Luggage Concierge (☎ 800/288–9818 ⊕ www.luggageconcierge.com). **Luggage Free** (☎ 800/361–6871 ⊕ www.luggagefree. com). **Luggage Forward** (☎ 866/416–7447 ⊕ www.luggageforward.com). **Sports Express** (☎ 800/357–4174 ⊕ www.sportsexpress.com) specializes in shipping golf clubs and other sports equipment.

▋ PASSPORTS AND VISAS

Citizens of the United States now need a passport to re-enter the United States from Canada. Passport requirements apply to minors as well.

Anyone under 18 traveling alone should carry a signed and dated letter from both parents or from all legal guardians authorizing the trip. It's also a good idea to include a copy of the child's birth certificate, custody documents if applicable, and death certificates of one or both parents, if applicable. Citizens of the United States, United Kingdom, Australia, and New Zealand do not need visas to enter Canada for a period of six months or less.

■TIP→ Before your trip, make two copies of your passport's data page (one for someone at home and another for you to carry separately). Or scan the page and e-mail it to someone at home and/or yourself.

If you're renewing a passport, you can do so by mail. Forms are available at passport-acceptance facilities and online.

▍TAXES

Before July 1, 2010, most purchases in BC will incur a Goods-and-Services Tax (GST) of 5% and a British Columbia Provincial Sales Tax (PST) of 7%. On July 1, 2010, these two taxes will be replaced with a single Harmonized Sales Tax (HST) of 12%. Before July 1, 2010, hotel rooms will be subject to the 5% GST plus an 8 % Hotel Tax; after July 1, 2010, they will be subject to the 12% HST instead.

Some municipalities levy an additional 1% or 2%. Wine, beer, and spirits purchased in bars and restaurants are subject to a 10% tax. Some restaurants build this into the price of the beverage, but others add it to the bill.

Prices in this book do not normally include taxes.

▍TIME

Vancouver, Victoria, Vancouver Island, and the nearby areas are within the Pacific time zone, on the same time as Los Angeles and Seattle. It's 19 hours behind Sydney, 8 hours behind London, 3 hours behind New York City and Toronto, 2

hours behind Chicago, and 1 hour ahead of Alaska.

▍TIPPING

Tips and service charges are not usually added to a bill in Canada. In general, tip 15% of the total bill. This goes for waiters, barbers and hairdressers, and taxi drivers.

TIPPING GUIDELINES FOR VANCOUVER AND VICTORIA AND AROUND	
Bartender	$1–$5 per round of drinks, depending on the number of drinks
Bellhop	$1–$5 per bag, depending on the level of the hotel
Hotel Concierge	$5 or more, if he or she performs a service for you
Hotel Doorman	$1–$2 if he helps you get a cab
Hotel Maid	1$–$3 a day (either daily or at the end of your stay, in cash)
Hotel Room-Service Waiter	$1 to $2 per delivery, even if a service charge has been added
Porter at Airport or Train Station	$1 per bag
Skycap at Airport	$1 to $3 per bag checked
Taxi Driver	15%–20%, but round up the fare to the next dollar amount
Tour Guide	10% of the cost of the tour
Valet Parking Attendant	$1–$2, but only when you get your car
Waiter	15%–20%, with 20% being the norm at high-end restaurants; nothing additional if a service charge is added to the bill

▍TOURS

GUIDED TOURS

Guided tours are a good option when you don't want to do it all yourself. You travel along with a group (sometimes large, sometimes small), stay in prebooked hotels, eat with your fellow travelers (the cost of meals sometimes included in the price of your tour, sometimes not), and follow a schedule.

But not all guided tours are an if-it's-Tuesday-this-must-be-Belgium experience. A knowledgeable guide can take you places that you might never discover on your own, and you may be pushed to see more than you would have otherwise. Tours aren't for everyone, but they can be just the thing for trips to places where making travel arrangements is difficult or time-consuming (particularly when you don't speak the language).

Whenever you book a guided tour, find out what's included and what isn't. A "land-only" tour includes all your travel (by bus, in most cases) in the destination, but not necessarily your flights to and from or even within it. Also, in most cases prices in tour brochures don't include fees and taxes. And remember that you'll be expected to tip your guide (in cash) at the end of the tour.

SPECIAL-INTEREST TOURS

BIKING

AOA Adventures, Rocky Mountain Cycle Tours, and Austin-Lehman Adventures run a variety of comfortable multiday bike trips in Whistler, the Gulf Islands, and the Okanagan.

■ TIP→ Most airlines accommodate bikes as luggage, provided they're dismantled and boxed.

Contacts AOA Adventures (☎ 480/945–2881 or 866/455–1601 ⊕ www.aoa-adventures.com). **Austin-Lehman Adventures** (☎ 800/575–1540 ⊕ www.austinlehman.com). **Rocky Mountain Cycle Tours** (☎ 800/661–2453 ⊕ www.rockymountaincycle.com).

CULINARY

Edible British Columbia can arrange everything from multiday kayaking trips through the Gulf Islands built around locally sourced gourmet meals, to short tours of Vancouver neighborhoods.

Contacts Edible British Columbia (☎ 604/812–9660 ⊕ www.edible-britishcolumbia.com).

DIVING

BC Dive and Kayak Adventures provides customized, multiday dive expeditions to view the eels, octopi, and fish in B.C.'s coastal waters.

Contacts BC Dive and Kayak Adventures (☎ 604/732–1344 or 800/960–0066 ⊕ www.bcdive.com).

ECO TOURS

British Columbians are known for their green-friendly practices, whether it's protecting endangered species, instituting responsible climate-change initiatives, or running local recycling programs. And it's all fed into tourism as well. Ecosummer Expeditions hosts a number of outdoor adventure trips in B.C., including week-long hiking trips along the West Coast Trail on Vancouver Island, kayaking tours amid orcas in Johnstone Strait, and inn-based kayaking trips in the Gulf Islands.

Contacts Ecosummer Expeditions (☎ 250/674–0102 or 800/465–8884 ⊕ www.ecosummer.com).

GOLF

BC Golf Safaris specializes in complete, customized golf vacations based around courses in Vancouver, Victoria, Whistler, the Okanagan, and the Rockies.

Contacts BC Golf Safaris (☎ 866/723–2747 ⊕ www.bcgolfsafaris.com).

SKIING

Contact Whistler Blackcomb, the host mountain resort of the 2010 Winter Games, to book a complete vacation at one of the world's most popular ski resorts.

Contacts Whistler Blackcomb (☎ 866/218–9690 ⊕ www.whistlerblackcomb.com).

❚ VISITOR INFORMATION

Regional Visitor information services are available in British Columbia. In addition, Downtown Ambassadors, sponsored by the Downtown Vancouver Business Improvement Association, are easily spotted on Vancouver streets in their red uniforms. They can provide information, directions, and emergency assistance to anyone visiting Vancouver's central business district.

Contacts Aboriginal Tourism Association of British Columbia (☎ 877/266–2822 ⊕ www.aboriginalbc.com). **Canadian Tourism Commission** (☎ 613/946–1000 ⊕ uscw.canada.travel). **Downtown Ambassadors** (☎ 604/689–4357 ⊕ www.downtownvancouver.net). **Hello BC (Tourism B.C.)** (☎ 800/435–5622 ⊕ www.hellobc.com). **Granville Island Information Centre** (☎ 604/666–5784 ⊕ www.granvilleisland.com). **Tourism Victoria InfoCentre** (☎ 250/953–2033 ⊕ www.tourismvictoria.com). **Vancouver Visitor Centre** (☎ 604/683–2000 ⊕ www.tourismvancouver.com).

ONLINE RESOURCES

All About Vancouver and British Columbia Information of particular interest to outdoorsy types is on the Web site for B.C. Parks (⊕ www.env.gov.bc.ca/bcparks), which outlines recreation, camping, and conservation initiatives at provincially operated reserves throughout British Columbia. At the site for Parks Canada (⊕ www.pc.gc.ca), you can learn about the seven national parks that fall within B.C.'s borders. The Great Outdoor Recreation Page (⊕ www.gorp.com) is another fount of information for hikers, skiers, and the like.

There are several useful general-interest sites that deal with travel in British Columbia. One good option is the ever-expanding VancouverPlus.ca (⊕ www.vancouverplus.ca), which provides tourism tips and travel suggestions for Vancouver. Among alternative newsweeklies, the *Georgia Straight* offers timely features about exploring the province in its "Outside" section (⊕ www.straight.com).

For outdoors enthusiasts, in addition to specific sites mentioned in the book, there are several Web sites that can provide information. These include the Canadian Cycling Association (⊕ www.canadian-cycling.com), the Canadian Recreational Canoeing Association (⊕ www.

paddlingcanada.com) for canoeing and kayaking, the Alpine Club of Canada (⊕ www.alpineclubofcanada.ca) for climbing and mountaineering, and the Royal Canadian Golf Association (⊕ www.rcga.org).

Safety Transportation Security Administration (⊕ www.tsa.gov).

Time Zones Timeanddate.com (⊕ www.timeanddate.com/worldclock) can help you figure out the correct time anywhere.

INDEX

A

Abbeymoore Manor Bed & Breakfast Inn ⊤, 224
Aberdeen Centre, 97–98
Abkhazi Garden, 202
Aboriginal art, 100
Aerie, The ✕⊡, 215, 226–227
Air tours, 190
Air travel, 324–325
Okanagan Wine Country, 283
Tofino, Ucluelet, and the Pacific Rim, 307
Victoria, 186
Apartment and house rentals, 160, 331–332
Araxi ✕, 265
Art Gallery of Greater Victoria, 202
Arts. ⇨ See Nightlife and the arts
Aura ✕, 207–208

B

B.C. Sports Hall of Fame and Museum, 47
Barbara-Jo's Books to Cooks (store), 103
Beaches
Sooke and the Southwest Coast, 242
Vancouver, 51, 54, 64–65, 73–75
Victoria, 203, 230
Beacon Hill Park, 199
Beaconsfield Inn ⊤, 219
Bear Mountain Golf & Country Club, 231, 234
Bearfoot Bistro ✕, 265–266
Ben Franklin submersible, 64
Bennett Bay Park, 255
Bicycles, 325
Mayne Island, 254
Okanagan Wine Country, 292
Oliver and Osoyoos, 305
Penticton and Naramata, 300
tours, 231, 340
Vancouver, 75–77, 81
Victoria, 230–231
Whistler, 271–272
Big Sky Golf and Country Club, 274–275
Bill Reid Gallery of Northwest Coast Art, 16, 33
Bird-watching, 77–78, 247–248
Black Hills Estate Winery, 301
Black Rock Oceanfront Resort ⊤, 320
Bloedel Floral Conservatory, 63

Blue Water Cafe ✕, 137
Boat and ferry travel, 325–326
Tofino, Ucluelet, and the Pacific Rim, 307
Vancouver, 29
Victoria, 182, 187
Boat tours, 190
Boating and sailing, 87, 272–273
Brasserie L'ecole ✕, 208–209
Brentwood Bay Lodge & Spa ⊤, 226
Brewpubs, 118–119
British Columbia Aviation Museum, 204
British Columbia Forest Discovery Centre, 247
British Columbia Orchard Industry Museum, 285
British Columbia Wine Information Centre, 295
Broken Group Islands, 322
Burgoyne Bay Provincial Park, 251
Burrowing Owl Estate Winery, 303
Bus tours, 190
Bus travel, 326–327
Okanagan Wine Country, 283
Vancouver, 29
Victoria, 187
Whistler, 261
Butchart Gardens, 17, 182, 204
Byrnes Block, 41

C

C Restaurant ✕, 140
Cafe Brio ✕, 209
Camille's ✕, 209
Canada Place, 33
Canadian Princess Resort (cruisers), 321
Canoeing, 87, 90
Canopy tours, 276–277
Capilano River Regional Park, 69–70, 83
Capilano Suspension Bridge, 67
Car rental, 329–330
Car travel, 327–330
Okanagan Wine Country, 283
Tofino, Ucluelet, and the Pacific Rim, 307
Whistler, 261
Carmanah Walbran Provincial Park, 241
Carriage and pedicab tours, 190
Casinos, 121
Cathedral Place, 34

Cedar Creek Estate Winery, 287
Centre of the Universe, 204–205
Chambar (bar), 117
Chateau Whistler Golf Club, 275
Chemainus, 248–249
Chemainus Theatre, 248
Children, attractions for
Okanagan Wine Country, 285, 287, 301
Vancouver, 20, 34, 46, 47, 50–51, 55, 58, 63, 64–65, 67, 69–70, 103, 171, 176–177
Victoria, 20, 189, 191, 197–198, 199, 200, 201, 204–205, 206–207, 247–248, 251, 253, 254
Whistler, 268–269, 276
Chinatown (Vancouver), 38–44, 95, 110
Chinatown (Victoria), 189, 191
Chinatown Night Market, 39, 110, 140
Chinese Freemasons Building, 41
Chinese Cultural Centre Museum and Archives, 41
Christ Church Cathedral, 33
Classical music, 124–125
Clayoquol Wilderness Resort: Outpost at Bedwell River ⊤, 313
Cleveland Dam, 69–70
CN IMAX Theatre, 33
Coastal Peoples Fine Arts Gallery (store), 98
Comedy clubs, 121
Contemporary Art Gallery, 47
Cowichan Bay, 246
Cowichan Bay Maritime Centre, 246
Cowichan Valley, 243–249
Cowichan Valley Museum, 247
Craigdarroch Castle, 202–203
Cruises, 330
Cuisine, 18–19, 130–135, 185
Culinary tours, 190, 340

D

Desert Centre, 301
Diamond, The (lounge), 117
Diving, 77, 235, 340
Downtown Historic Railway (Vancouver), 46
Dr. Sun Yat-Sen Classical Chinese Garden, 16, 39–40
Duncan, 246–247

E

Eagle-watching, *77–78*
East Sooke Regional Park, *242*
Ecotours, *77–79, 321, 340*
Elephant Island Orchard Wines, *295*
Emily Carr House, *199*
Emily Carr University of Art and Design, *57*
Empress Room ✕ , *209–210*

F

Fairholme Manor ☂ , *225*
Fairmont Château Whistler Resort ✕ , *268*
Fairmont Empress ☂ , *191, 196*
Fairmont Hotel Vancouver ☂ , *34, 36*
False Creek (Vancouver), *45–47*
Fan Tan Alley, *191*
Farmer's Market (Mayne Island), *254*
Festivals and special events, *22*
Pacific Rim, 312
Vancouver, 72, 115
Victoria, 185
Whistler, 260
Wine Islands, 245
First Nations culture, *22*
Fisherman's Wharf, *199*
Fishing
Tofino, 315
Ucluelet, 321
Vancouver, 79, 81
Whistler, 274
Flightseeing, *315*
Flores Island, *310*
Food and wine tours, *190, 340*
Fort Rodd Hill and Fisgard Lighthouse National Historic Sites of Canada, *206*
Four Seasons Resort Whistler ☂ , *268–269*
Fraserview Golf Course, *80*
Free attractions, *21*
French Beach Provincial Park, *242*
Fulford, *251*

G

Galiano Island, *252–253*
Galiano Oceanfront Inn & Spa ☂ , *253*
Galloping Goose Regional Trail, *230–231*
Gambling (casinos), *121*
Ganges, *251*
Gaoler's Mews, *40*
Gardens. ⇨ *See* Parks and gardens

Garibaldi Lift Company (bar), *278*
Gastown (Vancouver), *38–44, 95*
Gate of Harmonious Interest, *191*
Gay nightlife, *121–122*
Georgina Point Heritage Park, *254*
Goldstream Provincial Park, *206–207*
Golf
Okanagan Wine Country, 292–293
tours, 340
Vancouver, 79–80, 81
Victoria, 231, 234
Whistler, 274–275
Gordon MacMillan Southam Observatory, *64*
Government House Gardens, *203*
Gowlland Point Park, *255*
Granville Island, *16, 44, 56–59, 95*
Granville Island Brewing, *58*
Granville Island Public Market, *57, 109*
Granville Island Water Park, *58*
Grouse Mountain, *67, 69, 82–83*
Gulf Islands, *249–256*
Gulf Islands National Park Reserve, *255*

H

H.R. MacMillan Planetarium, *64*
Hainle Vineyards Estate Winery, *294*
Hastings House Country House Hotel ☂ , *252*
Hatley Park National Historic Site of Canada, *206*
Heli-skiing and heli-hiking, *274–275*
Helicopter travel, *261*
Helmcken House, *198*
Hester Creek Estate Winery, *303*
He-Tin-Kis Park, *319*
Hiking
Okanagan Wine Country, 292
Oliver and Osoyoos, 305
Pacific Rim, 322
Penticton and Naramata, 300
Vancouver, 82–85
Victoria, 234–235
Whistler, 271–272
Hill's Native Art (store), *98–99*
Hillside Estate Winery, *295*
Hockey, *85*
Holt Renfrew (store), *105*
Horseback riding, *276*
Hot Springs Cove, *309–310*
Hotel Europe, *40*

Hotel Grand Pacific ☂ , *220*
House Piccolo ✕ , *252*
HSBC Bank Building, *36*

I

Il Terrazzo ✕ , *210*
Inn at Laurel Point ☂ , *220–221*
Inner Harbour, *17, 182*
Itinerary suggestions, *22*

J

Japanese Garden, *255*
Juan de Fuca Marine Trail, *234, 241*
Juan de Fuca Provincial Park, *230, 241*

K

Kayaking
Mayne Island, 254
Tofino, Ucluelet, and the Pacific Rim, 306, 315, 321
Vancouver, 81, 87, 90
Victoria, 235
Kelowna, *285, 287, 289–293*
Kelowna Art Gallery, *285*
Kelowna Land & Orchard Company, *285, 287*
Kettle Valley Steam Railway, *294*
Kids' Market, *58*
Kidsbooks (store), *103*
Kitsilano, *60–65, 95*
Kitsilano Beach, *64–65, 74*

L

Lake Breeze Vineyards, *298*
Landing, The, *41*
Legacy Art Gallery and Café, *199–200*
Leone (store), *105*
Les Amis du Fromage (store), *109–110*
L'Hermitage Hotel ☂ , *168*
Library Square, *47*
Lighthouse Park, *84*
Limousines, *261*
Lodging, *331–332*
Gulf Islands, 252, 253, 255, 258
Okanagan Wine Country, 290–292, 295, 299–300, 304–305
Oliver and Osoyoos, 304–305
Penticton and Naramata, 299–300
price categories, 160, 185, 260, 282, 306
Sooke and the Southwest Coast, 243
Summerland and Peachland, 290–292

Tofino, 313–315
Ucluelet, 319–321
Vancouver, 160–180
Victoria, 185, 218–227, 243, 249, 252, 253, 255, 256
Whistler, 267–270
Long Beach, *322*
Long Beach Lodge Resort ⌸ **,** *313*
Longhorn Saloon & Grill, *278*
Lonsdale Quay, *70*
Lululemon Athletica (store), *105*
Lumbermen's Arch, *51*
Lynn Canyon Park, *70*

M

Marine Building, *33–34*
Maritime Museum of British Columbia, *200*
Market by Jean George, at Shangri La (bar), *119*
Markus' Wharfside Restaurant ✕ **,** *242*
Matisse ✕ **,** *211*
Max & Moritz Spicy Island Feast House ✕ **,** *253*
Mayne Island, *254–255*
Mayne Island Resort ⌸ **,** *255*
Meadow Park Sports Centre, *276*
Meares Island, *310*
Middle Beach Lodge ⌸ **,** *313–314*
Millennium Gate, *41, 44*
Miniature Railway and Children's Farmyard, *51*
Miniature World, *200*
Mission Hill Family Estate (winery), *287*
Mo:Lé ✕ **,** *211*
Montague Harbour Provincial Marine Park, *253*
Morning Bay Vineyard, *255–256*
Mortimer Spit, *255*
Mount Douglas Regional Park, *205*
Mountain Equipment Co-op, *112*
Movies, *125–126, 279*
Mt. Maxwell Provincial Park, *251*
Mt. Parke, *254*
Munro's Books (store), *237*
Museum of Anthropology, *16, 61–62*
Museums and galleries
Art Gallery of Greater Victoria, 202
B.C. Sports Hall of Fame and Museum, 47
Bill Reid Gallery of Northwest Coast Art, 16, 33
British Columbia Aviation Museum, 204

British Columbia Forest Discovery Centre, 247
British Columbia Orchard Industry Museum, 285
Charles H. Scott Gallery, 57
Chinese Cultural Centre Museum and Archives, 41
Contemporary Art Gallery, 47
Cowichan Bay Maritime Centre, 246
Cowichan Valley Museum, 247
how to buy Aboriginal art, 100
Kelowna Art Gallery, 285
Legacy Art Gallery and Café, 199–200
Maritime Museum of British Columbia, 200
Museum of Anthropology, 16, 61–62
Nk'Mip Desert Cultural Centre, 301
Old Hastings Mill Store Museum, 63
Plumper Pass Lockup, 254
Roedde House Museum, 34
Royal British Columbia Museum, 182, 197–198
Royal London Wax Museum, 201
Sooke Region Museum and Visitor Information Centre, 242
Squamish-Lil'wat Centre, 263
Vancouver Art Gallery, 36–37
Vancouver Maritime Museum, 65
Vancouver Museum, 65
Vancouver Police Centennial Museum, 41
Wine Museum, 285
Music, *122–125, 229*

N

Naramata, *295, 298–300*
Net Loft, *58*
Netherlands Centennial Carillon, *197–198*
Nine O'Clock Gun, *51*
Nita Lake Lodge ⌸ **,** *269*
Nitobe Memorial Garden, *62*
Nk'Mip Cellars, *303*
Nk'Mip Desert Cultural Centre, *301*
Noodle Box, The ✕ **,** *211*
North Shore, *66–70*

O

Oak Bay Village, *203*
Ocean Island Backpackers Inn ⌸ **,** *221*

Okanagan Wine Country, *12, 17, 282–305*
children, attractions for, 285, 287, 301
lodging, 290–292, 295, 299–300, 304–305
Okanagan wineries, 287–289, 294, 295, 298, 301–303
price categories, 282
restaurants, 289–290, 294–295, 298–299, 303–304
shopping, 293, 300
sports and outdoor activities, 292–293, 300, 305
tours, 282
transportation, 282
visitor information, 282
Old Hastings Mill Store Museum, *63*
Oliver, *300–301, 303–305*
Opus Bar, *119*
Opus Hotel ⌸ **,** *179–180*
Osoyoos, *300–301, 303–305*
Oswego Hotel, The ⌸ **,** *221, 223*
Outdoor Adventures Whistler, *276*

P

Pacific Northwest Raptors, *247–248*
Pacific Rim, *12, 306–308, 311, 312, 316, 322*
Pacific Rim National Park Reserve, *17, 310, 322*
Pacific Sands Beach Resort ⌸ **,** *314*
Pacific Undersea Gardens, *200*
Pan Pacific Hotel ⌸ **,** *33*
Paprika Bistro ✕ **,** *215*
Parks and gardens
Abkhazi Garden, 202
Beacon Hill Park, 199
Bennett Bay Park, 255
Bloedel Floral Conservatory, 63
Burgoyne Bay Provincial Park, 251
Butchart Gardens, 17, 182, 204
Capilano River Regional Park, 69–70, 83
Carmanah Walbran Provincial Park, 241
Dr. Sun Yat-Sen Classical Chinese Garden, 16, 39–40
East Sooke Regional Park, 242
French Beach Provincial Park, 242
Georgina Point Heritage Park, 254

Goldstream Provincial Park, 206–207
Government House Gardens, 203
Gowlland Point Park, 255
Gulf Islands National Park Reserve, 255
Hatley Park National Historic Site of Canada, 206
He-Tin-Kis Park, 319
Japanese Garden, 255
Juan de Fuca Provincial Park, 230, 241
Lighthouse Park, 84
Lynn Canyon Park, 70
Montague Harbour Provincial Marine Park, 253
Mount Douglas Regional Park, 205
Mt. Maxwell Provincial Park, 251
Nitobe Memorial Garden, 62
Pacific Rim National Park Reserve, 17, 310, 322
Pacific Undersea Gardens, 200
Queen Elizabeth Park, 63
Ruckle Provincial Park, 251
Sooke Potholes Provincial Park, 242
Stanley Park, 16, 48–55, 84–85, 165
Tofino Botanical Gardens, 310
University of British Columbia Botanical Garden, 63
VanDusen Botanical Garden, 63–64
Victoria Butterfly Gardens, 205
Willows Beach Park, 203
Parliament Buildings, 197
Peachland, 294–295
Pender Island, 255–256
Penticton, 295, 298–300
Plumper Pass Lockup, 255
Poets Cove Resort & Spa ⬚, 256
Point Ellice House, 200–201
Pointe, The ✕, 310
Poplar Grove (winery), 298
Port Renfrew, 242
Portobello West, 101
Pourhouse (bar), 117–118
Powows, 23
Prospect Point, 49

Q

Quail's Gate Estate Winery, 287, 289
Queen Elizabeth Park, 63
Quw'utsun' Cultural and Conference Centre, 248

R

RainCoast Café ✕, 310
Rapid-transit, 29
Red Rooster Winery, 298
Remote Passages Marine Excursions, 318
Restaurants, 7, 18–19, 334–335
Gulf Islands, 251–252
hours, 128
Okanagan Wine Country, 289–290, 294–295, 298–299, 303–304
Oliver and Osoyoos, 303–304
Penticton and Naramata, 298–299
price categories, 128, 185, 260, 282, 306
Sooke and the Southwest Coast, 242–243
Summerland and Peachland, 289–290
Tofino, 310, 312
Ucluelet, 319
Vancouver, 37, 47, 51, 55, 65, 128–158
Victoria, 185, 196–197, 199, 205, 207–215, 242–243, 248–249, 251–252, 253, 256
Whistler, 265–267
Richmond, 69, 96
Richmond Chinatown, 69
Richmond Olympic Oval, 81–82
Rim Rock Café ✕, 267
River rafting, 90
Robert Held Art Glass (store), 101
Robson Square, 36
Roedde House Museum, 34
Roesland, 256
Rogers' Chocolates (store), 237
Roots (store), 280
Royal British Columbia Museum, 182, 197–198
Royal London Wax Museum, 201
Ruckle Provincial Park, 251

S

Saanich Peninsula, 182, 203–205, 215, 226
Salt Spring Island, 250–252
Salt Spring Island Saturday Market, 251
Salt Tasting Room (wine bar), 121
Sam Kee Building, 44
Schooner on Second, The ✕, 310
Science World, 46
Scuba diving, 77, 235
Seaside route, 75–76
Seawall, 49–50
Second Beach, 51, 54

Shaw Ocean Discovery Centre, 205
Shopping
business hours, 92
Okanagan Wine Country, 293, 300
Penticton and Naramata, 300
Tofino, 318–319
Vancouver, 92–112
Victoria, 185, 236–239
Whistler, 280–281
Sidney and the Saanich Peninsula, 182, 203–205, 215, 226
Sidney Pier Hotel & Spa, The ⬚, 226
Sidney Spit, 205
Silk Road Aromatherapy & Tea Company & Spa, 238
Sinclair Centre, 36
Siwash Rock, 55
Skiing, 340
Vancouver, 81, 86–87
Whistler, 273–274
Skyride, 67, 69
Snowboarding, 86–87
Sobo ✕, 312
Sonora Room Restaurant at Burrowing Owl ✕, 304
Sooke and the Southwest Coast, 241–243
Sooke Harbour House ✕⬚, 243
Sooke Potholes Provincial Park, 242
Sooke Region Museum and Visitor Information Centre, 242
South Granville, 95
Spas
Kamloops, 293
Vancouver, 92, 106–107
Victoria, 238–239
Whistler, 280–281
Spinnakers Gastro Brewpub ✕, 212
Sports and outdoor activities
Okanagan Wine Country, 292–293, 300, 305
Oliver and Osoyoos, 305
Penticton and Naramata, 300
Tofino, Ucluelet, and the Pacific Rim, 306
Vancouver, 72–90
Victoria, 230–236, 255
Whistler, 270–277
Spotted Lake, 301
Springwater Lodge, 254
Squamish-Lil'wat Centre, 263
St. Ann's Academy National Historic Site, 201

Stanley Park, *16, 48–55, 84–85, 165*
Stanley Park Seawall, *49–50*
Steam Clock, *40*
Storm watching, *311*
Studio Tour, *251*
Sturdies Bay Bakery & Cafe ✕ , *253*
Sumac Ridge Estate Winery, *294*
Summerhill Estate Winery, *289*
Summerland, *294–295*
Sunmore Ginseng Spa, *293*
Surfing, *315–316, 318, 321*
Sushi Village ✕ , *267*
Sylvia Hotel 🔟 , *177*

T

Takaya Tours, *90*
Taxis
Okanagan Wine Country, 283
Tofino, Ucluelet, and the Pacific Rim, 307
Vancouver, 29
Victoria, 187
Terrace at Mission Hill, The ✕ , *290*
Theater
Okanagan Wine Country, 279
Vancouver, 126
Victoria, 229–230
Therapy Vineyards, *298*
Tla-ook Cultural Adventures, *318*
Tofino, *12, 306–319*
Tofino Botanical Gardens, *310*
Tojo's ✕ , *118*
Totem poles, *50*
Tours, *339–340*
Okanagan Wine Country, 282
Vancouver, 28
Victoria, 190, 231, 251
Train travel, *330*
Vancouver, 29
Victoria, 186
Whistler, 261
Transportation, *14, 20, 324–330*
Okanagan Wine Country, 282
Vancouver, 29, 160
Victoria, 182, 186–187, 240
Whistler, 260

U

Ucluelet, *12, 306–308, 319–321*
University of British Columbia Botanical Garden, *63*

V

Vancouver, *12, 26–180*
Alberni Street, 95
Cambie Village, 95–96

children, attractions for, 20, 34, 46, 47, 50–51, 55, 58, 63, 64–65, 67, 69–70, 103, 171, 176–177
Chinatown, 38–44, 95, 110
Commercial Drive, 44, 96
discounts and deals, 28
Downtown, 32–37, 137–149, 163–174
festivals and special events, 72, 115
free attractions, 21
Gastown, 38–44, 95
Granville Island, 16, 44, 56–59, 95
Greater Vancouver, 151–158
Harbor-front Shoreline, 44
history of, 31
itinerary recommendations, 22
Kitsilano, 60–65, 95
Library Square, 47
lodging, 160–180
Main Street/Mt. Pleasant, 44, 96
Marinaside, 44
nightlife and the arts, 114–126, 170
North Shore, 66–70
Punjabi Market, 96
restaurants, 37, 47, 51, 55, 65, 128–158
Richmond, 69, 96
Robson Square, 36
Robson Street, 34, 44, 95
shopping, 92–112
South Granville, 95
spas, 92, 106–107
sports and outdoor activities, 72–90
Stanley Park, 16, 48–55, 84–85, 165
top attractions, 16–17, 26–27
tours, 28
transportation, 29
West End, 32–37, 44, 165, 174–179
West Side, 60–65, 165, 179
Yaletown and False Creek, 45–47, 95, 165, 179–180
Vancouver Aquarium Marine Science Centre, *50–51*
Vancouver Art Gallery, *36–37*
Vancouver Convention and Exhibition Centre, *33*
Vancouver Lookout!, *34*
Vancouver Maritime Museum, *65*
Vancouver Museum, *65*
Vancouver Police Centennial Museum, *41*

VanDusen Botanical Garden, *63–64*
Vesuvius, *251*
Victoria, *12, 182–256*
afternoon tea, 213
Bastion Square, 198
children, attractions for, 20, 189, 191, 197–198, 199, 200, 201, 204–205, 206–207, 247–248, 251, 253, 254
Chinatown, 189, 191
Downtown, 182, 189–201, 206–212, 214–215, 218–224
festivals and special events, 185
free attractions, 21
Inner Harbour, 17, 182
itinerary recommendations, 22
lodging, 185, 218–227, 243, 249, 252, 253, 255, 256
Lower Johnson Street, 236
nightlife and the arts, 227–230
Oak Bay, Rockland, and Fairfield, 182, 201–203, 214–215, 224–225
restaurants, 185, 196–197, 199, 205, 207–215, 242–243, 248–249, 251–252, 253, 256
shopping, 185, 236–239
Sidney and the Saanich Peninsula, 182, 203–205, 215, 226
side trips from, 239–256
sports and outdoor activities, 230–236, 255
top attractions, 16–17
tours, 190, 231, 251
transportation, 182, 186–187, 240
visitor information, 184
waterfront, 196
West Shore and the Malahat, 182, 206–207, 215, 226–227
Victoria Bug Zoo, *201*
Victoria Butterfly Gardens, *205*
Vij's ✕ , *156–157*
Villa Marco Polo 🔟 , *225*
Visitor information, *340–341*
Okanagan Wine Country, 282
Tofino, Ucluelet, and the Pacific Rim, 306
Victoria, 184
Whistler, 260

W

Walking tours, *190*
Waterfront Restaurant & Wine Bar ✕ , *290*
Waterfront Station, *37*
Watermark on Kits Beach (bar), *118*

Weather, *311*
Wedgewood Hotel & Spa ⊤ , *173–174*
West ✕ , *158*
West Coast Trail, *322*
Whale-watching
Tofino, Ucluelet, and the Pacific Rim, *318, 321*
Vancouver, *78–79*
Victoria, *232–233*
Whalers on the Point Guest-house ⊤ , *314–315*
Whiffen Spit, *242*
Whistler, *12, 17, 258–280*
children, attractions for, *268–269, 276*
festivals and special events, *260*
free attractions, *21*
lodging, *267–270*
nightlife and the arts, *277–279*

restaurants, *265–267*
shopping, *280–281*
sports and outdoor activities, *270–277*
transportation, *260*
visitor information, *260*
Whistler Alpine Guides Bureau, *274*
Whistler Heli-Skiing, *276*
Whistler/Blackcomb Ski and Snowboard School, *274*
Wickaninnish Inn, The ⊤ , *315*
Wickaninnish Restaurant, The ✕ , *312*
Wild Pacific Trail, *319*
Wildlife viewing, *77–78*
Willows Beach Park, *203*
Winch Building, *36*
Windsurfing, *90*
Wine bars, *119, 121*

Wine Islands, *244–245*
Wine Museum, *285*
Wineries, *190, 244–245, 255–256, 287–289, 294, 295, 298, 301–303*
Wreck Beach, *65*

Y

Yaletown (Vancouver), *45–47, 95, 165, 179–180*
YEW Bar at the Four Seasons, *119*
Yoga, *80–82*

Z

Zip-trekking, *235–236*
Ziplining and canopy tours, *276–277*
Ziptrek Ecotours, *277*

ABOUT OUR WRITERS

Crai S. Bower has written more than a hundred stories about British Columbia in the past five years for *Alaska Airlines Magazine*, *Virtuoso Life*, MSN.com, *Journey Magazine*, and dozens of others. His "Excess is Enough: Riding Whistler-Blackcomb" (*Escape*) received the 2008 Northern Lights Award. He is the travel commentator for NPR affiliate, KUOW, and a contributing editor to SkiResorts. com. You can read more by and about him at www.FlowingStreamWriting.net.

Carolyn B. Heller, who updated the Vancouver Dining, Vancouver Shopping, and Okanagan Excursion chapters, has been enthusiastically exploring—and eating—her way across her adopted city of Vancouver since she relocated here in 2003. She's the author of *Living Abroad in Canada*, and her travel and food articles have appeared in publications ranging from the *Boston Globe* and the *Los Angeles Times*, to *FamilyFun*, *Real Weddings*, and *Perceptive Travel* magazines. She's contributed to more than 25 Fodor's guides for destinations from New England to New Zealand.

Vancouver-born freelance writer Sue Kernaghan has written about British Columbia for dozens of publications throughout North America and the United Kingdom. A fourth-generation British Columbian, she has contributed to several editions of *Fodor's Guide to Vancouver & British Columbia*, as well as to *Fodor's Alaska*, *Great Canadian Vacations*, *Healthy Escapes*, and *Escape to Nature Without Roughing It*. She lives on Salt Spring Island.

Award-winning freelance travel writer Chris McBeath's more than 25 years in the tourism industry have given her an insider's eye about what makes a great vacation. British Columbia is her home, so whether routing through backcountry, or discovering a hidden-away inn, Chris has combined history, insight, and anecdotes into her contribution to this book. Many of Chris's articles can be found at www. greatestgetaways.com; her destination videos are available on YouTube.